Doing Library Research

Other Titles in This Series

Introduction to Library Research in French Literature, Robert K. Baker

Aging and the Aged: An Annotated Bibliography and Library Research Guide, Linna F. Place, Linda Parker, and Forrest J. Berghorn

Also of Interest

† *A Practical Guide to the Conduct of Field Research in the Social Sciences,* Elliot J. Feldman

African International Relations: An Annotated Bibliography, Mark W. Delancey

A Select Bibliography on Economic Development: With Annotations, John P. Powelson

† *The Modern Middle East: A Guide to Research Tools in the Social Sciences,* Reeva S. Simon

The Librarians' Glossary and Reference Book, Leonard Montague Harrod

Bibliography on World Conflict and Peace: Second Edition, Elise Boulding, J. Robert Passamore, and Robert Scott Gassler

International Terrorism: An Annotated Bibliography and Research Guide, Augustus R. Norton and Martin H. Greenberg

International Bibliography of Jewish Affairs: A Select Annotated List of Books and Articles Published in the Diaspora, 1976-1977, edited by Elizabeth Eppler

A Subject Bibliography of the Second World War: Books in English 1939-1974, compiled by A.G.S. Enser

† Available in hardcover and paperback.

Westview Guides to Library Research
Robert K. Baker, Series Editor

Doing Library Research:
An Introduction for Community College Students
Robert K. Baker

Many college students remain puzzled by card catalogs, can't find books they need, and fail to use many of the important resources of the library despite tours, explanations, and much assistance from librarians.

In this book, a community college librarian provides the direction students need to utilize the resources typically found in a community college library. The author describes the way a library is organized, explains how to effectively use the catalog, tells how to obtain and evaluate potentially useful books and other materials, and discusses general and specialized references. The book concludes with an extensive list of standard references and guides for fields ranging from history to cosmetology, automotive maintenance to real estate – the entire gamut of subjects offered in a community college curriculum.

Though the book is directed at community college students and is most applicable to community college libraries, it will be helpful to any student pursuing information in a college or university library.

Robert K. Baker is technical services librarian at Spokane Community College, Spokane, Washington, and author of *Introduction to Library Research in French Literature* (Westview, 1978).

Doing Library Research: An Introduction for Community College Students

Robert K. Baker

Westview Press / Boulder, Colorado

Westview Guides to Library Research

Copyright © 1981 by Westview Press, Inc.

Published in 1981 in the United States of America by
  Westview Press, Inc.
  5500 Central Avenue
  Boulder, Colorado 80301
  Frederick A. Praeger, Publisher

Library of Congress Cataloging in Publication Data
Baker, Robert K   1948–
  Doing library research.
  (Westview guides to library research)
  Includes index.
  1. Libraries, Community college–Handbooks, manuals, etc.   2. Reference books.
I. Title.
Z675.J8B34   025.5'677   80-22943
ISBN 0-89158-778-0   AACR1

Printed and bound in the United States of America

To my parents, for their
love and support;
and to Werner Erhard, for his
vision of a world that
works for everyone, and
also for his love.

Contents

List of Figures and Photographs xiv
Preface xvi
Acknowledgments xx

Introduction 1

1 The Library and Access to Information 3

    Getting Yourself Oriented 3
    The Catalog 7
        The Main Entry 8
        Subject Searching 27
        Filing 30
    Finding and Evaluating Books 32
        Classification and Browsing 32
        Evaluating What You Find 38
    Beyond Your Library's Walls 39
    Your Most Important Resource 40
    Notes 41

2 The General Tools 43

    Dictionaries and Books on Language 46
        Unabridged 46
        Abridged 46
        Etymological and Historical 46
        New Words 47
        Slang 47
        Abbreviations 47
        Synonyms and Antonyms 48

Usage and Style 48
Encyclopedias 53
    Multivolume Adult Encyclopedias 53
    Multivolume Juvenile/Young Adult Encyclopedias 54
    One-volume Encyclopedias 54
Biographical Sources 57
    Ready Reference Dictionaries 57
    Current Sources 57
    Retrospective Sources 58
Geographical Sources 60
    Atlases 60
    Gazetteers 61
Ready Reference Sources 63
    Almanacs 63
    Yearbooks 64
    Handbooks 64
    Directories 64
Bibliographic Sources 67
    Trade Bibliographies 67
    Bibliographies of Periodicals 68
Indexing and Abstracting Services 70
    Periodicals 70
    Newspapers 70
    Current Events 70
    Book Reviews 70
    Biographical Information 71
Government Publications 79
    Indexes 79
    Guides 79
Media 82
    Microforms 82
    Films 82
    Filmstrips 83
    Transparencies 83
    Videotapes 83
    Slides 83
    Sound Recordings 83
    Reviews 84
Bibliographic Guides 89
Notes 91

3 The Specialized Tools 93

   Humanities 95
      Dance 96
      Drama 97
      Languages 100
      Literature 101
      Music 107
      Philosophy 110
      Religion 111
   Communications 114
      Journalism 115
      Radio and Television 116
      Speech 117
   Fine Arts 118
      Architecture 120
      Art 122
      Fashion Design 123
      Interior Decoration and Design 125
      Photography 126
   Social Sciences 128
      Afro-American Studies 129
      Anthropology 130
      Education 131
      Geography 134
      History 135
      Political Science 138
      Psychology 141
      Sociology 144
      Statistics 144
      Women's Studies 147
   Business and Office Occupations 148
      Accounting 150
      Advertising 151
      Business and Management 152
      Economics 155
      Hotel/Motel and Travel/Tourism .156
      Insurance 158
      Investments 159
      Legal Assistant 161
      Real Estate 162
      Secretarial Science 164

Pure Sciences 166
   Astronomy 168
   Biology 169
   Chemistry 171
   Computer Science 172
   Earth Sciences 174
   Ecology 175
   Mathematics 177
   Oceanography 178
   Physics 179
Health Sciences and Occupations 180
   Dental Assistant 185
   Dental Hygienist 186
   Dental Lab Technician 187
   Medical Assistant 187
   Medical Laboratory Assistant 189
   Medical Records Technician 190
   Nursing 191
   Paramedical Studies 193
   Physical Therapist Assistant 194
   Radiologic Technician 195
   Respiratory Therapist 196
   Surgical Assistant 198
Agricultural Technology 199
   Agribusiness 200
   Animal Science 202
   Conservation and Wildlife Management 204
   Culinary Arts 206
   Food Technology 207
   Forestry 208
   Horticulture/Floriculture 209
   Veterinary Science 212
Trade, Technical, and Industrial Occupations 213
   Air-conditioning, Heating, and Refrigeration 214
   Automotive Maintenance and Repair 215
   Aviation Occupations 217
   Construction Technology 219
   Cosmetology 221
   Electronics 222
   Fire Science 226
   Law Enforcement 227
   Library Technician 229

Mechanical Engineering 231
Mortuary Science 232
Printing 233
Transportation 235
Welding 236
Physical Education and Recreation 237

Appendix: Common Bibliographical Abbreviations 239
Index 241

Figures and Photographs

Figures

1.1 Author and Title Main Entries 11

1.2 Main Entry Card for a Corporate Author 12

1.3 A History Note for a Corporate Author 13

1.4 Main Entry Card for a Book 15

1.5 A Card Set Ready for Filing 19

1.6 Periodical Main Entry Cards 20

1.7 Main Entry Card for a Microfilm 21

1.8 Main Entry Cards for Media 23

1.9 Main Entry Cards for Sound Recordings 26

1.10 A Library of Congress Subject Heading 28

1.11 Filing Order 31

1.12 Library of Congress Classification 34

1.13 Dewey Decimal Classification 36

2.1 A Dictionary Entry 50

2.2 Sample Entry from the *Readers' Guide* 74

2.3 Sample Entry from the *New York Times Index* 77

2.4 Sample Entry from the *Monthly Catalog* 81

2.5 Sample from NICEM *Index to 16mm Educational Films:* Index to Subject Headings 86

2.6 Sample from NICEM *Index to 16mm Educational Films:* Subject Section 87

2.7 Sample from NICEM *Index to 16mm Educational Films:* Title Section...................................88

Photographs

1.1 Modern community college libraries 4

1.2 Student using a microfiche reader 6

2.1 Librarian using an on-line data base 75

Preface

Why another general guide to using libraries? The answer to that question is probably self-evident to most community college librarians: community college students – the designated audience for this book – have perceptibly different educational needs from their four-year-college counterparts. These needs are based on two separate but clearly related realities. The first has to do with the two-year college's traditional "open door" policy, which allows students of widely varying backgrounds to study for a degree, diploma, or certificate. The second revolves around the strikingly diverse curricular offerings in the comprehensive community college, where students can major in everything from English literature to automotive maintenance and repair.

Given those realities, it is clear that a more tailored work on libraries and library research has been needed. This is not to say, of course, that only a community college student can profit from using this book. Indeed, the very diversity of community college students makes this book an appropriate source of information for a general and equally diverse public.

This book is divided into three distinct parts. Chapter 1 addresses the structure and functions of the modern community college library. Here, *Doing Library Research* differs from some other guides in its attention to the catalog and to the cataloging of various media such as films and videotapes. It should be noted that the new second edition of the *Anglo-American Cataloging Rules* and the various implications of closed, frozen, or otherwise suspended catalogs have not been addressed. With the current state of U.S. cataloging in such flux and with catalogs, even in their present state, as difficult to describe as they are, I decided it would be inappropriate to burden a struggling student with overly descriptive – and possibly speculative – details. It is obvious, though, that those librarians who choose *Doing Library*

Research as a text will need to supplement the sections on the catalog with up-to-date and library-specific information if the student is to experience success in using the catalog.

Chapter 2 of *Doing Library Research* is devoted to an examination of general reference tools—including several indexes to media—with specific attention given to characteristics shared by particular types of reference works. The chapter opens with a discussion of the three main categories of reference works, what I have called "access-type" tools (such as periodical indexes, which point to where information is located), "source-type" tools (such as dictionaries, which provide information directly), and "source/access-type" tools (such as encyclopedias, which do both). This introductory discussion of the broad categories of tools, along with an illustrative examination of technical reading, is followed by sections devoted to types of general reference works—dictionaries, encyclopedias, periodical indexes—that most librarians would agree are useful to virtually all students, regardless of major. Each section of this chapter begins with standard bibliographic citations for the tools (arranged alphabetically by main entry) as well as subject headings for each type of tool so that the student may search out other works in the catalog. This is followed by a discussion in which each specific title cited is examined in light of how it exemplifies the particular type of tool in question. Thus, while the student does learn of many salient features of specific reference works, he or she is also learning about the distinctive characteristics of types of reference tools.

Chapter 3, "The Specialized Tools," lists reference works for specific areas of study, but unlike Chapter 2, does not include reference works for media. This decision was made for two reasons: first, many students can rely upon the National Information Center for Educational Media (NICEM) indexes listed in Chapter 2 in those situations where a particular nonprint medium is more appropriate to their information needs than a print source; and second, many community colleges have developed their own specialized access tools for media.

This last chapter represents a departure from the tradition set by most library guides in that the citations are not annotated. Instead, there are brief introductory remarks that broadly describe the types of tools available in the subject and then a listing of tools, again arranged alphabetically by main entry. Each citation is preceded by a code that indicates the category of tool being cited ("A" for access type, "S" for source type, and "SA" for source/access type), and each includes standard identifying information plus the number of pages (or volumes), an indication of whether a bibliography or bibliographical footnotes are present, the Library of Congress and Dewey classification numbers, and standard Library of Congress subject headings. Clearly, it would not be inaccurate to describe the citations in this chapter as abbreviated cataloging. And students are encouraged in the introduction to Chapter 3 to use this abbreviated cataloging – as well as cataloging available to them in their libraries – to devise their own "annotations" based on the subject headings, title, physical description, and other information.

Over 1,400 reference works were chosen for inclusion in *Doing Library Research,* and a word should be said here about how they were selected and, too, about the source of bibliographic and cataloging information. Many of the reference works listed were personally examined, but most were chosen for inclusion based on favorable reviews, which indicated that they would support the curriculum of a community college and would thus be prime candidates for acquisition. Hence, virtually all of the titles cited in Chapters 2 and 3 received favorable annotations or reviews in Eugene P. Sheehy's *Guide to Reference Books* (9th ed.; Chicago: American Library Association, 1976) or in one of the volumes – 1974 through 1980 – of *American Reference Books Annual* (Littleton, Colo.: Libraries Unlimited, 1970-). A smaller number of works – generally very recently published works – were included based on reviews in *Choice, Library Journal,* or *Booklist.* In a few cases, particularly for some specializations in the health sciences, agricultural technologies, and trade, technical, and industrial occupations, it was necessary to consult standard textbooks in the field to discover what sources were consistently identified in bibliographies as being of reference value to students. This particular selection procedure was necessary when the standard reviewing media did not adequately cover a particular field such as dental assisting or animal science.

As to bibliographic and cataloging information, in the vast majority of cases, this information corresponds to the bibliographic description, subject cataloging, and classification assigned by the Library of Congress and available through several sources: the *National Union Catalog,* the *American Book Publishing Record Cumulative 1950-1977* (15 v.; New York: R. R. Bowker, 1978), and the data base of the Washington Library Network. In only a few cases was information included in a citation that did not originate at the Library of Congress, and such information was generally gleaned from the original cataloging of a Washington Library Network member. If portions of information–like a Dewey number or possibly even subject headings–are missing from a citation, it is because no reliable information could be found in a standard source.

As already noted, this book represents somewhat of a departure in style and format from most library guides, Chapter 3 particularly so. This departure can, I think, be justified on the grounds of promoting a sense of self-sufficiency and responsibility in using the library. Students who have studied Chapter 2 and are aware of the varied characteristics of different types of reference works should be able to develop brief and meaningful annotations using the cataloging information provided. And while students are continually encouraged to make the library work for them by acting independently in using catalogs and reference sources, they are also encouraged to consult with librarians. Indeed, a student who has studied this book and used most of the general and appropriate subject-oriented reference tools is much more likely to seek the mediation of a reference librarian at times when the standard, and admittedly elementary, search strategies implied in this book have been exhausted.

The community college as an institution has long promoted the idea of the lifelong learner, and perhaps nowhere is this concept more appropriate than in the field of library and bibliographic instruction. To instill the realization that information is one's for the taking, any time and any place; to empower an individual to formulate a reasoned search strategy or an intelligent reference question; to aid an individual in the discovery that the library–any library–is central to the pursuit of knowledge are, I think, worthy goals. And to the extent that this book assists the individual student in becoming a true lifelong learner and in achieving those goals, it will be a success in this author's eyes.

Robert K. Baker

Acknowledgments

It is with pride and pleasure that I acknowledge the assistance of the following friends and colleagues who took the time to read and comment upon various portions of this book: Marjorie Havist, Skagit Valley College, Washington; Barbara Fulsaas, Spokane Falls Community College; Betty Waesche, Carlyn Spiker, Verona Southern, Charlotte Bageant, Jane Rehms, and Sunny and Mike Burns, all of Spokane Community College; Tim Aman, University of Washington School of Librarianship; Dave Nelson, Eastern Washington University; Mary Carr, Gonzaga University; and last, but by no means least, Liz Eisenbach, UCLA Graduate School of Library and Information Science, whose generosity and friendship during the summer of 1978 helped get this project off the ground.

A word of thanks must also go to the following three individuals: Al Webb, Spokane Community College, whose interior photographs of the SCC Library enrich this book; and Lynne Rienner and Miriam Gilbert, Westview Press, whose loyal friendship and encouragement saw me through more than just a few dry spells.

Finally, a grateful acknowledgment must go to Barry Taylor, a good friend who was willing to give generously of his vacation to assist me in proofreading the final page proofs.

R.K.B.

Introduction

Mrs. Roberts, aged forty-eight, has just enrolled in a refresher nursing program at her city's community college; Mr. Franklin, aged twenty-eight and a veteran, has just completed his first semester in the automotive maintenance program at his area's community college; Mr. Day and Ms. LaPointe, both aged nineteen, have just enrolled in their local community college's liberal arts transfer program – he will major in English literature, she in business.

Each of these persons represents in his or her own way the "typical" community college student. With differing educational backgrounds and goals, they have all come to one of the nation's community colleges seeking either to complete the first two years of a four-year college program or to learn the skills necessary for success in a particular occupation, be it trade, technical, or professional.

Regardless of why *you* have enrolled in your community college, you have something in common with the four typical students described above: you probably know very little about how to make effective use of your community college library. And inevitably that moment arrives when your English instructor tells you to begin gathering material for a term paper on the Watergate affair or your electronics instructor tells you to prepare an oral report on inverter circuits. At such a moment, the reaction of many students is sheer panic: Where to begin? How to proceed?

If you are like most people, you've probably never received any comprehensive education on how to do library research; so that sense of panic when confronted by the request to "find information on topic X, Y, or Z" is really quite natural and understandable. Why is it that the word research should inspire awe, and perhaps even anxiety, in most of us? Somehow, research is associated with scientists in long white coats or with musty old people who wander in and out of a library's stacks looking smug and self-satisfied; it's mysterious, and only those persons with exceptional intelligence are capable of doing it. But research is really a very simple word that comes from the Old French meaning "to seek out." Thus, every time you have consulted a telephone directory or a dictionary, you have been conducting research (although, of course, in an elementary form).

In order to dispel the myth that research is a "mystical" activity, consider some of the following typical questions that are asked every day and that involve a knowledge of how to do library research: "I'm looking for information on the latest stereo equipment in order to find out which is the best value for the money. Where can I find it?" "I need to find information on a new hairstyle developed by Vidal Sassoon for my cosmetology class. I know that there was a magazine article published a few months ago, but I don't remember where. Where do I start looking?" "I'm doing a term paper on population trends for my political science class. Where can I find some statistics on the birth and death rates in the United States in the 1960s?"

Such questions are not at all extraordinary, but the skills necessary to answer them are. And that's really quite surprising, for our modern world places a high premium on information: those who know how to find it efficiently and use it effectively are generally well rewarded. In the community college that reward may be better grades; in the "real world," it may be a better-paying job.

And so we come to the reason for this book: to assist you in developing the skills necessary to survive both in the community college setting and later on when you have graduated and are engaged in other pursuits (probably earning a living). *Doing Library Research* is divided into three broad areas. You will need to read carefully Chapters 1 and 2 since they contain information on general principles and tools that everybody needs to know. Chapter 3 is devoted to a discussion of some of the major tools in specialized areas; so you will only need to read through the sections that are of interest to you. For example, if you are majoring in agribusiness, you will only need to read through the general section in Chapter 3 on "Agricultural Technology" and the more specific section on "Agribusiness." You can safely ignore "Secretarial Science."

As you read *Doing Library Research*, however, keep in mind that its subtitle indicates a major limitation: it is only an introduction to the ins and outs of making effective use of the library and of the many different materials found there. Remember that the library is staffed with people—librarians—whose job it is to make *your* job of being a student as easy as possible. When in doubt, ask a librarian!

1
The Library and
Access to Information

Almost every day of your life, you receive and process information: you watch the evening news, you read a billboard, you go to a movie. Sometimes, you purposely welcome information (e.g., reading the daily newspaper), while at other times information is forced upon you (e.g., almost *any* television commercial). And as a community college student enrolled in various courses, you receive information from your instructors in their lectures and from the textbooks you read. But receiving and processing information are one thing; finding it is another. And this is precisely where the library comes in.

What *is* a library, anyway? It's a place—a building, room, or rooms—where information is collected and organized for study, reference, and reading, and from which you can borrow many materials for use at home and elsewhere. There are, of course, different kinds of libraries: public libraries (with general collections of materials for the average citizen), academic libraries (school, community college, college, and university, with collections designed to support their academic programs), and special libraries (such as those with collections of rare books and manuscripts or "corporate libraries" with materials for the specific use of their employees in day-to-day business). But regardless of type, every library can be distinguished as the principal agent in our society for giving you access to information—the subject of this chapter.

GETTING YOURSELF ORIENTED

It would be nice to be able to say that libraries are easy to use, but in fact, they can be very complicated. While such things as learning how

Photo 1.1: Modern community college libraries are both comfortable and functional places to study and conduct research. (Courtesy Spokane Community College Library, Washington State Community College District 17.)

to use the catalog, understanding classification, and becoming aware of the services available to you are critically important – and they will be discussed at length in this chapter – there is probably no better place to begin your study of library research than with a tour of the physical facility itself. While that may sound simplistic, few students take the half hour necessary to familiarize themselves with the layout, services, and people in their library. And that, as any reference librarian can confirm, is the source of endless confusion for far too many library users.

What should you expect to find in your library building? While the following may not describe every library, the list is representative of what you will find.

A Circulation Desk. Very often this desk is near the entrance or exit to your library building, and it often serves as the nerve center of the library—for this is where books and other materials are checked out and returned and where many informational questions are asked and answered. Usually, it is here that you should be able to obtain information on the library's hours, its fine policies, and its procedures for borrowing various materials. Many community college libraries publish handbooks that answer most of the frequently asked questions about their services, materials, and facilities; these are usually available at the circulation desk.

A Reference Area. This part of the library will contain all of those materials that are frequently consulted by students and faculty for quick answers to quick questions: encyclopedias, dictionaries, almanacs, handbooks, bibliographies, indexes. Note that you are not generally allowed to borrow reference materials for home use since they are usually in high demand. You will also usually find a reference librarian available somewhere near this area to help you make effective use of these and other library materials. Reference tools will be discussed in further detail in Chapters 2 and 3; the role of the librarian will be examined later in this chapter.

A Catalog. The catalog is your library's heart, for it gives you access—by subject, author, and title—to most of the materials owned by your library. The principal features of the catalog will be detailed shortly.

A Book Collection. Most of your library's books will be shelved in "call-number order" using either Dewey decimal or Library of Congress classification. Information on how classification works and how you can use it to browse is given later in this chapter.

A Periodical Collection. The term *periodical*—often also called *serial*—refers to those publications that are issued periodically (weekly, monthly, quarterly, and so on) such as *Newsweek* or *Time*. These publications contain the most current information available on a wide variety of subjects and thus are frequently more useful than books to many community college students, particularly those in the vocational fields. Many libraries have special areas set aside where you can read the latest issues of selected periodicals and newspapers. Older issues may be in call-number order either in a separate section or with the books, or they may be filed in a separate section alphabetically by title.

Vertical Files. Many libraries collect pamphlets and other pamphletlike materials that are too small to be fully cataloged and processed. These materials are often placed in manila folders or envelopes and then filed alphabetically by subject in filing cabinets called either "vertical files" or "pamphlet files."

Photo 1.2: Student using a microfiche reader. Microforms are an important part of the community college library collection. (Courtesy Spokane Community College Library, Washington State Community College District 17.)

A Microform Reading Center. These days, most libraries collect some materials in "microform": a filmlike material on which printed matter has been photographically reduced so that it is no longer readable with the naked eye. The two most common types of microform are microfilm (on reels) and microfiche (small postcard-sized sheets), both of which need special equipment to be read. Any library that collects materials in microform will, of course, have the necessary special readers so that you can comfortably use those materials. If you have never used a microfilm or microfiche reader, you might want to take a few minutes to learn how to operate it. Your library should have personnel available to show you how the machinery works, or simple instructions will have been posted near the readers.

A Media/Audiovisual Area. The term *media* is all encompassing, taking in everything from flashcards and slides to films and videotapes. While media will probably play a supplementary role in your search for different kinds of information, for some subjects a particular kind of nonprint material may be precisely what you seek. There is, after all, something to the old adage "One picture is worth a thousand words." Almost all community colleges collect media as well as the equipment necessary to use them. And it's increasingly common to find both the software (i.e., the media itself) and the hardware (i.e., the equipment) housed in the library building. Even if your college's media collection is housed separately, your librarians will generally be able to provide you with information on the kinds of materials available to you. You may also want to inquire as to whether or not your library makes such things as cassette recorders or calculators available for loan – a surprisingly large number do.

A Sound Recording Collection. Sound recordings – LPs, cassettes, and reel-to-reel tapes – are of major cultural, recreational, and informational value, and there are few community college libraries that will not have at least a minimal collection of musical and "spoken word" recordings available for your use. Near the collection itself, you may also find listening stations with instructions posted on how to operate the equipment, where to check out headphones, and other such matters.

A Reserve Collection. The materials in a community college library's reserve collection – books, periodicals, pamphlets, and sometimes even media – have been placed there by the librarians at the request of your instructors, who will probably assign or recommend certain readings as part of class assignments. Materials placed on reserve generally circulate for relatively short periods of time (two hours, twenty-four hours) since they will be in demand by a number of persons. Your library may have created a special file to let you know what has been placed on reserve.

As you wander around the library on your tour, you may also find some of the following: areas set aside for recreational reading materials or best-sellers, special sections for the shelving of oversize books (i.e., those books too large or too tall to fit on the regular shelves), "quiet" study areas, group-study rooms, typing rooms with coin-operated typewriters, photocopying machines, and exhibit or display areas.

Keep in mind that most librarians are inveterate signmakers: always look around you to find signs that may have been posted to help you locate materials or to inform you of one service or another offered by your library.

THE CATALOG

Having acquainted yourself with the layout of your library, you can now devote some attention to the heart of the library, its catalog. Perhaps the best way to define a library's catalog is to define first its second cousin, the index. At one time or another, you have certainly had occasion to use the index to a book: it's that alphabetical list at the back of the volume that indicates the specific pages you should turn to in the work to see where a subject or idea, person, place, or thing is discussed. For example, if you were to look in *this* book's index under the subject "catalog," you would be directed to this page and several others. The index, then, gives you *access to the intellectual contents* of a book.

Just as the index gives you access to the contents of a book, the catalog gives you access to the contents of the library. It will list, alphabetically: what the library has on a specific *subject*; those works by a specific *author*; and what *titles* the library owns. Thus, the catalog brings order to chaos by telling you what books are in the library. It may also sometimes give you access to other materials such as films, periodicals, government documents, and sound recordings, although this varies from library to library.

It is likely that you are familiar with the "card catalog," since it is still the most common kind of physical catalog in many libraries. Generally, the cards (or "index entries," if you prefer) are alphabetically arranged in one of two ways. If the catalog is a "dictionary catalog," all of the cards—author, title, and subject—will be interfiled in one alphabetical arrangement (hence the name *dictionary*). If the catalog is "divided," the subject cards are physically separated from all of the author and title cards, thus creating two separate catalogs. Some libraries may have a three-way divided catalog in which subject cards, author cards, and title cards are filed in separate drawers. This type of arrangement is slightly less common than the two-way divided catalog.

While the card catalog is still the most common physical type to be found, you should not be surprised to find other physical formats. Some libraries, for example, have book catalogs; others have microfiche or microfilm catalogs, often produced by computers; and others may even have their catalogs in a computer data base, in which case you would sit down at a computer terminal, type in your request on a keyboard (e.g., "Does the library have any books on Africa?"), and have your answer displayed on a screen or printed out for you. But regardless of physical format, any library catalog will generally contain the same kinds of information. For purposes of explanation and illustration, the examples used in the rest of this chapter will be from the card catalog.

The Main Entry

In order to discover how you can make effective use of your

library's catalog, we should examine closely what goes into it, namely the various entries: main entries, added entries, and subject entries. Both added and subject entries will be easily understood once you learn what a main entry is.

The discussion on main entry that follows deals first with books, then periodicals, microforms, media, and finally sound recordings. The entry examples shown in the figures all come from the Library of Congress, our national library, which makes them available to libraries across the country. Your own community college library, however, may not be using Library of Congress standardized cataloging for one or more of the types of materials that you will read about here. For example, many libraries do not catalog their periodicals, relying instead on simple title listings in a separate file.

The examples in this section are for the most part based on one set of cataloging rules, and these rules have changed – and will continue to change – over the years.[1] Once you have finished reading this section on main entry, you should plan to browse through your own library's catalog so that you can note what differences, if any, exist. And remember too that this is only an introduction to the concept of main entry; you may well have questions about the examples in this book or on catalog cards in your own library. Don't hesitate to seek assistance from your librarian if you have trouble in interpreting a particular catalog card. Also notice that the Appendix gives a list of some of the more common abbreviations used on catalog cards; you may want to refer to this appendix as you study the examples given below.

Books

The main entry is the basic, principal entry, usually the author entry, and sometimes contains the fullest amount of information on the book it describes. Thus, the main entry for this book is "Baker, Robert K., 1948– " because I'm the author of this book. Sounds simple, right? Well, it could be except for that part of the definition that says "*usually the author entry*": the *usually* causes many problems for librarians and library users alike. What will the main entry be if there is more than one author? And what about those publications that are authored by organizations? And, finally, *which* name do we use for personal authors, such as those who write under pseudonyms?

Let's examine first the problem posed by those publications authored by more than one person. Here's the general rule of thumb: if there are three authors or less, the main entry will be made under the author named first on the title page. If there are more than three authors, main entry will be made under the title of the work. (This is done because it is believed that you probably would remember the title rather than the names of the various authors.) As an example, imagine for a moment that this book had on its title page *"Doing Library Research . . . by Robert K. Baker and John Q. American."* There are less than three authors, so main entry goes to Baker, who's named first on the title page. Now, pretend instead that the title page reads "by Robert K. Baker, John Q., Sally L., and Floyd G. American." There are more than three authors here, so main entry will be made under the title, *"Doing Library Research."* Examples for author main entry and title main entry appear in Figure 1.1.

Now we turn to the second problem: what to do with those publications that are authored by an organization. Librarians call such organizations "corporate authors," a large category that includes everything from professional associations to governmental bodies. Corporate authors, like personal authors, are often main entries, and you will frequently see cards in the catalog under their official names, such as the American Society for Testing and Materials, the Modern Language Association of America, or the National Science Foundation. The major difficulty here is *how* (i.e., under what name) such authors will be entered in the catalog. Where, for example, would you expect to find a publication authored by the Manpower Administration of our nation's Department of Labor? It will be in the "U" drawer, under "United States. Department of Labor. Manpower Administration," as illustrated in Figure 1.2. Frankly, corporate authors are a real headache, principally because they often change their names. In Figure 1.3, you can read the history of the National Center for Air Pollution Control, a governmental body that has changed its name several times. Note that this "history card" tells you which entry is correct depending on the time period you're interested in.

There is no easy rule of thumb to guide you in the realm of corporate authorship—you simply need to be aware that many publications you may seek will have corporate authors, and that how a corporate author is entered in the catalog involves many considerations. When in doubt about the real name of an organization, however, you have two important alternatives: asking a librarian or looking for the publication under its title in the catalog.

The last difficulty with main entries (and with added entries too) involves the problem of *which* name we use in the catalog for personal authors. Where, for example, would you look to find Mark Twain's *The Adventures of Huckleberry Finn?* Under "Twain, Mark" (his pen name) or under "Clemens, Samuel" (his real name)? As with corporate

Figure 1.1

AUTHOR AND TITLE MAIN ENTRIES

Brennan, Lawrence David, 1915-
  Résumés for better jobs [by] Lawrence D.
Brennan, Stanley Strand [and] Edward C. Gruber.
New York, Simon and Schuster, [1973]
  187 p. illus. 24 cm. $2.95

  1. Applications for positions. I. Strand,
Stanley, joint author. II. Gruber, Edward C.,
joint author. III. Title.

HF5383.B68   331.1'28   73-174889

Eye to the future [by] Lorne Kelsey [and others]
  Pittsburgh, Stanwix House [1973]
  84 p. illus. 23 cm.

  1. Vocational guidance. 2. Applications for
positions. 3. Finance, Personal. I. Kelsey,
Lorne.

HF5381.E9   331.7'02   72-96333

Figure 1.2

MAIN ENTRY CARD FOR A CORPORATE AUTHOR

U.S. *Dept. of Labor. Manpower Administration.*
Health careers guidebook [by] U.S. Department of
Labor, Manpower Administration [and] U.S. Depart-
ment of Health, Education, and Welfare, National
Institutes of Health. 3d ed. [Washington, U.S.
Dept. of Labor; for sale by the Supt. of Docs.,
U.S. Govt. Print. Off.] 1972.
  xi, 166 p. illus. 27 cm. $2.25

First published in 1955 by the National Health
Council.
"Prepared in cooperation with the National
Health Council."

(Cont. on next card)

U.S. *Dept. of Labor. Manpower Administration.*
Health careers guidebook . . . 1972. Card 2.

Supt. of Docs. no.: L1.7/2:H34/972.

  1. Medicine as a profession. I. United States.
National Institutes of Health. II. National
Health Council. Health careers guidebook.
III. Title.

R690.U52 1972   610.'69   73-601166

Figure 1.3

A HISTORY NOTE FOR A CORPORATE AUTHOR

U.S. *National Center for Air Pollution Control.*
The Air Pollution Medical Branch and the Air
Pollution Engineering Branch, both of the Public
Health Service, were created in 1957. In 1960 these
two bodies merged to form the Division of Air
Pollution. The name was changed in Jan. 1967 to
National Center for Air Pollution Control; and in
July 1968 to National Air Pollution Control Admini-
stration.
Works by these bodies are found under the
following headings according to the name used at
the time of publication:

◯   (Cont. on next card)

U.S. *National Center for Air Pollution Control.*
History cross-reference note . . . Card 2.

U.S. *Air Pollution Engineering Branch.*
U.S. *Air Pollution Medical Branch.*
U.S. *Division of Air Pollution.*
U.S. *National Air Pollution Control Administra-
tion.*
U.S. *National Center for Air Pollution Control.*

◯

78-245616

authors, the answer may vary depending on when the book was cataloged, since rules have changed over the years. At one time, works were entered under the author's real name; today, they are entered under the name by which he or she is primarily identified in standard reference sources. In the case of "Twain" versus "Clemens," the main entry is "Clemens, Samuel Longhorne, 1835-1910." Happily, most libraries will have cross-references in their catalogs so that if you had looked under "Twain," you would have found a card that said *"see Clemens."*

You may have wondered about the life dates that are added to many personal names in the catalog. They are added to authors' names for one of two reasons: they could be easily found in some reference source, or such dates were needed to distinguish two authors with the same name. Imagine how many John or Mary Smiths may have written books and how useful such dates can be in your searching.

Now that we have finished looking at some of the quirks involved with main entries, we can turn our attention to what information is given on a main entry card, as illustrated in Figure 1.4. The first line of the card is, of course, the main entry "heading" (so called because it "heads up" or begins the description of the publication). Directly below the heading are the title and subtitle of the work, transcribed exactly as they appear on the title page. This in turn is followed by the authorship statement, which on our main entry card shows that there are two authors – Melvin W. Donaho and John L. Meyer. The authorship statement frequently includes the names of those persons or organizations that have contributed to the content of the work in other ways. For example, you may see such statements as "edited by . . . ," "compiled by . . . ," "illustrated by . . . ," or even "sponsored by . . . ."

In what way, you may ask, is such information going to be useful? This depends on what you're looking for. If, for example, you seek an illustrated *Adventures of Tom Sawyer* and you find a card that reads "illustrated by Norman Rockwell," this could be the deciding factor in your choice of one edition of *Tom Sawyer* over another. Or perhaps you're looking for an introduction to an area of your specialty that you've never previously studied, and you recognize the name of a coauthor to a book – it's the same person who wrote your elementary textbook, and you know that he writes well. In such situations, your choice is influenced by your own tastes, preferences, and knowledge, and by the information provided on the catalog card.

Following the authorship statement you will sometimes find an "edition" statement. There is no such statement on our sample main entry card, so we can probably assume that it's the first edition. An edition

Figure 1.4

MAIN ENTRY CARD FOR A BOOK

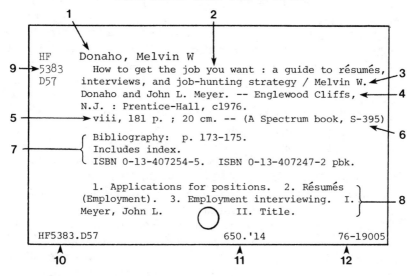

1 MAIN ENTRY HEADING (Choice of main entry based on authorship conditions)

2 TITLE & SUBTITLE (Transcribed from title page of work)

3 AUTHORSHIP STATEMENT (Persons who have contributed to the content of the work)

4 IMPRINT (Place of publication, publisher, date of publication)

5 COLLATION (Physical description of the book)

6 SERIES STATEMENT (Normally a publisher's series)

7 NOTES AREA (Other information which helps reader to identify the work)

8 TRACINGS (Show what other entries will appear in the catalog)

9 CALL NUMBER (Unique classification number assigned by library to this book)

10 LIBRARY OF CONGRESS CLASS NUMBER (Assigned at LC)

11 DEWEY DECIMAL NUMBER (For use by those libraries which use Dewey)

12 LIBRARY OF CONGRESS CARD NUMBER (For use by those libraries which wish to order card sets)

refers to all of the copies of a work produced from a single setting of type, and it doesn't mean the same thing as a "printing." Probably the best way to illustrate the difference between printing and edition is to examine a typical best-selling paperback. On the verso (i.e., reverse side) of the title page, you will probably find such information as "copyright © 1978, 1st printing, February 1978 . . . 5th printing, July 1978." Note that these are only printings since the text has not changed. With an edition, on the other hand, the text will have been revised, updated, or changed, and a more recent copyright date will appear. The edition statement, then, will be important to you when you seek the most current information available. If, for example, your library has two glossaries of terms used in automotive maintenance, one "copyright © 1973," and another "2d revised edition, copyright © 1977," you will be more likely to choose the later edition.

Following the edition statement you will find what librarians call the "imprint": the place of publication, the name of the publisher, and the date of publication or copyright date. Here, the date of publication is probably the most useful item of information. For example, if you're looking for books on the Civil War, and you find two—one dated in the 1920s, and the other in the 1960s—you can pick and choose depending on your need. If you wondered how historians in the early part of this century viewed the North-South conflict, the 1920s publication may be useful; more current viewpoints will obviously be found in the 1960s publication. As to the publisher information, this will become increasingly important to you the more you use books and libraries. For example, the electronics major will discover that McGraw-Hill publishes a number of reputable handbooks in that field. While the name of a publisher doesn't guarantee that a book with its imprint will be a reliable source of information, it is usually a good indicator.

Below the main descriptive portion of the main entry card, you will find a physical description of the book. In our case, the Donaho book is 189 pages long and stands twenty centimeters high. While this may not seem very useful at first glance, this portion of the card—called by librarians the "collation"—may help you choose one book over another. Consider the following collations for two different introductions to biochemistry:

xxvi, 145 p.; 24 cm.
2 v. in 3 : ill. (some col.); 36 cm.

The first work, containing just over 170 pages (26 preliminary pages—probably a preface or introduction—with 145 subsequent pages of text), is a brief introduction to the subject; the second work is in three *physical* volumes, with volumes one or two in two separate parts, contains illustrations (some in color), and stands markedly higher than the first book. This latter work is not by any means a *brief* introduction to biochemistry (unless, of course, each volume contained only 50 pages, which is unlikely). If you were seeking a concise overview of the subject, the second work has been ruled out by that intimidating collation; if, however, you already know something about biochemistry and wish to read an extensive "introduction," the second publication may be quite suitable.

On the same line and to the right of the collation, you will sometimes find some information in parentheses. This is the "series statement," and on our sample main entry card you will see that Donaho's book is a "Spectrum Book, S-395," as issued by Prentice-Hall. Many publishers issue books in series, sometimes thematic series such as "Issues in Philosophy" or "Contemporary Poets." This part of the description may influence your choice of one title over another depending on whether or not you are familiar with that series and have been favorably impressed in the past.

Below the collation and series statement, you will find the "notes area." On the Donaho card, we learn that the book has a three-page bibliography of other books and materials on the subject of job hunting and that there is an index (and books with indexes are *much* easier to use than those without them). We are also given the "international standard book numbers"—the ISBNs—for both the hardcover and paperback editions; these are useful if you wanted to order the book from the publisher. Other information that you may find in the notes area could be a summary of the contents of a work (particularly a work in more than one volume), explanatory notes on some aspect of the formal description that's already been given, and sometimes the price of the book.

At the bottom of the card you see several items preceded by either Arabic or Roman numerals. They are called the "tracings"—they indicate which other, extra entries will be made in the catalog for this particular book. The subject entries—those entries that indicate the subjects dealt with in the book, and that you will read about shortly—are preceded by Arabic numerals; the added entries—those for the title, any coauthors, and so on—by Roman numerals. Often, libraries will take their main entry cards, reproduce extra copies, and then type the subject and added entry headings at the top of the cards for filing in the catalog.

The complete card set for the Donaho title is displayed in Figure 1.5. Note that the subject entries are typed all in capital letters (although some libraries type their subject entries in red). In all, there are six access points in your catalog for the Donaho book: the main entry, three subject entries, and two added entries.

Periodicals

Since most periodicals consist of contributions by a number of different authors, the main entry is generally under title. Thus, you would look for *Sports Illustrated, Time,* and *Vogue* in the "S," "T," and "V" drawers respectively. The major exception to the title main entry rule occurs when the name of the organization that issues the publication is a part of the title; in this case, main entry will be under the organization's name. Thus, *JAMA* (the *Journal of the American Medical Association*) will be found in the "A" drawer, under American Medical Association.

In Figure 1.6, you will see examples of periodical main entry cards – one for *Time,* the other for *JAMA*. Notice that there are some differences between a main entry card for a book and that of a periodical, the primary one being that periodicals are issued in volumes ("v.1– ") beginning with a certain date ("July 1883– "), and thus the description reflects that fact. If either *Time* or *JAMA* should someday cease publication, these "open" entries would be "closed" (e.g., "v.1–100, July 1883–July 1983"). In the notes area of a periodical main entry card, you will often find information concerning the various editors and sometimes the various changes in title the publication may have undergone. This latter item – title change – is the source of many problems for both librarians and library users. There's probably little else more frustrating than to learn that *Transactions and Proceedings of the . . .* has become *Proceedings and Transactions of the. . . .* Don't hesitate to confer with a librarian if you have difficulty in locating a particular periodical title.

As a final note, remember that your library's catalog will *not* give you access to the individual articles in a magazine or journal. In Chapters 2 and 3, you will learn of the various tools that will help you to discover what information is available in periodicals.

Microforms

Since microforms are nothing but miniaturized versions of other library materials, such as books, the main entry rules are the same as those already mentioned. The only important difference will be found in the collation and notes area of the card, where the fact that the

Figure 1.5

A CARD SET READY FOR FILING

```
┌─────────────────────────────────────────────────────────────┐
│                                                               │
│        How to get the job you want                            │
│                                                               │
│     HF    Donaho, Melvin W                                    │
│     5383      How to get the job you want : a guide to résumés,│
│  ┌──────────────────────────────────────────────────────────┐│
│  │      Meyer, John L.                                        ││
│  │                                                            ││
│  │   HF    Donaho, Melvin W                                   ││
│  │   5383      How to get the job you want : a guide to résumés,│
│ ┌────────────────────────────────────────────────────────────┐│
│ │     EMPLOYMENT INTERVIEWING                                  ││
│ │                                                              ││
│ │  HF    Donaho, Melvin W                                      ││
│ │  5383      How to get the job you want : a guide to résumés, ││
│┌──────────────────────────────────────────────────────────────┐
││    RÉSUMÉS (EMPLOYMENT)                                        ││
││                                                                ││
││ HF    Donaho, Melvin W                                         ││
││ 5383      How to get the job you want : a guide to résumés,    ││
┌────────────────────────────────────────────────────────────────┐
│   APPLICATIONS FOR POSITIONS                                     │
│                                                                  │
│ HF    Donaho, Melvin W                                           │
│ 5383      How to get the job you want : a guide to résumés,      │
┌──────────────────────────────────────────────────────────────────┐
│                                                                    │
│ HF    Donaho, Melvin W                                             │
│ 5383      How to get the job you want : a guide to résumés,        │
│ D57    interviews, and job-hunting strategy / Melvin W.            │
│        Donaho and John L. Meyer. -- Englewood Cliffs,              │
│        N.J. : Prentice-Hall, c1976.                               │
│           viii, 181 p. ; 20 cm. -- (A Spectrum book S395)          │
│                                                                    │
│        Bibliography: p. 173-175.                                   │
│        Includes index.                                             │
│        ISBN 0-13-407254-5.  ISBN 0-13-407247-2 pbk.                │
│                                                                    │
│        1. Applications for positions.  2. Résumés                  │
│        (Employment).  3. Employment interviewing.  I.              │
│        Meyer, John L.        ◯     II. Title.                      │
│ HF5383.D57                         650.'14              76-19005   │
└────────────────────────────────────────────────────────────────────┘
```

Figure 1.6

PERIODICAL MAIN ENTRY CARDS

Time, the weekly newsmagazine. v.1-
Mar. 3, 1923-
[New York, N.Y.] 1923-
    v. illus. (incl. ports.) 28 cm.

Editors: 1923-   Briton Hadden, H.R. Luce.

    I. Hadden, Briton, ed. II. Luce, Henry
Robinson, 1898-   , ed.

Library of Congress   AP2.T37   25-11669

American medical association.
    The journal of the American medical association.
v.1-   July 1883-
Chicago [1883]-19
        v. illus, plates (part col.) ports. tables.
29½ cm. weekly.

    Editors: July 1883-Dec. 1888, N.S. Davis.--
Jan. 1889-Dec. 1890, ed. under the direction of
the board of trustees (Jan.5-Feb. 9, 1889, by J.
B. Hamilton)--Jan. 1891-June 1893, J.C. Culbertson.
--July 1893-Dec. 1898, J.B. Hamilton.--Jan. 1899-

            (Cont. on next card)

American medical association. The journal . . .
    1883-   Card 2.

            G. H. Simmons.
    Includes proceedings of the association, papers
read at the annual sessions, and lists of current
medical literature.

    1. Medicine--Societies, etc. 2. Medicine--Bibl.
I. Davis, Nathan Smith, 1817-1904, ed. II. Cul-
bertson, James Coe, 1840-1908, ed. III. Hamilton,
John Brown, 1847-1898, ed. IV. Simmons, George
Henry, 1852-1937, ed. V. Title.

R15.A48
                              7-37314

Figure 1.7

MAIN ENTRY CARD FOR A MICROFILM

Breines, Andrew Raymond, 1914-
  The Catholic layman in time of crisis; a study
in sociology of religion. Ann Arbor, Mich.,
University Microfilms [1959]
  Microfilm copy (positive) of typescript
  Collation of the original: vii, 276 l. illus.
  Thesis--University of Wisconsin.
  Abstracted in Dissertation abstracts, v. 19
(1959) no. 7, p. 1853-1854.
  Vita
  Bibliography: leaves 242-249.

(Cont. on next card)

Breines, Andrew Raymond, 1914-   . The Catholic
  layman in time of crisis . . . [1959] Card 2.

  1. Sociology, Christian (Catholic). I. Title.

Microfilm AC-1 no.58-5333
Wisconsin. Univ. Libr.   Mic 58-5333

work is on microfiche or microfilm will be noted, as illustrated in Figure 1.7.

Media

As already noted, the term *media* is very broad, and it would be difficult to talk about every type. Thus, we will look solely at films, filmstrips, and videotapes – three of the most common types of media collected by community college libraries. In Figure 1.8, you will see three sample main entry cards. Like periodicals, main entry for most types of media is under title because generally many persons have contributed in one way or another to the authorship of the material. The major difference you will find in the cataloging of media is in the collation. For example, the first card in Figure 1.8 is for a motion picture: it is fifty-nine minutes long, there is sound ("sd"), it is in black and white ("b&w"), and needs a sixteen-millimeter projector to be shown. The second card is for a filmstrip: there are six rolls of color ("col.") thirty-five-millimeter film, with six cassette tapes, and a guide. The last card represents a videorecording: it's in a cassette (as opposed to a tape), runs for fifty-six minutes, has sound and color, and is three-fourths inches wide.

Sound Recordings

Generally, main entry for musical sound recordings is made under composer, which, you may note, is *not* the same thing as performer. Thus, main entry for the Eagles' album in Figure 1.9 is under the title *Eagles: Their Greatest Hits.* Of course, if the Eagles had composed most or all of the songs they performed (as, for example, does Bob Dylan), main entry could have been made under "Eagles (Musical group)."[2]

In the bottom card in Figure 1.9, for Beethoven's *Emperor* Concerto, the main entry was easy to assign: Beethoven wrote the music, Beethoven gets the main entry. You will note, though, that below the main entry heading there is a title in brackets and printed in slightly smaller type. This is the concerto's "uniform title" – the title given to *all* recordings of this concerto so as to insure that all of the main entry cards for those recordings will file together in the catalog. To illustrate how this works, let's assume that we have three different recordings of the *Emperor* Concerto, each with the following titles: (1) Fifth Piano Concerto of Beethoven, (2) The *Emperor* Concerto, and (3) Piano Concerto no. 5. These will file under Beethoven, of course, but they *won't* file together because they begin with "F," "E," and "P" respectively. To remedy this problem, we use the concerto's uniform title – Concerto, piano, no. 5 . . ." – so that the three main entry cards will file together.

Figure 1.8

MAIN ENTRY CARDS FOR MEDIA

Leaders in American medicine--Karl F. Meyer, M.D.
  [Motion picture] Alpha Omega Alpha in coopera-
tion with the National Medical Audiovisual
Center, 1974. Released by National Medical
Audiovisual Center and National Audiovisual
Center.
59 min. sd. b&w. 16 mm.

CREDITS: John Z. Bowers, Edward B. Shaw.
SUMMARY: Dr. Meyer describes his early education and discusses his work in the field of microbiology and immunology. Points out his work in

(Cont. on next card)

Leaders in American medicine--Karl F. Meyer, M.D.
  [Motion picture] 1974. Card 2.

setting standards for quality control in the
canning industry; his research efforts in the
development of a vaccine against plague; and his
work in psittacosis, brucellosis, relapsing
fever, valley fever, and the toxic effects of
shellfish poisoning.

  1. Meyer, Karl Friedrich, 1884-1974. 2.
Pathologists--California--Biography. 3. Micro-

(Cont. on next card)

Leaders in American medicine--Karl F. Meyer, M.D.
  [Motion picture] 1974. Card 3.

biological research. I. Alpha Omega Alpha. II.
National Medical Audiovisual Center. III. National
Audiovisual Center.
[R154]   616.01092   75-704435

Figure 1.8 (cont.)

Leaders in American medicine, Matthew Walker,
   M.D. [Videorecording] / Alpha Omega Alpha ;
   in cooperation with National Medical Audio-
   visual Center. -- Atlanta : The Center ;
   Washington : distributed by National Audio-
   visual Center, 1974.
   1 cassette, 56 min. : sd., col. ; 3/4 in.

   Also issued as motion picture.
   CREDITS: John Z. Bowers, Louis J. Bernard.
   SUMMARY: Dr. Walker discusses his medical

   ○   (Cont. on next card)

Leaders in American medicine, Matthew Walker,
   M.D. [Videorecording] 1974. Card 2.

   education and tells about his efforts to
   train more surgeons, his responsibility for
   the success or failure of his students, and
   his concern for the delivery of comprehensive
   health care to ghettos and rural areas.

      1. Walker, Matthew. 2. Surgeons--Tennessee--
   Biography. 3. Surgery--Study and teaching.

   ○   (Cont. on next card)

Leaders in American medicine, Matthew Walker,
   M.D. [Videorecording] 1974. Card 3.

   4. Community health services. I. Alpha Omega
   Alpha.
[R154]   610.69   76-706147
National Audiovisual Center ○

Figure 1.8 (cont.)

Learning to sew. [Filmstrip] / Dynamic Educational Films. -- Glendale, Calif. : AIMS
Instructional Media Services, 1975.
6 rolls : col. ; 35 mm. & 6 cassettes and
guide.

CONTENTS: 1. An introduction to the sewing
machine.--2. Using the sewing machine.--3.
Selecting and understanding the pattern.--4.
Laying and cutting the pattern.--5. Sewing the
garment.--6. Finishing the garment.

(Cont. on next card)

Learning to sew. [Filmstrip] 1975. Card 2.

1. Sewing. 2. Sewing machines. [1. Sewing.]
I. Dynamic Educational Films (Firm).

[TT713]   646.2   76-731447
AIMS Instructional Media
  Services

Figure 1.9

MAIN ENTRY CARDS FOR SOUND RECORDINGS

Eagles: their greatest hits. [Sound recording]
Asylum 7E-1052. p1976
1 disc. 33-1/3 rpm. stereo 12 in.

Songs performed by the Eagles.
Durations on label.
CONTENTS: Take it easy.--Witchy woman.--Lyin'
eyes.--Already gone.--Desperado.--One of these
nights.--Tequilla sunrise.--Take it to the limit.--
Peaceful, easy feeling.--Best of my love.

1. Music, Popular (Songs, etc.)--United States.
I. Eagles (Musical group).

[M1630.18]   76-761093

Beethoven, Ludwig van, 1770-1827.
[Concerto, piano, no. 5, op. 73, E♭ major]
[Sound recording]
Piano concerto no. 5 in E flat (Emperor), op. 73.
Coriolanus overture in C minor, op. 62. [New York]
Funk & Wagnalls, 1976. FW 312.
1 disc. 33-1/3 rpm. stereo. 12 in. (Family
library of great music, album 12)

Hanae Nakajima, piano; Nuremberg Symphony
Orchestra; Zsolt Deàky, conductor.
Biographical and program notes by R. Jacobson

(Cont. on next card)

Beethoven, Ludwig van, 1770-1827. [Concerto,
piano, no. 5, op. 73, E♭ major] [Sound recording]
1976. Card 2.

(12 p. ill.) inserted in container.

1. Concertos (Piano). 2. Overtures. I. Beethoven, Ludwig van, 1770-1827. Coriolanus overture.
[Sound recording] 1976. II. Nakajima, Hanae,
1940-   III. Deàky, Zsolt. IV. Nürnberger Sym-
phoniker. V. Title: Coriolanus overture. VI.
Series: Family library of great music. [Sound
recording] album 12.

[M1010]   76-750804

Uniform titles for sound recordings are employed most often for classical music, and your librarian will be able to help you determine what the correct uniform title is.

Returning to the main entry cards in Figure 1.9, you will notice that the collation contains useful information. Here you will learn such things as whether the recording is on cassette tape or disc (LP), 33-⅓ RPM or 45 RPM, monaural ("mono"), stereo, or quadrophonic ("quad"). The notes area of the cards will generally highlight the contents, performers, and any other materials that may accompany the recording.

Subject Searching

So far, we have been talking about how to gain access to books and other materials in the catalog when you know the author, coauthor, or title. But you will often come to the catalog knowing neither author nor title, searching instead for materials on a subject. You have already learned that there are subject entries in your library's catalog, but what *are* those subject entries? If, for example, you were looking for information on choosing a career, you would need to consider if you should look under the entry "Careers" or "Business, Choice of," or possibly "Vocation" or "Occupational guidance." You may know very well what *you* want to find, but does the terminology you've picked coincide with the terminology used in the library catalog?

The difficulty described above is a common one for most library users and is usually called the problem of "vocabulary control" by librarians. This problem arises simply because the English language—or *any* language for that matter—is subject to interpretation. For one person, the term "Career choice" may be the perfect description of the subject of a book, while for another person examining the same book, "Occupational guidance" may seem more precise. Since librarians want to display together all the catalog cards for books on similar subjects, they need a specific, authoritative, and uniform list of terms that they can use. For most libraries, this list of terms is called the *Library of Congress Subject Headings* (commonly referred to as *LCSH*) and is usually available near the catalog or in the reference area of your library (although some libraries have their copies in their cataloging departments). Librarians have used *LCSH* for many years to create cross-reference cards for their catalogs, but these days more and more libraries are no longer making their own cross-references, but are instead referring their library users directly to *LCSH*.

To discover how to use *LCSH*, let's return to the situation described above, where you want to find information on choosing a career.

Figure 1.10

A LIBRARY OF CONGRESS SUBJECT HEADING

Vocational guidance (*Direct*)

   sa Blind--Education
      Counseling
      Deaf--Education
      Electronic data processing in vocational
        guidance
      Languages and vocational opportunities
      Medicine as a profession
      Occupations
      Occupations and race
      Personality and occupation
      Personnel service in education
      Professions
      Retraining, Occupational
      United States. Navy--Vocational
        guidance
      Vocation (in religious orders,
        congregations, etc.)
      Vocational interests
      Vocational qualifications
      Vocational rehabilitation
      subdivision Vocational guidance *under*
        fields of knowledge and industries
        and trades, e.g. Economics--
        Vocational guidance; Machine-shops
        --Vocational guidance; Plastics industry
        and trade--Vocational guidance; *also*
        Agriculture as a profession; Law as a
        profession; Music as a profession; *and*
        similar headings
   x Business, Choice of
      Careers
      Choice of profession
      Guidance, Student
      Guidance, Vocational
      Occupation, Choice of
      Student guidance
      Vocation, Choice of
  xx Counseling
      Occupations
      Personnel service in education
      Professions
      Vocation
      Vocational education
      Vocational rehabilitation
      Youth--Employment
  --Audio-visual aids
  --Information services
  --Juvenile literature
  --Religious aspects. *See* Vocation

You've decided to use "Careers" as a search term, and, finding it in *LCSH*, you discover a cross-reference that says "Careers. *See* Vocational guidance." Turning then to this latter term, you find the information displayed in Figure 1.10.

The heading "Vocational guidance," printed in boldface type, can be used to describe library materials in your catalog. But much more information you may find useful is provided in this excerpt. First, the word *"Direct,"* following "Vocational guidance," refers to what librarians call "method of geographic subdivision." If we have a book on, say, choosing careers in the Seattle, Washington, area, the subject heading would indicate the geographic location *directly*: "Vocational guidance – Seattle." If, however, you had seen *"Indirect"* following the subject heading, the place (Seattle) would have been indicated indirectly, following "Washington (State)": "Vocational guidance – Washington (State) – Seattle."

Of more importance to you will be the information provided *below* the subject heading, where you find a rather long list of terms. The first group, preceded by the *"sa,"* is a list of narrower, related subjects. Thus, if you are interested in finding materials on vocational guidance, you may also be interested in looking in your library's catalog under such authorized subject headings as "Professions," or "Machine shops – Vocational guidance." The *sa*, then, stands for "See also" and precedes a group of authorized subject terms that are generally more specific, and under which you may want to look. Below the *sa* group is another list of terms, preceded by *"x."* These are *not* authorized for use in the catalog, but are simple synonyms – terms with a similar meaning as that conveyed by "Vocational guidance." Notice that "Careers" appears here; this list created the reference that led you to "Vocational guidance" in the first place. Thus, if you looked under any of these terms in *LCSH*, you would find a note that said *"See* Vocational guidance." The third group of terms, preceded by the *"xx,"* is a list of broader authorized subject headings related to the subject vocational guidance. If you were to turn to one of the headings listed after the *xx* (such as "Vocational education"), you would find "Vocational guidance" listed under *sa*. Thus, the *xx* indicates a kind of backward reference to related subject headings.

After these three groups of terms have been presented, you will find a list of subdivisions of the subject, each preceded by a dash. For example, if you wanted materials on information services in vocational guidance, you would look under "Vocational guidance – Information services." Many subject headings you find in *LCSH* will have subdivisions under them, but there are also *general* subdivisions that can be used under almost *any* subject heading (such as "Bibliography"). The list of standard subdivisions appears in the introduction to *LCSH*.

In scanning the various lists that follow the authorized subject heading "Vocational guidance," you may be able to understand the major principle that underlies how subject headings are assigned, namely that the most *specific* terms are used in describing the contents of library materials. Thus, a book on a career as a machinist will be assigned the heading "Machine shops – Vocational guidance" and not necessarily "Vocational guidance."

This principle of "specificity" has an important implication: you must always try to find materials under the most appropriate heading, but if you fail to find that heading listed in your library's catalog, you will have to look under a broader heading. As an example of this, let's return to the situation in which you seek information on a career as a machinist. You look in the catalog under "Machine shops – Vocational guidance," but find nothing. Apparently your library has never bought any materials dealing solely, or at least primarily, with that subject. But your library may very well have some materials on vocational guidance in which a career as a machinist is discussed along with many other careers in various fields. Thus, you should probably try looking under "Vocational guidance" and then, assuming that you find some listings in the catalog, locate and examine those materials to see whether or not a career as a machinist is discussed.

The longer you use *LCSH*, the more you will find it to be indispensable to your subject searching in the catalog. Keep in mind, though, that *LCSH* does *not* list proper names (such as "Clemens, Samuel"). Your librarian can assist you in finding appropriate search terms in *LCSH*, as well as proper names that are not listed there, so that you can exploit your library's resources to their fullest extent.

Filing

In the introductory remarks to the section on the catalog, you may remember that the catalog was described as being filed alphabetically. Surely nothing could be simpler since everybody knows the alphabet, right? Would that it were so. In fact, most libraries use the *ALA Rules for Filing Catalog Cards* (2d ed.; Chicago: American Library Association, 1968), a book, well over 200 pages long, filled with rules and exceptions to rules.

The basic rule of which you need to be aware is that in a dictionary catalog, all entries – main, added, and subject – are alphabetically interfiled in the "word-by-word" mode, as illustrated in Figure 1.11.

Figure 1.11

FILING ORDER

Word by Word	Letter by Letter
San Diego's Historic Mission	Sanda, Albert
Sand Casting for Fun & Profit	Sandall, Robert
Sand Creek Baptist Association	Sandal Making
Sand Dollars on the Coast	The Sandarac Tree of Africa
Sand, Edward	Sandblasting in Urban Renewal
The Sand Grouse	Sandboxes
The Sand Rat in Song & Legend	Sandburg, Carl
Sanda, Albert	Sandby, William
Sandal Making	Sand Casting for Fun & Profit
Sandall, Robert	Sand Creek Baptist Association
The Sandarac Tree of Africa	Sand Dollars on the Coast
Sandblasting in Urban Renewal	Sand, Edward
Sandboxes	The Sand Grouse
Sandburg, Carl	San Diego's Historic Mission
Sandby, William	The Sand Rat in Song & Legend

Since you are probably most familiar with the "letter-by-letter" mode – the kind of alphabetization used in most dictionaries, telephone directories, and the like – you should study the examples in Figure 1.11 carefully. Note that in the word-by-word mode, "San Diego's Historic Mission" files first, while in the letter-by-letter mode, it files second to last. This is because the spaces between works are taken into account in the word-by-word mode of filing, whereas they are *not* in the letter-by-letter mode. Your library's catalog is not the only tool that employs the word-by-word mode; other reference tools, such as the *Encyclopedia Americana,* do so as well. Always check any alphabetically arranged tool to see which mode of alphabetization is used, since, as Figure 1.11 clearly illustrates, the difference is critical.

Once you have mastered the word-by-word mode of alphabetization, you can then concentrate on some of the more common filing problems experienced by many library users of the catalog. Here are a few filing rules that may save you time and frustration:

- Articles ("The," "A," "An," and their foreign equivalents) that appear at the beginning of entries are ignored in filing. Thus "The Sand Rat in Song & Legend" files in the "S"s, and *not* in the "T"s.
- Diacritical (i.e., accent) marks in foreign languages are ignored in filing. Thus "é," "ê," "à," and "ñ" will interfile with "e," "a," and "n" respectively.
- Common abbreviations and numbers will file as if spelled out in full. Thus "St." files as "Saint," "Dr." files as "Doctor," and "5" files as "five."
- Initials file as though each one were a word. Thus "IAA" is treated, and filed, as three separate words. The major exception to this occurs with those initials that are pronounced as words (they're called "acronyms"). Thus "UNESCO" files as a single word, not as six different ones.
- Personal names beginning with "Mac," "Mc," or "M'" all file *together* with the "Mac"s. Thus "McDonald" and "M'Donald" interfile with "MacDonald."
- In a dictionary catalog, cards representing books *by* an author are filed before cards representing books *about* an author. Thus you will find all of Samuel Clemens's works (i.e., main entries and added entries) in the catalog before you find the books *about* Samuel Clemens (i.e., subject entries).

Filing, as you may already have guessed, is a complicated matter. If you ever experience difficulty in finding an entry in the catalog, seek assistance from your librarian.

FINDING AND EVALUATING BOOKS

You now know something about how your library's catalog is structured and what kinds of information you can find on a catalog card. But the catalog not only tells you *what* books are in the library, it also tells you where those books are. The following two sections deal not only with how to locate books in the library, but also with how to evaluate what you find.

Classification and Browsing

Librarians do not simply buy materials and throw them onto the shelves in a willy-nilly fashion. After all, it is not going to be terribly useful to you if a book on Shakespeare is shelved next to a book on chemistry, which is in turn shelved next to a book on cooking. Instead, librarians attempt to put materials on related subjects next to each other so that you can browse. The process of analyzing the subject contents of a book and then assigning a shorthand notation—a series of numbers or letters and numbers—to the book is called classification.

There are two classification schemes used most often by U.S. libraries to arrange books on the shelves: Library of Congress classification (LC) and Dewey decimal classification (DDC, or just Dewey). Let's take a look first at the Library of Congress scheme, which is used mostly in college and university libraries and in about half of the nation's community college libraries. It is composed of a number of different individual classification schedules, each headed up by a letter (or letters) as shown in Figure 1.12. To each of these letters may be added extra letters and then numbers that will express the subject content of the book.

To get a better idea of how the LC classification system works, take a look again at Figure 1.4 (p. 15) where the main entry card for Melvin Donaho's book *How to Get the Job You Want* is displayed. In both the upper and lower left-hand corners, you see the LC classification number "HF5383.D57." The "H," as you can see from Figure 1.12, stands for social sciences. What you cannot see is that the "H" class is broken down into several subclasses, one of them being "HF," for "Commerce." Adding the number "5383" to "HF" indicates that Donaho's book deals with "Business—Popular works—Applications for positions." If your library uses the LC classification, then *any* books acquired on the subject of "Applications for positions" will be classified under "HF5383."

Now that the Donaho book has been classified, we have to deal with another problem—how to insure that the Donaho book will have a *unique* "address" on the library's shelves. Let's say, for example, that our imaginary community college library has five books on "Applications for positions": one by Baker, Donaho, Farley, Marlow, and Peters. Each book will receive the classification number "HF5383," but then to distinguish one book from another, we'll add a special designation for the author's name—a combination of the first letter of the author's last name, plus a decimal number (or numbers)—so that the books sit on the shelf alphabetically by the authors' names. Our imaginary arrangement would thus be:

HF	HF	HF	HF	HF
5383	5383	5383	5383	5383
.B2	.D57	.F23	.M225	.P37

The classification number plus the author designation (and perhaps a date, or other letters and numbers) forms what librarians term the "call number"—the unique address for a particular book.

Let's turn now to the Dewey decimal classification, which is used by most public libraries and almost half of the community college libraries in the United States. As you can see from examining Figure 1.13, Dewey divides knowledge into ten broad classes, each of which

Figure 1.12

LIBRARY OF CONGRESS CLASSIFICATION

A	General works
B-BJ	Philosophy. Psychology
BL-BX	Religion
C	Auxiliary Sciences of History
D	History: General and Old World (Eastern Hemisphere)
E-F	History: America (Western Hemisphere)
G	Geography. Anthropology. Recreation
H	Social Sciences
J	Political Science
K	Law. Philosophy of Law
KD	Law of the United Kingdom and Ireland
KF	Law of the United States
L	Education
M	Music. Books on Music
N	Fine Arts
P-PA	General Philology and Linguistics. Classical Languages and Literatures
PA Supplement	Byzantine and Modern Greek Literature. Medieval and Modern Latin Literature
PB-PH	Modern European Languages
PG	Russian Literature
PJ-PM	Languages and Literatures of Asia, Africa, Oceania. American Indian Languages. Artificial Languages.
P-PM Supplement	Index to Languages and Dialects
PN, PR, PS, PZ	General Literature. English and American Literature. Fiction in English. Juvenile Literature
PQ, Part 1	French Literature
PQ, Part 2	Italian, Spanish, and Portuguese Literatures
PT, Part 1	German Literature
PT, Part 2	Dutch and Scandinavian Literatures
Q	Science
R	Medicine
S	Agriculture
T	Technology
U	Military Science
V	Naval Science
Z	Bibliography. Library Science

is then broken down into more specific subclasses; thus the longer the number to the right of the decimal point, the more specific the subject being described. A relatively short Dewey number—"650.14"—was assigned to the Donaho book represented in Figure 1.4. The "650," as you can see from the Dewey outline, stands for "Managerial services" (which, you will note, is a part of the *broader* class "600: Applied Sciences"). What you cannot see is that the addition of ".1" to "650" indicates materials on "Success in business"; and the addition of the "4" to ".1" makes the Dewey number even more specific since it indicates "Success in obtaining jobs and promotions."

Since many books could have the same Dewey number, we need to construct unique call numbers, just as we did with the LC classification system. Again most libraries will use a special designation for the author's last name. Thus our imaginary library may have those same five books (by Baker, Donaho, Farley, Marlow, and Peters) each classified under "650.14," but each will have a unique address on the shelves:

650.14	650.14	650.14	650.14	650.14
.B245	.D683	.F267	.M321	.P473

Obviously, you need not know exactly what each number—either Dewey or LC—stands for in order to use your library and locate books. The point is that there is rhyme and reason to how books are shelved in the library. Since related materials are shelved together, you can consult the broad outlines of either Dewey or LC to find out where most of the books on your subject are shelved. Thus, if you were majoring in health occupations, you could browse through the "610"s in Dewey or the "R"s in LC to discover what your library had available for you.

While browsing is certainly one of the great advantages of classification, don't forget that each book has its own unique call number indicated in the upper left-hand corner of the catalog card. If you want one specific book—and *only* that book—you will need to copy down the entire call number so that if there were, say, some fifty books with the same *classification* number, you could easily and readily find the one you wanted. Also pay attention to any special indicators—such things as "Ref." to indicate "Reference"—that may have been added to the call number to tell you that the book is not shelved with the regular book collection.

As a final note, remember that *all* "author numbers"—such as ".D57"—are decimal integers and not whole numbers, even if your

Figure 1.13

DEWEY DECIMAL CLASSIFICATION

000 GENERALITIES
- 010 Bibliographies & catalogs
- 020 Library & information science
- 030 General encyclopedic works
- 040
- 050 General serial publications
- 060 General organizations & museology
- 070 Journalism, publishing, newspapers
- 080 General collections
- 090 Manuscripts & book rarities

100 PHILOSOPHY & RELATED DISCIPLINES
- 110 Metaphysics
- 120 Knowledge, cause, purpose, man
- 130 Popular & parapsychology, occultism
- 140 Specific philosophical viewpoints
- 150 Psychology
- 160 Logic
- 170 Ethics (Moral philosophy)
- 180 Ancient, medieval, Oriental
- 190 Modern Western philosophy

200 RELIGION
- 210 Natural religion
- 220 Bible
- 230 Christian doctrinal theology
- 240 Christian moral & devotional
- 250 Local church & religious orders
- 260 Social & ecclesiastical theology
- 270 History & geography of church
- 280 Christian denominations & sects
- 290 Other religions & comparative

300 THE SOCIAL SCIENCES
- 310 Statistics
- 320 Political science
- 330 Economics
- 340 Law
- 350 Public administration
- 360 Social pathology & services
- 370 Education
- 380 Commerce
- 390 Customs & folklore

400 LANGUAGE
- 410 Linguistics
- 420 English & Anglo-Saxon languages
- 430 Germanic languages / German
- 440 Romance languages / French
- 450 Italian, Romanian, Rhaeto-Romanic
- 460 Spanish & Portuguese languages
- 470 Italic languages / Latin
- 480 Hellenic Classical Greek
- 490 Other languages

Figure 1.13 (cont.)

500 PURE SCIENCES
510 Mathematics
520 Astronomy & allied sciences
530 Physics
540 Chemistry & allied sciences
550 Sciences of earth & other worlds
560 Paleontology
570 Life sciences
580 Botanical sciences
590 Zoological sciences

600 TECHNOLOGY (APPLIED SCIENCES)
610 Medical sciences
620 Engineering & allied operations
630 Agriculture & related
640 Domestic arts & sciences
650 Managerial services
660 Chemical & related technologies
670 Manufactures
680 Miscellaneous manufactures
690 Buildings

700 THE ARTS
710 Civic & landscape art
720 Architecture
730 Plastic arts / Sculpture
740 Drawing, decorative & minor arts
750 Painting & paintings
760 Graphic arts / Prints
770 Photography & photographs
780 Music
790 Recreational & performing arts

800 LITERATURE (BELLE-LETTRES)
810 American literature in English
820 English & Anglo-Saxon literatures
830 Literatures of Germanic languages
840 Literatures of Romance languages
850 Italian, Romanian, Rhaeto-Romanic
860 Spanish & Portuguese literatures
870 Italic languages literatures / Latin
880 Hellenic languages literatures
890 Literatures of other languages

900 GENERAL GEOGRAPHY & HISTORY
910 General geography / Travel
920 General biography & genealogy
930 General history of ancient world
940 General history of Europe
950 General history of Asia
960 General history of Africa
970 General history of North America
980 General history of South America
990 General history of other areas

library has dropped the decimal point in call numbers. Thus a call number that reads ".D2309" will be shelved *before* ".D231," because ".2309" is *smaller* than ".231."

Evaluating What You Find

You've been browsing through the catalog looking for books on vocational guidance. Following some of the suggestions offered earlier in this chapter, you've spent several minutes reading and evaluating the catalog cards with a critical eye: you've rejected one book because it was too long, another because it seemed too out of date, and another still because it had no illustrations. You've copied down the complete call numbers for five books that seem promising, and you now wander off to the "stacks" (a library word for shelves) where you hope to find the books you seek. You've found the five books (none were checked out), but you don't want to have to drag all of them home with you. So now what? Now it's time to make a personal evaluation of the books by using a technique some librarians call "technical reading."

Technical reading is nothing but a method of scanning certain important parts of a book in order to discover whether or not a book meets your needs. Before discussing which "important" parts you should examine, however, let's take a look at what a "typical" work of nonfiction contains.

- *The Preliminaries.* The pages of this part of a book are numbered with lowercased Roman numerals and usually include a title page, a copyright page, a dedication page, a table of contents (sometimes very detailed), a list of figures or illustrations, an acknowledgments page (on which the author thanks the persons or organizations that may have provided assistance), and a preface.
- *The Body of the Book.* Here the pagination is in Arabic numerals, often beginning with the introduction to the book and followed by the main text, which is usually divided into chapters.
- *The End Matter.* The regular pagination continues here, and you may find an appendix (supplementary material related to the subject of the book), a glossary (a list of terms and their definitions), a bibliography or list of references, and an index.

Let's return now to the topic at hand, technical reading. The best place to begin to evaluate a work of nonfiction is in the preliminaries, with the table of contents. If the contents are detailed, you will get an idea of how the book is structured and what broad topics are covered. For example, if you were specifically interested in résumé writing, you might find that one of the books you're examining has an entire chapter devoted to that topic or an appendix showing various résumés. If résumé writing is not mentioned specifically in the table of contents, you would then need to check the book's index to see if there are any references to this topic somewhere in the main body of the book. The table of contents will also lead you to any special appendixes, a bibliography, or other supplementary material that may significantly enhance the value of the book to you.

Once you have finished scanning the table of contents, you should skim through the preface and introduction to the work. In doing this, you should be able to discover the book's intended audience. For example, the book may have been written for senior business executives who are interested in a career change, or it could be written for students about to graduate from a community college. Sometimes, of course, the title of the book will give you a clue to the audience, but some books have deceptive titles, so that the only way to discover the author's intentions is by reading through the preface or introduction. Another advantage of skimming is that it will give you an idea of how well you may relate to the author's style. A book that uses language that is going to send you to the dictionary every few minutes may not be worth your time and effort. Alternately, you may feel that the author is talking down to you and that spending more than five minutes with his work would be unbearable.

Once you have finished examining the table of contents (with possibly a glance or two at the index) and reading the preface and introduction, you should have a feel for what the book is all about. You can, of course, continue to browse through the book—thumbing through various chapters, looking at some of the illustrations, scanning the bibliography—but the three-to-five minutes spent in your technical reading should have helped you to choose one book over another.

BEYOND YOUR LIBRARY'S WALLS

The English poet John Donne said that "no man is an island." Well, neither is a library. Thousands of new books and periodicals appear each year, and no community college library can hope to acquire more than a small percentage of them (although your librarians will go

out of their way to purchase the most important works). Because
library budgets have dwindled during the last decade and because the
price of most library materials continues to increase at an alarming
rate, many libraries are entering into cooperative agreements with
other libraries – locally, regionally, and sometimes nationally – so as to
stretch their library dollars.

What this means to you, the library user, is that information
resources are *not* by any means limited to the holdings of your own
library. You may find, for example, that your community college
library has entered a network through which the resources of many
other libraries are available to you. You may also find that you have
borrowing privileges at other academic libraries in your area. And, of
course, you may also be eligible to obtain materials from other
libraries using what is called an "interlibrary loan."

There is, of course, one slight drawback: obtaining materials from
other libraries will inevitably consume more time, time for which you
must allow. If your library has reciprocal agreements with local
libraries, the time necessary to obtain the materials you need may
amount to only two or three days; but if your library has to prepare an
actual interlibrary loan so as to obtain materials from outside your im-
mediate locality, the time will lengthen to two or perhaps three
weeks, sometimes even longer. This is, though, a small price to pay to
have virtually the entirety of human knowledge available to you.

YOUR MOST IMPORTANT RESOURCE

Many students come to the library, and if they don't immediately
find what they need in the catalog or in a periodical index, they leave,
under the assumption that the library has nothing for them. In so doing, they choose to ignore the most valuable resource available to
them: the librarian.

So what exactly *is* a librarian? Unfortunately, the popular mis-
conception is that of an old lady, usually with a bun on her head, who
either is checking out books behind the main desk or scowling at
students in an attempt (usually futile) to get them to be quiet. The
truth is that relatively few librarians check out books, much less
scowl – they generally work behind the scenes.

Most community college librarians in the United States hold a
master's degree in librarianship or information science, and some
have specialized in such areas as administration, technical services,
media, or public services. Administrators, as you might expect, see
to the overall functioning of the library and concern themselves with
such things as the budget, the library's relationship with various

academic and vocational departments, and other similar matters. Technical services librarians may work in cataloging (where they oversee the preparation of additions to the catalog), acquisitions (where they read reviews of new books and other materials and coordinate purchasing for the library's collections), or serials (where they oversee the purchasing and binding of old and new periodicals). Media librarians deal with the purchasing of films, videotapes, and other such nonprint materials and often work with the college faculty in designing materials and programs that will support classroom instruction. Public services librarians are generally the most visible librarians, since they may supervise the functioning of the circulation department, work at the reference desk, or teach a course in library orientation.

Now that you know a little bit about what librarians do, let's turn to a discussion of how they can help you. The primary function of any librarian, regardless of his or her specialty, is to help you wade through and sort out a veritable avalanche of information. Given that, you should feel free to turn to your librarian under a wide variety of circumstances. You may, for example, not be having any luck in finding appropriate search terms in *LCSH*. Your librarian will be able to suggest alternatives. You may have a specific question for which your librarian may be able to suggest a useful source of information. You may have doubts about a search strategy you adopted that seems to be failing. Your librarian should be able to get you back on the right track.

In the following two chapters, you will read about many different tools, both general and specialized, that are designed to answer a wide variety of questions. But that information, like the information on the catalog and on classification in this chapter, is introductory in scope. Your librarians have a comprehensive knowledge of your library's collection as well as an eye open for its new acquisitions. Don't ever hesitate to seek assistance from them, for they are, quite literally, your most important resource in the library.

NOTES

1. *Anglo-American Cataloging Rules.* (Chicago: American Library Association, 1967). A second edition of the *AACR* (as it is commonly known) was published in 1978 and will be adopted by most libraries in 1981.

2. Beginning in 1981, main entry under performer will be allowed under certain circumstances. This is a perfect example of rule changes mentioned earlier.

2
The General Tools

Tools. We use them everyday for a variety of purposes: an automobile for transportation, a stove for cooking, a pen for writing. The list is practically endless, for humankind is often characterized as being the species of "tool users." But there is a broad range of tools that only a small percentage of our society can use with any confidence and proficiency: reference tools. What they are and how you use them are the subject of this chapter.

Let's begin our discussion of reference tools by defining them: they are materials—most often in book format—that have generally been designed to be consulted for bits of information rather than read from cover to cover. This definition thus covers such things as dictionaries, encyclopedias, yearbooks, and periodical indexes, to name just a few. Within this broad spectrum, though, we can distinguish three principal categories: those reference tools that give you access to information rather than the information itself (such as bibliographies and periodical indexes), those that give you the information itself (such as dictionaries), and those that do both (such as many encyclopedias). Each of these three categories—which we'll call access type, source type, and source/access type—can in turn be either general in scope (such as a general-purpose dictionary) or limited in scope (such as a dictionary of literary terms).

In the first chapter, you read about how to evaluate books by examining the table of contents, preface, and introduction—a process called technical reading. You will find that this technique is particularly important when it comes to evaluating and using reference tools. As an example, let's take a look at a reference book that almost everybody has used at one time or another: the telephone directory. In the preliminaries of a typical telephone directory, you usually find the following: an index to information (sometimes inside the front cover);

a list of emergency numbers (such as for the police and fire departments); information on what communities are represented in the directory; information on how to place phone calls of different types (local, long distance, person-to-person); sample telephone rates for long distance calls; information on how the directory is organized (e.g., alphabetically, letter by letter); a list of area codes for cities and states; a list of telephone prefixes by location; information on how to pay telephone bills, how to obtain repair service, and how to have a new phone installed; and information on and advertising for special services of the company (such as vacation service).

Following the preliminaries come the "white pages": the alphabetical listing of persons and organizations with brief addresses and telephone numbers. At the end of the white pages, you can find such diverse things as public service information on how to be an intelligent consumer, more advertising, and even a calendar (!) for the years 1776 to 2000. The "yellow pages" of classified advertising sometimes begin with a map of postal codes and are usually followed by an alphabetical listing of products and services available in the geographical area covered by the directory. The yellow pages often end with more advertising for the phone company.

What can you learn from this technical reading of the telephone directory? Besides learning *how* the directory is organized for your use (e.g., entries are arranged alphabetically, governmental listings are found under the appropriate jurisdiction, abbreviations are filed as if spelled out), you can learn two important things. First, the phone book falls into all three categories of reference tool – source, access, and source/access. How so? Much of the material presented in the preliminary portion of the directory gives general information on telephone service; this portion of the phone book is a source type of reference tool. The white pages make the phone book an access type of tool because they give you access to the telephone numbers of most of the persons and businesses in the community (not *all* telephone customers allow their numbers to be listed). And finally, the yellow pages make the phone book a useful source/access type of reference tool because they contain information on what products and services are available (source) *plus* the telephone numbers for those establishments (access).

The second thing to be learned from a quick examination of the telephone directory is that it is limited in scope: you can't look in, say, the Milwaukee phone book for a telephone number of a business in New York City. You will only find listings for metropolitan Milwaukee and perhaps a few outlying communities.

Thus, after just a few minutes of careful examination, you should be able to discover what *type* of tool you have, what its *scope* is, and *how* it is arranged. And in so doing, you will learn what kinds of questions the tool was designed to answer. For example, you can turn to the phone directory to learn what businesses in your area will service typewriters and other office machines. You cannot, however, go to the telephone book with a phone number and find out *whose* number it is; the directory is simply not designed to give you that kind of information. And so it is with every reference tool that you will read about in this and the following chapter: each has its own scope and purpose; each is designed to impart certain kinds of information and not others. If you cultivate the habit of quickly scanning every new reference tool that you come across, your level of efficiency – and confidence – should rise tremendously.

Having discussed how you should evaluate reference tools, let's take a look at what this chapter is designed to do. As you may have noted if you scanned the Table of Contents, this chapter is divided into various sections, each devoted to a different type of general reference tool. Most of the source-type tools such as dictionaries and biographical sources are discussed first, followed by most of the access-type tools such as indexing services and bibliographic sources. Each section begins with a list of representative tools with full imprint information: author, title, place of publication, publisher's name, and date of publication (or copyright date). Also included are subject headings that you may use for further library searching. Following the list you will find an explanatory discussion, using the representative tools as examples, of how the particular type of tool will be helpful in providing you with information.

Note that the lists are arranged alphabetically by standard main entry so that you can quickly consult your library's catalog to find if your library owns the title. Further, after each title in the lists you will generally find two numbers in parentheses: both the Library of Congress and Dewey classification numbers (*not* full call numbers). These numbers may be used for browsing. But keep in mind that your library may not be using the standardized cataloging or classification made available from the Library of Congress; if either the main entry or classification numbers should differ in your library, you may want to make note of that fact in the margins of this book.

As a final point, be aware that while almost all of the titles listed in this and the following chapter are commonly accepted standard reference works, your library may not have them all. Your library should, however, have each *type* of reference tool mentioned in this book. Looking under the standard subject headings from *LCSH* will let you know what is available in your own library's collection. And, of course, if there's any doubt, *always* ask your librarian.

DICTIONARIES AND BOOKS ON LANGUAGE

Unabridged

Random House Dictionary of the English Language. Jess Stein, ed. in chief. New York: Random, 1966. (PE1625; 423)

Webster's New International Dictionary of the English Language. 2d ed., unabridged. . . . William Allan Neilson, ed. in chief. Springfield, Mass.: Merriam, 1934. (PE1625; 423)

Webster's Third New International Dictionary of the English Language. Ed. in chief, Philip Babcock Gove. Springfield, Mass.: Merriam, 1961. (PE1625; 423)

For other tools, look in your library's catalog under: "English language – Dictionaries."

Abridged

American Heritage Dictionary of the English Language. William Morris, ed. Boston: Houghton Mifflin; New York: American Heritage, 1969. (PE1625; 423)

Webster's New Collegiate Dictionary. [8th ed.] Springfield, Mass.: Merriam, c1976. (PE1628; 423)

Webster's New World Dictionary of the American Language. 2d college ed. David B. Guralnik, ed. in chief. New York: World, 1970. (PE1625; 423)

For other tools, look in your library's catalog under: "English language – Dictionaries."

Etymological and Historical

Craigie, Sir William Alexander, and Hulbert, James R. *Dictionary of American English on Historical Principles.* Chicago: University of Chicago Press, 1936–1944. (PE2835; 427.9)

A Dictionary of Americanisms on Historical Principles. Edited by Mitford M. Mathews. Chicago: University of Chicago Press, 1951. (PE2835; 427.9)

Murray, Sir James Augustus Henry. *New English Dictionary on Historical Principles.* Oxford: Clarendon Press, 1888–1933. And its *Supplement.* Edited by R. W. Burchfield. Oxford: Clarendon Press, 1972– . (PE1625; 423)

Onions, Charles Talbut. *Oxford Dictionary of English Etymology.* Oxford: Clarendon Press, 1966. (PE1580; 422.03)

For other tools, look in your library's catalog under: "English language in the U.S.–Dictionaries," "English language–Etymology–Dictionaries," or "Americanisms."

New Words

The Second Barnhart Dictionary of New English. Ed. by Clarence L. Barnhart, Sol Steinmetz, Robert K. Barnhart. Bronxville, N.Y.: Barnhart Books, 1980. (PE1630; 423)

6,000 Words: A Supplement to Webster's Third New International Dictionary. Springfield, Mass.: Merriam, c1976. (PE1630; 423)

For other tools, look in your library's catalog under: "Words, New–English–Dictionaries."

Slang

Partridge, Eric. *A Dictionary of Slang and Unconventional English.* 7th ed. New York: Macmillan, c1970. (PE3721; 427)

Wentworth, Harold, and Flexner, Stuart Berg. *Dictionary of American Slang.* 2d supplemented ed. New York: Crowell, 1975. (PE3729 *or* PE2846; 427.09)

For other tools, look in your library's catalog under: "English language–Slang–Dictionaries."

Abbreviations

Gale Research Company. *Acronyms, Initialisms, and Abbreviations Dictionary.* 5th ed. Ellen T. Crowley and Robert C. Thomas, eds. Detroit: Gale, 1976. (PE1693; 423.1)

Gale Research Company. *New Acronyms, Initialisms, and Abbreviations.* Detroit: Gale, 1971– . (PE1693; 423.1)

For other tools, look in your library's catalog under: "Abbreviations" or "Acronyms."

Synonyms and Antonyms

Roget's International Thesaurus. 3d ed. New York: Crowell, 1962. (PE1591; 424)
Webster's Collegiate Thesaurus. Springfield, Mass.: Merriam, 1976. (PE1591; 423.1)
Webster's New Dictionary of Synonyms. [Rev. ed.] Springfield, Mass.: Merriam, 1973. (PE1591; 423.1)

For other tools, look in your library's catalog under: "English language–Synonyms and antonyms."

Usage and Style

Chicago. University. Press. *A Manual of Style.* 12th rev. ed. Chicago: University of Chicago Press, 1969. (Z253; 655.25)
Copperud, Roy H. *American Usage and Style: The Consensus.* New York: Van Nostrand-Reinhold, 1980. (PE1460; 428)
Follett, Wilson. *Modern American Usage: A Guide.* Ed. and completed by Jacques Barzun [and others]. New York: Hill & Wang, 1966. (PE2835; 423.1)
Fowler, Henry Watson. *Dictionary of Modern English Usage.* 2d rev. ed. by Sir Ernest Gowers. Oxford: Clarendon Press, 1965. (PE1628; 423)
Modern Language Association of America. *MLA Handbook for Writers of Research Papers, Theses, and Dissertations.* New York: Modern Language Association, 1977. (LB2369; 808.02)
Morris, William. *Harper Dictionary of Contemporary Usage.* New York: Harper & Row, c1975. (PE1680; 428)
Strunk, William. *The Elements of Style.* With revisions, an introduction, and a chapter on writing by E. B. White. 3d ed. New York: Macmillan, 1979. (PE1408; 808)
Turabian, Kate L. *A Manual for Writers of Term Papers, Theses, and Dissertations.* 4th ed. Chicago: University of Chicago Press, 1973. (LB2369; 808.02)

For other tools, look in your library's catalog under: "English language–Idioms, corrections, errors," "English language–Usage," "English language–Rhetoric," "Dissertations, Academic," "Report writing," "Research," and "Authorship–Handbooks, manuals, etc."

* * *

Language. It's probably humanity's most important tool, for it pervades everything we do. And few of us use language as accurately and distinctly as we should, a fact decried for many years by educators, parents, and even politicians. How many times, for example, have you caught yourself using a word inaccurately – a word the meaning of which you *thought* you knew? But just as the ability to use language effectively is all important – and increasingly so as a marketable job skill – so too is it very difficult to achieve. Day in and day out new words come into the language and old ones lose their currency and value. Which words are acceptable and which are not? How is word X pronounced? Where did word Y come from?

If you scanned the list of dictionaries and books on language, you may have been surprised at the large number of titles. In fact, they represent only a small fraction of the works that are available. Thousands have been published – everything from rhyming dictionaries to lists of hard-to-spell words – simply because human beings *are* fascinated by language.

And so we come to the books themselves, starting with dictionaries. A dictionary, as noted earlier in this chapter, is a source type of reference tool: it provides you with information in a direct way. But what kinds of information? As you can see from examining the dictionary entry in Figure 2.1, you are given (1) an indication of how the word is divided (i.e., syllabification); (2) the correct pronunciation of the word; (3) an indication of what part of speech the word is; (4) the definition (definitions) of the word; (5) an indication of synonyms for the word; and (6) the etymology of the word (i.e., the history of its form) – although not necessarily in this particular order, which is used in the *American Heritage Dictionary*.

You are probably most familiar with the general language type of dictionary, represented by those titles listed under the headings "unabridged" and "abridged." You may not have realized, however, that there are differences from one dictionary to another. First, of course, is the matter of length: the unabridged dictionaries define anywhere from 600,000 (in *Webster's Second*) to 250,000 words (in *Random House*), while almost all the abridged dictionaries define approximately 155,000 words. Length, however, is probably not that important a consideration, since the definitions of most words you seek will very likely be found in an abridged dictionary. Of more importance to you will be the definitions themselves. In the unabridged dictionaries, you will find more expansive definitions and fuller illustrative quotations than in the abridged dictionaries.

As you use dictionaries, you should keep in mind that the arrangement of definitions varies from one work to another. For example, in

Figure 2.1

A DICTIONARY ENTRY

   1   2   3   4   5

pro·mote (prə-mōt') *tr.v.* -moted, -moting, -motes. 1.a. To
raise to a more important or responsible job or rank. b. To
advance (a student) to the next higher grade. 2. To contribute
to the progress or growth of; to further. 3. To urge the adop-
tion of; to advocate. 4. To attempt to sell or popularize by
advertising or by securing financial support. —See Synonyms ◀6
at advance. [Middle English *promoten*, from Latin *prōmovēre*
(past participle *prōmōtus*), to move forward, advance : *prō-* ◀7
forward, onward + *movēre*, to move (see -mew in Appendix*).]

1 MAIN ENTRY. Shows syllabification (i.e., how the
   word is divided).

2 PRONUNCIATION. The pronunciation "key" is at the
   bottom of the page.

3 PART OF SPEECH. The "functional" categories (e.g.,
   noun, verb, adjective) are always abbreviated.

4 INFLECTED FORMS. Shows any forms that may differ
   from the main word.

5 DEFINITIONS. Each definition is preceded by a number
   or by a letter and a number.

6 SYNONYMS. For "promote," the synonyms are not given
   here; instead you are referred to "advance."

7 ETYMOLOGY. The history of the form of the word.
   Note the cross-reference that directs you to
   "mew-" in the Appendix on "Indo-European Roots."

Webster's Second, Webster's Third, and *Webster's New Collegiate,* definitions are given in "historical" order, arranged with the oldest sense of
the word first and the current sense last. This is not true for a dictionary like *American Heritage,* which lists the central meaning first
and any other related meanings after.

An important consideration in using dictionaries is whether or not
usage is indicated. Will the dictionary indicate, for example, that the
use of a particular word is "slang" or "vulgar?" If it does—and *Webster's
Second, Webster's New World,* and *American Heritage* do—the dictionary is said to be "prescriptive"; if it doesn't—and both *Webster's
Third* and *Webster's New Collegiate* are in this category—it is "descrip-

tive." The *Random House* falls somewhere in between these two categories.

Your choice of one dictionary over another may also be based on its special features. Some dictionaries (like the *American Heritage*) are profusely illustrated, a feature that may greatly aid your comprehension of the definitions. Others may have special appendixes, making them encyclopedic in scope. The *Random House,* for example, has concise bilingual dictionaries (for French, Italian, Spanish, and German) as well as various lists (e.g., "Major rivers of the world," "Major dates in history"). Others still may be particularly strong in some aspect of the language. *Webster's New World,* for example, is good for Americanisms (which are indicated by a star) and for the language of technology. Scanning the preliminaries of any general language dictionary will clue you in to any special features or strengths that might make one title more useful to you than another.

You might think that the general language dictionary contains all the information you might ever need about words. But that's not true. Hundreds of specialized dictionaries answer questions that the unabridged and abridged dictionaries do not have the space to address. Let's begin by looking at the historical and etymological dictionaries, which trace the history of a word through its various meanings. The historical gives dates of use and quotations; the etymological shows the various forms and derivatives of the word.

The historical dictionary is best represented by that thirteen-volume masterwork the *New English Dictionary* (more commonly called, and later reissued as, the *Oxford English Dictionary,* or *OED*). In the *OED* and its supplements you can learn when a word first was used in print, who used it, and how the word was used (complete quotations are given). While it's not likely that you would need such information every day, knowing the historical development of a word can be useful when you're involved in writing a term paper or working on a project. Say, for example, that you're working on a term paper on abortion; you can turn to a general language dictionary to learn the precise contemporary sense of the word, to the etymological (such as the *Oxford Dictionary of English Etymology*) to get a more complete history of the form of the word, and to the historical to find out when the word was first introduced into the language and what it originally meant. Such information can give you an important historical context for your topic.

Note that there are two dictionaries—Craigie's *Dictionary of American English* and Mathew's *Dictionary of Americanisms*—that serve as U.S. counterparts to the *OED*. Craigie shows the difference between British and U.S. usage and meaning; Mathews lists words that developed on, and are peculiar to, our continent. Thus, both do the same thing for U.S. regional language that the *OED* does for the general English language.

Besides the historical and etymological dictionaries, there are other specialized tools that serve as supplements to the general language dictionaries. For example, dictionaries of new words (*6,000 Words* or the *Second Barnhart Dictionary of New English*) give the definitions of words and expressions that either have just recently come into the language or have changed in meaning. Dictionaries of slang (Partridge's *Dictionary of Slang and Unconventional English* or Wentworth and Flexner's *Dictionary of American Slang*) document the meanings of those words that might be too taboo for inclusion in a general language dictionary. And while the general dictionaries often spell out common abbreviations (either in the main alphabet or in an appendix), there are also dictionaries of abbreviations (Gale Research Company's *Acronyms, Initialisms, and Abbreviations Dictionary* and its *New Acronyms, Initialisms, and Abbreviations,* which appears annually.) Such tools decipher the latest, or more uncommon, abbreviations that are infiltrating our modern world.

One of the most useful supplements to the general dictionary is the dictionary of synonyms. Although most abridged and unabridged dictionaries indicate the principal synonyms, there is never enough room for an extensive listing of words with related meanings. Dictionaries of synonyms—*Roget's Thesaurus, Webster's Collegiate Thesaurus,* and *Webster's New Dictionary of Synonyms*—will be particularly useful to you when it comes time to write a paper, since they will help you vary your vocabulary, thus leading to a more interestingly written paper and possibly a better grade! These tools are also in heavy demand by crossword-puzzle addicts. Note that *Roget's Thesaurus,* unlike either of the Webster's titles, is *not* arranged alphabetically, but instead uses a classification system to group related words together. To make effective use of *Roget's,* then, you must use the index. If you have not used books of synonyms before, you may want to try either of the Webster's titles first since the alphabetical arrangement is probably more familiar to you. Further, the Webster's titles will give you an explanation of the different shades of meaning among words (the *Thesaurus,* by including a definition; the *Dictionary,* by using explanatory essays). *Roget's* does not do this and should be used with a general dictionary.

There is a final category of books on language that supplement the general dictionary: these are works on usage and style. Such works are essential to the term paper writer—and whether you're in an academic or a vocational program, you may need to write a term paper. First, let's talk about books on usage. They have been designed to deal with such questions as "Which do I use: *shall* or *will, that* or *which?*" They will also answer questions you may have on punctuation. Most of them—Fowler, Follett, Copperud, and Morris—are arranged alphabetically, which makes them easy to use. Fowler's *Dictionary of Modern English Usage* is probably the strictest usage manual, with Follett's *Modern American Usage* coming in second place. Copperud's *American Usage and Style* and (to a slightly lesser extent) Morris's *Harper Dictionary of Contemporary Usage* serve to bring together the opinions of language experts on correct usage. Any of these works, as well as Strunk and White's classic *The Elements of Style* (a very concise and indispensable guide to good writing), also makes entertaining and informative reading.

The books on style that have been listed—the Chicago *Manual of Style,* Turabian's *Manual for Writers,* and the *MLA Handbook*—do not deal with the style of prose (as does Strunk and White), but rather with the style or format that should be employed when constructing footnotes and bibliographies for your papers, as well as with other questions regarding the mechanics of writing. As such, they are truly indispensable to the community college student. The most widely used manual is Turabian (which is based on the larger Chicago *Manual of Style*), although your instructor may prefer that you use the *MLA Handbook* or some other manual of his or her choosing. Only when you have very technical questions not addressed by those shorter works will you need to refer to the Chicago *Manual of Style,* since it is designed for use by authors and editors.

Remember that all of the aforementioned dictionaries and books on language deal with *general* English that all of us use everyday. Many special subject and bilingual dictionaries, listed in Chapter 3, will give more expansive and exacting definitions that you will need as you learn more about your area of study.

ENCYCLOPEDIAS

Multivolume Adult Encyclopedias

Academic American Encyclopedia. Princeton: Aretê Publishing Co., 1979-1980. (AE5; 031)

Encyclopedia Americana. New York, Chicago: Americana Corporation. (AE5; 031)

The New Encyclopaedia Britannica. 15th ed. Chicago: Encyclopaedia Britannica, [1974]. (AE5; 031)

Multivolume Juvenile/Young Adult Encyclopedias

Encyclopedia International. New York: Grolier. (AE5; 031)
World Book Encyclopedia. Chicago: Field Enterprises Educational Corporation. (AE5; 031)

One-volume Encyclopedias

The New Columbia Encyclopedia. 4th ed. New York: Columbia University Press, 1975. (AG5; 031)
The Random House Encyclopedia. New York: Random House, 1977. (AG5; 031)

For other tools, look in your library's catalog under: "Encyclopedias and dictionaries."

*   *   *

The general purpose encyclopedia is an important source/access tool that not only provides information, but also sometimes leads you to other sources of information. It has two distinct uses as (1) a source of brief factual information about a person, place, or thing—what librarians call "ready reference"; and (2) a source of broader background information on a subject. In general, the one-volume encyclopedia is most useful for ready reference situations, while the multivolume sets are better suited as a source of background information.

Many students may remember their elementary or high school teachers telling them to write a term paper, but *not* to use the encyclopedia as a source of information. Indeed, the encyclopedia cannot be used as a primary source of information. It is, however, indispensable as a starting point for research since its summary information provides you with a beginning context on which to build. The fact that the larger encyclopedia articles also include references to the more important books available on your topic makes this general reference tool an ideal place to begin work on a research project or term paper.

If you scanned the list of encyclopedia titles, you may have noticed that most of the citations do not show dates of publication. This is because all of the multivolume sets—but not the single-volume encyclopedias—are continually revised. Each year, for example, a slightly revised version of the *Americana* appears, a version in which some of the articles have been rewritten or updated, particularly those dealing with national and world history. Only rarely does an entirely new edition of an encyclopedia appear, although two such events occurred recently: one in 1974 with the appearance of a newly designed fifteenth edition of the *Britannica* and another in 1979-1980 with the publication of the new *Academic American.*

The fact that the multivolume sets are continually revised has an important, and perhaps obvious, implication: you cannot expect to find recent information in an earlier dated set. For example, you can't look in the 1976 edition of the *World Book* for information on an event or development that occurred in 1977. Filling in the time gap between a particular revision of an encyclopedia and the present is the function of the encyclopedia yearbook, examples of which are discussed later in this chapter in the section devoted to ready reference sources.

So what of the encyclopedias themselves? Since you want to be able to rely on the information you find in one, you must consider how authoritative the encyclopedia is. This can be judged by examining the list of contributors and noting whether they are experts in their respective fields. Generally, you can safely assume that any of the multivolume encyclopedias that are published by one of the "big four" publishers are reliable, since they seek out qualified contributors. Those publishers are the Encyclopaedia Britannica Educational Corporation, Field Enterprises, Grolier Inc. (of which Americana Corporation is a subsidiary), and Macmillan Educational Corporation. Aretê Publishing (which issues *Academic American*) is also reputable. The one-volume encyclopedias—and the subject-oriented encyclopedias discussed in Chapter 3—are also considered to be authoritative. If you have occasion to use an encyclopedia not listed in this book or in another reference source, you may want to ask your librarian about its reputation, since it may fall into the category of the "supermarket encyclopedia," a category not particularly noted for its reliability.

If all of the encyclopedias listed here are authoritative, how, then, will you choose one over another? One criterion that you might apply is that of the encyclopedia's language level. The *World Book* and *Encyclopedia International,* for example, have been written for the high school level student; both the *Americana* and *Britannica,* as well as the one-volume encyclopedias, are designed for use by the average adult. The *Academic American,* although classed with the adult encyclopedias, falls in between the adult and juvenile categories since it is geared to the needs of the contemporary high school and college student. Thus, if you need information about a relatively technical subject, you might want to check in a juvenile or young adult encyclopedia first since the article is likely to be more easily readable. On the other hand, if you already know something about the subject, the adult encyclopedia – or even a subject-oriented encyclopedia – will be more suitable.

Another criterion you can apply is that of the encyclopedia's scope. While all encyclopedias attempt to deal with the universe of knowledge, some have particular strengths or editorial focal points. The *Americana,* for example, is frequently noted for its strong coverage of U.S. history and biography. The *Britannica,* originally a British work (as its title suggests), is now quite Americanized; it comes close to rivaling the *Americana* in its coverage of the United States. The *Academic American* is strong in science and technology. As to the juvenile and young-adult encyclopedias (*World Book* and *Encyclopedia International*), they often base their treatment of a subject on standard elementary and high school curricula, since their primary audience is the student at those grade levels. Because of this, the scope of articles and information in these encyclopedias is quite different from that of the adult sets. One-volume encyclopedias also cannot provide as vast a scope as that of the larger sets; thus they are useful as quick fact finders.

Once you have decided which encyclopedia to use, you will need to deal with the question of how to use it. First, there is the matter of whether the encyclopedia has a "specific-entry" or "broad-entry" approach to the subjects it treats. If an encyclopedia has a specific-entry approach, you will find separate, brief articles on smaller aspects of a subject. For example, if you were to look in the *Americana* index (volume 30) under the subject "Monkey," you would find indications that there is not only an article under the heading "Monkey," but also several different articles on specific kinds of monkeys. The broad-entry approach (formerly used throughout the *Britannica* and now used in only one section of that work) would discuss different kinds of monkeys under the single heading "Monkey." Because many encyclopedias are no longer entirely either of the specific-entry or broad-entry variety, it is absolutely essential to use the index when one is available. Note that all of the multivolume sets listed, with the exception of the new *Britannica,* have a separate index volume. The one-volume encyclopedias – the *Columbia* and the *Random House* – do not, although they contain numerous cross-references to related articles.

It probably goes without saying that, like the dictionary, entries in the encyclopedia are arranged alphabetically, some using the letter-by-letter mode, others the word-by-word mode. You may not have been aware, however, that two of the encyclopedias mentioned have more than one part. First, the new thirty-volume *Britannica* is divided into three parts. The first part is a single volume called the "Propaedia" and serves as an outline of knowledge and a guide to the whole set; it is *not* an index. The second part, in ten volumes, is called the "Micropaedia." It contains short (i.e., no longer than 750 words) articles and cross-references to the third part of the *Britannica,* the nineteen-volume "Macropaedia." The "Micropaedia" thus serves as an index to the large "Macropaedia," in which you will find long discursive articles on broader subjects as well as bibliographical references.

The other encyclopedia, the *Random House Encyclopedia,* is a new one-volume encyclopedia that has an arrangement similar to that of the *Britannica:* an "Alphapedia" of very short articles with references to the "Colorpedia," which is a series of seven articles on broad subjects (e.g., "The Universe"). The "Colorpedia" is so called because it is profusely illustrated with color photographs and drawings.

Keep in mind that the general purpose encyclopedias are supplemented by encyclopedias devoted to specific subjects, such as the *McGraw-Hill Encyclopedia of Science and Technology.* These subject-oriented encyclopedias, discussed in Chapter 3, give more specific information on topics within a particular field than the general works mentioned here.

BIOGRAPHICAL SOURCES

Ready Reference Dictionaries

Chamber's Biographical Dictionary. Edited by J. O. Thorne. Rev. ed. New York: St. Martin's, 1969. (CT103; 920.0203)

Webster's Biographical Dictionary: A Dictionary of Names of Noteworthy Persons, with Pronunciations and Concise Biographies. Springfield, Mass.: Merriam, 1972. (CT103; 920.02)

Current Sources

Current Biography Yearbook. New York: H. W. Wilson, 1940- , v.1- . (CT100; 920.02)

International Who's Who. London: Europa Publications and Allen & Unwin, 1935- . (CT120; 920.01)

Who's Who in America: A Biographical Dictionary of Notable Living Men and Women. Chicago: Marquis, 1899- , v.1- . (E176; 920.073)

Retrospective Sources

Dictionary of American Biography. Published under the auspices of the American Council of Learned Societies. New York: Scribner's; London: Milford, 1928–1937. (And other reprintings and editions.) And its *Supplements* 1–6. New York: Scribner's, 1944–1978. (E176; 920.073)

The McGraw-Hill Encyclopedia of World Biography. New York: McGraw-Hill, 1973. (CT103; 920.02)

For other tools (ready reference, current, or retrospective), look in your library's catalog under: "Biography – Dictionaries," Biography – 20th century," "United States – Biography," and "United States – Biography – Dictionaries."

*   *   *

If the popularity of newspaper gossip columns is any indication, we can safely say that people – their lives, personalities, and achievements – interest almost everybody. Indeed, in many classes a high percentage of students write term papers on famous or near-famous individuals.

And for as many times as people seek information about other people, there are probably as many tools available in the nation's libraries. Indeed, one author, Robert Slocum, has listed some 8,000 biographical sources in his work *Biographical Dictionaries and Related Works* (Detroit: Gale, 1967; *Supplement,* 1972). While your own community college library will have nowhere near 8,000 biographical sources, it is very likely that it will have more than the 7 source-type tools listed here.

Thus this section must begin with a caution: the seven reference tools discussed here are only examples of the thousands of biographical sources available. In fact, any library materials – books and encyclopedias, periodicals and newspapers, government documents, pamphlets, and films – may contain information about an individual whose life you're researching. This caution should also be broadened to note that it is not just the extraordinary number of biographical sources that occasionally leads to confusion, but also the various categories of sources. Some sources deal only with persons no longer living ("retrospective"), while others give information about those still alive ("current"). Some tools give very brief data-type information, while others feature long essaylike articles on their subjects. Some sources include persons of only one nationality, while others are international in scope. Some concentrate on persons in specific fields or persons who lived at specific times, while others include anyone who has achieved some degree of fame.

Given the fact that (1) there are thousands of biographical sources, (2) almost anything in your library could be a possible source of biographical information, and (3) the scope of the tools can vary greatly; it is particularly important that you examine any tool new to you carefully. While finding biographical information can, at times, seen rather overwhelming, you should also keep in mind that your librarian can be of great assistance.

Now let's take a look at the tools that have been listed, beginning first with the ready reference dictionaries, the two most famous of which are *Chamber's* and *Webster's*. You will usually turn to either of these tools when you seek brief identifying information about a person – birth and death dates, occupational field, and major accomplishments. *Chamber's* lists some 15,000 persons, while *Webster's* covers over 40,000. Both dictionaries vary the length of their entries, so that the articles on well-known persons receive more space than those on lesser-known individuals. Both also indicate pronunciation of the more difficult names.

The ready reference dictionary generally features more articles on historical figures than on contemporary (i.e., living) persons. When you want information on important persons who are still living, you should turn to a current biographical source: *Current Biography*, the *International Who's Who*, or *Who's Who in America*. The first title mentioned, *Current Biography*, is a periodical that appears every month, except August, featuring essay-type articles with photographs on prominent personalities regardless of nationality. At the end of each year, all of the articles are reprinted in an annual yearbook.

Unlike *Current Biography*, which gives more in-depth profiles, *International Who's Who* and *Who's Who in America* will give you only data-type information: names, birth dates, major accomplishments, educational background, current position, and addresses. Almost any current biographical source that has "who's who" as part of its title is structured in the same way. In fact, such a tool is often referred to as a "who's-who type" of directory. Your library will very likely have one or more of the regional directories (e.g., *Who's Who in the West*) in its collection and may also have the original *Who's Who*, a British publication (covering mostly British persons) that should not be confused with *Who's Who in America*.

If you are looking for information on a person whom you know is deceased, you may want to turn to a retrospective biographical

source: either the *Dictionary of American Biography* (usually called the
DAB) or the *McGraw-Hill Encyclopedia of World Biography*. The basic
DAB was originally issued in twenty volumes that contained over
13,000 essay-type articles on prominent dead Americans; the supplements, which cover those Americans who died from about 1928 up
through 1955, bring the total figure up to about 16,000. Other supplements to update the basic set will continue to be published occasionally. An important feature of the *DAB*–particularly for those doing term-paper research–is the fact that the articles include
bibliographies. The *McGraw-Hill Encyclopedia of World Biography*,
unlike the *DAB*, includes articles on famous deceased persons of all
nationalities. This twelve-volume set, which contains some 5,000 articles, also has many portraits, maps, and illustrations, as well as a
"study guide" in the last volume that can lead you to other sources of
information.

All of the biographical tools discussed so far are examples of source
tools–they directly give you the information you seek, either briefly
(as in *Who's Who in America*) or in a more extensive manner (as in the
DAB). When seeking information about people, however, you must
be aware of the existence of some important access-type tools to
biographical information–the indexes. Two such indexes–
Biographical Dictionaries Master Index and *Biography Index*–
are discussed later in this chapter in a section entitled "Indexing and
Abstracting Services."

GEOGRAPHICAL SOURCES

Atlases

Bartholomew (John) and Son, Ltd. *The Times Atlas of the World*.
  Comprehensive ed./5th ed. London: Times Books, 1975. (G1019;
  912)
Rand McNally & Co. *Rand McNally Cosmopolitan World Atlas*.
  Chicago: Rand McNally, c1979. (G1019; 912)
Rand McNally & Co. *Rand McNally Commercial Atlas and Marketing
  Guide*. Chicago: Rand McNally, 1876- . (G1019; 912)
Shepherd, William Robert. *Historical Atlas*. 9th ed. New York: Barnes
  & Noble, 1964. (G1030; 911)
U.S. Geological Survey. *The National Atlas of the United States
  of America*. Washington, D.C.: Government Printing Office, 1970.
  (G1200; 912.73)

For other tools, look in your library's catalog under: "Atlases," "Geography, Historical – Maps," and "United States – Maps."

Gazetteers

Columbia Lippincott Gazetteer of the World. (Includes the 1961 supplement.) Edited by Leon E. Seltzer. New York: Columbia University Press, 1962. (G103; 910.3)

Webster's New Geographical Dictionary. Springfield, Mass.: Merriam, c1977. (G103; 910.3)

For other tools, look in your library's catalog under: "Geography – Dictionaries."

*   *   *

At one time or another, almost everybody has a question about a place: What is the size of city X, the population of county Y, the predominant physical feature of province Z? While such information is sometimes available in encyclopedias and some of the ready reference sources (such as almanacs) discussed in the next section, there is an important set of source-type tools useful to students regardless of their major: the geographical sources.[1]

As you can see, two groups of tools are listed: atlases and gazetteers. Most people are familiar with atlases (although they are often unaware of the variety available). An atlas is nothing more than a collection of maps that has been bound together in a single physical volume for convenience's sake. The maps are generally one of three kinds: political, which indicate primarily the boundaries of countries, states, and counties; physical, which indicate landforms such as prairies or swamps; or thematic, which represent graphically such information as levels of precipitation, divorce rates, and energy resources. A gazetteer is a dictionary of geographical place-names – cities, towns, mountain ranges – that indicates location, pronunciation, and distinguishing characteristics (e.g., population).

In most libraries, atlases will be kept separate from other reference works in what is usually termed an "atlas case." This is done because most atlases are quite large and not easily accommodated on the regular bookshelves. Also note that most libraries will have at least some separate maps to supplement their atlas collection. Where maps are housed varies from library to library, but some of the more popular alternatives include filing them in the vertical file (see

Chapter 1), keeping them in a special "map case," or perhaps housing them adjacent to the atlas case. Gazetteers will generally be in the reference collection.

Now we shall turn our attention to the atlases themselves. Of the five titles listed, two—the *Times Atlas* and *Rand McNally Cosmopolitan World Atlas*—represent the general-purpose world atlas familiar to most people. The *Times Atlas* is usually judged to be the best English-language atlas available. As with most general-purpose atlases, the *Times Atlas* is divided into three parts: an introductory "encyclopedic" section, which includes information and small thematic maps on a variety of subjects—everything from food sources to volcanoes; the atlas proper, which consists of 128 double-page maps; and a 200,000-place-name index, which refers you to specific grid sections of individual maps. The *Times Atlas's* deservedly high reputation rests on the quality of its maps—both the color separation, which indicates both political boundaries and physical features, and the typography are highly detailed.

The *Rand McNally Cosmopolitan World Atlas* is in many ways representative of the typical U.S. world atlas, for it emphasizes North America and the United States, with individual maps of each of the states. The atlas contains much more encyclopedic-type information than does the *Times Atlas,* and there are several special indexes (e.g., to U.S. metropolitan area maps) as well as a 100-page general index at the back of the volume. While the maps in this atlas haven't the visual appeal of those in the *Times Atlas,* they are accurate and reliable, as are those for the many other atlases published by Rand McNally. Note that the atlases published by this firm, as well as those by C. S. Hammond, the National Geographic Society, and the British Oxford University Press, are quite reputable and generally well represented in the atlas collections of most U.S. libraries.

The remaining three atlases indicate in part the variety of special-purpose atlases that are available. The *National Atlas of the United States* is an atlas devoted to in-depth coverage of a single nation, the United States. It contains hundreds of thematic maps on such topics as U.S. history and culture, population structure, and land use. Virtually an illustrated almanac, the *National Atlas* is jammed with facts and figures not available in other atlases.

The *Rand McNally Commercial Atlas* is a tool designed to give up-to-date statistical information relating to business in the United States. Issued annually in a new edition, the *Commercial Atlas* contains detailed information on retailing, manufacturing, transportation, communications, agriculture, and related subjects for each of the fifty states. If you are not well versed in the terminology of business and statistics, you will need to spend some time studying the extensive introduction to this atlas.

Shepherd's *Historical Atlas* is, as its name suggests, an atlas filled with political maps of various areas of the world showing boundaries as they existed at earlier times in history. Thus, you can find maps of everything from the ancient Near East in 1375 B.C. to central Europe in 1547. Such maps can be particularly useful in assisting you to visualize past events and places. Note that the *Historical Atlas* has three indexes: the index proper, an index supplement, and a supplement to the supplement for the ninth edition.

In addition to atlases, almost every U.S. library owns two standard gazetteers: the 130,000-entry *Columbia Lippincott* and the 47,000-entry *Webster's*. Unlike the atlas index, which refers you to a map, the gazetteer describes the location of the place in question, sometimes including short tidbits of historical information where appropriate. Although it functions somewhat differently, a relatively comprehensive atlas index – such as the 200,000-entry index to the *Times Atlas* – can serve as a substitute for the gazetteer. Note that while the *Columbia Lippincott* is much larger than *Webster's*, it is also quite out of date, including only the names of places that existed prior to 1961. Note too that many libraries have one or more specialized place-name dictionaries.

Keep in mind that atlases – both general and special purpose – and gazetteers are not the only geographical sources available to you, although they are among the most frequently consulted. There also exist specialized guidebooks for specific countries, states, regions, and even cities. While these guidebooks are generally written with the prospective tourist in mind, quite often the general geographical or historical information included may not be found elsewhere. To discover what guidebooks your library may have, you should look in your library's catalog under the place-name you're interested in or consult a reference librarian.

READY REFERENCE SOURCES

Almanacs

Information Please Almanac. New York: Simon & Schuster, 1947- . (AY64; 031)

The World Almanac and Book of Facts. New York: Newspaper Enterprise Association, 1868- . (AY67; 317.3)

For other tools, look in your library's catalog under: "Almanacs, American" and "Statistics – Yearbooks."

Yearbooks

Americana Annual, An Encyclopedia of Current Events. New York: Americana Corporation, 1923- . (AE5; 031)
Britannica Book of the Year. Chicago: Encyclopaedia Britannica, 1938- . (AE5; 032)
Facts on File Yearbook. New York: Facts on File, Inc., 1940- . (D410)

For other tools, look in your library's catalog under: "Encyclopedias and dictionaries – Yearbooks" and "History – Yearbooks."

Handbooks

Guinness Book of World Records. New York: Sterling Publishing, 1955- . (AG243; 032)
Kane, Joseph Nathan. *Famous First Facts.* 3d ed. New York: H. W. Wilson, 1964. (AG5; 031)

For other tools, look in your library's catalog under: "Curiosities" and "Encyclopedias and dictionaries."

Directories

Encyclopedia of Associations. Detroit: Gale, 1956- . (AS22; 060)
Greenfield, Stanley R. *National Directory of Addresses and Telephone Numbers.* New York: Nicholas Publishing, 1977. (E154.5; 917.30025)

For other tools, look in your library's catalog under: "Associations, Institutions, etc. – Directories" and "United States – Directories."

*   *   *

The tools listed in this section share a common purpose: to provide quick answers to short factual questions such as "How tall is . . . ?" "How long is . . . ?" "How many . . . ?" or "Where is . . . ?" Because of this common purpose librarians frequently refer to these tools as ready reference sources.

The first type of ready reference source is the almanac, a source-type tool that could be described as a mini encyclopedia, containing many of the same facts, but without much of the language. The typical almanac is issued annually and is an excellent source of specific information and statistics on everything from religion and awards to foreign countries and news-making personalities. Note that the year on the cover and title page of an almanac refers to the year of publication, so that a 1979 almanac covers the history and events of 1978. Note too that in many almanacs smaller items of information are grouped under broad themes (e.g., "Nuclear Power Reactors in the United States" would be treated under "Energy"). Thus, using the almanac's index is essential.

Only two examples—*Information Please* and the *World Almanac*—have been listed, but there are many others, both U.S. and foreign. Since virtually all almanac publishers get their statistical information from government agencies and other background information from standard and generally reliable sources, it should come as no surprise that there is a great deal of duplication from one almanac to another. Thus, you will find motor-vehicle accident statistics listed in both *Information Please* and *World*. Where the individual titles differ is in relatively minor areas. For example, *Information Please* includes data on the airline-industry practice of "bumping" (i.e., denied boarding) while *World* does not. *World,* on the other hand, has information on the Battle of Lake Erie, while *Information Please* does not. So you should always consult more than one almanac if you don't find what you need the first time around.

The next type of tool is the yearbook (also referred to as an "annual"), so called because of the frequency of its appearance. Unlike the almanac, which includes a great deal of general information, the yearbook is a source tool devoted solely to information about the preceding year. Each of the first two titles—the *Americana Annual* and *Britannica Book of the Year*—is a typical encyclopedia yearbook that supplements the basic encyclopedia set with up-to-date information. As with the almanac, the year featured on the cover and title page refers to year of publication and not to year of coverage. Further, information in the encyclopedia yearbook is grouped under broad headings (e.g., "Economics and Industry") so that use of the index is necessary for access to individual items of information.

Later in this chapter, in the section on "Indexing and Abstracting Services," you will read about *Facts on File,* an index to current events. The *Facts on File Yearbook* is nothing but an annual cumulation of all of the news information that has originally appeared in the weekly issues of that indexing service. Like the encyclopedia annuals, *Facts on File Yearbook* uses the broad-category approach, but has an excellent and very specific index so that the information you seek is easily retrievable.

Keep in mind that these yearbooks, as many of the other reference sources discussed in this chapter, are general in scope. Some annuals—such as *The Women's Rights Almanac*—are devoted to special subjects, and many are listed in Chapter 3. Both the general and special-subject yearbooks are excellent tools for keeping abreast of current developments.

Another category of ready reference sources is the handbook, a source tool so named because traditionally it can fit easily and comfortably in one hand. These days, the actual size of the handbook is of little importance; what matters is the concise reference information it provides. Handbooks, sometimes also called "manuals" (particularly when they have a "how-to" approach), are prevalent in special subjects, and many are listed in Chapter 3.

The two general handbooks listed here—*Famous First Facts* and *Guinness Book of World Records*—are among the most interesting reference books published, particularly if you are a trivia lover. *Famous First Facts* is, as you might have guessed, a listing of firsts: everything from the first forest fire drenched by man-made rain to the first crossword puzzle. The work includes four indexes: by years, days of the month, personal names, and geographical terms. The other handbook, *Guinness Book of World Records*, is probably one of the best-known and most enjoyable reference works in print. It chronicles the largest, the deepest, the oldest, the newest, the longest—in fact, all of the superlatives in business, sports, science, the animal and plant world, and many other areas. It should be obvious that handbooks are an important supplement to both almanacs and yearbooks since they cover many miscellaneous facts those tools do not.

The last category of ready reference tool is an access-type tool, the directory. Directories are a simple alphabetical or classified listing of names of persons or organizations, usually with addresses and phone numbers. The best example of a directory is, of course, the telephone book, which you read about at the beginning of this chapter. Every library will have at least a few telephone directories available, and most will also have what is termed a "city directory." Most city directories are published by R. L. Polk & Company of Kansas City and are arranged with a buyer's guide and classified business directory (similar to the yellow pages) first, an alphabetical directory of householders and businesses second, and a numerical telephone directory last. This latter section is for use when all you have is a phone number and you need the name of the person or organization at that number.

Two other directories frequently found in the reference collections of libraries are the *Encyclopedia of Associations* and the *National Directory of Addresses and Telephone Numbers*. The first work, the *Encyclopedia of Associations*, appears in a new edition every two years and is issued in three volumes. Volume 1 is an alphabetical listing of national organizations in the United States by type of organization (e.g., trade, public affairs, veterans), with an index to organization names and keywords. Volume 2 is a geographical and executive index. Volume 3 is a periodical entitled *New Associations and Projects* that keeps the basic set up to date.

The other work, the *National Directory of Addresses and Telephone Numbers*, is composed of over 50,000 entries for the most-wanted addresses and telephone numbers in the United States. This list includes a wide variety of institutions such as hotels, hospitals, TV stations, government agencies, banks, and corporations. There is, of course, an index.

Note that to find other directories, you locate works listed in the catalog by place (e.g., "Los Angeles – Directories" or "Los Angeles – Directories – Telephone") or by type of subject field (e.g., "Engineers – Directories" or "Rubber industry and trade – Directories"). As usual, your reference librarian can also be of assistance in helping you to locate particular kinds of directories or directory-type information.

BIBLIOGRAPHIC SOURCES

Trade Bibliographies

Books in Print. New York: R. R. Bowker, 1948– . (Z1215; 015.73)

Cumulative Book Index. New York: H. W. Wilson, 1898– . (Z1219; 015.73)

Subject Guide to Books in Print. New York: R. R. Bowker, 1957– . (Z1215; 015.73)

For other tools, look in your library's catalog under: "U.S. – Imprints," "Catalogs, Publishers – U.S.," "U.S. – Bibliography," "American literature – Bibliography – Periodicals," or "English literature – Bibliography – Periodicals."

Bibliographies of Periodicals

Katz, William A., and Richards, Berry G. *Magazines for Libraries.*
3d ed. New York: R. R. Bowker, 1978. (Z6941; 016.05)
Ulrich's International Periodical Directory. 17th ed. New York: R. R.
Bowker, 1977. (Z6941; 011)

For other tools, look in your library's catalog under:
"Periodicals – Directories," "Bibliography – Bibliography – Periodicals,"
and "Periodicals – Bibliography – Union lists."

*   *   *

When you need information about books or periodicals – information such as who wrote what, when, and on what subject – you should
turn to the bibliographic source, one of the most important access-
type reference tools in the library. While often unfamiliar or obscure
to library users, the bibliographic source is really very simple to identify: it is a systematically arranged list of books or periodicals or both.
As you can see, only a few representative tools have been listed in
this category; but that may be misleading, for there are, in fact, many
different types of bibliographic sources. You may see, for example,
large, multivolume book catalogs such as the *National Union Catalog,*
which lists books and some other publications alphabetically by main
entry. And, too, there are national bibliographies of periodicals such
as the *Union List of Serials* or *New Serial Titles.* There are even
bibliographies of bibliographies, such as *Bibliographic Index.* These
and other such tools will not be discussed here simply because unless
you are conducting extensive in-depth research on a topic, you would
rarely have occasion to use them. If and when you do have need for
such tools, your librarian can explain their arrangement and scope.
There are, however, bibliographic sources that are consulted everyday by library users around the country and that you, too, may need
to use. Take, for example, the "trade bibliographies," so called because
they are the basic tools of the book trade and of libraries. The most
famous of the trade bibliographies is *Books in Print,* more commonly
called *BIP.* It is, as its name suggests, a listing of books that are still in
print and available for purchase. Each listing not only includes
author's name, title, publisher, and date of publication, but also the
ISBN (international standard book number – used for ordering purposes) and the price. *BIP* is an annual publication issued in two parts:
authors, *A* to *Z,* in two volumes and titles, *A* to *Z,* in two volumes.
Note that the second volume of the title portion of *BIP* includes the

names and addresses of some 5,300 U.S. publishers, a useful feature if you need to order a book directly from the publisher. Obviously,you will turn to the basic *BIP* when you know either an author's name or the title of a work. For access by subject to what's available for purchase, you can use the two-volume *Subject Guide to Books in Print.* This, too, is an annual publication.

Since *BIP* and the *Subject Guide to BIP* are only issued annually, you need to turn to other trade bibliographies for current information. One such bibliography found in most libraries is the *Cumulative Book Index*, commonly called *CBI*. The *CBI* is a serially issued publication that appears monthly and then cumulates quarterly, annually, and every five years. It lists authors, titles, and subjects in a single alphabetical arrangement, with the most complete information about a particular book to be found under the author entry. Note that the *CBI* is a *World List of Books in the English Language*, and thus you will find some prices listed in pound sterling rather than in dollars.

BIP, its *Subject Guide*, and *CBI* are all useful when you want to find out what books are available or have been published on a particular subject or by a particular author. But you also may want to find out what periodicals are available in your field of interest. The bibliography of periodicals will serve you here. Perhaps the most widely recognized standard in this area is *Ulrich's International Periodical Directory*. *Ulrich's* appears in a new edition every two years, and it lists some 60,000 periodical titles—both U.S. and foreign—alphabetically by subject. There is a title index at the back of the volume. *Ulrich's* includes not only the standard publishing information (e.g., name of the publisher, circulation figures, frequency of publication), but also includes the price of a subscription and the names of indexing or abstracting services that index the periodical's contents.

While *Ulrich's* doesn't list everything available in the periodical world, it does come close. Another bibliography of periodicals may even be more useful to you, however, despite the fact that it lists only some 6,500 periodical titles: William Katz's *Magazines for Libraries*. While this bibliography does not list the greater number of periodicals, it does list the best. *Magazines for Libraries* is used primarily by librarians to decide which periodicals to subscribe to, but you can use it to discover what are the most important and widely read periodicals available in your field of study. Katz's work includes not only all of the information *Ulrich's* does about the periodical in question, but also such information as audience level and pertinent facts about the scope of the periodical.

INDEXING AND ABSTRACTING SERVICES

Periodicals

Access: The Supplementary Index to Periodicals. Syracuse, N.Y.: Gaylord Bros., 1975- . (AI3; 016.051)
The Magazine Index. Los Altos, Calif.: Magazine Index, 1978- .
Monthly Periodical Index. Princeton: National Library Service Co., 1978–1979. (Beginning in 1980, *MPI* merged with *Access.*)
Popular Periodical Index. Camden, N.J.: Popular Periodical Index, 1973- . (AI3; 016.05)
The Readers' Guide to Periodical Literature. New York: H. W. Wilson, 1900- . (AI3; 050)

For other tools, look in your library's catalog under: "Periodicals – Indexes" and "American periodicals – Indexes."

Newspapers

The New York Times Index. New York: New York Times, 1913- . (AI21)

For other titles, look in your library's catalog under: "Newspapers – Indexes."

Current Events

Facts on File: Weekly World News Digest with Cumulative Index. New York: Facts on File, Inc., 1941- . (D410)

For other titles, look in your library's catalog under: "History – Yearbooks."

Book Reviews

Book Review Digest. New York: H. W. Wilson, 1905- . And its *Author/Title Index, 1905–1974.* 1976. (Z1219; 028.1)
Book Review Index. Detroit: Gale, 1965- . (Z1035; 016.0281)
Current Book Review Citations. New York: H. W. Wilson, 1976- . (Z1035; 016.0281)

For other tools, look in your library's catalog under: "Books – Reviews," "Bibliography – Periodicals," "Books – Reviews – Indexes," and "Books – Reviews – Bibliography – Periodicals."

Biographical Information

Biographical Dictionaries Master Index. 1st ed., 1975–1976. Detroit: Gale, 1976. (Z5303; 920.073)

Biography Index: A Cumulative Index to Biographical Material in Books and Magazines. New York: H. W. Wilson, 1946/49- , v.1- . (Z5301; 016.92)

For other tools, look in your library's catalog under: "Biography – Indexes" and "United States – Biography – Indexes."

*   *   *

The index is an access type of reference tool, indicating the contents of periodicals, newspapers, government documents, reports from private agencies, and parts of books – all of which are critically important sources of information for students. Because of this, indexes are perhaps the most useful – and most used – reference sources in the library. They are also sometimes the most bewildering, for reasons we will examine shortly.

Before we look at the specific tools listed above, we need to discuss the index as a type of tool more fully. We've already defined the index as an access type of tool. It functions in the same way as the library catalog or the index to a book: by listing alphabetically what has been published on a subject or by an author. Some indexes may also list titles, although this is rarer.

All of this probably sounds simple enough, so why is the index sometimes considered bewildering? First of all, almost all indexes are periodicals that cumulate. For example, the *Readers' Guide* is issued every two weeks (i.e., semimonthly) except during February, July, and August, when it appears monthly. Every three months the preceding three months' issues are discarded when the quarterly cumulation appears, since all of that previous indexing information – plus the latest indexing – are interfiled in a single alphabetical arrangement. Further, these quarterly cumulations are themselves cumulated into an annual volume. Always check to see how often an index is issued and how often it is cumulated since this has important implications for your own researching strategy.

The fact that indexes are cumulating periodicals poses two possible problems: In which issue should you begin to search for information, and how far back in time should you search? Imagine for a moment that you've decided to do a term paper on UFOs, a term paper for which you'll be needing information from magazines or newspapers or both. You sit down at an index table facing the annual, quarterly, and semimonthly issues of the *Readers' Guide*. Where should you start? Generally, you'll need to start with the latest issue of the index and keep searching earlier issues until you have all the citations to those articles that seem appropriate to your topic. But if you've decided to limit your topic to a discussion of how Americans in the 1950s viewed the UFO phenomenon, you may want to search only through issues of the *Readers' Guide* for the 1950s, gathering citations to articles published during that decade. Remember though that someone could have published an article entitled "UFOs in the 1950s" just last month; you'll miss the citation to that article if you've only searched through the 1950 issues of the *Readers' Guide*. Since the questions of where to start and where to stop can get very complicated, you should feel free to consult with a librarian whenever you have any doubt.

A second source of confusion about indexes is that they very often employ large numbers of abbreviations in order to save space. But such abbreviations are always deciphered in a list or lists that are usually found in the front of the index. A careful technical reading of the index will help you out here. It will also help you to discover what kind of arrangement is being used. For example, some indexes may have subjects and authors in a single alphabetical arrangement, while others will have separate alphabetical arrangements for subjects, authors, and titles. The variations from one index to another may be striking, so don't *assume* anything about a tool you've never used or you may end up wasting a great deal of time.

The last source of bewilderment involves the large number and variety of indexes available. Most students who have not had occasion to use libraries sometimes feel overwhelmed in the reference or index section of their library when they see how many different tools there are. Such students may depend on one index with which they're familiar (such as the *Readers' Guide*) in any and all situations and are inevitably disappointed when they don't find the information they need. But while the number and variety of indexes are large, they are by no means infinite. As already noted, indexes may be broken down by the type of material indexed: periodicals, parts of books, government documents, and so on. They may also be divided up into either general coverage or special-subject coverage. The *Reader's Guide, Monthly Periodical Index*, and the other periodical indexes listed in this section are examples of the general-coverage index. The indexes listed in Chapter 3, such as *Education Index* or *Business Periodicals Index*, are, of course, devoted to special subjects.

The problem posed by this great variety of indexing services is, of course, choice. Which index should you use? If, for example, you're well into a major in electronics and have to do some research on a topic, you'd probably be better advised to go to *Applied Science and Technology Index* rather than to a general-purpose index. An additional problem arises in those situations where you remember an article on a topic having been published in a particular periodical, say, for example, *Psychology Today*. In this situation, you would need to scan through the "List of Periodicals Indexed" in a few indexes to find out who does index it. *Psychology Today*, it turns out, is not indexed in *Access* or *Popular Periodicals Index;* it is indexed in the *Readers' Guide.*

It should be noted too that your library chooses the indexes it will receive, and so you may find that some of the indexes mentioned in this book are not available at your own community college library. This system does, however, make sense. If, for example, your own community college does not have a program in nursing, the library would have little need to subscribe to nursing periodicals, and hence no need for an index such as *Cumulative Index to Nursing Literature.*

So far we've discussed only the index and some of the problems associated with its use. But everything said so far also applies to the index's close relation, the abstract. The abstract does exactly the same thing as the index – it indicates the contents of periodicals and of other material. However, it goes one step further by also *summarizing* the contents of this material. As a source/access type of tool, the abstract can be a real time-saver since it may help you to choose more easily and readily between one document and another. In fact, abstracts may even give you enough information so that you need not consult the original document. Unfortunately, the true abstract is usually only published in special-subject areas – an example being *Psychological Abstracts* – and is often available only in larger public and college or university libraries.

Having discussed some of the characteristics of indexing and abstracting services in general, we can now turn our attention to the titles listed at the beginning of this section. Of all of the periodical indexes, H. W. Wilson's *Readers' Guide* is undoubtedly the best known and most widely used. In fact, probably no single tool more useful can be found in U.S. libraries. It is, in many ways, the prototype of the successful index and has served as a standard of excellent indexing for many years. The *Readers' Guide* is a cumulative subject and author index (in a single alphabetical arrangement) to some 180 general-interest periodicals published in the United States. It also includes a separate section for book reviews at the back of each issue. Such additional features as film and drama reviews (under "Motion pictures" and "Dramas") particularly enhance its usefulness. A sample entry from

Figure 2.2
SAMPLE ENTRY FROM THE READERS' GUIDE

Sample entry: CIVIL rights demonstrations
                 Day they didn't march. L. Bennett, Jr. il Ebony
                 32:128-30+ F'77

                 An illustrated article on the subject CIVIL
                 rights demonstrations entitled "Day they
                 didn't march," by L. Bennett, Jr., will be
                 found in volume 32 of Ebony, pages 128-30
                 (continued on later pages of the same issue)
                 the February 1977 number.

the *Readers' Guide* appears in Figure 2.2.

Three of the other periodical indexes listed—*Access, Monthly Periodical Index,* and *Popular Periodical Index*—are indexing services designed to fill in gaps in coverage left by the *Readers' Guide.* Since *Readers' Guide* indexes only 180 periodicals (and titles indexed are added and dropped on a continuing basis), a need has arisen for indexing of those popular periodicals not indexed by *Readers' Guide.*

Access, which appears three times a year (the third volume being an annual cumulation), is a periodical index in two sections: subject and author. As a supplement to the *Readers' Guide, Access* indexes some 125 titles and is particularly strong for its indexing of the new city and regional magazines that have become so popular. The *Monthly Periodical Index* (or *MPI*) began publication in 1978 when the *Readers' Guide* decided to discontinue the indexing of some 43 general-interest periodicals (such as *Backpacker, Harper's Bazaar,* and *People*). As its title indicates, *MPI* appeared monthly and was continuously cumulated into semiannual and then annual volumes. *MPI* indexed authors and subjects in a single alphabetical arrangement and covered some 84 periodicals. Beginning in 1980, *Access* took over *MPI*'s indexing program, certainly a convenience to library users. *Popular Periodical Index* indexes some 33 periodicals not indexed by the *Readers' Guide*—generally newer or more controversial publications. Unfortunately, this index is only published semiannually and is thus not greatly useful for timely, up-to-date information.

The last periodical index listed, *The Magazine Index,* illustrates perfectly how computer technology is beginning to affect the kinds of services available in modern libraries. *The Magazine Index,* first published in 1978, indexes over 370 periodicals, including *all* of those indexed by the *Readers' Guide.* Unlike the other indexes already discussed, *The Magazine Index* is published on microfilm or is obtainable via an on-line computer terminal using Lockheed Corporation's DIALOG system. Because this index is produced using computers, the microfilm version (which is issued monthly) is continuously cumulated up to five years. *The Magazine Index* also uses Library of Congress subject headings and includes both author and title access to periodical literature. There is, unfortunately, one catch to all of this—namely that *The Magazine Index* is quite expensive compared to the more traditional print indexes, and thus only larger libraries generally are able to subscribe to the service. If you live in a relatively large urban area where there is one or more large public or university library, you may be able to use *The Magazine Index.* Otherwise, you'll have a bit of a wait until smaller libraries can afford to purchase this kind of information technology.

Photo 2.1: Librarian conducting a search using an cn-line data base. Such computer-assisted searches will become more common in the future. (Courtesy Lockheed Information System DIALOG.)

So much for indexes to popular, general-interest periodicals. Now let's turn our attention to the newspaper index. Newspapers are, of course, a vital source of information on both national and international events and people. The most popular and widely used newspaper index is the *New York Times Index*, which indexes the late city edition of what is generally considered to be our national newspaper. Because the subject entries in the index are dated (see Figure 2.3), the *New York Times Index* can also indicate when a particular event might have been reported in your own local newspaper (although it will not, of course, indicate section, page, or column numbers). A particular advantage to the *New York Times Index* is that each subject entry also includes a summary of the event being reported; the *Index* is, in fact, an abstract. Unfortunately, the *New York Times Index* is published only semimonthly and only cumulates into a bound annual volume, which means that if you're uncertain about the date on which a particular event occurred, you may well have some extensive researching to do.

One particular problem with the *New York Times Index* is that it is late in appearing—the semimonthly issues by two to three months, the annual volume by six to eight months. What happens when you need information about an event that occurred only last week? Happily, there exist several indexes to current events such as *Facts on File*. *Facts on File* is a weekly service that condenses information (mostly on U.S. news) from several major newspapers into brief, factual reports. It, like the *New York Times Index,* is also more of an abstract than an index.

Facts on File is what is termed a "loose-leaf service." Each week, a subscribing library receives a number of loose white sheets—the digested news information itself—that are filed in a three-ring binder. Every two weeks, the library also receives several blue or yellow sheets—the index—to be filed at the back of the binder. Thus, the index to current events is never more than a few days behind the coverage of the news, since it is continually being updated with both the abstracts of the news and the indexes to them.

Another type of index we will examine in this section is the index to book reviews. Book reviews are important sources of information for students since they provide not only critical appraisals of the worth of newly published books, but also information about the author or authors of each book in question. Because thousands of book reviews are published each year, the specialized index to these reviews has developed.

The most famous and widely owned index to book reviews is actu-

Figure 2.3

SAMPLE ENTRY FROM THE <u>NEW YORK TIMES INDEX</u>

1   **2**

MIDDLE East.   See also country names
Israeli-Arab Conflict

3 ▶   Mar.1:   Cypriot police disclose that Samir
Mohammed Khadar, 1 of Arabs charged with murder
of Al Ahram editor Yousel el-Sebai, said Sebai was
killed because he was friend of Israel (S), Mr 1,8:4; **◀ 4**
Egyptian officials say there is no chance of agreeing
with Israel on declaration of peace principles before
Begin meets with Carter; Egyptian Foreign Min
Mohammed Ibrahim Kamel and special US envoy
Alfred L Atherton say future of Palestinians is still
main issue (M), Mr 1,9:1; PLO accuses Pres Sadat of
imposing 'mass punishment' on Palestinians in move
to disengage Egypt from Palestinian cause (S), Mr 1,
12:4; Roger N Baldwin lr disputes Feb 17 ed urging UN
Sec Gen Waldheim to remain neutral on Palestinian
issue (S), Mr 1, 26:3

  Mar.2:   Asst State Sec Alfred L. Atherton Jr meets in
Egypt with Foreign Min Kamel and Pres Sadat, then
returns unexpectedly to Israel to inform officials of
Egyptian reflections on Israeli proposals (M), Mr 2,
4:3; Israeli Defense Min Ezer Weizman forbids
Israelis to move into Kadesh Barnea settlement site in
Sinai Peninsula (S), Mr 2,4:4; Bernard Colodney
scores coalition of Arab-Amers opposing
imprisonment of Palestinian-Amer Sami Esmail in
Israel on pol charges (S), Mr 2,18:3

1 MAIN SUBJECT HEADING.   These headings may also
have subdivisions.

2 CROSS-REFERENCES.   Such references can lead you
to other related articles.

3 DATE.   The abstract of each day's articles begins
with the date of the final Late City Edition
of the paper.

4 LOCATION.   The date is repeated, followed by
page number ("8") and column number ("4").
The "S" in parentheses refers to the length
of the article: "S" for short, "M" for medium,
and "L" for long.

ally an abstracting service: *Book Review Digest*. The *BRD*, which appears monthly with annual cumulations, analyzes the reviews in eighty-three periodicals and includes brief excerpts from those reviews. Thus, if you do find a review listed in *BRD*, you may not even have to consult the review itself. As with the other indexes to book reviews, you can access the reviews by author, although there is also a title index. Unlike either *Book Review Index* or *Current Book Review Citations*, however, *BRD* also has a subject index. Further, *BRD* has an *Author/Title Index* for the years 1905 (the first year of publication of the *Digest*) to 1974. This latter index is an obvious time-saver.

Given all of the advantages of *Book Review Digest*, why, you might ask, would anyone ever consult any other index to book reviews? The answer is simple: *BRD* only indexes 83 periodicals, which represent only a small percentage of all of the reviews published each year. For more comprehensive coverage, you should turn to either *Book Review Index* (which indexes some 300 periodicals for reviews) or *Current Book Review Citations* (which indexes over 1,000 periodicals).

Also remember that the *Readers' Guide* and the other Wilson indexes referred to in Chapter 3 list book reviews and that there are also specialized, subject-oriented indexes to book reviews such as *Technical Book Review Index* or *Index to Book Reviews in the Humanities*. Your reference librarian can counsel you on which index may be most appropriate to your information need.

The last indexes to be discussed here were alluded to earlier in the section on biographical sources: the indexes to biographical information. The first tool, *Biographical Dictionaries Master Index*, gives you access to information about people who have been listed in any of the fifty-three biographical dictionaries covered by the index – everything from *Who's Who in America* and *Current Biography* to more specialized biographical sources such as *Who's Who in Professional Baseball* and *Standard & Poor's Register of Corporations, Directors, and Executives*. Since most of the tools indexed by the *Biographical Dictionaries Master Index* are of the who's-who variety, you will want to use this index when you seek data-type information on a living person.

The second tool listed, *Biography Index*, will give you access to biographical information that has appeared in approximately 2,000 periodicals and many books. *Biography Index* is published every three months (i.e., quarterly) and then is cumulated in annual volumes and eventually in volumes that cover three years. Thus, if you want the latest published information about a particular person, you would start with the latest issue of the index and work backward in time.

One feature of *Biography Index* particularly useful to many students is its "index to professions and occupations," which appears at the back of each issue and each volume of the index. Using it, you can look up a particular occupation, such as "radio and television performers" or "kidnapers," and find listed the names of persons in those categories about whom biographical information has been written. This part of the *Biography Index* will thus be most helpful when you wish to find information about persons in a specific field – perhaps your own field – but haven't any specific names in advance.

GOVERNMENT PUBLICATIONS

Indexes

U.S. Superintendent of Documents. *Monthly Catalog of United States Government Publications.* Washington, D.C.: Government Printing Office, 1895- . (Z1223; 015.73)

Guides

Morehead, Joe. *Introduction to United States Public Documents.* 2d ed. Littleton, Colo.: Libraries Unlimited, 1978. (Z1223; 015.73)

For other tools, look in your library's catalog under: "U.S. – Government publications," "U.S. – Government publications – Bibliography," and "U.S. Government Printing Office."

*   *   *

The largest publisher in this country – and possibly in the world – is our own Uncle Sam, the U.S. government, which each year issues some 24,000 to 35,000 documents through its various branches, departments, and agencies. Most of these documents are published by the Government Printing Office (GPO) and then distributed to institutions and individuals by the superintendent of documents (SUDOCS).

Those people who are unfamiliar with government publications often imagine that they are only useful to students of government or political science. Nothing could be further from the truth. While the U.S. government publishes information that is useful primarily to students and researchers in the social sciences or in the pure or applied sciences, it is possible to find a government document on almost every subject imaginable – everything from teenage acne or personnel management to drug abuse or strawberry marketing.

As useful as government publications are, however, there are some problems associated with their use. First there is the problem of the availability of the documents themselves (i.e., whether the publications you need are in your own library) and, second, the problem of learning what publications the government has issued. Both of these problems arise simply because government publications are issued outside the normal book-publishing channels.

First, then, let's take a look at document availability. Every U.S. library will have at least some government publications in its collection. But there are also some 1,200 libraries in the United States that have what is termed "depository" status. These depositories receive many government publications free from the superintendent of documents and are usually located in larger libraries—large city or county libraries, college or university libraries, or state libraries. A handful of community college libraries are designated as depositories. Your reference librarian will be able to tell you which libraries in your area are depositories.

Note that many depositories will keep their government publications in a separate area, often using a special classification scheme developed by SUDOCS rather than either Dewey or Library of Congress classification. Smaller libraries that purchase a limited number of government publications will usually treat them as though they were books, providing cataloging information and regular classification numbers so that the documents are found interspersed throughout the regular collection.

Now let's look at how you can learn what publications are being issued by the government. Documents are sometimes listed in various commercial indexes (some of which are discussed in this and the next chapter), but the most comprehensive listing appears in the *Monthly Catalog of United States Government Publications,* usually called simply the *Monthly Catalog* or even the *MoCat.* As its name suggests, *MoCat* appears monthly (although it appears several months late) and each issue includes a listing of government publications, arranged sequentially by entry number (e.g., "76-1435"), as well as indexes to author, title, subject, and series/report. These indexes refer you to the entry number where full information about the document in question is available. Cumulative indexes appear both semiannually and annually, thus saving you research time.

A sample entry from the *Monthly Catalog* appears in Figure 2.4. You'll immediately notice that the entry resembles a catalog card. This format is a relatively recent phenomenon, having been begun in

Figure 2.4

SAMPLE ENTRY FROM THE MONTHLY CATALOG

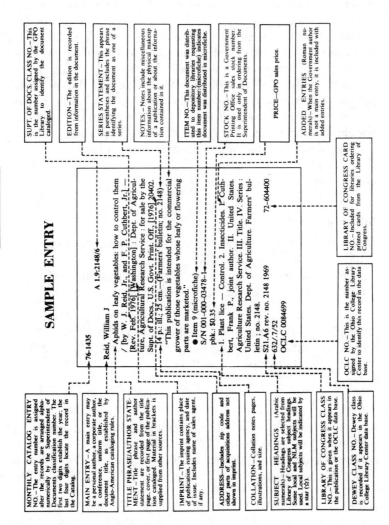

mid-1976. Prior to that time, the individual entries included only as much information as necessary to identify the document in question. Although neither the older nor the latest versions of the *Monthly Catalog* are difficult to use, you should spend the few minutes necessary to study the sample entry in Figure 2.4; it will save you time later.

Before leaving the subject of government publications, you should be aware that this brief section has only scratched the surface. If you anticipate or know that you will have need to use government publications frequently, you should read one of the many guides to the use of documents. The guide listed here, Morehead's *Introduction to United States Public Documents*, is one of the most popular and is widely available. It will serve to give you important background on the uses and functions of government publications.

MEDIA

Microforms

Guide to Microforms in Print. Weston, Conn.: Microcard Editions, 1961- . (Z1033.M5; 016.099)

Subject Guide to Microforms in Print. Washington, D.C.: Microcard Editions, 1962- . (Z1033.M5; 016.099)

For other tools, look in your library's catalog under: "Microfilms – Bibliography," "Microfilms – Catalogs," "Books on microfilm – Bibliography – Catalogs," and "Out of print books on microfilm – Bibliography – Catalogs."

Films

Educators Guide to Free Films. Randolph, Wis.: Educators Progress Service, 1941- . (LB1044; 371.335230838)

National Information Center for Educational Media. *Index to 8mm Motion Cartridges.* 6th ed. Los Angeles: NICEM, 1980. (LB1044.Z9; 011)

National Information Center for Educational Media. *Index to 16mm Educational Films.* 9th ed. Los Angeles: NICEM, 1980. (LB1044.Z9; 011)

For other tools, look in your library's catalog under: "Moving-pictures – Catalogs" and "Moving-pictures in education."

Filmstrips

Educators Guide to Free Filmstrips. Randolph, Wis.: Educators Progress Service, 1949- . (LB1043.8; 371.3352)

National Information Center for Educational Media. *Index to 35mm Educational Filmstrips.* 7th ed. Los Angeles: NICEM, 1980. (LB1043.8.Z9; 011)

For other tools, look in your library's catalog under: "Filmstrips – Catalogs."

Transparencies

National Information Center for Educational Media. *Index to Educational Overhead Transparencies.* 6th ed. Los Angeles: NICEM, 1980. (LB1043.7.Z9; 011)

For other tools, look in your library's catalog under: "Transparencies – Catalogs" and "Transparencies in education."

Videotapes

National Information Center for Educational Media. *Index to Educational Video Tapes.* 5th ed. Los Angeles: NICEM, 1980. (LB1044.75.Z9; 011)

For other tools, look in your library's catalog under: "Video tapes – Catalogs" and "Video tapes in education."

Slides

National Information Center for Educational Media. *Index to Educational Slides.* 4th ed. Los Angeles: NICEM, 1980. (LB1043.7.Z9; 011)

For other tools, look in your library's catalog under: "Lantern slides – Catalogs."

Sound Recordings

National Information Center for Educational Media. *Index to Educational Audio Tapes.* 5th ed. Los Angeles: NICEM, 1980. (LB1044.4.Z9; 011)

National Information Center for Educational Media. *Index to Educational Records.* 5th ed. Los Angeles: NICEM, 1980. (LB1044. 3.Z9; 011)

Schwann Record & Tape Guide. Boston: W. Schwann, 1949- . (ML156.2)

For other tools, look in your library's catalog under: "Phonorecords – Catalogs," "Phonorecords in education," "Phonotapes – Catalogs," "Phonotapes in education," and "Music – Discography."

Reviews

Media Review Digest. Ann Arbor, Mich.: Pierian Press, 1973/74- . (From 1970 until 1973/74 called *Multi-Media Reviews Index.*) (LB1043.Z9; 011)

For other tools, look in your library's catalog under: "Audio-visual materials – Catalogs – Periodicals," "Audio-visual materials – Reviews – Bibliography – Periodicals," "Moving-pictures – Reviews – Bibliography – Periodicals," "Filmstrips – Reviews – Bibliography – Periodicals," and "Phonorecords – Reviews – Bibliography – Periodicals."

*   *   *

You've already read in Chapter 1 about the organization of media (which here will also include microforms and sound recordings) in the community college library. You will remember that where the various forms of media are housed will vary from college to college; the same may be said about the tools listed in this section. Some may be shelved in the reference area, but it is more likely that most – if not all – of these tools will be kept in the media area since they are used extensively for selecting audiovisual materials for your college's collections.

You will note that fourteen different tools have been listed. This number may be misleading for two reasons. First, your own library may not have several of those tools, depending on how heavily it collects a particular type of medium. For example, a library that does not actively seek to build a strong collection of materials in microform is not likely to go to the expense of purchasing *Guide to Microforms in Print.* Second, these fourteen tools represent only a small percentage of the catalogs, bibliographies, and guides available to assist you in selecting from many different types of media. Only this small number has been included because, as important as media are, you are less likely to depend on them as sources of information as you would on print materials. Generally, media will serve as important supplementary sources of information, particularly appropriate in those situations where either visuals or sound could enhance communication. For example, the use of media to support oral reports and other presentations is nowadays quite common. Your reference or media personnel will be able to point you toward other sources of information about media when those listed here do not serve your purpose.

All of the tools listed are of the access type. Indeed, with the exception of *Media Review Digest,* they all function like *Books in Print,* indicating what is available for purchase and from what source. The analogy of *Books in Print* is particularly appropriate for the two tools listed under microforms: *Guide to Microforms in Print* and *Subject Guide to Microforms in Print. Guide to Microforms in Print* is an annual guide that alphabetically lists books, periodicals, and other print materials (but not theses or dissertations) that are available in microform from U.S. publishers. Its *Subject Guide* appears every two years (i.e., biennially) and lists the same works in a classified arrangement, with an index to the subject classifications included. Both tools include prices.

Turning to the other forms of media, you notice that almost all of the tools listed under each type of medium are published by the National Information Center for Educational Media (NICEM). Since each of the tools issued by NICEM is similar in arrangement, it is possible to choose one as an example.

In Figures 2.5, 2.6, and 2.7, you can see samples of some sections of NICEM's *Index to 16mm Educational Films.* An "Index to Subject Headings" appears in Figure 2.5. This index is used in somewhat the same fashion as you would use *LCSH* before looking for books on a subject in the library catalog. As an example, suppose that you wanted to find a biographical film on Thomas Jefferson. By using the subject heading index you learn that you should not look under "Presidents, U.S.," but rather under "Biography – Presidents of the U.S."

Once you know what heading or headings you should use, you can then turn to the "Subject Section," a sample of which is represented in Figure 2.6. Here, you can scan down the columns under "Biography – Presidents of the United States" and find the titles of various films. In the sample you will notice a film entitled *Administration of Thomas Jefferson* listed halfway down the column. Following the film title are some letters in parentheses – "(J-H)" – and then another abbreviation – "CORF" – all in capital letters. The letters in

Figure 2.5

SAMPLE FROM NICEM <u>INDEX TO 16MM EDUCATIONAL FILMS</u>:
INDEX TO SUBJECT HEADINGS

POVERTY
  Sociology
    Poverty

POWER
  Industrial And Technical Education
    Engines And Power Systems
  Social Science
    Resources--Power

PREHISTORIC TIMES
  History - World
    Prehistoric Times

PREJUDICE
  Sociology
    Human Relations
    Prejudices And Antipathies

PRENATAL CARE
  Psychology
    Child Growth And Development

PRESIDENT
  Civics And Political Systems
    Executive Power
    Government - U.S.

PRESIDENTS, U.S.
  Biography
    Presidents Of The U.S.

PRESS
  Literature And Drama
    Journalism
  Social Science
    Communication
    Newspaper

Source: National Information Center for Educational Media
(NICEM), <u>Index to 16MM Educational Films</u>, 7th ed. © 1967,
1980 by the University of Southern California. Reprinted
by permission.

Figure 2.6

SAMPLE FROM NICEM INDEX TO 16MM EDUCATIONAL FILMS:
SUBJECT SECTION

BIOGRAPHY

Presidents Of The United States

A Lincoln, A Story Of His Joys And Sorrow	SOP
A Lincoln, Fellow Citizen (J-C A)	SBRTC
Abraham Lincoln (I-H)	EBEC
Abraham Lincoln - A Background Study (I-H A)	CORF
Abraham Lincoln - A New Birth Of Freedom (I-C A)	HANDEL
Abraham Lincoln - The End And The Beginning (J-H T)	IQFILM
Abraham Lincoln - The Illinois Years (I-C A)	LINE
Abraham Lincoln - The War Years (J-C A)	LINE
Abraham Lincoln - Youth (P-C A)	LINE
Abraham Lincoln And The Emancipation Proclamation (I-C)	AMEDFL
Abraham Lincoln, Afro-Americans And The American Dream (H-C A)	HRAW
Absent Host, The - Thomas Jefferson, 1781 (I-J)	IU
Adams House, The (I-C T)	IQFILM
Administration of Thomas Jefferson (J-H)	CORF
Age Of Kennedy, Pt 1 - The Early Years (J-C A)	MGHT
Age Of Kennedy, Pt 2 - The Presidency (J-C A)	MGHT
America Buries A President	COUNFI

Source: National Information Center for Educational Media
(NICEM), Index to 16MM Educational Films, 7th ed. © 1967,
1980 by the University of Southern California. Reprinted
by permission.

parentheses refer to audience level (in this case, junior high to high
school level), and the other abbreviation refers to the producer (in this
case, Coronet Instructional Films). The lists of abbreviations and code
names are separate and appear in different places from one NICEM
index to another.

The last section we will look at is the "Title Section" represented in
Figure 2.7. As you can see, the title section is not just an alphabetical

Figure 2.7

SAMPLE FROM NICEM INDEX TO 16MM EDUCATIONAL FILMS:
TITLE SECTION

Administration Of Drugs To Sleep   C   23 min
            16MM FILM SILENT   PRO
Illustrates special equipment designed to administer medicine to sheep.
Shows the dosage employed and technique of administering
phenothiazine to a band of approximately 50 sheep.
Prod-CUNIV   Dist-AMVMA

Administration Of Plasma Components   B   20 min
            16MM FILM OPTICAL SOUND   PRO
Describes the preparation and application of cyro-free plasma
components, the conversion of these components in albumin and gamma
conditions previously calling for fresh plasma. From The Clinical
Pathology Series.
LC No. 74-706016
Prod-NMAC   Dist-USNAC   1970

Administration Of Projective Tests   B   19 min
            16MM FILM OPTICAL SOUND   C
Burgess Meredith acts as the subject to demonstrate standard projective
tests, such as TAT, Szondi and sentence completion, indiscriminate
showing may be inadvisable as actual tests are shown.
Prod-PSUPCR   Dist-PSUPCR   1951

Administration Of Thomas Jefferson   X   14 min
            16MM FILM OPTICAL SOUND   J-H
Presents the words of Thomas Jefferson describing the eight year
struggle between his political philosophies, the opposition and the
hard realities of life as President.
LC No. 72-702631
Prod-CORF   Dist-CORF   1972

Admiral Burke Takes Command   B   12 min
            16MM FILM OPTICAL SOUND
Presents portions of the 1955 Change of Command Speech at Annapolis
by the Secretary of the Navy, Admiral Carney, and the speech of Admiral
Burke as he is sworn in as the new Chief of Naval Operations.
LC No. FIE-56-9
Prod-USN   Dist-USNAC   1955

        Source: National Information Center for Educational Media
        (NICEM), Index to 16MM Educational Films, 7th ed. © 1967,
        1980 by the University of Southern California. Reprinted
        by permission.

listing of film titles, but also an abstract: each title includes a brief
description of the film's contents. The film *Administration of Thomas
Jefferson* is described in the sample, and you can see that it and the
other entries include the following information: the length (fourteen
minutes); whether the film has sound or not; whether the film is in
color ("C"), black and white ("B"), or both ("X"); the year of release, and

the distributor's name. The title section also includes audience level and producer's name. As mentioned earlier, each of the NICEM indexes is similar in scope and arrangement, so once you have used one, it is quite easy to use any of the others.

Besides the various NICEM indexes listed, your library may also own the two tools published by the Educators Progress Service: *Educators Guide to Free Films* and *Educators Guide to Free Filmstrips*. As their titles suggest, both tools list only films and filmstrips that are available at no cost. The bulk of each guide is composed of title listings with short summaries. Each guide also includes a title index, a subject index, and a "source and availability index," which lists the producing and distributing organizations. This latter index also indicates any restrictions on the availability of either films or filmstrips.

Another tool, the *Schwann Record & Tape Guide*, may be familiar to many audio buffs, for it is frequently used and seen in record stores. *Schwann* is the monthly *Books in Print* of the audio world. It lists about 45,000 stereo LP records, eight-track tapes, and cassette tapes. The listings are arranged alphabetically under broad categories such as classical, current popular, jazz, and musical shows.

The last tool listed, *Media Review Digest* (or *MRD*), is similar in scope to *Book Review Index*. *MRD* is an annually published work that is kept up to date with a mid-year supplement. It lists around 50,000 media reviews from over 150 periodicals. Some of the citations in *MRD* also include a short excerpt from the review itself or an indication of whether or not the review was favorable.

The variety of audiovisual materials available to you is indeed rich, and you should not hesitate to consult any of these tools if you believe that a particular type of medium would enhance the research you're doing. Be aware, however, that some media—particularly films and videotapes—are expensive, and few community college libraries will have everything you may desire. Your library's reference or media personnel are particularly important here, since they can assist you in choosing what may be immediately or at least readily available for your use.

BIBLIOGRAPHIC GUIDES

American Reference Books Annual. Littleton, Colo.: Libraries Unlimited, 1970– . (Z1035.1; 011.02)

Sheehy, Eugene Paul. *Guide to Reference Books.* 9th ed. Chicago: American Library Association, 1976. And its *Supplement,* 1980. (Z1035.1; 011.02)

Walford, Albert John. *Guide to Reference Materials.* 3d ed. London: Library Association, 1973–1977. (Z1035.1; 011.02)

For other tools, look in your library's catalog under: "Reference books – Bibliography" and "Reference books – Bibliography – Periodicals."

*   *   *

It is entirely appropriate that the last type of tool discussed in this chapter is the bibliographic guide, an important source type of reference work that lists and describes other reference sources in virtually every field of human endeavor. The bibliographic guide thus picks up where a book such as this leaves off: you will turn to it when you want to learn if a particular type of tool – say, for example, a who's who of chemists – exists.

Only three examples of the general bibliographic guide have been cited here, but there are others, most of which are devoted to special subjects (and some of these are listed in the next chapter). In fact, *Doing Library Research* could itself be called a bibliographic guide, although it is a very selective one.

Sheehy's *Guide to Reference Books* is often referred to as the American reference librarian's bible, for it lists and describes some 10,000 reference books, everything from Burmese-English dictionaries to handbooks of South African surnames. Although Sheehy's work emphasizes reference works that are useful to scholars in large research libraries, many popular reference tools are also included. The *Guide* lists reference works under one of five broad divisions: general reference works, humanities, social sciences, history and area studies, and pure and applied sciences. Each of these broad divisions is in turn broken down into specific subjects and further subdivided by type of tool. Such classification is a common arrangement in bibliographic guides, and you may note that a similar arrangement has been used in this book.

Walford's *Guide to Reference Materials* is Sheehy's British counterpart, listing and describing some 12,000 reference tools. It, too, is arranged by broad subject area: volume 1 deals with science and technology, volume 2 with social sciences, and volume 3 with generalities, the arts, and literature. While you will find Walford in just about every library of any size, you will probably not have occasion to use it as often as Sheehy simply because of its European emphasis.

As convenient as the bibliographic guide is, it has at least one serious drawback: it dates quickly and cannot be easily or readily republished in a new edition. *Guide to Reference Books,* for example, was published in 1976 and lists only those tools published up through October 1974. Its supplement continues this coverage through the fall of 1978. In order to discover what reference works may have been published in your area of interest since that time, you can turn to the *American Reference Books Annual,* more commonly called *ARBA.* The *ARBA* is an annual reviewing service that lists and evaluates virtually *all* reference books published in the United States during the preceding year. (Note that *ARBA 79* reviews the reference sources of 1978, *ARBA 78* the reference sources of 1977, and so on.) The entries in each *ARBA* are arranged under specific subjects and generally then subarranged by type of reference tool.

When you use either Sheehy's *Guide to Reference Books* or *ARBA,* keep in mind that their respective indexes do not refer you to page number but rather to item number. This is a common practice for those bibliographic guides wherein each reference work listed receives either a classification number (as in the *Guide*) or a sequential number (as in *ARBA*). Walford does not number items, so index entries refer you to page number.

NOTES

1. Other geographical-information sources useful specifically to students of geography are listed under the heading "Geography" in Chapter 3.

3
The Specialized Tools

In Chapters 1 and 2, you learned that after but a few minutes of examination, you could discover what *type* of tool you had, what its *scope* was, and *how* it was arranged. By now, it should be clear that researching a subject in a library is not at all a mystical activity – time consuming, yes; complicated, possibly; but not mystical. If you can read, you can use virtually any tool in the library with relative ease.

In this chapter you will learn of the various specialized tools available to you. Unlike Chapter 2, in which the citations were arranged by type of tool, the listings here are arranged first by broad area (e.g., "Humanities") and then by subject (e.g., "Literature"). Thus, if you're majoring in nursing, you'll want to consult not just the section on "Nursing," but also the broader area under which nursing falls, "Health Sciences." Depending on your major, you may also find it desirable to consult more than one area or section. If, for example, you are majoring in legal secretarial science, you will want to look under both "Legal Assistant" and "Secretarial Science."

Each area and subject begins with a brief discussion of the nature of the tools to be listed in that section. The list itself follows, arranged alphabetically by main entry. Each citation is preceded by a code that will tell you at a glance what type of tool you have: "S" stands for source, "A" stands for access, and "SA" stands for source/access. Thus, for example, if you want to find out what bibliographies or indexes exist in your field of study, you can quickly scan the codes preceding the entries to find those with an "A."

The entries themselves are actually similar to catalog cards, in that they contain the main entry, the title and publishing information, the number of pages or volumes, a notation as to whether or not a bibliography or bibliographical footnotes are included (both abbreviated "bibl."), classification numbers (when available), and the subject headings assigned by the Library of Congress. Thus, you may wish to review that portion of Chapter 1 where main entry cards are discussed.

To show you how the citations look and how to read them, here is an example taken from the health sciences section:

SA   American Hospital Association. *American Hospital Association Guide to the Health Care Field.* 1972– . Chicago: American Hospital Association, 1972– . Annual. (RA977.1; 362.11025 / 1. American Hospital Association – Yearbooks. 2. Hospitals – Directories – Yearbooks. 3. Hospitals – United States – Directories – Yearbooks. 4. Medical societies, etc. – Yearbooks. 5. Medical supplies – Directories – Yearbooks.)

The first thing to notice is that this is a source/access type of reference tool, which means, of course, that it not only gives you information directly, but also indicates where else you can find information. The citation begins with the main entry, in this case a corporate author, the American Hospital Association (AHA). The work is entitled *American Hospital Association Guide to the Health Care Field* and has been published since 1972 in Chicago by the association. Immediately following the publication date you should expect to find the number of pages and/or volumes, as well as an indication whether there is a bibliography present. Since the *AHA Guide to the Health Care Field* is a yearbook, all that appears in this area is the notation "Annual."

Following the publishing information you will find information in parentheses, beginning with both Library of Congress ("RA977.A1") and Dewey ("362.11025") classification numbers. Note that these are *not* full call numbers, which will vary from library to library. If your library follows standardized classification, however, this should be an accurate indication of where you could go to find a particular tool on the shelves. A slash separates the Dewey number from the subject headings, each of which is preceded by an arabic numeral. You should scan these headings, for they will give you clues as to the scope of the work. This particular tool is not just a yearbook for the AHA and for medical societies, but also an annual directory of medical supplies, hospitals generally, and U.S. hospitals particularly.

It is important to realize that the subject headings are not just important indications of the scope of the particular tool being listed, but also important access points for further subject searching in the catalog. Keep in mind that you may come across terms used in the subject headings that are unfamiliar to you such as "Bio-bibliography." Such terms will, of course, be defined in one of the general language dictionaries cited in Chapter 2. Note, too, that any abbreviations used in this chapter are decoded in the Appendix.

Once you have carefully read through the list of tools in your area and subject, it remains for you to actually find the tools and examine them so as to discover how they are arranged. Before doing so, you may want to reread the section on "Finding and Evaluating Books" in Chapter 1.

Finally the tools listed in this chapter, like those listed in Chapter 2, were the latest tools available in 1979 and early 1980 when this book was being written. Every book published is out of date as soon as the manuscript leaves the author and goes to the publisher, and this one is no exception. While that fact does not lessen the value of this or of other books, you should be aware that many of the titles listed here will have newer editions and also that new works are published every month. This is one important reason why you should rely as heavily on the subject headings in this and the preceding chapter as you do on the citations themselves. And, of course, there is absolutely no substitute for consulting a librarian.

HUMANITIES

The humanities traditionally have been concerned with the cultural aspects of human knowledge and activity. Because of this, many tools listed here and under specific subjects such as literature and music do not necessarily need to be current in order to be valuable. Indeed, the value of many older works of criticism in the humanities increases with age. Note that this is in distinct contrast with tools in the sciences where currency is almost always essential.

Unlike in some of the other broad areas of study, not very many reference tools deal in a general way with the specific subjects usually included in this category. The four titles listed here are, however, useful and important and generally found on the reference shelves of most libraries.

S   Benet, William Rose. *The Reader's Encyclopedia.* 2d ed. New
         York: Crowell, 1965. 1118p. (PN41; 803 / 1. Literature – Dic-
         tionaries. 2. Art – Dictionaries. 3. Music – Dictionaries.)
A   *Humanities Index.* v.1- , no.1- . New York: H. W. Wilson,
         1974- . Quarterly, with annual cumulations. From 1965 to 1974
         was called *Social Sciences and Humanities Index.* (AI3; 016.0013 / 1.
         Periodicals – Indexes. 2. Humanities – Periodicals – Indexes.)
A   *Index to Book Reviews in the Humanities.* Detroit: Phillip Thomson,
         1960- . Annual. (Z1035.A1; 028 / 1. Books – Reviews – Indexes. 2.

Humanities – Book reviews – Indexes.)
A   Rogers, A. Robert. *The Humanities: A Selective Guide to Information Sources.* Littleton, Colo.: Libraries Unlimited, 1974. 400p. (Z5579; 016.0013 / 1. Humanities – Bibliography.)

Dance

For the most part, the titles listed here deal with dance generally. There are, however, four tools noted that deal with specific forms of dance, namely ballet and modern dance. These tools have been included because ballet and modern dance are two of the more important forms of dance in the community college curriculum. They should also indicate to you, however, that there exist reference works devoted to other specialized forms of dance, which you can find listed in the catalog by using the appropriate subject headings.

Note that one of the titles listed – *Dance Magazine* – is a periodical and will not likely be found in the reference collection. It has been included because it is a recognized source for reviews, biographical information, and other general information on the various forms of dance.

SA   Chujoy, Anatole, and Manchester, P. W., comps. *The Dance Encyclopedia.* Rev. and enl. ed. New York: Simon & Schuster, 1967. 992p. bibl. (GV1585; 793.303 / 1. Dancing – Dictionaries.)

SA   *The Concise Oxford Dictionary of Ballet.* Compiled by Horst Koegler. New York: Oxford University Press, 1977. 583p. bibl. (GV1585; 792.803 / 1. Ballet – Dictionaries.)

SA   *The Dance Catalog.* Edited by Nancy Reynolds. New York: Harmony Books, c1979. 256p. bibl. (GV1594; 793.3 / 1. Dancing – Addresses, essays, lectures. 2. Dancing – Study and teaching – United States – Directories. 3. Dance companies – United States – Directories.)

S   *Dance Magazine.* New York: Dance Magazine, Inc., 1926- . Monthly. (GV1580; 793.3205 / 1. Dancing – Periodicals.)

S   *Dance World.* v.1- , 1966- . New York: Crown, 1966- . Annual. (GV1580; 793.320973 / 1. Dancing – United States – Yearbooks.)

SA   *The Encyclopedia of Dance & Ballet.* Edited by Mary Clarke and David Vaughan. New York: G. P. Putnam's, 1977. 376p. bibl. (GV1585; 793.303 / 1. Dancing – Dictionaries. 2. Ballet – Dictionaries.)

S   Grant, Gail. *Technical Manual and Dictionary of Classical Ballet.* 2d rev. ed. New York: Dover, 1967. 127p. (GV1787; 792.8014 / 1. Ballet – Terminology.)

A   Kaprelian, Mary H., comp. *Aesthetics for Dancers: A Selected*
     Annotated Bibliography. Washington, D.C.: American Alliance for
     Health, Physical Education and Recreation, 1976. 87p. (Z5931;
     016.7001 / 1. Art–Philosophy–Bibliography. 2. Danc-
     ing–Philosophy–Bibliography.)
S   Martin, John Joseph. *Book of the Dance.* New York: Tudor,
     1963. 192p. (GV1781; 793.32 / 1. Dancing. 2. Dancers.)
SA   McDonagh, Don. *The Complete Guide to Modern Dance.* New York:
     Doubleday, 1976. 534p. bibl. (GV1783; 793.32 / 1. Modern dance.)
S   Raffé, Walter George. *Dictionary of the Dance.* New York:
     Barnes & Noble, c1964. 583p. (GV1585; 793.303 / 1. Dancing–
     Dictionaries.)

Drama

As you scan the list of reference tools in drama, you will see that
most of the titles deal either with drama itself–including specific
plays–or with dramatists. There are also, however, a few tools that
may be useful in actual play production, such as *Modern Theatre Prac-*
tice.

Besides the tools listed here, several titles listed in the "Literature"
section may also be useful. Full citations will, of course, be found in
that section, but briefly, the most important titles are *MLA Interna-*
tional Bibliography of Books and Articles on the Modern Languages and
Literatures; Twentieth Century Literary Criticism; volume 2 of *The*
Reader's Adviser; Contemporary Literary Criticism; Cassell's En-
cyclopaedia of World Literature; and *A Dictionary of Literary, Dramatic,*
and Cinematic Terms.

SA   *The Best Plays [of 1894/99–] and Year Book of the Drama*
     in America. Boston: Small, 1920–1925; New York: Dodd, 1926– .
     Annual. bibl. (PN6112; 812.5082 / 1. Drama–20th century. 2.
     Theater–United States–Yearbooks. 3. Drama–Bibliography.)
S   Bowman, Walter Parker, and Ball, Robert Hamilton. *Theatre*
     Language: A Dictionary of Terms in English of the Drama and Stage
     from Medieval to Modern Times. New York: Theatre Arts Books,
     1961. 428p. (PN2035; 792.03 / 1. Theater–Dictionaries. 2.
     Drama–Dictionaries.)
A   Breed, Paul Francis, and Sniderman, Florence M. *Dramatic*
     Criticism Index: A Bibliography of Commentaries on Playwrights from
     Ibsen to the Avant-Garde. Detroit: Gale, 1972. 1022p. (Z5781;
     016.809204 / 1. Drama–20th century–History and
     criticism–Indexes.)
A   Brockett, Oscar Gross; Becker, Samuel L.; and Bryant,

Donald C. *A Bibliographical Guide to Research in Speech and Dramatic Art.* Chicago: Scott, Foresman, 1964. 118p. (Z1002; 016 / 1. Bibliography–Bibliography. 2. Bibliography–Bibliography–Speech. 3. Bibliography–Bibliography–Drama. 4. Bibliography–Bibliography–Mass media.)

S   *Crowell's Handbook of Contemporary Drama.* By Michael Anderson [and others]. New York: Crowell, 1971. 505p. (PN1861; 809.204 / 1. Drama–20th century–Dictionaries.)

A   Drury, Francis Keese Wynkoop. *Drury's Guide to Best Plays.* 3d ed. by James M. Salem. Metuchen, N.J.: Scarecrow, 1978. 421p. (Z5781; 016.80882 / 1. Drama–Bibliography. 2. Drama–Indexes. 3. Drama–Stories, plots, etc.)

A   Eddleman, Floyd Eugene. *American Drama Criticism: Interpretations, 1890–1977.* 2d ed. Hamden, Conn.: Shoe String Press, 1979. 488p. (Z1231.D7; 016.7920973 / 1. American drama–History and criticism–Bibliography. 2. Theater–United States–Reviews–Bibliography.)

SA *The Encyclopedia of World Theater.* With 420 illustrations and an index of play titles. Edited with an introduction by Martin Esslin. New York: Scribner's, 1977. 320p. bibl. (PN2035; 792.03 / 1. Theater–Dictionaries.)

A   Fidell, Estelle A. *Play Index 1961–1967.* New York: H. W. Wilson, 1968. 464p. (Z5781; 016.80882 / 1. Drama–Bibliography. 2. Drama–Indexes.)

A   Fidell, Estelle A. *Play Index 1968–1972.* New York: H. W. Wilson, 1973. 403p. (Z5781; 016.80882 / 1. Drama–Bibliography. 2. Drama–Indexes.)

A   Fidell, Estelle A. *Play Index 1973–1977.* New York: H. W. Wilson, 1978. 457p. (Z5781; 016.80882 / 1. Drama–Bibliography. 2. Drama–Indexes.)

A   Fidell, Estelle A., and Peake, Dorothy Margaret. *Play Index 1953–1960.* New York: H. W. Wilson, 1963. 404p. (Z5781; 016.80882 / 1. Drama–Bibliography. 2. Drama–Indexes.)

SA Gassner, John, and Quinn, Edward. *The Reader's Encyclopedia of World Drama.* New York: Crowell, 1969. 1030p. bibl. (PN1625; 809.2 / 1. Drama–Dictionaries.)

SA Hartnoll, Phyllis. *The Oxford Companion to the Theatre.* 3d ed. London: Oxford University Press, 1967. 1088p. bibl. (PN2035; 792.03 / 1. Theater–Dictionaries.)

SA Heffner, Hubert C. [and others]. *Modern Theatre Practice.* With an expansion of the scenery section by Tom Rezzuto and a chapter on sound by Kenneth K. Jones. 5th ed. New York: Appleton, 1973. 660p. bibl. (PN3151; 792.02 / 1. Amateur theatricals. 2. Theater–Production and direction.)

A   Keller, Dean H. *Index to Plays in Periodicals.* Rev. and

expanded ed. Metuchen, N.J.: Scarecrow, 1979. 824p.
(Z5781; 016.80882 / 1. Drama–Bibliography. 2.
Periodicals–Indexes.)

S   Lovell, John. *Digests of Great American Plays: Complete Summaries of More than 100 Plays from the Beginnings to the Present.* New York: Crowell, 1961. 452p. (PS338.P5; 812.0822 / 1. American drama–Stories, plots, etc.)

S   Matlaw, Myron. *Modern World Drama: An Encyclopedia.* New York: Dutton, 1972. 960p. (PN1851; 809.234 / 1. Drama–19th century–Dictionaries. 2. Drama–20th century–Dictionaries.)

SA   *McGraw-Hill Encyclopedia of World Drama: An International Reference Work.* New York: McGraw-Hill, 1972. 4v. bibl. (PN1625; 809.2 / 1. Dramatists–Biography–Dictionaries. 2. Drama–Bibliography.)

A   NCTE Liaison Committee. *Guide to Play Selection: A Selective Bibliography for Production and Study of Modern Plays.* 3d ed. Comp. by the NCTE Liaison Committee with the Speech Communication Association and the American Theatre Association. Joseph Mersand, editorial chairman. Urbana, Ill: Dist. by the National Council of Teachers of English, 1975. 292p. (Z5781; 016.822008 / 1. Drama–Bibliography.)

S   *Notable Names in the American Theatre.* New and rev. ed. Clifton, N.J.: James T. White, 1976. 1250p. (PN2285; 790.20973 / 1. Theater–United States–Biography.)

A   Ottemiller, John Henry. *Ottemiller's Index to Plays in Collections: An Author and Title Index to Plays Appearing in Collections Published Between 1900 and Early 1975.* 6th ed. rev. and enl. by John M. Connor and Billie M. Connor. Metuchen, N.J.: Scarecrow, 1976. 523p. bibl. (Z5781; 016.80882 / 1. Drama–Bibliography.)

S   Shipley, Joseph Twadell. *Guide to Great Plays.* Washington, D.C.: Public Affairs Press, 1956. 867p. (PN6112.5; 808.2 / 1. Drama–Stories, plots, etc. 2. Drama–History. 3. Theater–History.)

S   Sprinchorn, Evert, ed. *20th-Century Plays in Synopsis.* New York: Crowell, 1966. 493p. (PN6112.5; 808.8204 / 1. Drama–Stories, plots, etc. 2. Drama–20th century.)

SA   Vaughn, Jack A. *Drama A to Z: A Handbook.* New York: Ungar, c1978. 239p. bibl. (PN1625; 809.2 / 1. Drama–Dictionaries.)

SA   Vinson, James. *Contemporary Dramatists.* 2d ed. New York: St. Martin's, 1977. 1088p. bibl. (PR106; 822.91409 / 1. English drama–20th century–Bio-bibliography. 2. American drama–20th century–Bio-bibliography. 3. English drama–20th century–Addresses, essays, lectures. 4. American drama–20th century–Addresses, essays, lectures.)

A   West, Dorothy Herbert, and Peake, Dorothy Margaret. *Play
     Index 1949-1952.* New York: H. W. Wilson, 1953. 239p. (Z5781;
     016.80882 / 1. Drama–Bibliography. 2. Drama–Indexes.)

S   *Who Was Who in the Theatre, 1912-1976: A Biographical
     Dictionary of Actors, Actresses, Directors, Playwrights, and Producers
     of the English-speaking Theatre.* Detroit: Gale, c1978. 4v. (PN2597;
     792.0280922 / 1. Theater–Great Britain–Biography. 2.
     Theater–United States–Biography.)

Languages

Obviously, the most important tool for the foreign language student
is the dictionary. In this section, both bilingual dictionaries and
foreign language dictionaries are listed alphabetically by language.
The bilingual dictionary will be most useful when you wish to
translate a foreign language into English (or vice versa). The foreign
language dictionary may be used when you want a definition of a
foreign word in the language itself.

You will notice that only French, German, Italian, and Spanish are
covered. If you need either a bilingual or foreign language dictionary
in another language, look in your library's catalog under "[Name of
language]–Dictionaries–English" or "[Name of language]–Dictionaries."

French

S   Dubois, Marguerite-Marie. *Modern French-English Dictionary.*
     With the collaboration of Charles Cestre and others. New York:
     Larousse, 1978. 768p. (PC2640; 443.2 / 1. French language–Dic-
     tionaries–English. 2. English language–Dictionaries–French.)

S   *New Cassell's French Dictionary: French-English, English-
     French.* Rev. by Denis Girard [and others]. New York: Funk &
     Wagnalls, 1962. 762p. 655p. (PC2640; 443.2 / 1. French
     language–Dictionaries–English. 2. English language–Dic-
     tionaries–French.)

S   *Petit Larousse Illustré: Dictionnaire Encyclopédique pour Tous.*
     New York: Larousse, 1977, c1972. (AG25; 034.1 / 1. Encyclopedias
     and dictionaries, French. 2. French language–Dictionaries.)

German

S   Betteridge, Harold T. *Cassell's German-English, English-
     German Dictionary: Deutsch-Englisches, Englisch-Deutsches Wörter-
     buch.* Completely rev. ed. New York: Macmillan, 1978. 1580p.
     (PF3640; 433.2 / 1. German language–Dictionaries–English. 2.
     English language–Dictionaries–German.)

S   Messinger, Heinz. *Langenscheidt's Concise German Dictionary.*
       New York: Barnes & Noble, 1964. 2v. in 1. (PF3640; 433.2 / 1.
       German language – Dictionaries – English. 2. English language – Dictionaries – German.

S   Schöffler, Herbert. *The New Schöffler-Weis German and*
       English Dictionary: English-German/German-English. Completely rev.,
       greatly expanded, and fully updated by Erich Weis and Erwin
       Weis. Chicago: Follett, 1974, c1968. 562p., 500p. (PF3640; 433.2 /
       1. English language – Dictionaries – German. 2. German
       language – Dictionaries – English.)

Italian

S   *Cassell's Italian-English, English-Italian Dictionary.*
       Prepared by Piero Rebora, with the assistance of Francis M. Guer-
       cio and Arthur L. Hayward. 7th ed. London: Cassell, 1969. 1096p.
       (PC1640; 453.2 / 1. Italian language – Dictionaries – English. 2.
       English language – Dictionaries – Italian.)

S   Melzi, Gian Battista. *Il Novissimo Melzi: Dizionario*
       Enciclopedico Italiano. 35. ed. ampliamente aggiornata. Milano: An-
       tonio Vallardi, 1959. 2v. (PC1625; 453 / 1. Italian language –
       Dictionaries.)

S   Reynolds, Barbara, comp. *The Concise Cambridge Italian*
       Dictionary. New York: Cambridge University Press, 1975. 792p.
       (PC1640; 453.21 / 1. Italian language – Dictionaries – English. 2.
       English language – Dictionaries – Italian.)

Spanish

SA   Boggs, Ralph Steele, and Dixson, Joseph I. *Everyday*
       Spanish Idioms. New York: Regents Pub. Co., c1978. 258p. bibl.
       (PC4460; 468.3421 / 1. Spanish language – Idioms, corrections, er-
       rors – Dictionaries.)

S   Larousse, Pierre. *Pequeño Larousse Ilustrado.* By Ramon
       Garcia-Pelayo y Gross. Paris: Ediciones Larousse; dist., New York:
       Larousse, 1978, c1964. 1663p. (AG61; 036.1 / 1. Encyclopedias and
       dictionaries, Spanish. 2. Spanish language – Dictionaries.)

S   *The University of Chicago Spanish Dictionary.* 3d ed.,
       rev. and enl. Comp. by Carlos Castillo and Otto F. Bond. Chicago:
       University of Chicago Press, 1977. 488p. (PC4640; 463.21 / 1.
       Spanish language – Dictionaries – English. 2. English language – Dictionaries – Spanish.)

Literature

It may be true to say that there is actually more criticism of
literature than there is literature itself. This phenomenon would at

least partially explain why you find as many reference tools listed in this section as you do. But it is not the only reason. Another reason has already been mentioned in the section on "Humanities"; namely, many tools do not go out of date. Thus, a tool such as the *Cambridge History of American Literature,* originally published in four volumes in 1917–1921, was reprinted in one volume in 1972 because of demand.

In this section, you will find reference works that deal not only with English, American, and world literature in general, but also with various genres, such as the short story, poetry, and science fiction. You will also find several titles that indicate the source of quotations and proverbs. Besides these works, there is also listed an index of a type not examined in detail in Chapter 2, the index to collections. The particular tool is *Essay and General Literature Index,* and it gives you access to individual essays and other short pieces of general literature in collective works such as anthologies.

Believe it or not, the list of reference works included here only begins to scratch the surface of what is available to you. Your catalog and a librarian can assist if you don't find the information you need in the works listed here.

A   Altick, Richard Daniel, and Wright, Andrew. *Selective
        Bibliography for the Study of English and American Literature.* 5th ed.
        New York: Macmillan, 1975. 168p. (Z2011; 016.82 / 1. English
        literature – Study and teaching – Bibliography. 2. American
        literature – Study and teaching – Bibliography.)

S   Barnet, Sylvan; Berman, Morton; and Burton, William.
        A Dictionary of Literary, Dramatic, and Cinematic Terms. 2d ed.
        Boston: Little, Brown, 1971. 124p. (PN44.5; 801.4 / 1.
        Literature – Terminology. 2. Moving-pictures – Terminology.)

S   Bartlett, John. *Familiar Quotations: A Collection of
        Passages, Phrases, and Proverbs Traced to Their Sources in Ancient
        and Modern Literature.* 15th and 125th anniversary ed., rev. and
        enl. Emily Morison Beck, ed. Boston: Little, Brown, 1980. 1540p.
        (PN6081; 808.882 / 1. Quotations, English.)

SA   *Cambridge History of American Literature.* Ed. by William
        Peterfield Trent [and others]. New York: Putnam, 1917–1921.
        Reprinted, New York: Macmillan, 1972. 4v. in 1. bibl. (PS88; 810.9
        / 1. American literature – History and criticism.)

SA   *Cambridge History of English Literature.* Edited by A. W.
        Ward and A. R. Waller. Cambridge: University Press; New York:
        Putnam, 1919–1933. 15v. bibl. (PR83; ____ / 1. English
        literature – History and criticism. 2. English
        literature – Bibliography.)

SA   *Cassell's Encyclopaedia of World Literature.* Rev. and enl.

General ed., J. Buchanan-Brown. London: Cassell, 1973. 3v. bibl.
(PN41; 803 / 1. Literature – Dictionaries. 2. Literature – Bio-
bibliography.)

SA *Columbia Dictionary of Modern European Literature*. Horatio
Smith, gen. ed. New York: Columbia University Press, 1947. 899p.
bibl. (PN41; 803 / 1. Literature, Modern – Dictionaries, indexes,
etc.)

SA *Contemporary Authors: A Bio-bibliographical Guide to Current
Authors and Their Works*. Detroit: Gale, 1962- , v.1- . Annual.
(Z1224; 928.1 / 1. United States – Bio-bibliography. 2. Authors,
American.)

SA *Contemporary Literary Criticism: Excerpts from Criticism
of the Works of Today's Novelists, Poets, Playwrights, and Other
Creative Writers*. Detroit: Gale, 1973- . bibl. (PN771; 809.04 / 1.
Literature, Modern – 20th century – History and
criticism – Periodicals.)

SA *Contemporary Poets*. James Vinson, ed. 2d ed. New York:
St. Martin's, 1975. 1849p. bibl. (PR603; 821.9109 / 1. English
poetry – 20th century – Bio-bibliography. 2. American poetry – 20th
century – Bio-bibliography. 3. English poetry – 20th century – Addresses, essays, lectures. 4. American poetry – 20th century – Addresses, essays, lectures.)

A Contento, William. *Index to Science Fiction Anthologies
and Collections*. Boston: G. K. Hall, 1978. 608p. (Z131.F4;
016.8130876 / 1. Science fiction, American – Bibliography. 2.
Science fiction, English – Bibliography. 3. Science fiction – Bibliography.)

A Cook, Dorothy Elizabeth, and Monro, Isabel Stevenson. *Short
Story Index*. New York: H. W. Wilson, 1953. And its *Supplements,*
1950-1954, 1955-1958, 1959-1963, 1964-1968, 1969-1973. And its
Annuals for 1974, 1975, 1976, and 1977. (Z5917.S5; 016.80883 / 1.
Short stories – Bibliography.)

S Cuddon, John A. *A Dictionary of Literary Terms*. Garden City,
N.Y.: Doubleday, 1977. 745p. (PN41; 803 / 1. Literature –
Dictionaries.)

SA Elrick, George. *Science Fiction Handbook for Readers and
Writers*. 1st ed. Chicago: Chicago Review Press, c1978. 315p. bibl.
(PN3448.S45; 809.3876 / 1. Science fiction – Dictionaries.)

A English Association. *The Year's Work in English Studies.*
1919/20- . Publ. for the English Association. London: Murray,
1921- , v.1- . Annual. (PE58; ____ / 1. English philology – History.
2. English philology – Bibliography. 3. English literature – History
and criticism. 3. English literature – Bibliography.)

A *Essay and General Literature Index*. 1900-1933. An index
to essays and articles in collections of essays and miscellaneous
works. New York: H. W. Wilson, 1934. Kept up to date by sup-

plements: 7-year cumulations (1934–1940, 1941–1947, 1948–1954);
5-year cumulations (1955/59–); and semiannual and annual
cumulations. (AI3; 016 / 1. Literature–Indexes. 2.
Essays–Indexes.)

SA   Gaster, Adrian, ed. *The International Authors and Writers
     Who's Who.* 8th ed. Cambridge, Eng.: International Biographical
     Centre, 1977. 1167p. (Z1010; 808 / 1. Bio-bibliography–Collected
     works.)

A   Granger, Edith. *Granger's Index to Poetry.* 6th ed. Ed.
     by William James Smith. New York: Columbia University Press,
     1973. 2223p. (PN1021; 808.810016 / 1. Poetry–Indexes. 2. English
     poetry–Indexes.)

SA   Hart, James David. *The Oxford Companion to American Literature.*
     4th ed. New York: Oxford University Press, 1965. 991p. bibl.
     (PS21; 810.3 / 1. American literature–Dictionaries. 2. American
     literature–Bio-bibliography.)

SA   Harvey, Sir Paul. *The Oxford Companion to English Literature.*
     4th ed. Rev. by Dorothy Eagle. Oxford: Clarendon Press, c1967.
     961p. bibl. (PR19; 820.3 / 1. English literature–Dictionaries. 2.
     English literature–Bio-bibliography. 3. American literature–Dic-
     tionaries. 4. American literature–Bio-bibliography.)

S   Holman, Clarence Hugh. *A Handbook to Literature.* 4th ed.
     Indianapolis, Ind.: Bobbs-Merrill, c1980. 537p. (PN41; 803 / 1.
     Literature–Dictionaries. 2. English literature–Outlines, syllabi,
     etc. 3. American literature–Outlines, syllabi, etc.)

S   Keller, Helen Rex. *Reader's Digest of Books.* New and
     greatly enl. ed. New York: Macmillan, 1929. 1447p. (PN44; ____ /
     1. Literature–Dictionaries, indexes, etc. 2. Books–Reviews.)

SA   Kunitz, Stanley J., and Colby, Vineta. *European Authors:
     1000–1900.* New York: H. W. Wilson, 1967. 1016p. bibl. (PN451;
     920.04 / 1. Literature, Modern–Bio-bibliography. 2. Authors,
     European.)

SA   Kunitz, Stanley J., and Haycraft, Howard. *American
     Authors, 1600–1900: A Biographical Dictionary of American
     Literature.* Complete in one volume with 1,300 biographies and 400
     portraits. New York: H. W. Wilson, 1938. 846p. bibl. (PS21; 928.1 /
     1. Authors, American. 2. United States–Biography–Dictionaries.)

SA   Kunitz, Stanley J., and Haycraft, Howard. *British Authors
     Before 1800: A Biographical Dictionary.* New York: H. W. Wilson,
     1952. 584p. bibl. (PR105; 928.2 / 1. Authors, English.)

SA   Kunitz, Stanley J., and Haycraft, Howard. *British Authors
     of the 19th Century.* New York: H. W. Wilson, 1936. 677p. bibl.
     (PR451; ____ / 1. Biography–Dictionaries. 2. Authors, English.)

SA   Kunitz, Stanley J., and Haycraft, Howard. *Twentieth Century
     Authors: A Biographical Dictionary of Modern Literature.* New York:

H. W. Wilson, 1942. 1577p. bibl. And by the same authors with
Vineta Colby, *Twentieth Century Authors: First Supplement.* New
York: H. W. Wilson, 1955. 1123p. bibl. (PN771; 928 / 1. Literature,
Modern – 20th century – Bio-bibliography.)

A   Magill, Frank Northen. *Magill's Bibliography of Literary Criticism:
Selected Sources for the Study of More than 2,500 Outstanding Works
of Western Literature.* Englewood Cliffs, N.J.: Salem Press, c1979.
4v. (Z6511; 016.8 / 1. Literature – History and criticism – Indexes.)

S   Magill, Frank Northen. *Masterpieces of World Literature
in Digest Form.* New York: Harper, 1952–1969, ser. 1–4. (PN44;
808.8 / 1. Literature – Collections. 2. Literature – Stories, plots, etc.).
Kept up to date by *Masterplots Annual Volume,* 1954- . Ed. by
Frank N. Magill. New York: Salem Press, 1955- , v.1- . (Z1219;
015 / 1. Books – Reviews.)

S   Magill, Frank Northen. *Survey of Contemporary Literature:
Updated Reprints of 2,300 Essay-Reviews from Masterplots Annuals,
1954–1976, and Survey of Contemporary Literature Supplement.* Rev.
ed. Englewood Cliffs, N.J.: Salem Press, 1977. 12v. (PN44; 809.04 /
1. Literature – Stories, plots, etc.)

A   Modern Humanities Research Association. *Annual Bibliography
of English Language and Literature.* 1920- . Cambridge: University
Press, 1921- , v.1- . Annual. (Z2011; ____ / 1. English
philology – Bibliography. 2. English literature – Bibliography.)

A   Modern Language Association of America. *MLA International
Bibliography of Books and Articles on the Modern Languages and
Literatures.* 1921- . Annual. (Z7006; ____ / 1. Languages,
Modern – Bibliography. 2. Literature – History and
criticism – Bibliography.)

A   *The New Cambridge Bibliography of English Literature.*
Cambridge: University Press, 1969–1977. 5v. (Z2011; 016.82 / 1.
English literature – Bibliography.)

S   *Oxford Dictionary of English Proverbs.* 3d ed. Rev. by F. P.
Wilson. Oxford: Clarendon Press, 1970. 930p. (PN6421; 398.9203 /
1. Proverbs, English.)

S   *The Oxford Dictionary of Quotations.* 3d ed. New York:
Oxford University Press, 1979. 907p. (PN6081; 808.88 / 1. Quotations. 2. Quotations, English.)

SA *The Penguin Companion to American Literature.* Edited by
Malcolm Bradbury, Eric Mottram, and Jean Franco. New York:
McGraw-Hill, 1971. 384p. bibl. (PN843; 809 / 1.
America – Literatures – Bio-bibliography.)

SA *The Penguin Companion to Classical, Oriental & African
Literature.* Edited by D. M. Lang and D. R. Dudley. New York:
McGraw-Hill, 1971, c1969. 359p. bibl. (PA31; 809 / 1. Classical
literature – Bio-bibliography. 2. Oriental literature – Bio-

bibliography. 3. African literature – Bio-bibliography.)
SA   *The Penguin Companion to English Literature.* Edited by
        David Daiches. New York: McGraw-Hill, 1971. 575p. bibl. (PN849;
        820.9 / 1. Commonwealth of Nations – Literature – Bio-
        bibliography.)
SA   *The Penguin Companion to European Literature.* Edited by
        Anthony Thorlby. New York: McGraw-Hill, c1969. 907p. bibl.
        (PN41; 809.894 / 1. Literature – Bio-bibliography. 2.
        Literature – Dictionaries.)
SA   *Princeton Encyclopedia of Poetry and Poetics.* Alex
        Preminger, ed. Princeton: Princeton University Press, 1974. 992p.
        bibl. (PN1021; 808.103 / 1. Poetry – Dictionaries. 2. Poetics – Dic-
        tionaries. 3. Poetry – History and criticism.)
A   *The Reader's Adviser.* 1st- . New York: R. R. Bowker,
        1921- . 3v. (Z1035; 016.42 / 1. Bibliography – Best books.)
S   *The Science Fiction Encyclopedia.* General ed., Peter Nicholls.
        1st ed. New York: Doubleday, 1979. 672p. (PN3448.S45; 809.3876 /
        1. Science fiction – Dictionaries.)
SA   Seymour-Smith, Martin. *Funk & Wagnalls Guide to Modern*
        World Literature. New York: Funk & Wagnalls, 1973. 1206p. bibl.
        (PN761; 809.034 / 1. Literature, Modern – 19th century – History
        and criticism. 2. Literature, Modern – 20th century – History and
        criticism.)
A   Smith, William James, ed. *Granger's Index to Poetry,*
        1970-1977. New York: Columbia University Press, 1978. 635p.
        (PN1021; 808.810016 / 1. Poetry – Indexes. 2. English
        poetry – Indexes.)
SA   Spiller, Robert E., [and others], eds. *Literary History*
        of the United States. 4th ed. New York: Macmillan, 1974. 2v. bibl.
        (PS88; 810.9 / 1. American literature – History and criticism. 2.
        American literature – Bibliography.)
SA   Stark, John O. *Almanac of British and American Literature.*
        Littleton, Colo.: Libraries Unlimited, 1979. 218p. bibl. (PR87;
        820.202 / 1. English literature – Chronology. 2. American
        literature – Chronology. 3. Literary calendars.)
S   Stevenson, Burton. *The Home Book of Proverbs, Maxims and*
        Familiar Phrases. New York: Macmillan, 1948. 2957p. (PN6405;
        808.88 / 1. Proverbs. 2. Maxims.)
S   Stevenson, Burton. *The Home Book of Quotations, Classical*
        and Modern. 10th ed. rev. New York: Dodd, 1967. 2816p. (PN6081;
        808.882 / 1. Quotations.)
SA   Tuck, Donald H., comp. *The Encyclopedia of Science Fiction*
        and Fantasy Through 1968. Chicago: Advent, 1974- , v.1- . bibl.
        (Z5917.S36; 016.80883876 / 1. Science fiction – Bibliography. 2.
        Fantastic fiction – Bibliography.)

S   *Twentieth-Century Literary Criticism: Excerpts from*
     Criticism of the Works of Novelists, Poets, Playwrights, Short Story
     Writers, and Other Creative Writers 1900-1960. Detroit: Gale,
     1978- , v.1- . (___; 809.04 / 1. Literature – History and criticism.)
SA   Vinson, James. *Contemporary Novelists.* 2d ed. New York:
     St. Martin's, 1976. 1636p. bibl. (PR883; 823.03 / 1. English fic-
     tion – 20th century – Bio-bibliography. 2. American fiction – 20th
     century – Bio-bibliography.)
A   Vitale, Philip H. *Basic Tools of Research: An Annotated*
     Guide for Students of English. 3d ed. rev. and enl. Woodbury, N.Y.:
     Barron's, 1975. 279p. (Z2011; 016.8208 / 1. English
     literature – Bibliography. 2. American literature – Bibliography. 3.
     Reference books – Bibliography.)
A   Watson, George, ed. *The Concise Cambridge Bibliography of*
     English Literature, 600-1950. 2d ed. Cambridge: University Press,
     1965. 269p. (Z2011; 016.82 / 1. English literature – Bibliography.)
SA   *Webster's New World Companion to English and American*
     Literature. Ed. by Arthur Pollard. New York: Popular Library,
     c1973. 850p. bibl. (PR19; 820.9 / 1. English literature – Dictionaries.
     2. American literature – Dictionaries. 3. English literature – Bio-
     bibliography. 4. American literature – Bio-bibliography.)
A   Wilson, H. W., Firm, Publishers. *Fiction Catalog.* 9th
     ed. by Estelle A. Fidell. New York: H. W. Wilson, 1976. 797p.
     (Z5916; 016.823008 / 1. Fiction – Indexes. 2. Bibliography – Best
     books – Fiction.)
SA   *World Authors, 1970-1975.* Ed., John Wakeman. New York: H. W.
     Wilson, 1980. 894p. bibl. (PN451; 809.04 / 1. Literature,
     Modern – 20th century – Bio-bibliography. 2. Literature,
     Modern – 20th century – History and criticism.)

Music

The tools listed in this section should assist you in answering a wide
variety of questions. There are several biographical sources for information on famous composers and musical artists, as well as a number
of source and source/access tools that cover various periods of music
and various types of music such as opera, musical theater, jazz, and
rock. You will also find sources of information devoted specifically to
musical instruments. And there are access tools such as *Music Index,*
which lists periodical literature, and discographies, which list sound
recordings. Remember, too, to consult the Schwann catalog already
listed in the "Media" section of Chapter 2.

SA   Apel, Willi. *Harvard Dictionary of Music.* 2d ed., rev.

and enl. Cambridge, Mass.: Harvard University Press, Belknap
Press, 1969. 935p. bibl. (ML100; 780.3 / 1. Music–Dictionaries.)

SA   Baker, Theodore. *Baker's Biographical Dictionary of
Musicians.* 6th ed., rev. by Nicolas Slonimsky. New York: Shirmer,
1978. 1955p. bibl. (ML105; 780.92 / 1. Music–Bio-bibliography.)

S   Blom, Eric. *Everyman's Dictionary of Music.* Rev. by Sir
Jack Westrup. New York: St. Martin's, 1971. 793p. (ML100; 780.3 /
1. Music–Dictionaries.)

S   Bordman, Gerald. *American Musical Theatre: A Chronicle.*
New York: Oxford University Press, 1978. 749p. (ML1711;
782.810973 / 1. Musical revue, comedy, etc.–United States.)

A   Bull, Storm. *Index to Biographies of Contemporary Composers,
Volume II.* Metuchen, N.J.: Scarecrow, 1974. 567p. (ML105;
016.9278 / 1. Music–Bio-bibliography–Indexes.)

SA   Diagram Group. *Musical Instruments of the World: An
Illustrated Encyclopedia.* New York: Bantam Books, 1978, c1976.
320p. bibl. (____; 781.9103 / 1. Musical instruments–Dictionaries.)

A   Duckles, Vincent Harris. *Music Reference and Research
Materials: An Annotated Bibliography.* 3d ed. New York: Free Press,
1974. 526p. (ML113; 016.78 / 1. Music–Bibliography. 2.
Bibliography–Bibliography–Music.)

SA   *The Encyclopedia of Jazz.* Rev. and enl. New York:
Horizon Press, 1960. 527p. bibl. (ML3561.J3; 785.42 / 1. Jazz
music. 2. Musicians. 3. Jazz music–Discography.)

SA   Ewen, David. *Musicians Since 1900: Performers in Concert
and Opera.* New York: H. W. Wilson, 1978. 974p. (ML105;
780.922 / 1. Music–Bio-bibliography. 2. Opera–Bio-bibliography.)

S   Ewen, David. *New Complete Book of the American Musical
Theater.* New York: Holt, Rinehart, and Winston, 1970. 800p.
(ML1711; 782.810973 / 1. Musical revue, comedy, etc.–United
States. 2. Musical revue, comedy, etc.–Stories, plots, etc.)

S   Ewen, David. *The New Encyclopedia of the Opera.* New York:
Hill & Wang, 1971. 759p. (ML102.O6; 782.103 / 1. Opera–
Dictionaries.)

SA   Grout, Donald Jay. *A History of Western Music.* Rev. ed.
New York: W. W. Norton, 1973. 818p. bibl. (ML160; 780.9 / 1.
Music–History and criticism.)

A   Halsey, Richard Sweeney. *Classical Music Recordings for
Home and Library.* Chicago: American Library Association, 1976.
340p. (ML111.5; 016.789912 / 1. Phonorecord collection. 2.
Phonorecord libraries. 3. Music–Discography.)

A   Havlice, Patricia P. *Popular Song Index.* Metuchen, N.J.:
Scarecrow, 1975. 933p. And its *First Supplement.* Metuchen, N.J.:
Scarecrow, 1978. (ML128.S3; 016.784 / 1. Songs–Indexes.)

SA   Kinkle, Roger D. *The Complete Encyclopedia of Popular*

Music and Jazz, 1900–1950. New Rochelle, N.Y.: Arlington House, 1974. 4v. bibl. (ML102.P66; 780.420973 / 1. Music, Popular (Songs, etc.) – Dictionaries. 2. Jazz music – Dictionaries. 3. Musicians, American – Biography. 4. Jazz musicians – Biography.)

S Kobbé, Gustave. *The New Kobbé's Complete Opera Book.* Ed. and rev. by the Earl of Harewood. London; New York: G. P. Putnam's, c1976. 1694p. (MT95; 782.13 / 1. Opera – Stories, plots, etc.)

SA Marcuse, Sibyl. *Musical Instruments: A Comprehensive Dictionary.* Corrected ed. New York: W. W. Norton, 1975. 608p. bibl. (ML105.I5; 781.9103 / 1. Musical instruments – Dictionaries.)

SA Marcuse, Sibyl. *A Survey of Musical Instruments.* New York: Harper & Row, 1975. 863p. bibl. (ML460; 781.9109 / 1. Musical instruments. 2. Musical instruments – History.)

A *Music Index: The Key to Current Music Periodical Literature.* Detroit: Information Coordinators, 1950– . Monthly, with annual cumulations. (ML118; 016.78 / 1. Music – Indexes. 2. Subject headings – Music.)

A Music Library Association. Subcommittee on Basic Music Collection. *A Basic Music Library: Essential Scores and Books.* Ed. by Pauline Shaw Bayne. Chicago: American Library Association, 1978. 173p. (ML113; 016.78 / 1. Music – Bibliography.)

SA *The New Grove Dictionary of Music and Musicians.* Edited by Stanley Sadie. Washington, D.C.: Grove's Dictionaries of Music, 1980. 20v. bibl. (ML100; 780.3 / 1. Music – Dictionaries. 2. Music – Bio-bibliography.)

SA *New Oxford History of Music.* London; New York: Oxford University Press, 1954– , v.1– . bibl. (ML160; 780.9 / 1. Music – History and criticism.)

SA Randel, Don Michael, comp. *Harvard Concise Music Dictionary.* Cambridge: Harvard University Press, 1978. 577p. bibl. (ML100; 780.3 / 1. Music – Dictionaries. 2. Music – Bio-bibliography.)

SA Rosenthal, Harold, and Warrack, John. *The Concise Oxford Dictionary of Opera.* 2d ed. New York: Oxford University Press, 1979. 561p. bibl. (ML102; 782.103 / 1. Opera – Dictionaries.)

SA Roxon, Lillian. *Rock Encyclopedia.* New York: Grosset & Dunlap, 1971. 611p. bibl. (ML102.P66; 784 / 1. Music, Popular (Songs, etc.) – Dictionaries. 2. Music – Bio-bibliography.)

A Sears, Minnie Earl. *Song Index: An Index to more than 12,000 Songs in 177 Song Collections Comprising 262 Volumes.* New York: H. W. Wilson, 1926. 650p. And its *Supplement: An Index to More than 7,000 Songs in 104 Song Collections Comprising 124 Volumes.* New York: H. W. Wilson, 1934. 367p. (ML128; 016.784 / 1. Songs – Indexes.)

SA Stambler, Irwin. *Encyclopedia of Pop, Rock and Soul.* Rev.

ed. New York: St. Martin's, 1977. 609p. bibl. (ML102.P66;
784.0922 / 1. Music, Popular (Songs, etc.) – Dictionaries. 2. Music,
Popular (Songs, etc.) – Bio-bibliography. 3. Rock music – Dictionaries. 4. Rock music – Bio-bibliography. 5. Blues (Songs,
etc.) – Dictionaries. 6. Blues (Songs, etc.) –
Bio-bibliography.)

S   Stambler, Irwin, and Landon, Grelun. *Encyclopedia of*
Folk, Country and Western Music. New York: St. Martin's, 1969.
396p. (ML102.J3; 781.773 / 1. Music, Popular (Songs, etc.) –
Dictionaries. 2. Musicians, American. 3. Folk music – United
States.)

SA   Vinton, John, ed. *Dictionary of Contemporary Music.*
New York: Dutton, 1974. 834p. bibl. (ML100; 780.904 / 1.
Music – Dictionaries. 2. Music – Bio-bibliography. 3.
Music – History and criticism – 20th century.)

S   *Who's Who in Opera: An International Biographical Directory*
of Singers, Conductors, Directors, Designers, and Administrators, Also
Including Profiles of 101 Opera Companies. Maria F. Rich, ed. New
York: New York Times Co., 1976. 684p. (ML102.O6; 782.10922 / 1.
Opera – Biography – Dictionaries. 2. Opera – Directories.)

S   *The Year in Music.* New York: Columbia House, 1977- .
Annual. (ML1; 780.973 / 1. Music – United States – Yearbooks.)

SA   York, William, comp. and ed. *Who's Who in Rock Music.*
Seattle: Atomic Press, c1978. 260p. bibl. (ML102.P66; 784.0922 / 1.
Rock music – Bio-bibliography. 2. Rock music – Discography.)

Philosophy

As you can see, only a few titles have been cited for philosophy. The
list, therefore, is slightly misleading, for many more tools are
available. They are likely to be found, however, only in larger
libraries since many of them are devoted to individual philosophers or
schools of philosophy. Thus, the works listed here are among the
more general and commonly available reference works. Beyond these
titles, keep in mind that you may also have occasion to use the
reference works of other subjects such as history, psychology, or
literature.

SA   Baldwin, James Mark. *Dictionary of Philosophy and*
Psychology. . . . New York: Macmillan, 1901–1905. Reprinted,
Gloucester, Mass.: Peter Smith, 1960. 3v. in 4. bibl. (B41; 103 / 1.
Philosophy – Dictionaries. 2. Philosophy – Bibliography. 3.
Psychology – Dictionaries. 4. Psychology – Bibliography.)

A   Borchardt, Dietrich Hans. *How to Find Out in Philosophy*

and Psychology. Oxford: Pergamon, 1968. 97p. (Z7125; 016.1 / 1.
Philosophy – Bibliography. 2. Psychology – Bibliography.)

SA   Bréhier, Émile. *The History of Philosophy.* Trans. by
Joseph Thomas. Chicago: University of Chicago Press, 1963-1969.
7v. bibl. (B77; 109 / 1. Philosophy – History.)

SA   *Dictionary of the History of Ideas: Studies of Selected
Ideas.* Philip P. Wiener, ed. in chief. New York: Scribner's,
1973-1974. 5v. bibl. (CB5; 901.9 / 1. Civilization – Collected
works.)

SA   *Encyclopedia of Philosophy.* Paul Edwards, ed. in chief.
New York: Macmillan, 1967. 8v. bibl. (B41; 103 / 1.
Philosophy – Dictionaries.)

S   Lacey, Alan Robert. *A Dictionary of Philosophy.* New
York: Scribner's, 1976. 239p. (B41; 103 / 1. Philosophy –
Dictionaries.)

Religion

The reference tools in religion range from broad general works that
embrace the religious experience of humankind to more specialized
works in theology, Judaism, Buddhism, Islam, Hinduism, and Christianity. You will also find some biographical and bibliographical
sources as well as several atlases that portray the religious world at
various points in history.

Included in this list are also several works that deal with the Bible
and Bible studies. Because the Bible figures centrally in many
religious studies programs, you should be aware that the main entry
for the Bible follows rules somewhat different from those for main entry you read about in Chapter 1. Since there are many different versions (e.g., King James, Douay, Jerusalem), librarians use what is
called a uniform title for the main entry so that you can find these different versions in a single place in the catalog, under the word "Bible."
Here is an example of a uniform-title heading: "Bible. N.T. English.
1961. New English." The first element of this heading is, of course, the
word "Bible." It is followed by "N.T.," which stands for New Testament
("O.T." stands for Old Testament), and then by the language, the date,
and the version. If you have questions about such headings in your
library's catalog, make sure to consult a librarian.

A   Adams, Charles J., ed. *A Reader's Guide to the Great
Religions.* 2d ed. New York: Free Press, 1977. 521p. (BL80.2;
016.2 / 1. Religions – Bibliography.)

S   Attwater, Donald. *The Penguin Dictionary of Saints.*

Baltimore: Penguin, 1965. 362p. (BX4655.8; 235.20922 / 1.
Saints – Dictionaries.)

S   Barker, William Pierson. *Who's Who in Church History.*
Grand Rapids, Mich.: Baker Book House, 1977. 319p. (BR1700.2;
209.22 / 1. Christian biography.)

A   Bollier, John A. *The Literature of Theology: A Guide
for Students and Pastors.* Philadelphia: Westminster, 1979. 208p.
(Z7751; 016.23 / 1. Theology – Bibliography.)

SA   Douglas, James Dixon, general ed. *The New International
Dictionary of the Christian Church.* 2d ed. Exeter, Eng.: Paternoster
Press, 1978. 1074p. bibl. (BR95; 203 / 1. Christianity – Dictionaries.)

SA   *Encyclopaedia Judaica.* Jerusalem: Encyclopaedia Judaica;
New York: Macmillan, 1972. 16v. bibl. (DS102.8; 909.04924 / 1.
Jews – Dictionaries and encyclopedias. 2. Jews – Yearbooks.)

SA   *Encyclopaedia of Religion and Ethics.* Ed. by James
Hastings, with the assistance of John A. Selbie and other scholars.
New York: Scribner's, 1951. 12v. bibl. (BL31; 200.4 / 1.
Religion – Dictionaries. 2. Ethics – Dictionaries. 3. Theology –
Dictionaries.)

SA   Gaustad, Edwin Scott. *Historical Atlas of Religion in
America.* Rev. ed. New York: Harper & Row, 1976. 189p. bibl.
(G1201.E4; 912.1200973 / 1. Ecclesiastical geography – United
States – Maps. 2. United States – Church history.)

S   Harvey, Van Austin. *A Handbook of Theological Terms.* New
York: Macmillan, 1964. 253p. (BR95; 230.03 / 1. Theology – Dictionaries.)

S   Humphreys, Christmas. *A Popular Dictionary of Buddhism.*
London: Arco; New York: Citadel, 1963. 223p. (BL1403; 294.303 /
1. Buddha and Buddhism – Dictionaries.)

S   *Interpreter's Bible: The Holy Scriptures in the King James and Revised
Standard Versions with General Articles and Introduction, Exegesis, Ex-
position for Each Book of the Bible.* New York: Abingdon,
1951-1957. 12v. (BS491.2; 220.7 / 1. Bible – Commentaries.)

SA   *The Interpreter's Dictionary of the Bible: An Illustrated
Encyclopedia Identifying and Explaining All Proper Names and Signifi-
cant Terms and Subjects in the Holy Scriptures, Including the
Apocrypha, with Attention to Archaeological Discoveries and Re-
searches into the Life and Faith of Ancient Times.* New York:
Abingdon, 1962. And its *Supplementary Volume.* Nashville, Tenn.:
Abingdon, 1976. 5v. bibl. (BS440; 220.3 / 1. Bible – Dictionaries.)

SA   Julian, John. *A Dictionary of Hymnology Setting Forth the
Origin and History of Christian Hymns of All Ages and Nations.* Rev.
ed. with new supplement. London: Murray; New York: Scribner's,
1907. Reprinted, New York: Dover, 1957. 1768p. bibl. (BV305;
245.03 / 1. Hymns – Dictionaries. 2. Hymns – Indexes.)

A   Kennedy, James R. *Library Research Guide to Religion and*
     Theology: Illustrated Search Strategy and Sources. Ann Arbor, Mich.:
     Pierian Press, 1974. 53p. (BL41; 200.72 / 1. Religion – Re-
     search – Handbooks, manuals, etc. 2. Reference books – Theology.
     3. Libraries – Handbooks, manuals, etc.)
S   Kraeling, Emil Gottlieb Heinrich. *Rand McNally Bible Atlas.*
     2d ed. Chicago: Rand McNally, 1962. 487p. (BS630; 220.91 / 1.
     Bible – Geography.)
SA   Mathews, Shailer, and Smith, Gerald Birney. *Dictionary*
     of Religion and Ethics. New York: Macmillan, 1921. 513p. bibl.
     (BL31; _____ / 1. Religion – Dictionaries. 2. Ethics – Dictionaries.)
S   Meer, Frederic van der, and Mohrmann, Christine. *Atlas*
     of the Early Christian World. Tr. and ed. by Mary F. Hedlund and
     H. H. Rowley. London: Nelson, 1958. 215p. (G1046.E4; _____ / 1.
     Ecclesiastical geography – Maps. 2. Church history – Primitive and
     early church. 3. Christian antiquities.)
SA   Melton, J. Gordon. *The Encyclopedia of American Religions.*
     Wilmington, N.C.: McGrath, 1978. 2v. bibl. (BL2530.U6; 200.973 /
     1. Sects – United States – Dictionaries. 2. Cults – United States –
     Dictionaries.)
S   Miller, Madeleine Sweeny, and Miller, John Lane. *Harper's*
     Bible Dictionary. 8th ed. New York: Harper & Row, 1973. 853p.
     (BS440; 220.3 / 1. Bible – Dictionaries.)
SA   *New Catholic Encyclopedia.* Prep. by an editorial staff at
     the Catholic University of America. New York: McGraw-Hill,
     1967. 15v. bibl. (BX841; 282.03 / 1. Catholic
     Church – Dictionaries.)
SA   *The Oxford Dictionary of the Christian Church.* 2d ed.
     by F. L. Cross and E. A. Livingstone. London: Oxford University
     Press, 1974. 1518p. bibl. (BR95; 203 / 1. Theology – Dictionaries.)
A   *The Religious Life of Man: Guide to Basic Literature.*
     Comp. by Leszek M. Karpinski. Metuchen, N.J.: Scarecrow, 1978.
     399p. (Z7751; 016.2 / 1. Religion – Bibliography.)
S   Rice, Edward. *Eastern Definitions: A Short Encyclopedia*
     of Religions of the Orient. 1st ed. New York: Doubleday, 1978.
     433p. (BL31; 290.3 / 1. Religions – Dictionaries. 2.
     Asia – Religion – Dictionaries.)
SA   *Shorter Encyclopaedia of Islam.* Ed. on behalf of the Royal
     Netherlands Academy by H.A.R. Gibb and J. H. Kramers. Ithaca,
     N.Y.: Cornell University Press, 1953. 671p. bibl. (DS37; 297.03 / 1.
     Mohammedanism – Dictionaries.)
S   Stevenson, Burton Egbert. *The Home Book of Bible Quotations.*
     New York: Harper, 1949. 645p. (BS432; 220.2 / 1. Bible – Indexes,
     Topical.)
S   Strong, James. *Exhaustive Concordance of the Bible.*

London: Hodder; New York: Hunt, 1894. Reprinted, New York:
Abingdon, 1961. 1807p. (BS425; 220.2 / 1. Bible – Concordances,
English. 2. Hebrew language – Dictionaries – English. 3. Greek
language, Biblical – Dictionaries – English.)

SA   Stutley, Margaret, and Stutley, James. *Harper's Dictionary*
      of Hinduism: Its Mythology, Folklore, Philosophy, Literature, and
      History. 1st U.S. ed. New York: Harper & Row, 1977. 372p. bibl.
      (____; 294.5 / 1. Hinduism – Dictionaries.)

S   *Who's Who in Religion.* 1st- ed. Chicago: Marquis
      Who's Who, 1975/76- . (BL2530.U6; 200.922 / 1. United
      States – Religion – Biography. 2. United States – Biography.)

S   *Yearbook of American and Canadian Churches.* 41st- ,
      1973- . Nashville, Tenn.: Abingdon, 1973- . Continues *Year Book*
      of American Churches. (BR513; 277.05 / 1. Sects – United
      States – Directories. 2. Sects – Canada – Directories.)

COMMUNICATIONS

The broad area of communications, sometimes also referred to as
mass media or just media, is meant here to include journalism, radio,
and television. Speech has been included as well since it is frequently
an important part of preparation for a career in mass media. The tools
listed here under communications, however, will not be as directly
useful to the speech student as they will be to the journalism or radio
and television major. Among the titles included below are two useful
bibliographical tools as well as some source tools on trends and
statistics in the field of communications.

A   Blum, Eleanor. *Basic Books in the Mass Media: An Annotated*
      Selected Booklist Covering General Communications, Book Publishing,
      Broadcasting, Film, Magazines, Newspapers, Advertising, Indexes, and
      Scholarly and Professional Periodicals. Urbana: University of Illinois
      Press, 1972. 252p. (Z5630; 016.301161 / 1. Mass
      media – Bibliography.)

S   Diamant, Lincoln, ed. *The Broadcast Communications*
      Dictionary. Rev. and expanded ed. New York: Hastings House,
      1978. 201p. (P87.5; 384.54014 / 1. Communications – Dictionaries.)

A   Gordon, Thomas Frank, and Verna, Mary Ellen. *Mass*
      Communication Effects and Processes: A Comprehensive Bibliography,
      1950-1975. Beverly Hills, Calif.: Sage Publications, c1978. 229p.
      (Z5630; 016.301161 / 1. Mass media – Psychological
      aspects – Bibliography. 2. Mass media – Social
      aspects – Bibliography. 3. Television and children – Bibliography.)

A   La Beau, Dennis. *Theatre, Film and Television Biographies*
      Master Index. Detroit: Gale, 1979. 477p. (PN1583; 016.7910922 / 1.

Performing arts – Biography – Dictionaries – Indexes.)
SA   Sterling, Christopher H., and Haight, Timothy R. *The Mass Media: Aspen Institute Guide to Communication Industry Trends.* New York: Praeger, published with the Aspen Institute for Humanistic Studies, 1978. 457p. bibl. (P92.U5; 301.1610973 / 1. Mass media – United States.)
SA   *World Communications: A 200-Country Survey of Press, Radio, Television and Film.* 5th ed. Epping, Eng.: Gower Press; New York: Unipub, 1975. 533p. bibl. (P90; 301.161 / 1. Mass media.)
S   *Writer's Market.* Cincinnati: Writer's Digest, [1931?]– . Annual. (PN161; 051 / 1. Publishers and publishing – United States. 2. Publishers and publishing – Great Britain. 3. Authorship – Handbooks, manuals, etc.)

Journalism

The tools listed here represent a good cross section of what is available both to the journalism student and to the working journalist concerned with his or her profession. Perhaps more than other professionals, the journalist needs to acquire a thorough working knowledge of libraries early on since research skills are as essential to the field as writing ability. Hence, you should work as carefully with the general tools listed in Chapter 2 as you do with the sources of information listed here.

A   Anderson, Peter Joseph. *Research Guide in Journalism.* Morristown, N.J.: General Learning Press, 1974. 229p. (PN4775; 070.4 / 1. Journalism – Handbooks, manuals, etc.)
A   *Journalist Biographies Master Index: A Guide to More than 90,000 Sketches of and References to Historical and Modern Journalists in over 200 Biographical Directories and Other Sources.* Alan E. Abrams, ed. 1st ed. Detroit: Gale, c1979. 380p. (Z6940; 016.070922 / 1. Journalists – Biography – Indexes.)
SA   Kent, Ruth K. *The Language of Journalism: A Glossary of Print Communication Terms.* Kent, Ohio: Kent State University Press, 1971. 186p. bibl. (PN4728; 070.03 / 1. Journalism – Dictionaries. 2. Printing – Dictionaries.)
A   Nordland, Rod. *Names and Numbers: A Journalist's Guide to the Most Needed Information Sources.* New York: Wiley-Interscience, 1978. 560p. (AS22; 061.3 / 1. Associations, institutions, etc. – United States – Directories. 2. Associations, institutions, etc. – Directories.)
A   Price, Warren C. *The Literature of Journalism: An Annotated Bibliography.* Minneapolis: University of Minnesota Press, 1959. 489p. (Z6940; 016.07 / 1. Journalism – Bibliography.)

A   Price, Warren C., and Pickett, Calder M. *An Annotated*
       Journalism Bibliography, 1958–1968. Minneapolis: University of
       Minnesota Press, 1970. 285p. (Z6940; 016.07 / 1. Jour-
       nalism – Bibliography.)
SA   Weiner, Richard. *Syndicated Columnists.* 3d ed. New
       York: Weiner, c1979. 295p. bibl. (PN4888.S9; 070.4420922 / 1.
       Newspapers – Sections, columns, etc. 2. Syndicates
       (Journalism) – United States. 3. Journalists – United States –
       Directories.)
S   White, Jan V. *Editing by Design: Word-and-Picture*
       Communication for Editors and Designers. New York: R. R. Bowker,
       1974. 230p. (Z253.5; 070.572 / 1. Magazine design.)
S   *The Working Press of the Nation.* 1945– .
       Burlington, Iowa: National Research Bureau, 1945– . (Z6951;
       071.49 / 1. American newspapers – Directories. 2. Jour-
       nalists – United States – Directories. 3. Radio – United States – Direc-
       tories. 4. American newspapers – New York (City) – History.)

Radio and Television

The student majoring in either radio or television broadcasting may
experience everything from writing copy to producing graphics. And
the kinds of tools available in your library can assist you with all of it.
There are texts on methods of videotaping as well as dictionaries of
specialized terms in broadcasting. You will also find directories of FM
radio stations and of production equipment in film studios. The
general tools listed under "Communications" are also of great value to
the radio or television major.

SA   Barnouw, Erik. *A History of Broadcasting in the United*
       States. New York: Oxford University Press, 1966–1970. 3v. bibl.
       (HE8689.8; 384.540973 / 1. Broadcasting – United States – History.)
S   Brooks, Tim, and Marsh, Earle. *The Complete Directory to*
       Prime Time Network TV Shows, 1946–Present. 1st ed. New York:
       Ballantine Books, 1979. 848p. (PN1992.18; 791.45703 / 1. Televi-
       sion broadcasting – United States – Dictionaries.)
SA   Brown, Les. *The New York Times Encyclopedia of*
       Television. New York: Times Books, 1977. 492p. bibl. (PN1992.18;
       791.4503 / 1. Television broadcasting – Dictionaries.)
S   Ellmore, R. Terry. *The Illustrated Dictionary of*
       Broadcast-CATV-Telecommunications. Blue Ridge Summit, Pa.: G/L
       Tab Books, 1977. 396p. (TK6634; 384.5403 / 1. Television – Dic-
       tionaries. 2. Radio – Dictionaries. 3. Television broadcasting – Dic-
       tionaries. 4. Radio broadcasting – Dictionaries.)
S   Elving, Bruce F. *FM Atlas and Station Directory.* 5th ed.

Adolph, Minn.: FM Atlas Publishing, 1978. 112p. (HE8664;
384.5453 / 1. Radio stations – United States – Directories. 2. FM
broadcasting – Directories.)

SA   Field, Stanley. *Professional Broadcast Writer's Handbook.*
Blue Ridge Summit, Pa.: G/L Tab Books, 1974. 396p. bibl.
(PN1922.7; 808.06679144 / 1. Television authorship. 2. Radio
authorship.)

S   *Focal Encyclopedia of Film and Television Techniques.*
Raymond Spottiswoode, gen. ed. London; New York: Focal, 1969.
1100p. (TR847; 778.503 / 1. Cinematography – Dictionaries. 2.
Television – Dictionaries.)

S   Hurrel, Ron. *Van Nostrand Reinhold Manual of Television
Graphics.* New York: Van Nostrand Reinhold, 1974. 136p. (TR146;
770.28 / 1. Graphic arts (Television). 2. Photography.)

S   *International Television Almanac.* New York: Quigley,
1956– . Annual. (HE8698; 384.058 / 1. Television broadcasting – United States – Yearbooks. 2. Television broadcasting – United States – Biography.)

SA   Legge, Nancy. *Access, Film and Video Equipment: A
Directory.* Washington, D.C.: Distributed by the American Film Institute, c1978. 121p. bibl. (TR847.5; 778.5028 / 1. Moving-picture
studios – United States – Directories.)

A   McCavitt, William E., comp. *Radio and Television:
A Selected, Annotated Bibliography.* Metuchen, N.J.: Scarecrow,
1978. 229p. (Z4221; 016.38454 / 1. Broadcasting – Bibliography.)

S   *The Radio Amateur's Handbook.* 1st– ed. Newington,
Conn.: American Radio Relay League, 1926– . Annual. (TK6550;
621.3841 / 1. Radio – Amateurs' manuals. 2. Radio, Short
wave – Handbooks, manuals, etc.)

S   Steinberg, Cobett. *TV Facts.* New York: Facts on File,
1980. 350p. (PN1992.18; 384.550973 / 1. Television broadcasting – United States – Dictionaries. 2. Television industry – United States – Statistics.)

S   *Television Factbook.* 1977 ed. No. 46. Washington, D.C.:
Television Digest, 1977. (____; 338.4739455 / 1. Television – Periodicals. 2. Electronics – Periodicals.)

SA   Weiner, Peter Mark. *Making the Media Revolution: A
Handbook for Video-Tape Production.* New York: Macmillan, 1973.
217p. bibl. (TK6655.V5; 778.59 / 1. Videotape recorders and
recording.)

Speech

The student majoring in speech certainly wants the kinds of tools
that are available to students in other disciplines, such as histories,
dictionaries, and bibliographical guides. But he or she can also profit

from using such tools as *1400 Ideas for Speakers and Toastmasters* or *Vital Speeches of the Day.* As with the journalism student, the speech major has frequent occasion to research a topic, usually in preparation for a debate or other oral report. Thus, the general tools listed in Chapter 2 are at least as important as the specialized tools listed here. Time spent in becoming acquainted with both will be well spent.

SA   Auer, John Jeffery, and Ewbank, Henry Lee. *Handbook for Discussion Leaders.* Rev. ed. New York: Harper, 1954. 153p. bibl. (LC6519; 808.53 / 1. Discussion.)

A   Kruger, Arthur N. *Argumentation and Debate: A Classified Bibliography.* 2d ed. Metuchen, N.J.: Scarecrow, 1975. 520p. (Z7161.5; 016.80853 / 1. Debates and debating – Bibliography.)

S   Prochnow, Herbert Victor. *1400 Ideas for Speakers and Toastmasters: How to Speak with Confidence.* Natick, Mass.: W. A. Wilde, 1964. 158p. (PN4193.I5; 808.88 / 1. Quotations. 2. Anecdotes. 3. American wit and humor.)

SA   Speech Association of America. *A History and Criticism of American Public Address.* 1st ed. New York: McGraw-Hill, 1943-1955. 3v. bibl. (PS400; 808.5108073 / 1. American orations – History and criticism.)

A   Sutton, Roberta Briggs. *Speech Index: An Index to 259 Collections of World Famous Orations and Speeches for Various Occasions.* 4th ed. rev. and enl. New York: Scarecrow, 1966. And its *Supplement, 1966-1970.* By Roberta Briggs Sutton and Charity Mitchell. Metuchen, N.J.: Scarecrow, 1972. And its *Supplement, 1971-1975.* By Charity Mitchell. Metuchen, N.J.: Scarecrow, 1977. 3v. (AI3; 016.051 / 1. Speeches, addresses, etc. – Indexes. 2. Orations – Indexes. 3. American orations – Indexes.)

A   Tandberg, Gerilyn. *Research Guide in Speech.* Morristown, N.J.: General Learning Press, 1974. 226p. (PN4121; 808.51 / 1. Public speaking.)

S   *Vital Speeches of the Day.* v.1- , Oct. 8, 1934- . New York: City News Publishing Co., 1934- . Monthly. And its *25 Year Index, Oct. 8, 1934-Oct. 1, 1959.* Pelham, N.Y.: City News Publishing Co., 1963. (PN6121; 808.85 / 1. Speeches, addresses, etc. – Periodicals.)

SA   Woodson, Linda. *A Handbook of Modern Rhetorical Terms.* Urbana, Ill.: National Council of Teachers of English, c1979. 78p. bibl. (PN172; 808.003 / 1. Rhetoric – Dictionaries.)

FINE ARTS

The tools listed under the broad area of fine arts should be of interest to those students majoring in architecture, art, fashion design,

interior design, and photography. Included in this section you will
find listings for dictionaries, encyclopedias, handbooks, histories, and
biographical tools. Also cited is *Art Index,* the major access tool to
periodical literature in the fine arts. As with materials in the
humanities, you should not be surprised to find that your library will
have older works in the fine arts; they are frequently as valuable as
current titles.

S *American Art Directory.* v.1- , 1898- . New York:
    R. R. Bowker, 1899- . Triennial, 1952- . (N50; 705.8 / 1.
    Art – United States – Directories. 2. Art – Canada – Directories. 3.
    Art – Spanish – America – Directories.)

A *Art Index.* v.1- , Jan. 1929/Sept. 1932- . New
    York: H. W. Wilson, [1933]- . Quarterly, with annual cumulations.
    (Z5937; 016.7 / 1. Art – Periodicals – Indexes. 2. Art – Bibliography.)

A Bowker (R. R.) Company, New York. *Art Books, 1950–1979:*
    Including an International Directory of Museum Permanent Collection
    Catalogs. New York: R. R. Bowker, c1979. 1500p. (Z695.1.A7;
    025.497 / 1. Subject headings – Art – Catalogs. 2. Art
    museums – Catalogs – Directories.)

SA *The Britannica Encyclopedia of American Art.* Chicago:
    Encyclopaedia Britannica Educational Corp., [1976?]. 669p. bibl.
    (N6505; 709.73 / 1. Art, American – Dictionaries. 2. Artists – United
    States – Biography.)

A Chamberlin, Mary Walls. *Guide to Art Reference Books.*
    Chicago: American Library Association, 1959. 418p. (Z5931; 016.7 /
    1. Art – Bibliography. 2. Art libraries.)

A Ehresmann, Donald L. *Fine Arts: A Bibliographic Guide*
    to Basic Reference Works, Histories, and Handbooks. 2d ed. Littleton,
    Colo.: Libraries Unlimited, 1979. 349p. (Z5931; 016.7 / 1.
    Art – Bibliography.)

SA *Encyclopedia of World Art.* New York: McGraw-Hill,
    1959-1968. 15v. bibl. (N31; 703 / 1. Art – Dictionaries.)

SA Gardner, Helen. *Gardner's Art Through the Ages.* 6th ed.
    Rev. by Horst de la Croix and Richard G. Tansey. New York: Har-
    court Brace Jovanovich, 1975. 959p. bibl. (N5300; 709 / 1.
    Art – History.)

SA Janson, Horst Woldemar, and Janson, Dora Jane. *History*
    of Art: A Survey of the Major Visual Arts from the Dawn of History to
    the Present Day. 2d ed. New York: Abrams, 1977. 767p. bibl.
    (N5300; 709 / 1. Art – History.)

SA Mayer, Ralph. *A Dictionary of Art Terms and Techniques.*
    New York: Crowell, 1969. 447p. bibl. (N33; 703 / 1. Art –
    Dictionaries.)

SA *McGraw-Hill Dictionary of Art.* Ed. by Bernard S. Myers.

New York: McGraw-Hill, 1969. 5v. bibl. (N33; 703 / 1. Art –
Dictionaries.)

SA   Muehsam, Gerd. *Guide to Basic Information Sources in the
Visual Arts.* Santa Barbara, Calif: Jeffrey Norton/ABC-Clio, 1977.
266p. bibl. (N7425; 700.7 / 1. Art – Sources.)

SA   *The Oxford Companion to Art.* Edited by Harold Osborne.
Oxford: Clarendon Press, 1970. 1277p. bibl. (N33; 703 / 1.
Art – Dictionaries. 2. Artists – Dictionaries.)

SA   Quick, John. *Artists' and Illustrators' Encyclopedia.*
2d ed. New York: McGraw-Hill, 1977. 327p. bibl. (N33; 703 / 1.
Art – Dictionaries.)

SA   Stafford, Maureen, and Ware, Dora. *An Illustrated Dictionary
of Ornament.* New York: St. Martin's, 1975, c1974. 246p.
bibl. (NK1165; 745.403 / 1. Decoration and ornament –
Dictionaries.)

SA   Walker, John A. *Glossary of Art, Architecture and Design Since 1945:
Terms and Labels Describing Movements, Styles and Groups Derived
from the Vocabulary of Artists and Critics.* 2d rev. ed. Hamden,
Conn.: Linnet Books, 1977. 352p. bibl. (N34; 709.04 / 1. Art –
Terminology.)

S   *Who's Who in American Art.* v.1- , 1936/37- . New
York: R. R. Bowker, 1935- . Biennial (irregular). (N6536; 927 / 1.
Artists, American.)

Architecture

For the student of architecture, a variety of tools are available,
everything from handbooks of information on building and construction to works that deal specifically with drawing and building calculations. There are also dictionaries of terms, histories, and even a
biographical source tool for information on notable architects, both
past and present. Besides the general works listed under "Fine Arts,"
you may also find many useful reference works listed under the
heading "Construction Technology" later in this book.

S   American Institute of Architects. *Handbook of Architectural
Practice.* 8th ed. Washington, D.C.: American Institute of Architects, 1958. 1v. (NA2570; 720.69 / 1. Architecture – Handbooks,
manuals, etc. 2. Building – Contracts and specifications – United
States.)

S   Briggs, Martin Shaw. *Everyman's Concise Encyclopaedia of
Architecture.* London: Dent; New York: Dutton, 1959. 372p. (NA31;
720.3 / 1. Architecture – Dictionaries.)

SA   *Contemporary Architects.* Ed., Muriel Emanuel. New York:

St. Martin's, 1980. 932p. bibl. (NA40; ____ / 1. Architects – Biography.)

SA Cowan, Henry J. *Dictionary of Architectural Science.*
New York: Wiley, 1973. 354p. bibl. (NA31; 721.03 / 1. Architecture – Dictionaries. 2. Building – Dictionaries.)

S *Encyclopedia of Architectural Technology.* Ed. by Pedro
Guedes. New York: McGraw-Hill, c1979. 313p. (NA31; 720 / 1. Architecture – Dictionaries.)

SA Hamlin, Talbot Faulkner. *Architecture Through the Ages.*
Rev. ed. New York: G. P. Putnam's, 1953. 684p. (NA200; 720.9 / 1.
Architecture – History.)

SA Hamlin, Talbot Faulkner, ed. *Forms and Functions of*
Twentieth-Century Architecture. New York: Columbia University
Press, 1952. 4v. bibl. (NA680; 724.91 / 1. Architecture,
Modern – 20th century.)

S Harris, Cyril M., ed. *Dictionary of Architecture and*
Construction. New York: McGraw-Hill, 1975. 553p. (NA31; 720.3 /
1. Architecture – Dictionaries. 2. Building – Dictionaries.)

S *Historic Architecture Sourcebook.* Edited by Cyril M.
Harris. New York: McGraw-Hill, 1977. 581p. (NA31; 720.3 / 1. Architecture – Dictionaries.)

S Hunt, William Dudley. *Encyclopedia of American Architecture.*
New York: McGraw-Hill, 1980. 640p. (NA705; 720.973 / 1. Architecture – United States – Dictionaries.)

S Pevsner, Nikolaus; Fleming, John; and Honour, Hugh. *A Dictionary*
of Architecture. Rev. and enl. Woodstock, N.Y.: Overlook Press,
1976. 556p. (NA31; 720.3 / 1. Architecture – Dictionaries.)

A Phillips, Margaret. *Guide to Architectural Information.*
Lansdale, Pa.: Design Data Center, 1971. 89p. (Z7914.B9; 016.721 /
1. Building – Bibliography. 2. Architecture – Bibliography. 3.
Building – Information services.)

SA Putnam, R. E., and Carlson, G. E. *Architectural*
and Building Trades Dictionary. 3d ed. Chicago: American Technical
Society, 1974. 510p. (TH9; 721.03 / 1. Building – Dictionaries. 2.
Architecture – Dictionaries.)

S Ramsey, Charles George, and Sleeper, Harold R.
Architectural Graphic Standards. Ed. by Joseph N. Boaz. 6th ed.
New York: Wiley, 1970. 695p. (TH2031; 692.2 / 1.
Building – Details – Drawings.)

SA *Time-Saver Standards for Architectural Design Data.* John
Hancock Callender, ed. in chief. 5th ed. New York: McGraw-Hill,
1974. 1042p. bibl. (TH151; 721.0202 / 1. Building – Tables, calculations, etc. 2. Building – Handbooks, manuals, etc.)

S *Who's Who in Architecture from 1400 to the Present Day.*
Ed. by J. M. Richards. 1st ed. New York: Holt, Rinehart, and

Winston, 1977. 368p. (NA40; 720.922 / 1. Architects – Biography.)

Art

The art student will find the tools listed under "Fine Arts" almost quite as useful as those listed here. Most of the reference works cited below deal with painting or sculpture, and there are also some works that will be useful to the graphics and commercial artist. Also included here are some catalogs of art reproductions. These latter access tools are helpful if you need to locate a reproduction of a particular artwork.

S   *Artist's Market.* Cincinnati: Writer's Digest Books,
     1979- . Annual. (N8600; 380.145702573 / 1. Art – United
     States – Marketing – Directories.)
S   Bazin, Germain. *The History of World Sculpture.*
     Greenwich, Conn.: New York Graphic Society, 1968. 459p. (NB60;
     730.9 / 1. Sculpture – History.)
A   Clapp, Jane. *Art Reproductions.* New York: Scarecrow,
     1961. 350p. (N4000; 708.1 / 1. Art – Catalogs. 2.
     Photographs – Catalogs. 3. Color prints – Catalogs.)
A   Clapp, Jane. *Sculpture Index.* Metuchen, N.J.: Scarecrow,
     1970-1971. 2v. in 3. (NB36; 730.16 / 1. Sculpture – Indexes.)
S   Daniel, Howard. *Encyclopedia of Themes and Subjects in
     Painting: Mythological, Biblical, Historical, Literary, Allegorical and
     Topical.* New York: Abrams, 1971. 252p. (ND1288; 759.9403 / 1.
     Painting – Themes, motives – Dictionaries.)
S   *Dictionary of Modern Painting.* General eds. Carlton
     Lake and Robert Maillard. 3d ed. rev. and enl. New York: Tudor,
     1964. 416p. (ND30; 759.05 / 1. Painting – Dictionaries.)
S   *Dictionary of Modern Sculpture.* Gen. ed. Robert Maillard.
     New York: Tudor, 1962. 310p. (NB50; 730.3 / 1. Sculpture –
     Dictionaries.)
SA   Dreyfuss, Henry. *Symbol Sourcebook: An Authoritative
     Guide to International Graphic Symbols.* New York: McGraw-Hill,
     1972. 292p. bibl. (AZ108; 001.56 / 1. Signs and symbols.)
S   *Encyclopedia of Painting: Painters and Painting of the
     World from Prehistoric Times to the Present Day.* Bernard S. Myers,
     ed. 4th rev. ed. New York: Crown, c1979. 511p. (ND30; 750.3 / 1.
     Painting – Dictionaries. 2. Painters – Biography.)
S   Gaunt, William. *Everyman's Dictionary of Pictorial Art.*
     New York: Dutton, 1962. 2v. (N31; 703 / 1. Art – Dictionaries. 2.
     Artists – Dictionaries.)
SA   Mayer, Ralph. *The Artist's Handbook of Materials and
     Techniques.* 3d ed., rev. and expanded. New York: Viking Press,

1970. 750p. bibl. (ND1500; 751.4 / 1. Painting – Technique. 2. Artists' materials.)

SA   Modley, Rudolf. *Handbook of Pictorial Symbols: 3,250 Examples from International Sources.* New York: Dover, 1976. 143p. bibl. (AZ108; 001.56 / 1. Signs and symbols.)

A   New York Graphic Society. *Fine Art Reproductions of Old & Modern Masters: A Comprehensive Illustrated Catalog of Art Through the Ages.* Greenwich, Conn.: New York Graphic Society, 1978. 598p. (N4035; 380.145769 / 1. Art – Catalogs.)

SA   *Phaidon Dictionary of Twentieth-Century Art.* 2d ed. London; New York: Phaidon Press, 1977, c1973. 420p. bibl. (N6490; 709.04 / 1. Art, Modern – 20th century – Dictionaries. 2. Artists – Biography – Dictionaries.)

SA   Richardson, Edgar Preston. *Painting in America: The Story of 450 Years.* New York: Crowell, 1956. 447p. bibl. (ND205; 750.973 / 1. Painting – United States – History.)

S   Snyder, John. *Commercial Artist's Handbook.* New York: Watson-Guptill, 1973. 264p. (NC1000; 741.6028 / 1. Commercial art – Handbooks, manuals, etc. 2. Artists' materials – Handbooks, manuals, etc.)

A   Special Libraries Association. Picture Division. *Picture Sources: Collections of Prints and Photographs in the U.S. and Canada.* A project of Picture Division, SLA, and American Society of Picture Professionals. Ann Novotny, ed. 3d ed. New York: Special Libraries Association, 1975. 387p. (N4000; 025.21 / 1. Pictures – Catalogs.)

S   Taubes, Frederic. *The Painter's Dictionary of Materials and Methods.* New York: Watson-Guptill, 1971. 253p. (ND1505; 703 / 1. Artists' materials – Dictionaries. 2. Painting – Technique – Dictionaries.)

SA   *A Visual Dictionary of Art.* Ed. by Ann Hill and others. Greenwich, Conn.: New York Graphic Society, 1974. 640p. bibl. (N33; 703 / 1. Art – Dictionaries. 2. Artists – Biography – Dictionaries.)

SA   Wehlte, Kurt. *The Materials and Techniques of Painting.* New York: Van Nostrand Reinhold, 1975. 678p. bibl. (ND1500; 751 / 1. Artists' materials. 2. Painting – Technique.)

Fashion Design

The student of fashion design is interested not just in costume and its history, but also in textiles and the textile industry. And these are precisely the topics covered by the tools listed in this section. You will also find dictionaries of terms for the clothing and fashion industry as well as a bibliography of works on aesthetics and clothing. Since many

of the tools are of the source/access variety, you should also be able to
explore a far wider range of resources than just those listed here.

A   American Home Economics Association. Textiles and Clothing
      Section. *Aesthetics and Clothing: An Annotated Bibliography.*
      Washington, D.C.: American Home Economics Association,1972.
      159p. (Z5691; 016.391001 / 1. Clothing and dress – Bibliography. 2.
      Aesthetics – Bibliography.)
SA   American Home Economics Association. Textiles and Clothing
      Section. *Textile Handbook.* 5th ed. Washington, D.C.: American
      Home Economics Association, 1974. 121p. bibl. (TS1445; 677.00202
      / 1. Textile industry and fabrics.)
S   *The Butterick Fabric Handbook: A Consumer's Guide to
      Fabrics for Clothing and Home Furnishings.* Edited by Irene Cum-
      ming Kleeberg. New York: Butterick, 1975. 210p. (TS1765;
      677.02864 / 1. Textile fabrics. 2. Textile fabrics – Dictionaries.)
SA   Davenport, Millia. *The Book of Costume.* New York:
      Crown, 1966, c1948. 958p. bibl. (GT513; 391.09 / 1.
      Costume – History.)
S   *Encyclopedia of Textiles.* By the editors of *American
      Fabrics Magazine.* 3d ed. Englewood Cliffs, N.J.: Prentice-Hall,
      c1980. 656p. (TS1445; 677 / 1. Textile industry. 2. Textile fabrics.
      3. Textile industry – Dictionaries. 4. Textile fabrics – Dictionaries.)
S   *Fairchild's Dictionary of Textiles.* Isabel B. Wingate,
      ed. 6th ed. New York: Fairchild Publications, c1979. 691p.
      (TS1309; 677.00321 / 1. Textile industry – Dictionaries. 2. Textile
      fabrics – Dictionaries.)
SA   Gioello, Debbie Ann, and Berke, Beverly. *Fashion
      Production Terms.* New York: Fairchild Publications, c1979. 340p.
      bibl. (TT494; 687.014 / 1. Clothing trade – Terminology. 2.
      Fashion – Terminology.)
SA   Gioello, Debbie Ann, and Berke, Beverly. *Figure Types
      & Size Ranges.* New York: Fairchild Publications, c1979. 108p. bibl.
      (TT499; 687.0218 / 1. Clothing and dress measurements – Tables,
      calculation, etc. 2. Metric systems.)
SA   Hardingham, Martin. *The Fabric Catalog.* New York: Pocket
      Books, c1978. 159p. bibl. (TS1309; 677.0286403 / 1. Textile
      fabrics – Dictionaries.)
S   Klapper, Marvin. *Fabric Almanac.* 2d ed. New York:
      Fairchild Publications, 1971. 191p. (TS1451; 677.00202 / 1. Textile
      industry and fabrics – Handbooks, manuals, etc.)
SA   Lambert, Eleanor. *World of Fashion: People, Places,
      Resources.* New York: R. R. Bowker, 1976. 361p. bibl. (TT515;
      746.92 / 1. Fashion.)
SA   Linton, George E. *The Modern Textile and Apparel*

Dictionary. 4th rev. enl. ed. Plainfield, N.J.: Textile Book Service, 1973. 716p. bibl. (TS1309; 677.003 / 1. Textile industry and fabrics–Dictionaries. 2. Clothing and dress–Dictionaries.)

S   Picken, Mary (Brooks). *The Fashion Dictionary: Fabric, Sewing, and Dress as Expressed in the Language of Fashion.* Rev. and enl. New York: Funk & Wagnalls, 1973. 434p. (TT503; 391.003 / 1. Clothing and dress–Dictionaries. 2. Fashion–Dictionaries. 3. Textile industry and fabrics–Dictionaries.)

S   Schoeffler, O. E., and Gale, William. *Esquire's Encyclopedia of 20th Century Men's Fashions.* New York: McGraw-Hill, 1973. 709p. (TT617; 391.0710904 / 1. Men's clothing. 2. Costume–History–20th century.)

SA   Tolman, Ruth. *Guide to Fashion Merchandise Knowledge.* Bronx, N.Y.: Milady, 1973. 2v. bibl. (TT518; 391 / 1. Fashion. 2. Costume–History. 3. Decoration and ornament–History.)

SA   Wilcox, Ruth Turner. *The Dictionary of Costume.* New York: Scribner's, 1969. 406p. bibl. (GT507; 391.003 / 1. Costume–Dictionaries.)

SA   Wingate, Isabel B. *Textile Fabrics and Their Selection.* 7th ed. Englewood Cliffs, N.J.: Prentice-Hall, c1976. 620p. bibl. (TS1449; 677 / 1. Textile industry. 2. Textile fabrics.)

SA   Yarwood, Doreen. *The Encyclopedia of World Costume.* New York: Scribner's, c1978. 471p. bibl. (GT507; 391.003 / 1. Costume–Dictionaries.)

Interior Decoration and Design

The interior designer frequently needs information about furniture styles, and so it should be no surprise that several of the titles to be found in the library's reference collection address that very need. Besides these tools, you will also find encyclopedic source tools that deal generally with decoration and ornament as a function of interior decoration. You may also want to consult the titles on textiles in the section on "Fashion Design." Some of the tools listed under "Architecture" may also be of interest since space planning is a concern of the interior designer.

SA   Aronson, Joseph. *The Encyclopedia of Furniture.* 3d ed., completely rev. New York: Crown, 1965. 484p. bibl. (NK2205; 749.03 / 1. Furniture–Dictionaries.)

SA   Boger, Louise Ade. *The Complete Guide to Furniture Styles.* Enl. ed. New York: Scribner's, 1969. 500p. bibl. (NK2270; 749.2 / 1. Furniture–History.)

SA   *The Encyclopedia of Decorative Arts, 1890–1940.* Ed.

by Philippe Garner, New York: Van Nostrand Reinhold, 1978. 320p. bibl. (NK775; 745.0904 / 1. Art, Decorative – History – 19th century – Dictionaries. 2. Art, Decorative – History – 20th century – Dictionaries.)

S   Fleming, John, and Honour, Hugh. *Dictionary of the Decorative Arts*. New York: Harper & Row, 1977. 895p. (_____; 745.03 / 1. Decoration and ornament – Dictionaries. 2. Furniture – Dictionaries. 3. Interior decoration – Dictionaries. 4. Art industries and trade – Dictionaries. 5. Art, Decorative – Dictionaries.)

SA   Gloag, John. *A Short Dictionary of Furniture, Containing 1767 Terms Used in Britain and America*. New York: Holt, Rinehart, and Winston, 1965. 565p. bibl. (NK2205; 749.03 / 1. Furniture – Dictionaries.)

A   Lackschewitz, Gertrud. *Interior Design and Decoration: A Bibliography*. Comp. for the American Institute of Decorators. New York: New York Public Library, 1961. 86p. (Z5956.D3; 658.917 / 1. Interior decoration – Bibliography. 2. Art – Bibliography.)

S   Pegler, Martin. *The Dictionary of Interior Design*. New York: Crown, 1966. 500p. (NK1165; 747.03 / 1. Decoration and ornament – Dictionaries.)

S   *Studio Dictionary of Design and Decoration*. Ed. by Robert Harling. Rev. and enl. ed. New York: Viking Press, 1973. 538p. (NK1165; 745.403 / 1. Decoration and ornament – Dictionaries. 2. Design, Decorative – Dictionaries. 3. Architecture – Dictionaries.)

SA   Weiss, Lillian. *The Concise Dictionary of Interior Decorating*. Garden City, N.Y.: Doubleday, 1973. 188p. bibl. (NK1165; 747.03 / 1. Decoration and ornament – Dictionaries. 2. Interior decoration – Dictionaries.)

S   Wheeler, Gershon J. *Interior Painting, Wallpapering, and Paneling: A Beginner's Approach*. Reston, Va.: Reston, 1974. 171p. (TT323; 698 / 1. House painting – Amateurs' manuals. 2. Paperhanging – Amateurs' manuals. 3. Paneling – Amateurs' manuals.)

Photography

The photography student will be as concerned with equipment and processing as he or she is with style and technique. The tools listed below cover all those aspects of photographic art and more. There is even a tool listed, *Photographer's Market*, that will tell you where you can market your photographs. Several of the titles also include either bibliographies or bibliographic references so that you can access other, more extensive works. And, finally, two catalogs listed in the section on "Art" will allow you to locate photographs: Jane Clapp's *Art*

Reproductions and the Special Libraries Association Picture Division's *Picture Sources.*

SA   *Camera Work: A Pictorial Guide, with Reproductions of*
     All 559 Illustrations and Plates. From the original magazine ed. by
     Alfred Stieglitz. New York: Dover, 1978. 157p. bibl. (TR653;
     779.0922 / 1. Photography, Artistic.)
SA   *Focal Encyclopedia of Photography.* Fully rev. ed.
     London; New York: Focal Press, c1965. 2v. bibl. (TR9; 770.3 / 1.
     Photography – Dictionaries.)
SA   Gassan, Arnold. *A Handbook for Contemporary Photography.*
     4th ed. Rochester, N.Y.: Light Impressions, 1977. 257p. bibl.
     (TR330; 770.28 / 1. Photography – Printing processes.)
S   Harwood, Mary. *Running Press Glossary of Photography*
     Language. Philadelphia: Running Press, c1978. 95p. (TR9; 770.3 / 1.
     Photography – Dictionaries.)
S   Hedgecoe, John. *The Photographer's Handbook: A Complete*
     Reference Manual of Techniques, Procedures, Equipment and Style.
     New York: Knopf, c1977. 352p. (TR150; 770.202 / 1.
     Photography – Handbooks, manuals, etc.)
S   *Illustrated Dictionary of Photography.* By Duncan Backhouse
     [and others]. London: Fountain Press; New York: Morgan &
     Morgan, 1972. 213p. (TR9; 770.3 / 1. Photography – Dictionaries.)
A   Moss, Martha. *Photography Books Index: A Subject Guide*
     to Photo Anthologies. Metuchen, N.J.: Scarecrow, 1980. 286p.
     (TR199; 779.016 / 1. Photographs – Catalogs. 2.
     Photographs – Indexes.)
S   Neblette, Carroll Bernard. *Neblette's Handbook of*
     Photography and Reprography: Materials, Processes and Systems. 7th
     ed. Ed. by John M. Sturge. New York: Van Nostrand Reinhold,
     1976. 641p. (TR145; 770 / 1. Photography. 2. Copying processes.)
S   *Photographer's Market.* Cincinnati: Writer's Digest
     Books, 1978– . Annual. (TR12; 381.457702573 / 1.
     Photographs – Marketing – United States – Directories.)
S   *Photography Year.* 1975 ed. By the editors of Time-Life
     Books. New York: Time-Life Books, 1975. (TR9; 770.15 / 1.
     Photography – Yearbooks.)
S   *Photo-Lab-Index: The Cumulative Formulary of Standard*
     Recommended Photographic Procedures. Ed. 1– . New York: Morgan
     and Lester, 1939– . Loose-leaf annual with quarterly supplements.
     (TR151; 770 / 1. Photography formulae, tables, etc.)
SA   Spencer, Douglas Arthur. *The Focal Dictionary of Photographic*
     Technologies. London: Focal Press; Englewood Cliffs, N.J.: Prentice-
     Hall, 1973. 725p. bibl. (TR9; 770.3 / 1. Photography – Dictionaries.)
S   Stroebel, Leslie, and Todd, Hollis N. *Dictionary of*

Contemporary Photography. Dobbs Ferry, N.Y.: Morgan & Morgan,
1974. 217p. (TR9; 770.3 / 1. Photography–Dictionaries.)
SA   Taylor, Herb. Encyclopedia of Practical Photography.
      Edited by and published for Eastman Kodak. Garden City, N.Y.:
      Amphoto, 1977. 3v. bibl. (TR9; 770.3 / 1. Photography–
      Dictionaries.)
SA   Thomas, Woodlief, ed. SPSE Handbook of Photographic
      Science and Engineering. New York: Wiley, 1973. 1416p. bibl.
      (TR150; 770.15 / 1. Photography–Handbooks, manuals, etc.)

SOCIAL SCIENCES

The social sciences document the history and behavior of humanity
from a variety of perspectives. These perspectives are represented by
many specialized fields, everything from Afro-American studies to
psychology. The titles listed below indicate what is available in many
libraries. There are two major encyclopedias as well as two important
periodical indexes, one of which–Public Affairs Information Service–even indexes selected government publications. There are also
dictionaries, bibliographical guides, and even a biographical source
for information about significant figures in the social sciences.

As with works in the humanities, do not automatically assume that
an older work in the social sciences is outdated and worthless. Many
older titles have significant historical and research value.

S   American Men and Women of Science. Social and Behavioral
      Sciences. 12th- ed. New York: R. R. Bowker, 1971- . Irregular.
      (Q141; 509.22 / 1. Scientists–United States–Biography. 2. Scien-
      tists–United States–Directories. 3. Scientists–Canada–Biography.
      4. Scientists–Canada–Directories.)
S   Encyclopaedia of the Social Sciences. Editor in chief, Edwin R. A.
      Seligman. New York: Macmillan, c1930–1935. 15v. (H41; 303 / 1.
      Social sciences–Dictionaries.)
SA   International Encyclopedia of the Social Sciences.
      David L. Sills, ed. New York: Macmillan and the Free Press, 1968.
      And its Biographical Supplement. New York: Free Press, 1979. 18v.
      bibl. (H40.A2; 300.3 / 1. Social sciences–Dictionaries.)
A   McInnis, Raymond G., and Scott, James W. Social Science
      Research Handbook. New York: Barnes & Noble, 1975. 395p. bibl.
      (Z7161.A1; 016.3 / 1. Reference books–Social
      sciences–Bibliography. 2. Reference books–Area
      studies–Bibliography.)
S   Mitchell, Geoffrey Duncan. A New Dictionary of the Social
      Sciences. New York: Aldine Publishing Co., 1979. 244p. (HM17;

300.321 / 1. Sociology – Dictionaries. 2. Social sciences –
Dictionaries.)

A   Public Affairs Information Service. *Bulletin of the*
Public Affairs Information Service. 1st- . 1915- . White Plains, N.Y.:
H. W. Wilson, 1915- . Weekly, with five cumulations per year,
and an annual cumulation. (Z7163; 016.3 / 1. Social
sciences – Bibliography – Periodicals. 2. Political science –
Bibliography – Periodicals. 3. Legisla-
tion – Bibliography – Periodicals. 4. Economics –
Bibliography – Periodicals.)

S   Reading, Hugo F. *A Dictionary of the Social Sciences.*
London; Boston: Routledge and Kegan Paul, 1977. 231p. (H41;
300.3 / 1. Social sciences – Dictionaries.)

A   *Social Sciences Index.* v.1- , 1974/75- . New
York: H. W. Wilson, 1974- . Quarterly, with annual cumulations.
From 1965 to 1974 was called *Social Sciences and Humanities Index.*
(AI3; 016.3 / 1. Periodicals – Indexes. 2. Social
sciences – Periodicals – Indexes.)

A   White, Carl Milton. *Sources of Information in the Social*
Sciences: A Guide to the Literature. 2d ed. Chicago: American
Library Association, 1973. 702p. (Z7161; 016.3 / 1. Social
sciences – Bibliography.)

S   Zadrozny, John Thomas. *Dictionary of Social Science.*
Washington, D.C.: Public Affairs Press, 1959. 367p. (H41; 303 / 1.
Social sciences – Dictionaries.)

Afro-American Studies

The tools listed below are representative of the kinds of resources
available that document the black experience. Several of the works
are almost almanacs, containing miscellaneous cultural and statistical
information about Afro-Americans. And the majority of titles are of
the source/access variety so that you can easily learn of other
resources available to you.

When you are using the catalog to find information by subject, you
should be aware that there are two basic headings assigned by the
Library of Congress. "Afro-American" describes works that concern
black people of the United States, while "Blacks" describes works that
concern black people outside of the United States.

SA   Baskin, Wade, and Runes, Richard N. *Dictionary of Black*
Culture. New York: Philosophical Library, 1973. 493p. bibl.
(E185.96; 917.30696003 / 1. Afro-Americans – Bibliography. 2. Afro-
Americans – Dictionaries and encyclopedias.)

SA   *The Black American Reference Book.* Edited by Mabel M.
     Smythe. Englewood Cliffs, N.J.: Prentice-Hall, 1976. 1026p. bibl.
     (E185; 301.45196073 / 1. Afro-Americans.)
SA   Dunn, Lynn P. *Black Americans: A Study Guide and Sourcebook.*
     San Francisco: R and E Research Associates, 1975. 112p. bibl.
     (E185; 973.0496073 / 1. Afro-Americans – History – Outlines,
     syllabi, etc.)
S   *The Ebony Handbook.* By the editors of *Ebony.* Chicago:
     Johnson Publishing Co., 1974. 553p. (E185; 917.30696073 / 1. Afro-
     Americans – Handbooks, manuals, etc.)
S   *The Negro in American History.* Rev. ed. Chicago:
     Encyclopaedia Britannica Educational Corp., 1972. 3v. (E185;
     973.097496 / 1. Afro-Americans – History – Sources.)
A   Peavy, Charles D. *Afro-American Literature and Culture
     Since World War II: A Guide to Information Sources.* Detroit: Gale,
     1979. 302p. (Z1229.N39; 016.81080896073 / 1. American
     literature – Afro-American authors – Bibliography. 2. American
     literature – 20th century – Bibliography. 3. Afro-
     Americans – Bibliography. 4. Reference books – Afro-
     Americans – Bibliography. 5. United States – Civilization – 1945-
     – Bibliography.)
SA   Ploski, Harry A., and Marr, Warren, comps. and eds. *The
     Negro Almanac: A Reference Work on the Afro American.* Bicenten-
     nial ed. New York: Bellwether, 1976. 1206p. bibl. (E185;
     973.0496073 / 1. Afro-Americans – Dictionaries and encyclopedias.)
SA   Race Relations Information Center, Nashville. *Directory
     of Afro-American Resources.* Ed. by Walter Schatz. New York: R. R.
     Bowker, 1970. 485p. bibl. (Z1361.N39; 917.30696073 / 1. Library
     resources on Afro-American studies.)

Anthropology

The tools devoted to anthropology will assist you in your study of
the physical and cultural development of man. Listed below you will
find a bibliographic guide as well as atlases that document the
physical distribution of humanity. There are also dictionaries, encyclopedic works, and handbooks. You should be aware that many
more resources are available to you than are listed. These resources
most frequently deal with specific races and specific peoples such as
individual California Indian tribes. To access these works, you will
need to look up the specific name of the ethnic group, tribe, or people.

S   *Annual Review of Anthropology.* v.1- , 1972- . Palo
     Alto, Calif.: Annual Reviews, 1972- . Annual. (GN1; 301.205 / 1.
     Anthropology – Periodicals.)

SA   Coon, Carleton Stevens. *The Origin of Races.* New York:
      Knopf, 1962. 724p. bibl. (GN350; 573.2 / 1. Man–Origins. 2. Man,
      Prehistoric. 3. Race.)

SA   *Encyclopedia of Anthropology.* Edited by David E. Hunter
      and Phillip Whitten. New York: Harper & Row, 1976. 411p. bibl.
      (GN11; 301.203 / 1. Anthropology–Dictionaries.)

S   *The Encyclopedia of Prehistoric Life.* Edited by Rodney
      Steel and Anthony P. Harvey. New York: McGraw-Hill, 1979.
      218p. (QE711.2; 560 / 1. Paleontology.)

A   Frantz, Charles. *The Student Anthropologist's Handbook:*
      A Guide to Research, Training, and Career. Cambridge,
      Mass.: Schenkman Publishing Co., 1972. 228p. bibl. (GN42; 301.2 /
      1. Anthropology–Study and teaching. 2. An-
      thropology–Bibliography.)

SA   Honigmann, John Joseph. *Handbook of Social and Cultural*
      Anthropology. Chicago: Rand McNally, 1973. 1295p. bibl. (GN315;
      301.2 / 1. Ethnology.)

SA   *The Illustrated Encyclopedia of Mankind.* London; New York:
      M. Cavendish, 1978. 20v. bibl. (GN307; 301.203 / 1.
      Ethnology–Dictionaries. 2. Man–Dictionaries.)

SA   Murdock, George Peter. *Ethnographic Atlas.* Pittsburgh:
      University of Pittsburgh Press, 1967. 128p. bibl. (GN405;
      301.2012 / 1. Ethnology–Classification.)

SA   Naroll, Raoul, and Cohen, Ronald, eds. *A Handbook of*
      Method in Cultural Anthropology. Garden City, N.Y.: Published for
      the American Museum of Natural History by the Natural History
      Press, 1970. 1017p. bibl. (GN345; 301.2 / 1.
      Ethnology–Methodology.)

S   Spencer, Robert F., and Johnson, Elden. *Atlas for*
      Anthropology. Dubuque, Iowa: W. C. Brown, 1960. 52 leaves.
      (G1046.E1; _____ / 1. Anthropology–Maps.)

S   Winick, Charles. *Dictionary of Anthropology.* New York:
      Philosophical Library, 1956. 579p. (GN11; 572.03 / 1. An-
      thropology–Dictionaries.)

Education

Many community colleges have two-year programs for students
who are interested either in becoming an educational paraprofes-
sional or in specializing in a specific area such as early childhood
education. Many tools are available to the education major, only a few
of which are listed here. There are, for example, a large number of
specialized bibliographies to narrower subjects within education such
as immigrant children, reading disabilities, or vocational education.
There are also many more guides to two-year and four-year col-

leges – and to financial aid – than are listed here, and your library will probably have several.

One of the titles listed below deserves some special attention. It is *Resources in Education,* a monthly abstracting service of a national information network called the Educational Research Information Center, or ERIC for short. Various universities and other educational institutions across the country have been designated as ERIC clearinghouses for a specific area of education (e.g., UCLA is the clearinghouse for documents on junior college education). Each ERIC clearinghouse receives informational materials in its area and then indexes and abstracts those documents in *Resources in Education.* The documents themselves are available either in hard copy or, more often, in microform. Larger libraries sometimes own the entire ERIC collection on microfiche, and your reference librarian will be able to tell you which libraries in your area have the ERIC documents collection.

S   *American Junior Colleges.* Ed.1- . Washington, D.C.:
     American Council on Education, 1940- . Quadrennial. (L901;
     378.73 / 1. Junior colleges – Directories.)
S   *American Universities and Colleges.* 1st ed.- , 1928- .
     Washington, D.C.: American Council on Education, 1928- .
     Quadrennial. (LA226; 378.73 / 1. Universities and colleges – United
     States. 2. Education – United States – Directories.)
SA   Association for Educational Communications and Technology.
     Task Force on Definition and Terminology. *Educational Technology:
     Definition and Glossary of Terms.* Washington, D.C.: Association for
     Educational Communications and Technology, c1977- . In prog-
     ress. bibl. (LB1028.3; 371.3078 / 1. Educational technology.)
SA   Council of Chief State School Officers. *Education in the
     States.* Ed. by Jim B. Pearson and Edgar Fuller. Washington, D.C.:
     National Education Association, 1969. 2v. bibl. (LA205; 370.973 /
     1. Education – United States – History.)
S   *Digest of Educational Statistics.* 1962- . Washington,
     D.C.: Government Printing Office, 1962- . Annual. (L111; ____ / 1.
     Education – United States – Statistics.)
S   *Directory of American Scholars: A Biographical Directory.*
     1st- . New York: Jaques Cattell Press/R. R. Bowker, 1942- . Ir-
     regular. (LA2311; ____ / 1. Scholars, American – Directories.)
A   *Education Index: A Cumulative Subject Index to a Selected
     List of Educational Periodicals, Proceedings, and Yearbooks.* January
     1929/1932- . New York: H. W. Wilson, 1932- . Monthly, except
     July and August, cumulating throughout the year, with an annual
     cumulation. (Z5813; 016.3705 / 1. Education –

Bibliography – Periodicals. 2. Education – Periodicals – Indexes.)
S *Education Yearbook.* 1972/1973–1974/1975. New York:
Macmillan, 1972–1975. 3v. (L101.U6; 370.973 / 1. Education – United States – Yearbooks.)

SA *The Encyclopaedia of Educational Media Communications and Technology.* Edited by Derick Unwin and Ray McAleese. Westport, Conn.: Greenwood Press, 1978. 800p. bibl. (LB1042.5; 371.3078 / 1. Audio-visual materials – Dictionaries. 2. Educational technology – Dictionaries.)

SA *The Encyclopedia of Education.* Lee C. Deighton, editor in chief. New York: Macmillan, 1971. 10v. bibl. (LB15; 370.3 / 1. Education – Dictionaries.)

A Foskett, D. J. *How to Find Out: Educational Research.* Oxford; New York: Pergamon, 1966. 132p. bibl. (LB1028; 370.78 / 1. Educational research.)

S Good, Carter Victor, ed. *Dictionary of Education.* 3d ed. Prepared under the auspices of Phi Delta Kappa. New York: McGraw-Hill, 1973. 681p. (LB15; 370.3 / 1. Education – Dictionaries.)

SA *Handbook on Contemporary Education.* Comp. and ed. by Steven E. Goodman in association with Reference Development Corporation. New York: R. R. Bowker, 1976. 622p. bibl. (LB17; 370 / 1. Education – 1965- – Handbooks, manuals, etc. 2. Education – United States – 1965- – Handbooks, manuals, etc. 3. Education – 1965- – Addresses, essays, lectures.)

SA Hillway, Tyrus. *Handbook of Educational Research: A Guide to Methods and Materials.* Boston: Houghton, 1969. 117p. bibl. (LB1028; 370.78 / 1. Educational research – Handbooks, manuals, etc.)

SA *International Encyclopedia of Higher Education.* Editor in chief, Asa S. Knowles. San Francisco: Jossey-Bass Publishers, 1978, c1977. 10v. bibl. (LB15; 378.003 / 1. Education, Higher – Dictionaries.)

S Page, G. Terry, and Thomas, J. B. *International Dictionary of Education.* London: Kogan Page; New York: Nichols, 1977. 381p. (LB15; 370.3 / 1. Education – Dictionaries.)

A *Resources in Education.* v.10- , January 1975- . Washington, D.C.: U.S. Department of Health, Education, and Welfare, 1975- . Until 1974, called *Research in Education.* Monthly. (Z5813; 016.37078 / 1. Educational research – Bibliography. 2. Education – Bibliography.)

S *Sourcebook of Equal Educational Opportunity.* 2d- ed. Chicago: Marquis Academic Media/Marquis Who's Who, 1977- . Continues *Yearbook of Equal Educational Opportunity.* (LC213.2; 370.190973 / 1. Educational organization – United States – Yearbooks.)

S   *Standard Education Almanac.* 1968- . Los Angeles: Academic
      Media, 1968- . Biennial? (L101.U6; 370.5 / 1. Education – United
      States – Yearbooks.)
SA   Stoops, Emery; Rafferty, Max; and Johnson, Russell E.
      Handbook of Educational Administration: A Guide for the Practitioner.
      Boston: Allyn & Bacon, 1975. 899p. bibl. (LB2805; 371.2 / 1. School
      management and organization – United States.)
S   United States. Office of Education. *Education Directory.*
      v.1- . Washington, D.C.: Government Printing Office, 1912- . An-
      nual. (L111; _____ / 1. Education – United States – Directories.)
A   Woodbury, Marda. *A Guide to Sources of Educational
      Information.* Washington, D.C.: Information Resources Press, 1976.
      371p. (Z5811; 016.37 / 1. Education – Bibliography. 2. Educational
      research – Bibliography. 3. Education – Dictionaries – Bibliography.)
S   *Yearbook of Higher Education.* Chicago: Marquis Academic
      Media/Marquis Who's Who, 1969- . Annual. (LB2300; 378.73 / 1.
      Education, Higher – Yearbooks.)

Geography

As you probably remember, a number of general geographical
sources have already been listed in Chapter 2. The tools cited here are
somewhat more specialized and will be primarily useful to the student
of geography: bibliographical guides, dictionaries of terms in both
geography and cartography, specialized handbooks of place-names,
and even a biographical dictionary of cartographers. If you are particularly interested in physical geography, you may also find some
useful resources listed later in this chapter under "Earth Sciences."

A   Brewer, J. Gordon. *The Literature of Geography: A Guide
      to Its Organization and Use.* 2d ed. Hamden, Conn.: Linnet Books,
      1978. 264p. (Z6001; 016.91 / 1. Geography – Bibliography. 2.
      Geography – Methodology.)
SA   *A Dictionary of Basic Geography.* By Allen A. Schmieder
      [and others]. Boston: Allyn & Bacon, 1970. 299p. bibl. (G108.A2;
      910.003 / 1. Geography – Terminology.)
SA   Durrenberger, Robert W. *Geographical Research and
      Writing.* New York: Crowell, 1971. 246p. bibl. (G73; 808.06691 / 1.
      Geographical writing. 2. Technical writing.)
S   Gannett, Henry. *Dictionary of Altitudes in the United
      States.* 4th ed. Washington, D.C.: Government Printing Office,
      1906. 1072p. (QE75; 917.302 / 1. United States – Altitudes.)
A   Harris, Chauncy D. *Bibliography of Geography: Part I,
      Introduction to General Aids.* Chicago: Department of Geography,
      University of Chicago, 1976. 276p. (H31; 910 / 1. Geography –

Bibliography. 2. Bibliography – Bibliography – Geography.)
S   *The International Geographic Encyclopedia and Atlas.*
       Boston: Houghton Mifflin, 1979. 1005p. (G105; 910.3 / 1.
       Geography – Dictionaries.)
S   Kane, Joseph Nathan. *The American Counties.* 3d ed.
       Metuchen, N.J.: Scarecrow, 1972. 608p. (E180; 917.303 / 1. United
       States – History, Local.)
S   Monkhouse, Francis John, and Small, John. *A Dictionary
       of the Natural Environment.* New York: Wiley, c1978. 320p. (GB10;
       910.0203 / 1. Physical geography – Dictionaries.)
SA   Room, Adrian. *Place-name Changes Since 1900: A World
       Gazetteer.* Metuchen, N.J.: Scarecrow, 1979. 202p. bibl. (G103.5;
       910.3 / 1. Gazetteers.)
A   Sealock, Richard Burl, and Seely, Pauline Augusta.
       Bibliography of Place-name Literature: United States and Canada. 2d
       ed. Chicago: American Library Association, 1967. 352p. (Z6824;
       016.9294 / 1. Names, Geographical – North America – Bibliography.
       2. Names, Geographical – Indexes.)
SA   Stewart, George Rippey. *American Place Names: A Concise
       and Selective Dictionary for the Continental United States of America.*
       New York: Oxford University Press, 1970. 550p. bibl. (E155;
       917.3003 / 1. Names, Geographical – United States.)
SA   Thompson, Morris Mordecai. *Maps for America: Cartographic
       Products of the U.S. Geological Survey and Others.* Washington, D.C.:
       Government Printing Office, 1979. 265p. bibl. (GA405; 526.0973 /
       1. Cartography – United States. 2. United States. Geological
       Survey.)
SA   Tooley, Ronald Vere. *Tooley's Dictionary of Mapmakers.*
       New York: A. R. Liss, c1979. 684p. bibl. (GA198; 526.0922 / 1.
       Cartographers – Biography.)
S   United States. Army Topographic Command. *Glossary of
       Mapping, Charting, and Geodetic Terms.* 2d ed. Washington, D.C.:
       Government Printing Office, 1969. 281p. (GA102; 526.803 / 1. Car-
       tography – Dictionaries. 2. Geodesy – Dictionaries.)
SA   Van Zandt, Franklin K. *Boundaries of the United States
       and the Several States, with Miscellaneous Geographic Information
       Concerning Areas, Altitudes, and Geographic Centers.* Washington,
       D.C.: Government Printing Office, 1976. 191p. bibl. (E179.5;
       911.73 / 1. United States – Boundaries.)

History

History is a broad field with many tools available to the student.
Only a relative handful are listed here, but they cover both world
history and U.S. history. There are several bibliographical guides and

guides to writing as well as major multivolume reference histories such as the *Cambridge Ancient History*. Also, you will find several useful chronologies and handbooks, and even some historical atlases. Since there are several access- and source/access-type reference works, you should also have little difficulty in expanding your searches for other informational tools.

S   American Heritage. *The American Heritage Pictorial Atlas of United States History.* By the editors of *American Heritage*. New York: American Heritage, 1966. 424p. (G1201.S1; 796.54074 / 1. United States – Historical geography – Maps.)

A   American Historical Association. *Guide to Historical Literature.* George Frederick Howe, chairman, Board of Editors. New York: Macmillan, 1961. 962p. (Z6201; 016.9 / 1. History – Bibliography. 2. Bibliography – Best books – History.)

S   Barraclough, Geoffrey, ed. *The Times Atlas of World History.* Maplewood, N.J.: Hammond, 1978. 360p. (G1030; 911 / 1. Geography, Historical – Maps.)

SA   Barzun, Jacques, and Graff, Henry F. *The Modern Researcher.* 3d ed. New York: Harcourt, Brace, Jovanovich, 1977. 378p. bibl. (D13; 808.023 / 1. Historiography. 2. Report writing.)

SA   Bickerman, Elias Joseph. *Chronology of the Ancient World.* London: Thames & Hudson; Ithaca, N.Y.: Cornell University Press, 1968. 253p. bibl. (D54.5; 529.32 / 1. History, Ancient – Chronology.)

SA   Boatner, Mark Mayo. *The Civil War Dictionary.* New York: McKay, 1959. 974p. bibl. (E468; 973.703 / 1. United States – History – Civil War – Dictionaries.)

SA   Boatner, Mark Mayo. *Encyclopedia of the American Revolution.* Bicentennial ed. New York: McKay, 1974. 1290p. bibl. (E208; 973.303 / 1. United States – History – Revolution, 1775–1783 – Dictionaries.)

SA   *Cambridge Ancient History.* Cambridge: University Press; New York: Macmillan, 1923–1939. 12v. and 5v. plates. bibl. 3d ed. in progress, 1970- . (D57; 913 / 1. History – Ancient.)

SA   *Cambridge Mediaeval History.* Planned by J. B. Bury. Cambridge: University Press; New York: Macmillan, 1922–1936. 8v. bibl. 2d ed. in progress, 1966- . (D117; 909.07 / 1. Middle ages – History.)

S   Carruth, Gorton, and associates. *The Encyclopedia of American Facts and Dates.* 6th ed. with a supplement of the 70s. New York: Crowell, 1972. 922p. (E174.5; 973.02 / 1. United States – History – Chronology.)

S   Clements, John. *Chronology of the United States.* New York: McGraw-Hill, 1975. 247p. (E174.5; 973 / 1. United States – History – Chronology.)

S   Commager, Henry Steele, ed. *Documents of American History.*
     9th ed. New York: Appleton, 1973. 2v. (E173; 973.08 / 1. United
     States–History–Sources.)

SA   *Dictionary of American History.* Rev. ed. New York:
     Scribner's, 1976-1978. 8v. bibl. (E174; 973.03 / 1. United
     States–History–Dictionaries.)

S   *Everyman's Dictionary of Dates.* 6th ed. rev. by Audrey
     Butler. London: Dent; New York: Dutton, 1971. 518p. (D9; 903 / 1.
     History–Dictionaries.)

A   Freidel, Frank, ed. *Harvard Guide to American History.*
     Rev. ed. . . . with the assistance of Richard K. Showman. Cam-
     bridge, Mass.: Harvard University Press, Belknap Press, 1974. 2v.
     (Z1236; 016.917303 / 1. United States–History–Bibliography.)

S   *Harper Encyclopedia of the Modern World: A Concise
     Reference History from 1760 to the Present.* Ed. by Richard B. Morris
     and Graham W. Irwin. New York: Harper, 1970. 1271p. (D205;
     903 / 1. History, Modern–Dictionaries.)

S   Hochman, Stanley. *Yesterday and Today: A Dictionary
     of Recent American History.* New York: McGraw-Hill, 1979. 407p.
     (E838.6; 973.9 / 1. United States–History–1945- –Dictionaries.)

A   Irwin, Leonard Bertram. *A Guide to Historical Reading:
     Non-Fiction; For the Use of Schools, Libraries and the General Reader.*
     9th rev. ed. Brooklawn, N.J.: McKinley Publishing Co., 1970. 276p.
     (Z6201; 016.9 / 1. History–Bibliography.)

SA   Johnson, Thomas Herbert. *The Oxford Companion to American
     History.* New York: Oxford University Press, 1966. 906p. bibl.
     (E174; 973.03 / 1. United States–History–Dictionaries.)

A   Krikler, Bernard, and Laqueur, Walter, eds. *A Reader's
     Guide to Contemporary History.* 1st U.S. ed. Chicago: Quadrangle
     Books, c1972. 259p. (Z6204; 909.82 / 1. History, Modern–1945-
     –Bibliography.)

S   Langer, William Leonard. *An Encyclopedia of World History,
     Ancient, Medieval, and Modern, Chronologically Arranged.* 5th ed.
     rev. and enl. Boston: Houghton Mifflin, 1972. 1569p. (D21;
     902.02 / 1. History–Outlines, syllabi, etc.)

S   Morison, Samuel Eliot. *The Oxford History of the American
     People.* New York: Oxford University Press, c1965. 1150p. (E178;
     973 / 1. United States–History.)

S   Morris, Richard Brandon, ed. *Encyclopedia of American
     History.* Bicentennial ed. New York: Harper & Row, 1976. 1245p.
     (E174.5; 973.03 / 1. United States–History–Chronology. 2. United
     States–History–Dictionaries.)

SA   *The New Cambridge Modern History.* Cambridge: University
     Press, 1957-1979. 14v. bibl. (D208; 940.2 / 1. History, Modern.)

SA   *The Oxford Classical Dictionary.* Edited by N.G.L. Hammond
     and H. H. Scullard. 2d ed. Oxford: Clarendon Press, 1970. 1176p.
     bibl. (DE5; 913.38003 / 1. Classical dictionaries.)

S   Paullin, Charles Oscar. *Atlas of the Historical Geography
       of the United States*. Ed. by John K. Wright. Washington, N.Y.:
       Published jointly by Carnegie Institute of Washington and the
       American Geographical Society, 1932. 162p. (G1201.S1; 911.73 / 1.
       United States – Historical geography – Maps. 2. United
       States – Historical geography. 3. United States – Description and
       travel. 4. Cartography – America. 5. Maps, Early – Facsimiles.

A   Poulton, Helen J. *The Historian's Handbook: A Descriptive
       Guide to Reference Works*. Norman: University of Oklahoma Press,
       1972. 304p. (Z6201; 016.9 / 1. History – Bibliography. 2.
       Bibliography – Bibliography – History.)

S   Previté-Orton, Charles William. *The Shorter Cambridge
       Medieval History*. Cambridge: University Press, 1952. 2v. (D117;
       940.1 / 1. Middle Ages – History.)

SA   Rand McNally and Company. *Atlas of World History*. Ed.
       by R. R. Palmer. Chicago: Rand McNally, 1965. 216p. bibl.
       (G1030; 911 / 1. Geography, Historical – Maps.)

SA   Sanderlin, David. *Writing the History Paper: How to
       Select, Collect, Interpret, Organize, and Write Your Term Paper*.
       Woodbury, N.Y.: Barron's, 1975. 126p. bibl. (D16; 907.2 / 1.
       Historical research.)

SA   Shafer, Robert Jones, ed. *A Guide to Historical Method*.
       Rev. ed. Homewood, Ill.: Dorsey, 1974. 255p. bibl. (D16; 907.2 / 1.
       History – Methodology.)

S   *Webster's Guide to American History: A Chronological,
       Geographical, and Biographical Survey and Compendium*. Springfield,
       Mass.: Merriam, 1971. 1428p. (E174.5; 973 / 1. United
       States – History – Chronology. 2. United States – Biography. 3.
       United States – Historical geography – Maps.)

Political Science

The tools of political science are many and varied. Besides the
kinds of resources you would expect in any subject – dictionaries of
specialized terms, bibliographical guides, and biographical sources –
there are also some important statistical handbooks for information on elections and directories to government officials and
agencies at the federal, state, and municipal levels. Besides the titles
listed here, the political science student is also likely to make extensive use of government publications, so a review of that section in
Chapter 2 is advisable.

S   *America Votes: A Handbook of Contemporary American Election
       Statistics*. New York: Macmillan, 1956- . Biennial. (JK1967;
       324.73 / 1. Elections – United States – Statistics.)

S Barone, Michael; Ujifusa, Grant; and Matthews, Douglas.
The Almanac of American Politics: The Senators, the Represen-
tatives — Their Records, States and Districts. 2d ed. Boston: Gambit,
1973. 1240p. (JK271; 328.73 / 1. United
States — Congress — Registers. 2. United States. Congress.
House — Election districts — Handbooks, manuals, etc. 3. United
States — Politics and government — 1945-1965.)

S *Book of the States.* v.1- , 1935- . Chicago: Council
of State Governments, 1935- . Biennial. (JK2043; 353.9 / 1. State
governments — Yearbooks.)

A Brock, Clifton. *The Literature of Political Science: A*
Guide for Students, Librarians, and Teachers. New York: R. R.
Bowker, 1969. 232p. (Z7161; 016.32 / 1. Political
science — Bibliography.)

S Commager, Henry Steele, ed. *Documents of American History.*
9th ed. Englewood Cliffs, N.J.: Prentice-Hall, 1973. 2v. (E173;
973.08 / 1. United States — History — Sources.)

S *Congressional Quarterly Almanac: A Service for Editors*
and Commentators. v.1- , Jan./Mar. 1945- . Washington, D.C.: Congressional Quarterly News Features, 1945- . Annual. (JK1; 328.73 /
1. United States — Politics and government — Periodicals.)

S Congressional Quarterly, Inc. *Congress and the Nation:*
A Review of Government and Politics in the Postwar Years.
Washington, D.C.: Congressional Quarterly Service, 1965- , v.1- .
Quadrennial. (KF49; 320.973092 / 1. Legislation — United States. 2.
United States — Politics and government — 1945-1965.

SA Congressional Quarterly, Inc. *Congressional Quarterly's*
Guide to Congress. 2d ed. Washington, D.C.: Congressional Quar-
terly, 1976. 1v. in various pagings. bibl. (JK1021; 328.73 / 1.
United States. Congress.)

SA Congressional Quarterly, Inc. *Politics in America.* Washington,
D.C.: Congressional Quarterly, 1979. 314p. bibl. (E743;
329.00973 / 1. Elections — United States. 2. United States — Politics
and government — 1945-1965. 3. United States — Foreign
relations — 1945- .)

S *Congressional Staff Directory.* Indianapolis: Bobbs-
Merrill, 1959- . Annual. (JK1012; 328.738 / 1. United States. Congress — Directories. 2. United States. Congress — Biography.)

A Council of State Governments. *State Bluebooks and*
Reference Publications (A Selected Bibliography). Lexington, Ky.:
Council, 1972. Unpaged. (____; 028.7 / 1. Reference books — State
governments.)

SA *Countries of the World and Their Leaders.* 3d ed. Detroit:
Gale, 1977. 1141p. bibl. (G122; 909.827 / 1. Geography. 2.
Statesmen.)

S *CQ Weekly Report.* Washington, D.C.: Congressional Quarterly,
1947- . Weekly. (JK1; ____ / 1. United States — Politics and govern-

ment – Periodicals.)

S   *The Europa Year Book: A World Survey.* London: Europa
     Publications, 1959- . Annual. (JN1; 341.184 / 1.
     Europe – Politics – Yearbooks. 2. European federation – Yearbooks.)

A   Holler, Frederick L. *The Information Sources of Political
     Science.* 2d ed. Santa Barbara, Calif.: ABC-Clio, 1975. 5v. (Z7161;
     016.32 / 1. Political science – Bibliography.)

S   *International Yearbook and Statesmen's Who's Who.* London:
     Burke's Peerage, 1953- . Annual. (JA51; 305.8 / 1. Political
     science – Yearbooks. 2. Statesmen – Biography. 3. Biography.)

A   Kalvelage, Carl; Segal, Morley; and Anderson, Peter J.
     Research Guide for Undergraduates in Political Science. Morristown,
     N.J.: General Learning Press, 1972. 140p. (JA86; 320.072 / 1.
     Political science research. 2. Political science – Bibliography.)

S   Kane, Joseph Nathan. *Facts About the Presidents: A
     Compilation of Biographical and Historical Data.* 2d ed. New York:
     H. W. Wilson, 1968. 384p. (E176.1; 973 / 1. Presidents – United
     States.)

SA   Kurian, George Thomas. *Encyclopedia of the Third World.*
     New York: Facts on File, c1978. 2v. bibl. (HC59.7; 909.09724 / 1.
     Underdeveloped areas – Dictionaries.)

S   Morris, Dan, and Morris, Inez. *Who Was Who in American
     Politics: A Biographical Dictionary of over 4,000 Men and Women
     Who Contributed to the United States Political Scene from Colonial
     Days up to and Including the Immediate Past.* New York: Hawthorn
     Books, 1974. 637p. (E176; 329.00922 / 1. Statesmen – United
     States – Biography – Dictionaries.)

S   *Municipal Year Book: The Authoritative Résumé of Activities
     and Statistical Data of American Cities.* Chicago: International City
     Management Association, 1934- . Annual. (JS342.A2; ____ / 1.
     Municipal government – United States – Yearbooks. 2. Municipal
     government by city manager – Yearbooks.)

S   Plano, Jack C. [and others] *Political Science Dictionary.*
     Hinsdale, Ill.: Dryden Press, 1973. 418p. (JA61; 320.03 / 1. Political
     science – Dictionaries.)

S   Plano, Jack C., and Greenberg, Milton. *The American
     Political Dictionary.* 5th ed. New York: Holt, Rinehart, and
     Winston, c1979. 488p. (JK9; 320.973 / 1. United States – Politics
     and government – Dictionaries.)

S   *Political Handbook and Atlas of the World: Parliaments,
     Parties and Press.* New York: Harper & Row for Council on Foreign
     Relations, 1927- . Annual. (JF37; 320.0202 / 1. Political
     science – Handbooks, manuals, etc. 2. Newspapers – Directories. 3.
     Political parties.)

SA   Raymond, Walter J. *Dictionary of Politics: Selected
     American and Foreign Political and Legal Terms.* 6th ed., rev.
     Lawrenceville, Va.: Brunswick Publishing, 1978. 956p. bibl. (JA61;

320.03 / 1. Political science – Dictionaries.)

SA   Safire, William L. *Safire's Political Dictionary*. 3d ed.
New York: Random House, c1978. 845p. bibl. (JK9; 320.03 / 1.
United States – Politics and government – Dictionaries.)

SA   Sperber, Hans, and Trittschuh, Travis. *American Political
Terms: An Historical Dictionary*. Detroit: Wayne State University
Press, 1962. 516p. bibl. (JK9; 320.3 / 1. United States – Politics and
government – Dictionaries.)

SA   Taylor, Charles Lewis, and Hudson, Michael C. *World
Handbook of Political and Social Indicators*. 2d ed. New Haven,
Conn.: Yale University Press, 1972. 443p. bibl. (HN15; 301.018 / 1.
Social history – 20th century.)

S   United States. Bureau of the Census. *Congressional
District Data Book*. Washington, D.C.: Government Printing Office,
1961- . Irregular. 3d ed., 1973/74. (HA205; ____ / 1. United States.
Congress. House – Election districts – Statistics. 2. United
States – Statistics.)

S   United States. Central Intelligence Agency. *National
Basic Intelligence Factbook*. Washington, D.C.: Government Printing
Office, 1978. 228p. Semiannual. (G122; 910.5 / 1.
Geography – Periodicals.)

S   United States. Congress. *Official Congressional Directory*.
Washington, D.C.: Government Printing Office, 1809- . Irregular.
(JK1011; 328.73 / 1. United States. Congress – Registers. 2. United
States. Congress – Biography.)

S   *United States Government Manual*. 1935- . Washington,
D.C.: Government Printing Office, 1935- . Annual. (JK421; 353 / 1.
United States – Executive departments – Handbooks, manuals, etc.
2. United States – Politics and government – Handbooks, manuals,
etc.)

A   *Washington Information Directory*. Washington, D.C.:
Congressional Quarterly, 1975/76- . Annual. (F192.3; 975.30025 /
1. Washington metropolitan area – Directories. 2. Washington,
D.C. – Directories. 3. United States – Executive departments –
Directories.)

S   *Who's Who in American Politics: A Biographical Directory
of United States Political Leaders*. New York: R. R. Bowker, 1967- .
Biennial. (E176; 320.0922 / 1. United States – Biography.)

SA   *Worldmark Encyclopedia of the Nations*. 5th ed. New York:
Worldmark Press, 1976. 5v. bibl. (G63; 910.3 / 1. United Nations.
2. Geography – Dictionaries. 3. History – Dictionaries. 4.
Economics – Dictionaries. 5. Political science – Dictionaries.)

Psychology

The titles listed below are representative of the resources available to the psychology student. There are dictionaries of specialized terms, a biographical directory of living psychologists, some useful bibliographical access tools, and a number of handbooks and encyclopedic sources. As you scan the list of tools for psychology, you will notice that many of the titles deal not just with psychology, but also with the related fields of psychiatry, psychoanalysis, and mental health generally. Further, some of the handbooks cited concern various aspects of psychology such as personality theory. Similar related titles will be listed in the access and source/access tools cited below.

SA   Alexander, Franz Gabriel, and Selesnick, Sheldon T. *The History of Psychiatry: An Evaluation of Psychiatric Thought and Practice from Prehistoric Times to the Present.* New York: Harper, 1966. 471p. bibl. (RC438; 616.89009 / 1. Psychiatry – History.)

SA   *American Handbook of Psychiatry.* 2d ed. Silvano Arieti, editor in chief. New York: Basic Books, 1974-1975. 6v. bibl. (RC435; 616.89008 / 1. Psychiatry – Collected works.)

S   *Annual Review of Psychology.* Palo Alto, Calif.: Annual Reviews, 1950- , v.1- . Annual. (BF30; 150.58 / 1. Psychology – Yearbooks.)

A   Bell, James Edward. *A Guide to Library Research in Psychology.* Dubuque, Iowa: W. C. Brown, 1971. 211p. (BF76.8; 016.15 / 1. Psychological literature. 2. Psychology – Bibliography.)

SA   Borgatta, Edgar F., and Lambert, William W. *Handbook of Personality Theory and Research.* Chicago: Rand McNally, 1968. 1232p. bibl. (BF698; 155.2 / 1. Personality – Addresses, essays, lectures.)

SA   Brussel, James Arnold, and Cantzlaar, George La Fond. *The Layman's Dictionary of Psychiatry.* New York: Barnes & Noble, 1967. 269p. bibl. (RC437; 616.89003 / 1. Psychiatry – Dictionaries.)

A   Communications/Research/Machines, Inc. *Psychosources: A Psychology Resource Catalog.* By the editors of CRM, Inc. New York: Bantam Books, 1973. 215p. (BF131; 150.8 / 1. Psychology – Bibliography. 2. Social sciences – Bibliography.)

S   *Directory of the American Psychological Association.* Washington, D.C.: Association, 1978- . Continues American Psychological Association. *Biographical Directory.* Irregular. (BF11; 150.6273 / 1. Psychologists – United States – Directories – Periodicals.)

S   Drever, James. *A Dictionary of Psychology.* Rev. by Harvey Wallerstein. Baltimore: Penguin, 1964. 320p. (BF31; 150.3 / 1. Psychology – Dictionaries.)

SA   *Encyclopedia of Psychology.* Editors: H. J. Eysenck, W. Arnold, and R. Meili. New York: Herder and Herder, 1972. 3v. bibl. (BF31; 150.3 / 1. Psychology – Dictionaries.)

S   English, Horace Bidwell, and English, Ava C. *A Comprehensive Dictionary of Psychological and Psychoanalytical Terms: A Guide to Usage.* New York: Longmans, 1958. 594p. (BF31; 150.3 / 1. Psychology – Dictionaries. 2. Psychoanalysis – Dictionaries.)

SA   Eysenck, Hans Jürgen, ed. *Handbook of Abnormal Psychology.* 2d ed. San Diego: R. R. Knapp, 1973. 906p. bibl. (RC454.4; 157 / 1. Psychology, Pathological. 2. Psychology, Experimental.)

SA   Goldenson, Robert M. *The Encyclopedia of Human Behavior: Psychology, Psychiatry, and Mental Health.* Garden City, N.Y.: Doubleday, 1970. 2v. bibl. (BF31; 150.3 / 1. Psychology – Dictionaries. 2. Psychiatry – Dictionaries.)

S   Harriman, Philip Lawrence. *Handbook of Psychological Terms.* Totowa, N.J.: Littlefield, Adams, 1965. 222p. (BF31; 150.3 / 1. Psychology – Dictionaries.)

SA   *International Encyclopedia of Psychiatry, Psychology, Psychoanalysis & Neurology.* Ed. by Benjamin B. Wolman. New York: Published for Aesculapius by Van Nostrand Reinhold, 1977. 12v. bibl. (RC334; 616.89003 / 1. Psychiatry – Dictionaries. 2. Psychology – Dictionaries. 3. Psychoanalysis – Dictionaries. 4. Neurology – Dictionaries.)

S   Klein, Barry T., ed. *Reference Encyclopedia of American Psychology and Psychiatry.* Rye, N.Y.: Todd Publications, 1975. 459p. (RC437; 616.89002573 / 1. Psychiatry – Information Services. 2. Psychiatry – Directories. 3. Psychology – Information services. 4. Psychology – Directories.)

SA   *The Mental Health Almanac.* Robert D. Allen, ed. New York: Garland, 1978. 403p. bibl. (RA790.6; 362.20973 / 1. Mental health services – United States. 2. Mental health services – Vocational guidance. 3. Mental health services – Information services.)

SA   *The Mental Health Yearbook/Directory.* New York: Van Nostrand Reinhold, 1979/80- . Annual. bibl. (RA790.6; 362.202573 / 1. Mental health facilities – United States – Directories. 2. Mental retardation services – United States – Directories. 3. Mental health – United States – Directories.)

S   Milt, Harry. *Basic Handbook on Mental Illness.* New York: Scribner's, 1974. 125p. (RC454; 616.89 / 1. Mental illness.)

SA   Watson, Robert Irving. *The Great Psychologists, from Aristotle to Freud.* 2d ed. Philadelphia: Lippincott, 1968. 613p. bibl. (BF81; 150.922 / 1. Psychology – History.)

S   Wolman, Benjamin, B., comp. and ed. *Dictionary of Behavioral Science.* New York: Van Nostrand Reinhold, 1973. 478p. (BF31; 150.3 / 1. Psychology – Dictionaries.)

SA   Wolman, Benjamin B. *Handbook of Clinical Psychology.* New York: McGraw-Hill, 1965. 1596p. bibl. (RC467; 157.9 / 1. Clinical psychology.)

SA   Wolman, Benjamin B. *Handbook of General Psychology.*

Englewood Cliffs, N.J.: Prentice-Hall, 1973. 1006p. bibl. (BF121; 150 / 1. Psychology.)

Sociology

As you can see, only a few titles have been listed under sociology, although those listed represent the types of reference tools you would expect to find: dictionaries, encyclopedias, handbooks, and bibliographic guides. The reason so few tools are cited here is twofold. First, the sociology student tends to rely heavily on the more general reference works listed under "Social Sciences." And, second, many more specialized tools are available, but they are devoted to a wide range of individual topics such as prostitution, marriage and family life, or homosexuality. Some of these works will, of course, be noted in the access and source/access tools cited below. You will find others by looking directly under the appropriate headings in your library's catalog.

SA   *Annual Review of Sociology.* Alex Inkeles, ed. Palo
     Alto, Calif.: Annual Reviews, 1975- . Annual. bibl. (HM51; 301 / 1.
     Sociology.)
SA   *Encyclopedia of Sociology.* Guilford, Conn.: Dushkin, 1974.
     330p. bibl. (HM17; 301.03 / 1. Sociology–Dictionaries.)
A   Mark, Charles. *Sociology of America: A Guide to*
     Information Sources. Detroit: Gale, 1976. 454p. (Z7164.S66;
     016.309173092 / 1. Sociology–United
     States–History–Bibliography. 2. United States–Social condi-
     tions–1960- –Bibliography.)
SA   Sanders, William B., ed. *The Sociologist as Detective:*
     An Introduction to Research Methods. New York: Praeger, 1974.
     263p. bibl. (HM48; 301.072 / 1. Sociological research–Addresses,
     essays, lectures. 2. Social science research–Addresses, essays, lec-
     tures. 3. Criminal investigation–Addresses, essays, lectures.)
S   Theodorson, George A., and Theodorson, Achilles G.
     A Modern Dictionary of Sociology. New York: Crowell, 1969. 469p.
     (HM17; 301.03 / 1. Sociology–Dictionaries.)

Statistics

The tools listed in this section fall roughly into two different categories. The first is composed either of access tools that will lead you to sources of statistics or to source tools filled with statistics themselves. Some of the source tools in this latter grouping are com- posed almost entirely of population statistics. Since the primary source of most statistics are governments, or international governmental bodies such as the United Nations, it should not be surprising that many of the works in this first category will have corporate authors. The second category of reference work is composed of those titles that treat statistics as a science. Here, you will find such resources as handbooks of tables for probability and statistics and an encyclopedia. As with the other social sciences, you will find some access and source/access tools to lead you to other information sources. And, too, you will find some statistical compilations listed elsewhere in this book under specific subjects such as business.

S   Beyer, William., ed. *CRC Handbook of Tables for*
        Probability and Statistics. 2d ed. Cleveland: Chemical Rubber Co.,
        1968. 642p. (QA276.25; 519.0212 / 1. Mathematical
        statistics – Tables, etc. 2. Probabilities – Tables, etc.)
SA   Burington, Richard Stevens, and May, Donald Curtis.
        Handbook of Probability and Statistics. 2d ed. New York: McGraw-
        Hill, 1970. 462p. bibl. (QA273; 519.0202 / 1. Probabilities – Hand-
        books, manuals, etc. 2. Statistics – Handbooks, manuals, etc.)
S   *Demographic Yearbook/Annuaire démographique.* New York:
        United Nations, 1949- . Annual. (HA17; 312.058 / 1. Popula-
        tion – Yearbooks.)
S   Ernst, Morris Leopold. *The Comparative International*
        Almanac. Judith A. Posner, ed. New York: Macmillan, 1967. 239p.
        (HA42; 910.03 / 1. Statistics.)
SA   Freund, John E., and Williams, Frank J. *Dictionary/Outline*
        of Basic Statistics. New York: McGraw-Hill, 1966. 195p. bibl.
        (HA17; 310.03 / 1. Statistics – Dictionaries.)
A   *Guide to U.S.Government Statistics.* By John L. Andriot.
        4th ed. McLean, Va.: Documents Index, 1973. 431p. (Z7554.U5;
        016.3173 / 1. United States – Statistics – Bibliography. 2. United
        States – Government publications – Bibliography.)
SA   *International Encyclopedia of Statistics.* Edited by
        William H. Kruskal and Judith M. Tanur. New York: Free Press,
        c1978. 2v. bibl. (HA17; 001.42203 / 1. Statistics – Dictionaries. 2.
        Social sciences – Statistical methods – Dictionaries.)
SA   Judge, Clark S. *The Book of American Rankings.* New York:
        Facts on File, c1979. 324p. bibl. (HA217; 317.3 / 1. United
        States – Statistics.)
SA   Kurian, George Thomas. *The Book of World Rankings.* New
        York: Facts on File, c1979. 430p. bibl. (HN25; 309.072 / 1. Social
        indicators.)
S   Kurtz, Albert K., and Edgerton, Harold A. *Statistical*
        Dictionary of Terms and Symbols. New York: Wiley; London: Chap-
        man and Hall, 1939, reprinted 1967. 191p. (HA17; 310.3 / 1.

Statistics – Dictionaries.)

SA   McEvedy, Colin, and Jones, Richard. *Altas of World*
Population History. New York: Penguin, 1978. 368p. bibl. (HB851;
301.329 / 1. Population – History. 2. Population – Statistics. 3.
Population – Charts, diagrams, etc.)

S   Murdoch, John, and Barnes, John A. *Statistical Tables*
for Science, Engineering, Management and Business Studies. 2d ed.
New York: Wiley, Halsted Press, 1973, c1970. 40p. (QA276.25;
519.50212 / 1. Mathematical statistics – Tables, etc.)

SA   Owen, Donald Bruce. *Handbook of Statistical Tables.*
Reading, Mass.: Addison-Wesley, 1962. 580p. bibl. (HA48; 310.84 /
1. Statistics – Charts, tables, etc.)

SA   *Pocket Book of Statistical Tables.* Comp. by Robert E.
Odeh [and others]. New York: Marcel Dekker, 1977. 166p. bibl.
(QA276.25; 519.50212 / 1. Mathematical statistics – Tables.)

SA   Showers, Victor. *World Facts and Figures: A Unique,*
Authoritative Collection of Comparative Information About Cities,
Counties, and Geographic Features of the World. New York: Wiley,
1979. 757p. bibl. (G109; 910.212 / 1. Geography – Tables. 2. Cities
and towns – Statistics.)

SA   *Statesman's Year-Book: Statistical and Historical Annual*
of the States of the World. London; New York: Macmillan, 1864- ,
v.1- . Annual. bibl. (JA51; 310.58 / 1. Political
science – Yearbooks.)

A   *Statistics Sources: A Subject Guide to Data on Industrial,*
Business, Social, Educational, Financial, and Other Topics for the
United States and Internationally. Ed. by Paul Wasserman and Jacqueline Bernero. 5th ed. Detroit: Gale, 1977. 976p. (Z7551; 016.31 /
1. Statistics – Bibliography.)

S   United Nations. Statistical Office. *Statistical Yearbook/*
Annuaire statistique. 1948- . New York: United Nations, 1949- ,
v.1- . Annual. (HA12.5; 310.58 / 1. Statistics – Yearbooks.)

S   United States. Bureau of the Census. *County and City*
Data Book. 1949- . Washington, D.C.: Government Printing Office,
1952- . Irregular. (HA202; 317.3 / 1. Cities and towns – United
States. 2. United States – Statistics.)

SA   United States. Bureau of the Census. *Historical Statistics*
of the United States: Colonial Times to 1970. Washington, D.C.:
Government Printing Office, 1976. 1200p. bibl. (HA202; 317.3 / 1.
United States – Statistics.)

S   United States. Bureau of the Census. *Statistical Abstract*
of the United States. 1878- . Washington, D.C.: Government Printing Office, 1879- , v.1- . Annual. (HA202; 317.3 / 1. United
States – Statistics.)

S   United States. Department of Commerce. Office of the
Assistant Secretary for Economic Affairs. *Dictionary of Economic*

and Statistical Terms. Washington, D.C.: Government Printing Office, 1973. 83p. (HB61; 330.03 / 1. Economics – Dictionaries. 2. Statistics – Dictionaries.)

Women's Studies

The field of women's studies is relatively young in comparison with the other social sciences, but as you can see by scanning the list below many tools are already available. Besides the books of quotations, statistical sources, biographical tools, and encyclopedic sources, there are also numerous access tools such as bibliographies and indexes. Because women's studies are so comparatively new, the demand on publishers for materials to support two-year and four-year college programs is great, and you should continue to check under the appropriate subject headings in your catalog to find new materials.

S   *Feminist Quotations: Voices of Rebels, Reformers, and Visionaries.* Compiled by Carol McPhee, Ann FitzGerald. 1st ed. New York: Crowell, c1979. 271p. (HQ1154; 301.41208 / 1. Feminism – Quotations, maxims, etc.)

SA *Handbook of International Data on Women.* By Elise Boulding [and others]. Beverly Hills, Calif.: Sage Publications, c1976. 468p. bibl. (HQ1115; 301.4120212 / 1. Women – Statistics – Handbooks, manuals, etc.)

A   Hughes, Marija Matich. *The Sexual Barrier: Legal, Medical, and Social Aspects of Sex Discrimination.* Enl. and rev. ed. Washington, D.C.: Hughes Press, c1977. 843p. (KF4758.A1; 016.3014120973 / 1. Sex discrimination against women – Law and legislation – United States – Bibliography. 2. Women – Legal status, laws, etc. – Bibliography. 3. Women – Bibliography.)

A   Krichmar, Albert. *The Women's Rights Movement in the United States, 1848-1970: A Bibliography and Sourcebook.* Metuchen, N.J.: Scarecrow, 1972. 436p. (Z7964.U49; 016.3014120973 / 1. Women's rights – United States – Bibliography. 2. Women's rights – United States – History – Sources.)

A   McKee, Kathleen Burke. *Women's Studies: A Guide to Reference Sources.* Storrs, Conn.: University of Connecticut Library, 1977. 112 p. (Z7965; 016.301412 / 1. Connecticut. University. Library. 2. Women's studies – Bibliography – Catalogs.)

S   *The Quotable Woman, 1800-1975.* Compiled and edited by Elaine Partnow. Los Angeles: Corwin Books, c1977. 539p. (PN6081.5; 082 / 1. Quotations, English.)

S   *Who's Who of American Women.* v.1- . Chicago: Marquis Who's Who, 1958/59- . Biennial. (CT3260; 920.7 / 1.

Women – United States – Biography.)
SA   *Woman's Almanac: Twelve How-To Handbooks in One.*
      Compiled and edited by Kathryn Paulsen and Ryan A. Kuhn.
      Philadelphia: Lippincott, 1976. 624p. bibl. (HQ1115; 301.412 / 1.
      Women's encyclopedias and dictionaries. 2. Women – Societies and
      clubs – Directories.)
A   *Women, 1965-1975.* Cynthia Crippen, ed. Glen Rock, N.J.:
      Microfilming Corp. of America, 1978. 1150p. (Z7961; 016.301412 /
      1. New York Times – Indexes. 2. Women – Indexes. 3.
      Women – Biography – Indexes.)
S   *The Women's Book of World Records and Achievements.* Ed.
      by Lois Decker O'Neill. Garden City, N.Y.: Anchor/Doubleday,
      1979. 798p. (CT3234; 920.72 / 1. Women – Biography. 2.
      Biography – 19th century. 3. Biography – 20th century.)
S   *Women's Organizations & Leaders Directory.* Washington,
      D.C.: Today Publications & News Service, 1973- . Irregular.
      (HQ1883; 301.41206273 / 1. Women – Societies – Directories.)
S   *Women's Rights Almanac.* v.1- . Bethesda, Md.:
      Elizabeth Cady Stanton Publishing Co., 1974- . Annual. (HQ1406;
      301.4120973 / 1. Women – United States – Yearbooks. 2. Women's
      rights – United States – Yearbooks. 3. Almanacs, American.)
A   *Women Studies Abstracts.* v.1- . Rush, N.Y.: Rush
      Publishing Co., 1972- . Quarterly. (Z7962; 016.30141205 / 1.
      Women – Abstracts.)

BUSINESS AND OFFICE OCCUPATIONS

The need for current information in the business world is ever present, and many of the tools listed here and under the specific subjects
within the business area will fill that need. In this section, the tools
cited should be useful to any business student, regardless of major, for
there are guides to writing, dictionaries of general business and industrial management, a widely available periodical index, as well as
planning tables and statistical sources. (Note that the tools listed in the
section "Business and Management" are more specifically geared to
such topics as personnel administration, business law, and finance.)

If you scanned the Table of Contents, you probably noticed that
many of the subjects listed under "Business and Office Occupations"
are very closely related. It is vitally important to recognize that you
will very likely need to consult more than one section. For example,
the student interested in "Investments" will more than likely also want
to check the tools listed under "Business and Management,"
"Economics," and possibly even "Accounting." It goes without saying
that the same student will also examine the resources listed here

under "Business and Office Occupations."

SA   Bursaw, Charles T.; Alred, Gerald J.; and Oliu, Walter E.
     The Business Writer's Handbook. New York: St. Martin's, 1976.
     575p. bibl. (HF5726; 651.75 / 1. Commercial cor-
     respondence – Handbooks, manuals, etc.)

A   *Business Books and Serials in Print.* New York: R. R.
     Bowker, 1973– . Annual. (Z7164.C81; 016.33 / 1.
     Business – Bibliography.)

A   *Business Periodicals Index.* New York: H. W. Wilson,
     1958– . Monthly (except August) with annual cumulation.
     (Z7164.C81; 016.6505 / 1. Business – Periodicals – Indexes. 2. In-
     dustry – Periodicals – Indexes.)

A   Coman, Edwin Truman. *Sources of Business Information.*
     Rev. ed. Berkeley: University of California Press, 1964. 330p.
     (Z7164.C81; 016.65 / 1. Bibliography – Best books – Economics. 2.
     Bibliography – Best books – Industrial management. 3. Reference
     books – Bibliography. 4. Economics – Bibliography. 5. Industrial
     management – Bibliography.)

S   Cox, Edwin Burk, ed. *Basic Tables in Business and Economics.*
     New York: McGraw-Hill, 1967. 399p. (HG5699; 511.8 / 1. Ready-
     reckoners. 2. Business mathematics – Tables, etc. 3. United
     States – Statistics.)

S   Dow Jones-Irwin. *Dow Jones–Irwin Business Almanac.*
     Homewood, Ill.: Dow Jones–Irwin, 1977– . Annual. (HF5003;
     330.904 / 1. Business – Yearbooks. 2. Economic history – 1945–
     – Yearbooks. 3. United States – Economic conditions – 1971–
     – Yearbooks. 4. United States – Commerce – Yearbooks.)

S   Institute for Business Planning, Inc. *Business and*
     Financial Planning Tables Desk Book. By the IBP Research and
     Editorial Staff. Englewood Cliffs, N.J.: Institute for Business Plan-
     ning, 1975. 282p. (HF5699; 332.0212 / 1. Ready-reckoners.)

S   Lasser, Jacob Kay. *Business Management Handbook.* 3d ed.,
     rev. and expanded. Bernard Greisman, ed. New York: McGraw-
     Hill, 1968. 770p. (HF5351; 658.00202 / 1. Business. 2. Industrial
     management.)

S   Prentice-Hall, Inc. *Encyclopedic Dictionary of Systems*
     and Procedures. Prepared by the Prentice-Hall Editorial Staff.
     Englewood Cliffs, N.J.: Prentice-Hall, 1966. 673p. (HD19;
     658.5003 / 1. Industrial management – Dictionaries.)

S   Rosenberg, Jerry Martin. *Dictionary of Business and*
     Management. New York: Wiley, c1978. 564p. (HF1002; 330.03 / 1.
     Business – Dictionaries. 2. Management – Dictionaries.)

SA   Sabin, William A. *The Gregg Reference Manual.* 5th ed.
     New York: Gregg Division of McGraw-Hill, 1977. 326p. bibl.

(PN147; 808.042 / 1. Authorship – Handbooks, manuals, etc.)
S   Sloan, Harold Stephenson, and Zurcher, Arnold J. *Dictionary*
       of Economics. 5th ed. New York: Barnes & Noble, 1971. 520p.
       (HB61; 330.03 / 1. Economics – Dictionaries.)
A   *The Use of Economics Literature.* Edited by John Fletcher.
       Hamden, Conn.: Archon Books, 1971. 309p. (Z7164.E2; 016.33 / 1.
       Economics – Bibliography – Addresses, essays, lectures.)

Accounting

Most of the tools listed here have been designed to answer the kinds
of accounting questions both the student and the professional en-
counter daily. Besides the ready reference handbook, which accounts
for many of the citations below, there are also two dictionaries, two
encyclopedic sources, and a bibliographic guide for access to other
sources of information in the field. One of the things you will notice as
you read through the citations is that the tools listed below deal not
just with accounting, but also with auditing and statistical sampling.
The accounting major may find it useful to consult some of the tools
listed under "Statistics" in the social sciences.

SA   *Accountants' Handbook.* 5th ed., ed. by Rufus Wixon,
       Walter G. Kell, and Norton M. Bedford. New York: Ronald, 1970.
       1v. in various pagings. bibl. (HF5621; 657 / 1. Accounting.)
S   American Institute of Ce ..ified Public Accountants.
       AICPA Professional Standards. Chicago: Commerce Clearing House,
       c1975- . v. (HF5667; 657.61 / 1. Auditing – Standards. 2. Business
       ethics. 3. Accounting – Standards.)
SA   Arkin, Herbert. *Handbook of Sampling for Auditing and Accounting.*
       2d ed. New York: McGraw-Hill, 1974. 510p. bibl. (HF5657;
       519.52024657 / 1. Sampling (Statistics). 2. Accounting. 3. Auditing.)
SA   Casey, William J. *Accounting Desk Book: The Accountant's*
       Everyday Instant Answer Book. 5th ed., completely revised by
       Stephen R. Novak. Englewood Cliffs, N.J.: Institute for Business
       Planning, 1977. 434p. bibl. (HF5635; 657.0202 / 1. Accounting.)
A   Demarest, Rosemary R. *Accounting: Information Sources.*
       Detroit: Gale, 1971. 420p. (Z7164.C81; 016.657 / 1. Account-
       ing – Bibliography.)
S   *Encyclopedia of Accounting Systems.* Rev. and enl.
       Jerome K. Pescow, ed. Englewood Cliffs, N.J.: Prentice-Hall, 1976.
       3v. (HF5635; 657 / 1. Accounting.)
SA   *Handbook for Auditors.* James A. Cashin, ed. in chief.
       New York: McGraw-Hill, 1971. 1v. in various pagings. bibl.
       (HG5667; 657.45 / 1. Auditing – Handbooks, manuals, etc.)

SA   *Handbook of Modern Accounting.* 2d ed. Sidney Davidson,
       ed. New York: McGraw-Hill, 1977. 1372p. bibl. (HF5635; 657 / 1.
       Accounting–Handbooks, manuals, etc.)

S   Kohler, Eric Louis. *A Dictionary for Accountants.* 5th
       ed. Englewood Cliffs, N.J.: Prentice-Hall, 1975. 497p. (HF5621;
       657.03 / 1. Accounting–Dictionaries.)

SA   Lasser (J. K.) Institute, New York. *J. K. Lasser's Standard
       Handbook for Accountants.* New York: McGraw-Hill, 1956. 1v. in
       various pagings. bibl. (HF5621; 657.02 / 1. Accounting. 2.
       Auditing.)

S   March, Robert T. *Running Press Glossary of Accounting
       Language.* Philadelphia: Running Press, c1978. 78p. (HF5621;
       657.03 / 1. Accounting–Dictionaries.)

S   Prentice-Hall, Inc. *Encyclopedia of Auditing Techniques.*
       Jennie M. Palen, ed. Englewood Cliffs, N.J.: Prentice-Hall, 1967.
       2v. (HF5667; 657.6 / 1. Auditing–Addresses, essays, lectures.)

Advertising

The advertising student has several different types of resources available. Besides the standard source tools such as dictionaries and encyclopedic works, there are also directories of both advertisers and advertising agencies, handbooks of advertising management, and a bibliography for those students interested in the history of advertising. You will note that one of the tools listed deals as much with printing as it does with promotion and advertising. Indeed, the advertising student should scan the list of tools cited under "Printing" later in this book.

Not listed here, but also of interest to you, will be many of the works issued by the Standard Rate and Data Service, which lists rates for various advertising media. Most will be found under the heading "Standard Rate and Data Service," including such periodicals as *Direct Mail List Rates and Data, Weekly Newspaper Rates and Data,* and *Network Rates and Data.*

S   *Ayer Glossary of Advertising and Related Terms.* Comp.
       and publ. by the Ayer Press. 2d ed. Philadelphia: Ayer Press, 1977.
       219p. (HF5803; 659.103 / 1. Advertising–Dictionaries.)

S   Barton, Roger, ed. *Handbook of Advertising Management.*
       New York: McGraw-Hill, 1970. 1v. in various pagings. (HF5823;
       659.10202 / 1. Advertising management–Handbooks, manuals,
       etc.)

S   Graham, Irvin. *Encyclopedia of Advertising.* 2d ed.

New York: Fairchild, 1969. 494p. (HF5803; 659.103 / 1. Advertising – Dictionaries.)

SA   Lavidge, Arthur W. _A Common Sense Guide to Professional Advertising._ Blue Ridge Summit, Pa.: Tab Books, 1973. 318p. bibl. (HF5823; 659.1 / 1. Advertising.)

S   Melcher, Daniel, and Larrick, Nancy. _Printing and Promotion Handbook: How to Plan, Produce, and Use Printing, Advertising, and Direct Mail._ 3d ed. New York: McGraw-Hill, 1966. 451p. (Z118; 655.03 / 1. Printing – Dictionaries.)

A   Pollay, Richard W. _Information Sources in Advertising History._ Westport, Conn.: Greenwood Press, 1979. 330p. (Z7164.C81; 016.6591 / 1. Advertising – History – Bibliography.)

A   _Standard Directory of Advertisers._ 1964– . New York: National Register Publishing Co., 1964– . Frequency varies. (HF5805; 659.102573 / 1. Advertising – United States – Directories.)

A   _Standard Directory of Advertising Agencies._ New York: National Register Publishing Co., 1964– . Three times a year. (HF5805; 659.105873 / 1. Advertising – United States – Directories.)

S   Stansfield, Richard H. _The Dartnell Advertising Manager's Handbook._ Chicago: Dartnell, 1969. 1503p. (HF5823; 659.1 / 1. Advertising – Handbooks, manuals, etc.)

S   Tatham-Laird and Kudner. _Dictionary of Advertising Terms._ Laurence Urdang, ed. Chicago: Tatham-Laird and Kudner, 1977. 209p. (HF5803; 659.103 / 1. Advertising – Dictionaries.)

Business and Management

If you have read the introductory remarks to the broad area of business and office occupations, you are already aware that the tools listed there and here are closely related. In this section, you will find tools that deal with various aspects of business and management such as personnel administration, business law, finance, and commerce and trade. Besides the standard source and access tools, you will also find a commercial and marketing atlas, a who's-who biographical dictionary of financial and industrial leaders, and directories of trade and professional associations and of manufacturers. There is even a dictionary of trade names. You will probably find it useful also to scan the titles listed in the sections "Economics" and "Investments."

SA   Brown, Stanley M., and Doris, Lillian. _Business Executive's Handbook._ 4th ed. New York: Prentice-Hall, 1953. 1496p. bibl. (HF5356; 650.2 / 1. Business.)

S   Clark, Donald Thomas, and Gottfried, Bert A. _Dictionary of Business and Finance._ New York: Crowell, 1957. 409p. (HF1002;

650.3 / 1. Business – Dictionaries. 2. Finance – Dictionaries.)

S Crowley, Ellen T. *Trade Names Dictionary: A Guide to Consumer-Oriented Trade Names, Brand Names, Product Names, Coined Names, Model Names, and Design Names, with Addresses of Their Manufacturers, Importers, Marketers, or Distributors.* 2d ed. Detroit: Gale, c1979. 2v. (T223.V4; 602.75 / 1. Tradeworks – United States. 2. Business names – United States.)

SA Dartnell Corporation. *Dartnell International Trade Handbook.* By G. R. Richter [and others]; ed. by Leslie L. Lewis. 2d ed. Chicago: Dartnell, 1965. 1023p. bibl. (HF1010; 382.02 / 1. Commerce – Handbooks, manuals, etc.)

S *The Dartnell Personnel Administration Handbook.* Edited by Wilbert E. Scheer. 2d ed. Chicago: Dartnell, c1979. 1088p. (____; 658.3 / 1. Personnel management – Handbooks, manuals, etc.)

A *Encyclopedia of Business Information Sources.* 4th ed. Paul Wasserman, managing editor. Detroit: Gale, 1980. 778p. (HF5353; 016.33 / 1. Business – Information services. 2. Information services.)

S French, Derek, and Saward, Heather. *Dictionary of Management.* New York: International Publications Service, 1975. 447p. (HD19; 658.4003 / 1. Management – Dictionaries. 2. Economics – Dictionaries.)

SA Heyel, Carl. *The Encyclopedia of Management.* 2d ed. New York: Van Nostrand Reinhold, 1973. 1161p. bibl. (HD19; 658.003 / 1. Industrial management – Dictionaries.)

SA Lindemann, A. J.; Lundgren, Earl F.; and Von Kaas, H. K. *Dictionary of Management Terms.* Dubuque, Iowa: W. C. Brown Book Co., 1966. 81p. bibl. (HD19; 658.003 / 1. Industrial management – Dictionaries.)

SA Maynard, Harold Bright, ed. *Handbook of Business Administration.* New York: McGraw-Hill, 1967. 1v. in various pagings. bibl. (HD31; 658 / 1. Business – Addresses, essays, lectures. 2. Industrial management – Addresses, essays, lectures.)

S Moffat, Donald W., ed. *Concise Desk Book of Business Finance.* Englewood Cliffs, N.J.: Prentice-Hall, 1975. 387p. (HG151; 332.03 / 1. Finance – Terminology. 2. Business enterprises – Finance – Terminology.)

S *National Trade and Professional Associations of the United States, and Labor Unions.* Ed.1- , 1966- . Washington, D.C.: Columbia Books, 1966- . Annual. (HD2425; 650.58 / 1. Trade and professional associations – United States – Directories.)

S *Poor's Register of Corporations, Directors and Executives, United States and Canada.* New York: Standard and Poor's Corporation, 1928- . Annual. (HG4057; 658.151 / 1. Directors of corpora-

tions – United States – Directories. 2. Directors of corporations –
Canada – Directories. 3. Capitalists and financiers – United
States – Directories. 4. Capitalists and financiers – Canada – Directories.)

S   Prentice-Hall, Inc. *Encyclopedic Dictionary of Business
Finance.* Prepared by the editorial staff. Englewood Cliffs, N.J.:
Prentice-Hall, 1961. 658p. (HG151; 332.03 / 1. Finance – Dic-
tionaries. 2. Business – Dictionaries.)

S   Prentice-Hall, Inc. *Encyclopedic Dictionary of Business
Law.* Prepared by the editorial staff. Englewood Cliffs, N.J.:
Prentice-Hall, 1961. 608p. (____; 347.70973 / 1. Commercial
law – United States – Dictionaries.)

S   Rand McNally & Co. *Rand McNally Commercial Atlas and
Marketing Guide.* Chicago: Rand McNally, 1876– . Annual. (G1019;
912 / 1. Atlases. 2. United States – Maps.)

S   Ross, Martin J. *New Encyclopedic Dictionary of Business
Law – With Forms.* Englewood Cliffs, N.J.: Prentice-Hall, 1975.
289p. (KF887; 346.730703 / 1. Commercial law – United
States – Dictionaries.)

S   Schwartz, Robert J. *The Dictionary of Business and
Industry.* New York: B. C. Forbes, 1954. 561p. (T9; 603 / 1.
Technology – Dictionaries. 2. Economics – Dictionaries.)

S   *Thomas Register of American Manufacturers and Thomas
Catalog File.* 1st– ed. 1905/1906– . New York: Thomas Publishing
Co., 1906– . Annual. (T12; 338.7602573 / 1. United
States – Manufacturers – Directories.)

S   United Nations. Statistical Office. *World Trade Annual.*
1963– . New York: Walker, 1964– . Annual. (HF53; 650.06 / 1.
Commerce – Yearbooks. 2. Commerce – Directories.)

S   United Nations. Statistical Office. *Yearbook of
International Trade Statistics.* 1950– . New York: United Nations,
1951– . Annual. (HF91; 382.058 / 1. Commercial statistics.)

S   United States. Bureau of Economic Analysis. *Survey of
Current Business.* v.1, Aug. 1921– . Washington, D.C.: Government
Printing Office, 1921– . Monthly, with weekly supplements.
(HC101; 330 / 1. Business. 2. Commerce. 3. Prices – United States.
4. United States – Commerce. 5. United States – Industries.)

A   Washington Researchers. *How to Find Information About
Companies.* Editor, Donna M. Jablonski. Washington, D.C.: Researchers, c1979. 284p. (HD2791; 016.338740973 / 1. Corporations – Information services – United States. 2. Corporations – United States – Directories.)

S   *Who's Who in Finance and Industry.* Ed.17– . Chicago:
Marquis, 1972/1973– . Irregular. Continues *World Who's Who in
Finance and Industry.* (HF3023.A2; 338.00922 / 1. United
States – Biography – Dictionaries. 2. Canada – Biography – Dic-

tionaries. 3. Capitalists and financiers – United States.)

Economics

While both the economics student and the economist will frequently have occasion to turn to many of the resources listed under "Business and Office Occupations" and "Business and Management," several tools are directly appropriate to the field itself. Besides the standard source tools, there are also economic atlases, handbooks of both labor and general economic statistics, economic indicators, and even the annual economic report of the president. Keep in mind that some of the general statistical sources listed in Chapter 2 as well as those listed under "Statistics" in this chapter may also be useful to you.

SA   Ammer, Christine, and Ammer, Dean S. *Dictionary of Business
      and Economics.* New York: Free Press, 1977. 461p. bibl. (HB61;
      330.03 / 1. Economics – Dictionaries. 2. Business – Dictionaries.)
S   Bannock, G., Baxter, R. E., and Rees, R. *The Penguin
      Dictionary of Economics.* 2d ed. Harmondsworth, N.Y.: Penguin,
      1978. 463p. (HB61; 330.03 / 1. Economics – Dictionaries.)
SA   *Economics: Encyclopedia.* 1973/74– . Guilford, Conn.:
      Dushkin, 1974– . v. bibl. (HB61; 330.03 / 1. Economics –
      Dictionaries.)
SA   Mai, Ludwig H. *Men and Ideas in Economics: A Dictionary
      of World Economists Past and Present.* Totowa, N.J.: Rowman and
      Littlefield, 1977, c1975. 270p. bibl. (HB76; 330.0922 / 1.
      Economists – Biography.)
S   *The McGraw-Hill Dictionary of Modern Economics: A
      Handbook of Terms and Organizations.* Douglas Greenwald, ed. 2d
      ed. New York: McGraw-Hill, 1973. 792p. (HB61; 330.03 / 1.
      Economics – Dictionaries.)
S   *Oxford Regional Economic Atlas: The United States
      and Canada.* Prepared by the Cartographic Department of Oxford
      University Press. 2d ed. London: Oxford University Press, 1975.
      128p. (____; 330.97053 / 1. United States – Economic condi-
      tions – Maps. 2. Canada – Economic conditions – Maps.)
SA   Oxford University Press. *Oxford Economic Atlas of the
      World.* Prepared by the Cartographic Department of the Clarendon
      Press. 4th ed. London: Oxford University Press, 1972. 239p. bibl.
      (G1046.G1; 912.133 / 1. Geography, Economic – Maps.)
S   United States. Bureau of Labor Statistics. *Handbook of
      Labor Statistics.* Washington, D.C.: Government Printing Office,
      1926– . Annual. (HD8051; ____ / 1. Labor and laboring
      classes – United States – Statistics.)

S   United States. Bureau of the Census. *Long Term Economic
     Growth, 1860–1965: A Statistical Compendium*. Washington, D.C.:
     Government Printing Office, 1966. 256p. (HA203; ____ / 1. United
     States–Statistics. 2. Time-series analysis.)
S   United States. Council of Economic Advisers. *Economic
     Indicators*. May 1948– . Washington, D.C.: Government Printing
     Office, 1948– . Monthly. (HC101; ____ / 1. United
     States–Economic conditions–1945– .)
S   United States. President. *Economic Report of the President
     Transmitted to the Congress*. Washington, D.C.: Government Print-
     ing Office, 1947– . Annual. (HC106.5; 330.973 / 1. United
     States–Economic policy–Periodicals. 2. United States–Economic
     conditions–1945– –Periodicals.)

Hotel/Motel and Travel/Tourism

Most often, programs in hotel/motel management and in tourism
are separate in community colleges. But given how closely related
these programs are, the tools listed below will likely be of interest to
students in either one. Most of the sources in this section are designed
primarily for use by professionals in the industry, such tools as
timetables for airlines, railways, and steamships or directories of
hotels, travel agents, and convention facilities. Other sources will be
of interest to travelers themselves, such as *Traveler's Almanac*. Not
listed, but of interest to professional and traveler alike, will be *Fodor's
Modern Guides*. Issued annually since 1953, the guides are devoted to
individual countries and may be found in the catalog by looking either
under *Fodor's Modern Guides* or under the name of the country you are
interested in.

S   *Encyclopedia of World Travel*. Ed. by Nelson Doubleday
         and C. Earl Cooley. Rev. by Marjorie Zelko and Diana Powell
         Ward. 2d rev. ed. Garden City, N.Y.: Doubleday, 1973. 2v. (G153;
         910.202 / 1. Voyages and travels–Guide-books.)
S   *Hotel and Motel Red Book*. 1886– . New York: American
         Hotel Association Directory Corporation, 1886– . Annual. (TX907;
         ____ / 1. Hotels, taverns, etc.–Directories. 2. Tourist camps,
         hostels, etc.–Directories.)
A   *Hotel & Travel Index*. New York: Ziff-Davis, 1938– .
         Quarterly. (TX907; 647.025 / 1. Hotels, taverns, etc.–Directories.
         2. Motels–Directories.)
SA   Lundberg, Donald E. *The Tourist Business*. Jule Wilkinson,
         ed. 3d ed. Boston: Cahners Books International, c1976. 323p. bibl.
         (G155.A1; 338.479104 / 1. Tourist trade.)

S   *Official Airline Guide. Worldwide Edition.* v.1- , March
1976- . Oak Brook, Ill.: R. H. Donnelley, 1976- . (HE9768;
387.7420212 / 1. Air lines – Time-tables – Periodicals. 2. Air
lines – Rates – Periodicals.)

S   *The Official Guide of the Railways and Steam Navigation
Lines of the United States, Puerto Rico, Canada, Mexico and Cuba.*
New York: National Railway Publication Co., [1868?]- . (HE2727;
_____ / 1. Railroads – United States – Time-tables. 2.
Railroads – Canada – Time-tables. 3. Railroads – Mexico – Time-
tables. 4. Railroads – Cuba – Time-tables. 5. Railroads – Puerto
Rico – Time-tables.)

S   *Official Meeting Facilities Guide.* New York: Ziff-Davis,
1974- . (TX907; 647.94 / 1. Convention facilities – Directories. 2.
Hotels, taverns, etc. – Directories.)

S   *Official Steamship Guide.* International. v.1- . New
York: Transportation Guides, 1932- . Monthly. (_____; 387.2405 / 1.
Steamboats – Time-tables – Periodicals.)

S   *Pan Am's World Guide.* 24th ed. New York: McGraw-Hill, 1978.
1058p. (G153.4; 910.202 / 1. Voyages and travels – 1951-
– Guidebooks.)

S   *Russell's Official National Motor Coach Guide.* v.9- ,
October 1936- . Cedar Rapids, Iowa: Russell's Guides, 1936- .
Monthly. (HE5623.A1; _____).

S   *Traveler's Almanac.* 2d- ed. Los Angeles: B. Muster,
1976- . Annual. (G153.4; 910.202 / 1. Voyages and travels – 1951-
– Guide-books – Periodicals.)

A   *Travel Guidebooks in Review.* Edited by Jon O. Heise [and
others]. 3d ed. rev. Syracuse, N.Y.: Gaylord Professional Publications, 1978. 187p. bibl. (Z6016.T7; 016.9102 / 1. Voyages and
travels – 1951- – Guidebooks – Bibliography.)

S   *Travel Marketing.* Stamford, Conn.: Marketing Handbooks,
1978- . Annual. Continues *Travel Market Yearbook.* (G155.A1;
338.4791 / 1. Tourist trade – Yearbooks.)

S   *Travel Weekly's World Travel Directory.* v.9- , 1978- .
New York: Ziff-Davis, 1978- . Annual. Continues *World Travel
Directory.* (G154; 380.14591025 / 1. Travel agents – Directories.)

S   *Who's Who Among Innkeepers: A Biographical Reference
Work About Hotel, Motel and Resort Managers and Owners in
America.* 1st ed. New York: Rating Publications, 1974. 210p.
(TX910.3; 647.940922 / 1. Hotel management – United
States – Biography. 2. Motel management – United
States – Biography.)

S   Ziff-Davis Publishing Company. Public Transportation and
Travel Division. *The Official Hotel & Resort Guide.* New York: Ziff-
Davis, 1978- . 3v. Loose-leaf. (TX907; 647.94 / 1. Hotels, taverns,
etc. – Directories. 2. Resorts – Directories.)

Insurance

Students preparing for a career in the insurance business will find a variety of useful resources cited below. There are annuals devoted not only to insurance in general, but also to life and health insurance as well as property and casualty insurance. There are dictionaries, an encyclopedic source for information on inspection and underwriting, handbooks, and even an annual bibliography of books on life and health insurance. As in several other fields in business, students in insurance may need statistical information from tools listed in Chapter 2 and under "Statistics" in this chapter.

S   *Best's Insurance Reports. Life-Health Edition.* 1906– . Morristown, N.J.:
        A. M. Best, 1906– . Annual. (____; ____ / 1. Insurance, Life.)
S   *Best's Insurance Reports. Property-Casualty Edition.*
        1899/1900– . Morristown, N.J.: A. M. Best, 1900– . Annual.
        (HG9655; 368.1006573 / 1. Insurance, Property–United
        States–Periodicals. 2. Insurance, Property–Canada–Periodicals. 3.
        Insurance companies–United States–Periodicals. 4. Insurance
        companies–Canada–Periodicals.)
S   Casey, William J. *Life Insurance Desk Book.* 3d ed.
        Englewood Cliffs, N.J.: Institute for Business Planning, 1974. 382p.
        (HG8771; 368.32 / 1. Insurance, Life–Handbooks, manuals, etc.)
S   Crobaugh, Clyde J. *Handbook of Insurance.* New York:
        Prentice-Hall, 1949. 1v. (HG8025; 368.03 / 1. Insurance–
        Dictionaries.)
S   Davids, Lewis E. *Dictionary of Insurance.* 5th ed.
        Paterson, N.J.: Littlefield, Adams, 1977. 291p. (HG8025; 368.003 /
        1. Insurance–Dictionaries.)
S   Ferguson, Elizabeth, ed. *Sources of Insurance Statistics.*
        New York: Special Libraries Association, 1965. 191p. (HG8045;
        368.00212 / 1. Insurance–Statistics.)
SA   Gregg, Davis W., and Lucas, Vane B., eds. *Life and Health
        Insurance Handbook.* 3d ed. Homewood, Ill.: R. D. Irwin, 1973.
        1336p. bibl. (HG8769; 368.300202 / 1. Insurance, Life. 2. Insurance, Health.)
S   Heath, Gerald R. *Insurance Words and Their Meanings.*
        10th ed. Indianapolis, Ind.: Rough Notes Co., 1972. 120p.
        (HG8025; 368.03 / 1. Insurance–Dictionaries. 2. Insurance,
        Fire–Dictionaries. 3. Insurance, Casualty–Dictionaries.)
S   *Insurance Almanac: Who, What, When and Where in Insurance, An Annual of Insurance Facts.* Ed. 1– , 1913– . New York: Underwriter
        Press and Publishing, 1912– . Annual. (HG8019; ____ / 1. Insurance–Yearbooks.)
S   Levy, Michael H. *A Handbook of Personal Insurance*

      Terminology. Lynbrook, N.Y.: Farnsworth, 1968. 595p. (HG8759;
      368.320014 / 1. Insurance, Life – Dictionaries. 2. Insurance,
      Health – Dictionaries.)

S   *Life Insurance Fact Book.* New York: Institute of Life
      Insurance, 1946- . Annual. (HG8943; 368.3058 / 1. Insurance,
      Life – Yearbooks. 2. Insurance, Life – United States.)

S   Lincoln, Walter Osborn, and Tisdale, George W. *Insurance*
      Inspection and Underwriting: A Non-Technical Encyclopedic
      Handbook. 8th ed., rev., condensed, and fully illustrated.
      Philadelphia: Spectator, 1965. 1290p. (HG9715; 368.1 / 1.
      Insurance, Fire – Inspectors. 2. Insurance, Fire. 3. Fire
      prevention.)

A   *A List of Worthwhile Life and Health Insurance Books.*
      By the Institute of Life Insurance, New York, and Health In-
      surance Institute, New York. New York: Institutes, 1968- . An-
      nual. (Z7164.I7; 016.36832 / 1. Insurance,
      Life – Bibliography – Periodicals. 2. Insurance,
      Health – Bibliography – Periodicals.)

S   *Who's Who in Insurance: A Section of the Insurance*
      Almanac. New York: Underwriter Press and Publishing,
      1948- . Annual. (HG8523; 368.058 / 1. Insurance – Biography. 2.
      United States – Biography.)

Investments

For the business student interested in investments, many reference
works are available. There are guides to securities and corporations,
handbooks of stocks and bonds, directories to brokers and to the stock
exchange, as well as works devoted to banks and banking, personal
finance, and the stock market. Statistics can be important to the investor, so you should also consult the statistical sources listed both in
Chapter 2 and in this chapter under the heading "Statistics." As mentioned in the introductory remarks to the section on "Business and Office Occupations," the student of investments may also want to consult
the tools listed under "Business and Management," "Economics," and
possibly even "Accounting."

S   Badger, Ralph E. *The Complete Guide to Investment Analysis.*
      New York: McGraw-Hill, 1967. 504p. (HG4521; 332.6 / 1.
      Securities – United States. 2. Finance – United States. 3. Corpora-
      tions – United States.)

SA   Balachandran, M. *A Guide to Trade and Securities Statistics.*
      Ann Arbor, Mich.: Pierian Press, 1977. 185p. bibl. (Z7165.U5;
      016.3326 / 1. Securities – United
      States – Statistics – Periodicals – Indexes. 2. Commercial

statistics – Periodicals – Indexes. 3. United States – Statistical services – Periodicals – Indexes.)

S   Batz, Laila. *Running Press Glossary of Banking Language.*
      Philadelphia: Running Press, 1977. 85p. (HG151; 332.103 / 1.
      Banks and banking – Dictionaries.)

S   Collins, George William, ed. *Stock Exchange: International
      Directory.* Washington, D.C.: 1965. 101p. (HG4509; 332.61 / 1.
      Stock-exchange – Directories. 2. Brokers – Directories.)

S   *Dun & Bradstreet's Guide to Your Investments.* 19th- ed.
      New York: Crowell, 1974/1975- . Continues *Your Investments: How
      to Increase Your Capital and Income.* (HG4905; 332.670973 / 1.
      Securities – United States – Periodicals.)

S   Farrell, Maurice, L., ed. *The Dow Jones Investor's Handbook.*
      Princeton: Dow Jones Books, 1966- . Annual. (HG4921; 332.678 /
      1. Stocks – United States. 2. Bonds – United States.)

SA   *Handbook of Wealth Management.* Edited by Leo Barnes and
      Stephen Feldman. New York: McGraw-Hill, 1977. 1012p. bibl.
      (HG4521; 332.678 / 1. Investments – Handbooks, manuals, etc. 2.
      Finance, Personal.)

S   *Investment Companies: Mutual Funds and Other Types.*
      New York: Wiesenberger Services, 1941- . Annual. (HG4497;
      332.670973 / 1. Investment trusts – United States – Yearbooks. 2.
      Investment trusts – Canada.)

S   *Moody's Handbook of Widely Held Common Stocks.* New York:
      Moody's Investors Service, 1956- . Annual. (HG4905; 332.670973 /
      1. Stocks – United States.)

S   Moore, Norman D. *Dictionary of Business Finance and
      Investment.* Dayton, Ohio: Investor's Systems, 1975. 543p. (HF1001;
      332.03 / 1. Business – Dictionaries. 2. Finance – Dictionaries. 3. In-
      vestments – Dictionaries.)

SA   Munn, Glenn Gaywaine. *Encyclopedia of Banking and Finance.*
      6th ed. by F. L. Garcia. Boston: Bankers Publishing, 1962. 788p.
      bibl. (HG151; 332.03 / 1. Banks and banking – Dictionaries. 2.
      Finance – Dictionaries. 3. Banks and banking – United States.)

S   *Security Dealers of North America.* New York: Standard and
      Poor's Corp., 1922- . Annual. (HG4907; 332.620257 / 1.
      Brokers – Directories.)

S   Standard and Poor's Corporation. *Stock Market Encyclopedia.*
      New York: Standard and Poor's Corp., [1961?]- . Annual. (HG4921;
      332.630973 / 1. Securities – United States. 2. Stocks – United States.
      3. Corporations – United States.)

S   *The Stock Market Handbook: Reference Manual for the
      Securities Industry.* Ed. by Frank G. Zarb and Gabriel T. Kerekes.
      Homewood, Ill.: Dow Jones-Irwin, 1970. 1073p. (HG4921;
      332.60973 / 1. Securities – United States – Handbooks, manuals,
      etc.)

S   Wyckoff, Peter. *The Language of Wall Street.* New York:

Hopkinson & Blake, 1973. 247p. (HG4513; 332.603 / 1. Investments – Dictionaries. 2. Stock-exchange – Dictionaries.)

Legal Assistant

The student preparing for a career as a legal assistant will need to
develop a familiarity not just with the law and legal research – and
there are two bibliographic guides to legal research cited below – but
also with office administration. To that end, works are listed here that
deal with both aspects of this field of study. There are handbooks of
forms, legal dictionaries, and citations to the law itself, as well as
works for the legal secretary. Since your community college library
may not have an overly large legal collection, your reference librarian
can point you toward larger law libraries in your area, as well as to
depository collections of government documents, which frequently
prove useful to the legal assistant.

S   Bailey, F. Lee, and Rothblatt, Henry B. *Complete Manual*
      of Criminal Forms: Federal and State. 2d ed. Rochester, N.Y.:
      Lawyers Co-operative Publishing; San Francisco: Bancroft-
      Whitney, 1974. 2v. plus supplement. (KF9616; 345.73050269 / 1.
      Criminal procedure – United States – Forms.)

S   Ballentine, James Arthur. *Ballentine's Law Dictionary*
      with Pronunciations. 3d ed., ed. by William S. Anderson. Rochester,
      N.Y.: Lawyers Co-operative Publishing, 1969. (KF156; 340.03 / 1.
      Law – Dictionaries. 2. Law – Terms and phrases.)

S   Black, Henry Campbell. *Black's Law Dictionary.* 5th ed.
      St. Paul, Minn.: West Publishing, 1979. 1511p. (KF156; 340.03 / 1.
      Law – Dictionaries.)

SA   Casey, William J. *Lawyer's Desk Book: The Lawyer's*
      Everyday Instant Answer Book. 3d ed. Englewood Cliffs, N.J.: In-
      stitute for Business Planning, 1979. 859p. bibl. (KF386; 340.0973 /
      1. Law – United States – Compends. 2. Practice of law – United
      States.)

SA   Cohen, Morris L. *Legal Research in a Nutshell.* 2d ed.
      St. Paul, Minn.: West Publishing, 1971. 259p. (KF240; 340.072073 /
      1. Legal research – United States.)

S   *Corpus Juris Secundum: A Complete Restatement of the*
      Entire American Law as Developed by All Reported Cases. By William
      Mack and Donald J. Kiser. . . . Brooklyn, N.Y.: American Law
      Book Co., 1936–1974. 101v. in 136. Kept up to date by cumulative
      annual parts and revised volumes. Five-volume index issued in
      1959–1960. (___; 345.5 / 1. Law – United States. 2. Law reports,
      digests, etc. – United States.)

S   Cunningham, William E. *The Para-Legal and the Lawyer's*

       Library: A Handbook for the Para-Legal Designed to Give a Basic
Understanding of Legal Publications, the Structure of the Law Library,
and Commonly Used Legal Terms. Colorado Springs, Colo.: Shepard's
Citations, 1973. 64p. (KF319; 651.93400973 / 1. Law offices – United States – Handbooks, manuals, etc. 2. Law
libraries – United States – Handbooks, manuals, etc. 3. Law – United
States – Terms and phrases.)

S   Gifis, Steven H. *Law Dictionary.* Woodbury, N.Y.: Barron's,
1975. 227p. (KF156; 340.03 / 1. Law – United States – Dictionaries.)

S   Gordon, Frank S., and Hemnes, Thomas M. S., comps. *The*
Legal Word Book. Boston: Houghton Mifflin, 1978. 296p. (KF156;
340.14 / 1. Law – Terms and phrases.)

A   *Index to Legal Periodicals.* New York: H. W. Wilson,
1909- . Monthly, except September. Annual and triennial cumulations. (K9; 016.34705 / 1. Law – Periodicals – United
States – Indexes. 2. Law – Periodicals – Indexes.)

S   *Legal Secretary's Encyclopedic Dictionary.* 2d ed.
Prepared by the Prentice-Hall Editorial Staff. Rev. by Betty Kennedy Thomae. Englewood Cliffs, N.J.: Prentice-Hall, 1977. 450p.
(KF319; 340.03 / 1. Legal secretaries – United States – Handbooks,
manuals, etc.)

S   *Martindale-Hubbell Law Directory.* New York:
Martindale-Hubbell, 1931- . Annual in 5v. (___; 340.0973 / 1.
Lawyers – United States – Directories.)

SA   Pollack, Ervin Harold. *Ervin H. Pollack's Fundamentals*
of Legal Research. 4th ed. by J. Myron Jacobstein and Roy M. Mersky. Mineola, N.Y.: Foundation Press, 1973. 565p. (KF240;
340.072073 / 1. Legal research – United States.)

S   Reilly, Theresa M. *Legal Secretary's Word Finder and*
Desk Book. West Nyack, N.Y.: Parker, 1974. 263p. (KF319;
340.024651 / 1. Legal secretaries – United States – Handbooks,
manuals, etc. 2. Law – Terms and phrases.)

S   Sletwold, Evangeline. *Sletwold's Manual of Documents and*
Forms for the Legal Secretary. 2d ed. Englewood Cliffs, N.J.:
Prentice-Hall, 1976. 199p. (KF319; 340.024651 / 1. Legal
secretaries – United States – Handbooks, manuals, etc.)

S   United States. Laws, statutes, etc. *United States Code*
Annotated. St. Paul, Minn.: West Publishing, 1927- , v.1- . Kept up
to date by pocket parts. (___; 345.21)

Real Estate

    Most of the resources cited below are source tools: dictionaries of
real estate and appraisal terminology, tables, forms, handbooks, and
housing statistical sources. There are also two bibliographic access
tools that will lead you to other information sources, as well as some

source/access handbooks on real estate investment and practice. Besides these works, you will also find a source tool for information on housing and building materials; other similar and potentially useful tools are listed in this chapter under "Construction Technology." Keep in mind that the number of information sources in real estate is quite large and will include tools specifically devoted to real estate practice in your home state.

A   American Institute of Real Estate Appraisers. *Real Estate Appraisal Bibliography.* 2d ed. Chicago: Institute, 1973. 346p. (Z7164.L3; 016.333332 / 1. Real property – Valuation – Bibliography.)

S   Arnold, Alvin L., and Kusnet, Jack. *The Arnold Encyclopedia of Real Estate.* Boston: Warren, Gorham and Lamont, c1978. 1055p. (HD1365; 333.33 / 1. Real estate business – Dictionaries.)

A   Babb, Janice B., and Dordick, Beverly F. *Real Estate Information Sources.* Detroit: Gale, 1963. 317p. (Z7164.L3; 016.33333 / 1. Real estate business – Bibliography.)

S   Boyce, Byrl N. *Real Estate Appraisal Terminology.* Cambridge, Mass.: Ballinger, 1975. 306p. (HD1387; 333.33203 / 1. Real property – Valuation – Terminology.)

SA   Campbell, Don G. *The Handbook of Real Estate Investment.* Indianapolis, Ind.: Bobbs-Merrill, 1968. 306p. bibl. (HD1375; 333.330973 / 1. Real estate investment – United States.)

S   Casey, William J. *Real Estate Investment Tables.* 5th ed. Englewood Cliffs, N.J.: Institute for Business Planning, 1974. 89p. (HF5716; 674.083 / 1. Real estate business – Tables and ready-reckoners.)

S   Ellwood, L. W. *Ellwood Tables for Real Estate Appraising and Financing.* 4th ed. Cambridge, Mass.: Published for the American Institute of Real Estate Appraisers of the National Association of Realtors by Ballinger Pub. Co., c1977. 642p. (HD1387; 333.332076 / 1. Real property – Valuation – Problems, exercises, etc. 2. Real estate business – Finance – Problems, exercises, etc.)

S   Gross, Jerome S. *Concise Desk Guide to Real Estate Practice and Procedure.* Englewood Cliffs, N.J.: Prentice-Hall, 1976. 300p. (HD1375; 658.9133333 / 1. Real estate business – Handbooks, manuals, etc. 2. Real estate business – United States – Handbooks, manuals, etc.)

S   Gross, Jerome S. *Encyclopedia of Real Estate Forms.* Englewood Cliffs, N.J.: Prentice-Hall, 1973. 458p. (KF568.1; 346.730437 / 1. Real property – United States – Forms. 2. Real estate business – United States – Forms.)

S   Gross, Jerome S. *Illustrated Encyclopedic Dictionary of Real Estate Terms.* Englewood Cliffs, N.J.: Prentice-Hall, 1969.

468p. (HD1375; 333.3303 / 1. Real estate business—Dictionaries.)

S   Harrison, Henry S. *Houses: The Illustrated Guide to
    Construction, Design, and Systems.* Chicago: National Institute of
    Real Estate Brokers of the National Association of Realtors, 1973.
    412p. (NA7110; 728.3 / 1. Architecture, Domestic—Handbooks,
    manuals, etc. 2. Building materials—Handbooks, manuals, etc.)

S   Johnsich, John Robert. *Modern Real Estate Dictionary.*
    San Francisco: Canfield Press, 1975. 261p. (HD1375; 333.33 / 1.
    Real estate business—Dictionaries.)

S   McMahan, John. *The McGraw-Hill Real Estate Pocket Guide:
    Up-to-Date Tables for the Real Estate Professional.* New York:
    McGraw-Hill, c1979. 283p. (HD1388; 333.33 / 1. Business
    mathematics—Real estate business—Tables.)

S   Prentice-Hall, Inc. *Encyclopedic Dictionary of Real
    Estate Practice.* Rev. and enl. Englewood Cliffs, N.J.: Prentice-Hall,
    1962. 533p. (HD1375; 333.3303 / 1. Real estate business—
    Dictionaries.)

SA *The Real Estate Handbook.* Ed. by Maury Seldin. Homewood,
    Ill.: Dow Jones–Irwin, c1980. 1186p. bibl. (HD255; 333.330202 / 1.
    Real estate business—United States—Handbooks, manuals, etc.)

S   Realtors National Marketing Institute. *Real Estate Sales
    Handbook.* 8th ed. Chicago: National Association of Realtors, 1979.
    221p. (HD1375; 333.330688 / 1. Real estate business—Handbooks,
    manuals, etc.)

S   Seward, Peter G., and Cantor, M. Catherine. *Manual for
    Lawyers and Legal Assistants: Real Estate.* 2d ed. Ann Arbor, Mich.:
    Institute of Continuing Legal Education, c1980. 476p. (KF570.Z9;
    346.73043 / 1. Real property—United States.)

S   United States. Bureau of the Census. *Housing Construction
    Statistics, 1889 to 1964.* Washington, D.C.: Government Printing
    Office, 1966. 805p. (HD7293; 338.4769080973 / 1. Housing—United
    States—Statistics. 2. Construction industry—United
    States—Statistics.)

S   United States. Bureau of the Census. *1970 Census of
    Housing.* Washington, D.C.: Government Printing Office, 1972. 7v.
    (HD7293; 301.5409791 / 1. Housing—United States—Statistics.)

Secretarial Science

With the exception of two source/access handbooks, the reference
works devoted to secretarial science are all source-type handbooks
that deal with correspondence and letter writing, office administration, and filing. But the resources available, and necessary to, the
modern secretary do not stop here. Today's secretary is frequently
asked to conduct research in almost any field, and so the student of
secretarial science should be aware that any and every tool listed in

this book may on occasion prove useful. Also, students who are preparing to work in a specific work setting such as a law or dental office should consult the appropriate sections in this book for other tools that will prove useful on the job.

S   Blumenthal, Lassor A. *The Complete Book of Personal Letter-Writing and Modern Correspondence.* Garden City, N.Y.: Doubleday, 1969. 313p. (PE1483; 808.6 / 1. Letter-writing.)

S   *The Dartnell Office Administration Handbook.* 4th- ed. Chicago: Dartnell, 1967- . v. (HF5547; 651 / 1. Office management – Periodicals.)

S   Doris, Lillian, and Miller, Besse May. *Complete Secretary's Handbook.* 4th ed. rev. by Mary A. De Vries. Englewood Cliffs, N.J.: Prentice-Hall, 1977. 555p. (HF5547.5; 651.4 / 1. Office practice – Handbooks, manuals, etc. 2. Secretaries – Handbooks, manuals, etc.)

S   *Encyclopedia of Business Letters in Four Languages.* New York: Arco, 1972. 3v. (____; 651.75 / 1. Commercial correspondence – Dictionaries – Polyglot. 2. Dictionaries – Polyglot.)

S   Hoffman, Herbert H. *Alphanumeric Filing Rules for Business Documents.* Santa Ana, Calif.: Hoffman, 1977. 118p. (HF5736; 651.53 / 1. Files and filing (Documents). 2. Alphabeting.)

SA Nanassy, Louis C.; Selden, William; and Lee, Jo Ann. *Reference Manual for Office Workers.* Beverly Hills, Calif: Glencoe Press, 1977. 348p. bibl. (HF5547.5; 651.4 / 1. Office practice – Handbooks, manuals, etc. 2. Secretaries – Handbooks, manuals, etc.)

S   *Office Management Handbook.* Ed. by Harry L. Wylie. 2d ed. New York: Ronald, 1958. 1v. in various pagings. (HF5547; 651 / 1. Office management.)

S   Parkhurst, Charles Chandler. *Business Communication for Better Human Relations.* 7th ed. Englewood Cliffs, N.J.: Prentice-Hall, 1966. 519p. (HF5721; 651.75 / 1. Commercial correspondence. 2. English language – Business English.)

SA Simpson, Marian G. *Tested Secretarial Techniques for Getting Things Done.* West Nyack, N.Y.: Parker, 1973. 220p. bibl. (HF5547.5; 651.3741 / 1. Secretaries – Handbooks, manuals, etc.)

S   Taintor, Sarah Augusta, and Monro, Kate M. *The Secretary's Handbook: A Manual of Correct Usage.* 9th ed. fully rev. by Kate M. Munro and Margaret D. Shertzer. New York: Macmillan, 1969. 530p. (HF5547; 651.74 / 1. Office practice.)

SA *Webster's Secretarial Handbook.* Anna L. Eckersley-Johnson, ed. Springfield, Mass.: Merriam, 1976. 550p. bibl. (HF5547.5; 651.4 / 1. Office practice – Handbooks, manuals, etc. 2. Secretaries – Handbooks, manuals, etc.)

PURE SCIENCES

In the field of science, the need for current, up-to-date information is critical, perhaps more so than in any other area of human endeavor. Thus, the two periodical indexes cited here will be of value to you regardless of your specialized major in the sciences, since they give you quick access to the latest literature on your topic. In this section you will also find listed several biographical sources, three yearbooks (which are often useful for a quick overview of recent developments), some dictionaries, a guide to writing scientific papers, three bibliographic guides, and a books in print for scientific and technical materials. You will also find citations for two encyclopedias, one of which is a major multivolume set, and, finally, an index to handbooks. Note that while there are no true handbooks listed here under "Pure Sciences," you will find them cited under the more specific subjects that follow, since they are widely used by both students and practicing scientists.

While you will probably be able to satisfy most of your information needs with the tools listed here and under the subjects that follow, you should be aware that many other reference sources exist for the science student. Chief among these are automated data-base searches as discussed in Chapter 2. Your librarian will be able to assist you in determining if such computerized searches would be necessary to you and where in your area they could be conducted if not in your own community college library.

S   *American Men and Women of Science.* Ed.12- . New York:
     Jaques Cattell Press/R. R. Bowker, 1971- . (Q141; 509.22 / 1. Scientists, American – Directories.)
A   *Applied Science and Technology Index.* New York: H. W.
     Wilson, 1913- . Monthly, except July. Quarterly and annual
     cumulations. (Z7913; 016.6 / 1. Engineering – Periodicals – Indexes.
     2. Technology – Periodicals – Indexes. 3. Industrial
     arts – Periodicals – Indexes.)
S   *Britannica Yearbook of Science and the Future.* 1969- .
     Chicago: Encyclopaedia Britannica, 1968- . Annual. (Q9; 505 / 1.
     Science – Yearbooks.)
A   *Composite Index for CRC Handbooks.* 2d ed. Cleveland:
     Chemical Rubber Co., 1977. 1111p. (QD65; 540.202 / 1.
     Chemistry – Handbooks, manuals, etc. – Indexes. 2.
     Mathematics – Handbooks, manuals, etc. – Indexes.)
S   Crispin, Frederic Swing. *Dictionary of Technical Terms.*
     11th ed., rev. New York: Bruce, 1970. 455p. (T9; 603 / 1.

Technology – Dictionaries.)

S   *Dictionary of Science and Technology.* Ed. T. C. Collocott.
New York: Barnes & Noble, 1972. 1328p. (Q123; 503 / 1.
Science – Dictionaries. 2. Technology – Dictionaries.)

SA   *Dictionary of Scientific Biography.* Charles Coulston
Gillispie, ed. in chief. New York: Scribner's, 1970–1976. 13v. bibl.
(Q141; 509.22 / 1. Scientists – Biography – Dictionaries.)

S   Elliott, Clark A. *Biographical Dictionary of American
Science: The Seventeenth Through the Nineteenth Centuries.* Westport,
Conn.: Greenwood Press, 1979. 360p. (Q141; 509.22 / 1. Scien-
tists – United States – Biography.)

A   *General Science Index.* v.1– , July 1978– . Bronx,
N.Y.: H. W. Wilson, 1978– . (____; ____)

A   Grogan, Denis Joseph. *Science and Technology: An
Introduction to the Literature.* 2d ed. rev. Hamden, Conn.: Linnet
Books, 1973. 254p. bibl. (Q223; 507 / 1. Scientific literature.)

S   Lapedes, Daniel N., ed. in chief. *McGraw-Hill Dictionary
of Scientific and Technical Terms.* 2d ed. New York: McGraw-Hill,
1978. 1771 p. (Q123; 503 / 1. Science – Dictionaries. 2.
Technology – Dictionaries.)

A   Malinowsky, Harold Robert; Gray, Richard A.; and Gray,
Dorothy A. *Science and Engineering Literature: A Guide to Reference
Sources.* 2d ed. Littleton, Colo.: Libraries Unlimited, c1976. 368p.
(Z7401; 016.5 / 1. Reference books – Science. 2.
Science – Bibliography. 3. Reference books – Engineering. 4.
Engineering – Bibliography.)

SA   *McGraw-Hill Encyclopedia of Science and Technology: An
International Reference Work.* Daniel N. Lapedes, ed. in chief. 4th
ed. New York: McGraw-Hill, 1977. 15v. bibl. (Q121; 503 / 1.
Science – Dictionaries. 2. Technology – Dictionaries.)

SA   *McGraw-Hill Yearbook of Science and Technology.* New York:
McGraw-Hill, 1962– . Annual. bibl. (Q1; 505.8 / 1. Science – Yearbooks. 2. Technology – Yearbooks.)

S   *Science Year: The World Book Science Annual.* Chicago:
Field Enterprises, 1965– . Annual. (Q9; 505 / 1. Science –
Yearbooks.)

A   *Scientific and Technical Books and Serials in Print.*
New York: R. R. Bowker, 1972– . Annual. (Z7401; 016.5 / 1.
Science – Indexes. 2. Engineering – Indexes. 3.
Technology – Indexes.)

SA   Trelease, Sam Farlow. *How to Write Scientific and
Technical Papers.* 3d ed. Baltimore: Williams and Wilkins, 1958.
185p. bibl. (PE1425; 808.060296 / 1. Authorship – Handbooks,
manuals, etc. 2. Technical writing.)

SA   *Van Nostrand's Scientific Encyclopedia.* Ed. by Douglas

M. Considine. 5th ed. New York: Van Nostrand Reinhold, 1976.
2370p. bibl. (Q121; 503 / 1. Science–Dictionaries.)
A   Walford, Albert John. *Guide to Reference Material.*
Volume 1: Science and Technology. 3d ed. London: Library Association, 1973. (Z1035.1; 011.02 / 1. Reference books–Bibliography.)

Astronomy

Of the various types of tools available to the astronomy student and
amateur astronomer, by far the most predominant is the handbook,
containing miscellaneous information on all aspects of the stars,
planets, and other heavenly phenomena. Besides the handbooks,
however, there are also several dictionaries, two encyclopedic source
tools, a yearbook, and a bibliographic guide, which will give you access to many other reference sources. Not listed here, but widely
regarded as an important source of astronomical information at the intermediate level, are the *Harvard Books on Astronomy.* The individual
works in this series, each devoted to a separate topic, may be accessed
under the series title in your library's catalog.

S   Callatäy, Vincent de, and Dollfus, Audouin. *Atlas of*
the Planets. Toronto: University of Toronto Press, 1974. 152p.
(QB601; 523.4 / 1. Planets.)
S   *The Cambridge Encyclopaedia of Astronomy.* Editor in
chief, Simon Mitton. New York: Crown, 1977. 481p. (QB43.2; 520
/ 1. Astronomy.)
S   *The Facts on File Dictionary of Astronomy.* Ed. by Valerie
Illingworth. New York: Facts on File, 1979. 378p. (QB14; 520.3 / 1.
Astronomy–Dictionaries.)
S   Flammarion, Camille. *Flammarion Book of Astronomy.* New
York: Simon & Schuster, 1964. 670p. (QB44; 523 / 1. Astronomy.)
S   Hopkins, Jeanne. *Glossary of Astronomy and Astrophysics.*
Chicago: University of Chicago Press, 1976. 169p. (QB14; 520.3 / 1.
Astronomy–Dictionaries. 2. Astrophysics–Dictionaries.)
SA   Howard, Neale E. *The Telescope Handbook and Star Atlas.*
Updated ed. New York: Crowell, 1975. 226p. bibl. (QB63;
523.00202 / 1. Astronomy–Observers' manuals.)
SA   Jackson, Joseph Hollister. *Pictorial Guide to the Planets.*
2d ed. New York: Crowell, 1973. 248p. bibl. (QB601; 523.4 / 1.
Planets.)
S   Moore, Patrick. *The Amateur Astronomer's Glossary.* London:
Butterworth; New York: W. W. Norton, 1967. 162p. (QB14; 520.3 /
1. Astronomy–Dictionaries.)
S   Moore, Patrick. *The A-Z of Astronomy.* Rev. ed. New

York: Scribner's, 1976. 192p. (QB14; 520.3 / 1. Astronomy –
Dictionaries.)

S Moore, Patrick. *The Concise Atlas of the Universe*. Completely
rev. New York; Chicago: Rand McNally, 1978. 190p. (QB44.2; 523
/ 1. Astronomy – Popular works.)

S Murdin, Paul, and Allen, David. *Catalog of the Universe*.
New York: Crown, 1979. 256p. (QB44.2; 523 / 1.
Astronomy – Popular works. 2. Astronomy – Pictorial works.)

S Norton, Arthur Philip. *Star Atlas and Reference
Handbook (Epoch 1950) for Students and Astronomers*. 15th ed. The
reference handbook by J. Gall Inglis and A. P. Norton, and ed. by
R.M.G. Inglis. Cambridge, Mass.: Sky Publishing Corp., 1964. 57p.
(QB65; 523.89 / 1. Stars – Atlases.)

S Robinson, J. Hedley, and Muirden, James. *Astronomy Data
Book*. 2d ed. New York: Wiley, c1979. 272p. (QB64; 523 / 1.
Astronomy – Observers' manuals.)

SA Roth, Günter Dietmar, ed. *Astronomy: A Handbook*. Rev. ed.
by Arthur Beer. New York: Springer-Verlag, 1975. 567p. bibl.
(QB64; 520 / 1. Astronomy – Handbooks, manuals, etc.)

A Seal, Robert A. *A Guide to the Literature of Astronomy*.
Littleton, Colo.: Libraries Unlimited, 1977. 306p. bibl. (Z5151;
016.52 / 1. Astronomy – Bibliography.)

S United States. Aeronautical Chart and Information Center,
St. Louis. *The Times Atlas of the Moon*. Ed. by H.A.G. Lewis. London: Times, 1969. 110p. (QB595; 523.39 / 1. Moon – Maps.)

S Wallenquist, Åke. *Dictionary of Astronomical Terms*.
Edited and translated from the Swedish by Sune Engelbrektson.
Garden City, N.Y.: Natural History Press, 1966. 265p. (QB14;
520.3 / 1. Astronomy – Dictionaries.)

S Weigert, A., and Zimmerman, H. *Concise Encyclopedia
of Astronomy*. 2d English ed. London: Adam Hilger, 1976, c1975.
532p. (QB14; 520.3 / 1. Astronomy – Dictionaries.)

SA *Yearbook of Astronomy*. New York: W. W. Norton, 1962– . Annual.
bibl. (QB1; 523.058 / 1. Astronomy – Yearbooks.)

Biology

The tools listed in this section cover a variety of topics that fall
roughly into the domain of biology, everything from natural history
and zoology to biochemistry and genetics. You will also find two encyclopedic sources devoted to animal life as well as a reference source
on microscopy (i.e., the use of the microscope as a scientific tool in
biology). As to types of tools, you will find the usual variety, from dictionaries and a periodical index to bibliographic guides. Note that you

may also find useful tools listed later on in this chapter under "Animal Science" and "Horticulture."

S   Abercrombie, Michael; Hickman, C. J.; and Johnson, M. L.
     A Dictionary of Biology. 6th ed. Baltimore: Penguin, 1973. 306p.
     (QH13; 574.03 / 1. Biology – Dictionaries.)
SA   Altman, Philip L., and Bittmer, Dorothy S., comps. and eds.
     Biology Data Book. 2d ed. Bethesda, Md.: Federation of American
     Societies for Experimental Biology, 1974. 3v. bibl. (QH310;
     574.0212 / 1. Biology – Handbooks, manuals, etc.)
A   *Biological & Agricultural Index: A Cumulative Subject
     Index to Periodicals in the Fields of Biology, Agriculture, and Related
     Sciences.* v.50- , 1964- . New York: H. W. Wilson, 1964- .
     Monthly, except August. Annual cumulations. Continues
     Agricultural Index. (Z5073; 016.57405 / 1.
     Agriculture – Periodicals – Indexes. 2.
     Agriculture – Bibliography – Periodicals. 3.
     Biology – Periodicals – Indexes. 4.
     Biology – Bibliography – Periodicals.)
S   *A Dictionary of Life Sciences.* Edited by E. A. Martin.
     New York: Pica Press, 1977. 374p. (QH302.5; 574.03 / 1.
     Biology – Dictionaries.)
SA   Gray, Peter. *The Dictionary of the Biological Sciences.*
     New York: Reinhold, 1967. 602p. bibl. (QH13; 574.03 / 1.
     Biology – Dictionaries.)
SA   Gray, Peter. *The Encyclopedia of Microscopy and Microtechnique.*
     New York: Van Nostrand, 1973. 638p. bibl. (QH203; 502.8 / 1.
     Microscope and microscopy – Technique – Dictionaries.)
S   Gray, Peter. *Student Dictionary of Biology.* New York:
     Van Nostrand Reinhold, 1973. 194p. (QH13; 574.03 / 1.
     Biology – Dictionaries.)
SA   Gray, Peter, ed. *The Encyclopedia of the Biological
     Sciences.* 2d ed. New York: Van Nostrand Reinhold, 1970. 1027p.
     bibl. (QH13; 574.03 / 1. Biology – Dictionaries.)
SA   Grzimek, Bernhard. *Grzimek's Animal Life Encyclopedia.*
     New York: Van Nostrand Reinhold, 1972-1975. 13v. bibl. (QL3;
     591 / 1. Zoology – Collected works.)
SA   King, Robert C. *A Dictionary of Genetics.* 2d ed., rev.
     New York: Oxford University Press, 1974. 375p. bibl. (QH427;
     575.103 / 1. Genetics – Dictionaries.)
A   Kirk, Thomas G., Jr. *Library Research Guide to Biology:
     Illustrated Search Strategy and Sources.* Ann Arbor, Mich.: Pierian
     Press, 1978. 84p. (QH315; 574.07 / 1. Biological research – Hand-
     books, manuals, etc. 2. Biology – Bibliography. 3. Reference
     books – Biology.)

SA   *Larousse Encyclopedia of Animal Life.* New York: McGraw-Hill,
       1967. 640p. bibl. (QL50; 591 / 1. Zoology.)

S   *McGraw-Hill Dictionary of the Life Sciences.* Daniel N.
       Lapedes, ed. in chief. New York: McGraw-Hill, 1976. 907p.
       (QH302.5; 570.3 / 1. Life sciences – Dictionaries. 2. Biology – Dic-
       tionaries. 3. Science – Dictionaries.)

S   Palmer, E. Laurence. *Fieldbook of Natural History.* 2d
       ed. Rev. by H. Seymour Fowler. New York: McGraw-Hill, c1975.
       779p. (QH45.2; 500.9 / 1. Natural history.)

S   Pennak, Robert William. *Collegiate Dictionary of Zoology.*
       New York: Ronald, 1964. 583p. (QL9; 590.3 / 1. Zoology –
       Dictionaries.)

A   Smith, Roger Cletus, and Reid, W. Malcolm. *Guide to the*
       Literature of the Life Sciences. 8th ed. Minneapolis: Burgess, 1972.
       166p. (Z5320; 016.574 / 1. Biology – Bibliography.)

S   Williams, Roger John, and Lansford, Edwin M. *The*
       Encyclopedia of Biochemistry. New York: Reinhold, 1967. 876p. bibl.
       (QP512; 574.19203 / 1. Biological chemistry – Dictionaries.)

Chemistry

The tools listed here for chemistry include some dictionaries, two
encyclopedic sources, a biographical source, and then a number of
ready-reference handbooks for the practicing chemist or the
chemistry student. Note that one of the handbooks is expressly
designed to assist the technician in using chemicals and performing
experiments in a laboratory setting. Finally, there are two
bibliographic guides listed that will lead you to other sources of information.

A   Antony, Arthur. *Guide to Basic Information Sources in*
       Chemistry. New York: J. Norton Publishers, c1979. 219p. (QD8.5;
       540.7 / 1. Chemical literature.)

S   Chen, Philip S. *A New Handbook of Chemistry.* Camarillo,
       Calif.: Chemical Elements, 1975. 212p. (QD65; 540 / 1.
       Chemistry – Handbooks, manuals, etc.)

S   *The Condensed Chemical Dictionary.* 9th ed. Rev. by
       Gessner G. Hawley. New York: Van Nostrand Reinhold, 1977.
       971p. (QD5; 540.3 / 1. Chemistry – Dictionaries.)

SA   *The Encyclopedia of Chemistry.* Ed. by Clifford A. Hampel
       and Gessner G. Hawley. 3d ed. New York: Van Nostrand
       Reinhold, 1973. 1198p. bibl. (QD5; 540.3 / 1. Chemistry –
       Dictionaries.)

SA   Farber, Eduard. *Great Chemists.* New York: Interscience, c1961. 1642p. bibl. (QD21; 925.4 / 1. Chemists.)

SA   Gordon, Arnold J., and Ford, Richard A. *The Chemist's
      Companion: A Handbook of Practical Data, Techniques, and
      References.* New York: Wiley, 1972. 537p. bibl. (QD65; 542 / 1.
      Chemistry – Handbooks, manuals, etc.)

S   Hampel, Clifford A., and Hawley, Gessner G. *Glossary of
      Chemical Terms.* New York: Van Nostrand Reinhold, 1976. 281p.
      (QD5; 540.3 / 1. Chemistry – Dictionaries.)

S   *Handbook of Chemistry and Physics: A Ready-Reference
      Book of Chemical and Physical Data.* Ed.1- . Cleveland: Chemical
      Rubber Co., 1913- . Irregular. (QD65; 541.9 / 1.
      Chemistry – Tables. 2. Physics – Tables.)

S   *International Encyclopedia of Chemical Science.* Princeton:
      Van Nostrand, 1964. 1331p. (QD5; 540.3 / 1. Chemistry –
      Dictionaries.)

S   Lange, Norbert Adolph. *Lange's Handbook of Chemistry.*
      Editor, John A. Dean. 11th ed. New York: McGraw-Hill, 1973. 1v.
      in various pagings. (QD65; 540 / 1. Chemistry – Handbooks,
      manuals, etc.)

A   Maizell, Robert E. *How to Find Chemical Information:
      A Guide for Practicing Chemists, Teachers, and Students.* New York:
      Wiley, 1979. 261p. (QD8.5; 540.7 / 1. Chemical literature.)

SA   *Merck Index: An Encyclopedia of Chemicals and Drugs.*
      9th ed. Martha Windholz, ed. Rahway, N.J.: Merck, 1976. 1835p.
      bibl. (RS51; 615.103 / 1. Drugs – Dictionaries. 2. Chemicals –
      Dictionaries.)

S   Miall, Laurence Mackenzie, and Sharp, D.W.A. *A New
      Dictionary of Chemistry.* 4th ed. New York: Wiley, 1968. (QD5;
      540.03 / 1. Chemistry – Dictionaries.)

S   Shugar, Gershon J.; Shugar, Ronald A.; and Bauman, Lawrence.
      Chemical Technicians' Ready Reference Handbook. New York:
      McGraw-Hill, 1973. 463p. (QD61; 542 / 1. Chemistry – Manipula-
      tion – Handbooks, manuals, etc.)

S   Strauss, Howard J. *Handbook for Chemical Technicians.* New
      York: McGraw-Hill, 1976. 455p. (TP151; 542 / 1. Chemistry,
      Technical – Handbooks, manuals, etc.)

Computer Science

The tools listed here under computer science also cover the related
fields of information science and data processing. Several dictionaries
and encyclopedic sources are listed, as well as a yearbook and handbook. Keep in mind that both computer hardware and software are
continually evolving and so reference sources can date quickly. Also
note that many useful tools may be found by looking under the ap-

propriate subject headings for specific programming languages such as FORTRAN or BASIC.

S   Chandor, Anthony; Graham, John; and Williamson, Robin.
    Dictionary of Computers. 2d ed. New York: Penguin, 1977. 440p.
    (QA76.15; 001.6403 / 1. Electronic data processing–Dictionaries. 2.
    Electronic digital computers–Dictionaries.)

S   *Computer Yearbook.* Detroit: International Electronics
    Information Services, 1972– . Irregular. Continues *Computer Year-*
    book and Directory. (QA76; 001.6405510 / 1. Electronic data pro-
    cessing–Yearbooks. 2. Computers–Yearbooks. 3. Electronic data
    processing–Directories. 4. Computers–Directories.)

SA   *Encyclopedia of Computer Science.* Anthony Ralston, ed.
    New York: Petrocelli/Charter, 1976. 1523p. bibl. (QA76.15;
    001.6403 / 1. Computers–Dictionaries. 2. Electronic data process-
    ing–Dictionaries. 3. Information science–Dictionaries.)

SA   *Encyclopedia of Computer Science and Technology.* New
    York: Marcel Dekker, 1975– , v.1– . bibl. (QA76.15; 001.6403 / 1.
    Computers–Dictionaries.)

SA   Greenstein, Carol Horn. *Dictionary of Logical Terms and*
    Symbols. New York: Van Nostrand Reinhold, 1978. 188p. bibl.
    (QA9; 511.303 / 1. Logic, Symbolic and mathematical–
    Dictionaries.)

SA   Jordain, Philip B., and Breslau, Michael. *Condensed*
    Computer Encyclopedia. New York: McGraw-Hill, 1969. 605p. bibl.
    (QA76.15; 651.803 / 1. Computers–Dictionaries.)

SA   Laird, Eleanor S. *Data Processing Secretary's Complete*
    Handbook. West Nyack, N.Y.: Parker, 1973. 240p. bibl. (HF5547.5;
    651.3741 / 1. Secretaries–Handbooks, manuals, etc. 2.
    Business–Data processing.)

S   Maynard, Jeff. *Dictionary of Data Processing.* London:
    Newnes-Butterworths, 1975. 269p. (QA76.15; 001.6403 / 1. Elec-
    tronic data processing–Dictionaries.)

S   Prenis, John. *Running Press Glossary of Computer Terms.*
    Philadelphia: Running Press, 1977. 86p. (QA76.15; 001.6403 / 1.
    Electronic data processing–Dictionaries. 2. Computers–
    Dictionaries.)

S   Schmalz, Larry C., and Sippl, Charles J. *Computer Glossary*
    for Students and Teachers. Newport Beach, Calif.: Newport Com-
    puter Information, 1972. 248p. (QA76.15; 001.6403 / 1. Electronic
    data processing–Dictionaries.)

S   Sippl, Charles J., and Sippl, Charles P. *Computer Dictionary*
    and Handbook. 2d ed. Indianapolis, Ind.: Sams, 1972. 778p.
    (QA76.15; 001.6403 / 1. Computers–Dictionaries. 2. Electronic
    data processing–Dictionaries.)

S   Van Amerongen, C. *The Way Things Work Book of the Computer:*

      An Illustrated Encyclopedia of Science, Cybernetics, and Data Processing. New York: Simon & Schuster, 1974. 245p. (Q315;001.53 / 1. Cybernetics. 2. Information theory. 3. Computers.)

SA   Weik, Martin H. *Standard Dictionary of Computers and Information Processing.* Rev. 2d ed. Rochelle Park, N.J.: Hayden Book Co., 1977. 390p. bibl. (QA76.15; 001.6403 / 1. Electronic data processing – Dictionaries. 2. Electronic digital computers – Dictionaries.)

Earth Sciences

    In the field of earth sciences or geology, several interesting reference sources are available. There are four dictionaries of specialized terms, an annual, and even two atlases depicting various features of the physical world. Besides these, there are also five encyclopedic sources, two of which are general in scope; the other three are devoted to different aspects of the earth: rivers and lakes, mountains, and oceans and islands. Although one of the encyclopedias deals with oceans, note that there are other more specific tools listed in this chapter under "Oceanography."

S   American Geological Institute. *Dictionary of Geological Terms.* Rev. ed. Garden City, N.Y.: Anchor Press/Doubleday, 1976. 472p. (QE5; 550.3 / 1. Geology – Dictionaries.)

S   *Annual Review of Earth and Planetary Sciences.* Palo Alto, Calif.: Annual Reviews, 1973- , v.1- . Annual. (QE1; 550.5 / 1. Earth sciences – Periodicals. 2. Planets – Periodicals.)

S   Challinor, John. *A Dictionary of Geology.* 5th ed. Cardiff: University of Wales Press. 1978. 365p. (QE5; 550.3 / 1. Geology – Dictionaries.)

SA   Gary, Margaret; McAfee, Robert; and Wolf, Carol L. *Glossary of Geology.* Washington, D.C.: American Geological Institute, 1973, c1972. 872p. bibl. (QE5; 550.3 / 1. Geology – Dictionaries.)

S   Gresswell, R. Kay, and Huxley, Anthony Julian. *Standard Encyclopedia of the World's Rivers and Lakes.* New York: G. P. Putnam's, c1965. 384p. (GB1203; 910.091693 / 1. Rivers – Dictionaries. 2. Lakes – Dictionaries.)

S   Huxley, Anthony Julian. *Standard Encyclopedia of the World's Mountains.* New York: G. P. Putnam's, 1962. 383p. (GB501; 551.4303 / 1. Mountains. 2. Mountaineering.)

SA   Huxley, Anthony Julian. *Standard Encyclopedia of the World's Oceans and Islands.* New York: G. P. Putnam's, 1962. 383p. bibl. (GB471; 910.3 / 1. Islands. 2. Oceans.)

S   *McGraw-Hill Encyclopedia of the Geological Sciences.*

Daniel N. Lapedes, ed. in chief. New York: McGraw-Hill, 1978.
915p. (QE5; 550.3 / 1. Geology – Dictionaries.)

S   Nelson, Archibald, and Nelson, Kenneth Davies. *Dictionary of Applied Geology: Mining and Civil Engineering.* New York: Philosophical Library, 1967. 421p. (QE5; 550.3 / 1. Geology – Dictionaries. 2. Mining engineering – Dictionaries. 3. Civil engineering – Dictionaries.)

SA   *Our Magnificent Earth: A Rand McNally Atlas of Earth Resources.* New York: Rand McNally, 1979. 208p. bibl. (G1046.G3; ___ / 1. Atlases. 2. Natural resources – Atlases.)

S   *The Planet We Live On: Illustrated Encyclopedia of the Earth Sciences.* Ed. by Cornelius S. Hurlbut, Jr. New York: Abrams, 1976. 527p. (QE5; 550.3 / 1. Earth sciences – Dictionaries.)

SA   United States. Military Academy, West Point. Department of Earth, Space, and Graphic Sciences. *Atlas of Landforms.* 2d ed. Ed. by H. Allen Curran [and others]. New York: Wiley, 1974. 140p. bibl. (G1046.C2; 912.15514 / 1. Landforms – Maps.)

Ecology

The student of ecology has a variety of tools available, only a few of which are listed here. There are handbooks, dictionaries, encyclopedic sources, an annual, a directory, and even two miscellaneous source tools similar to almanacs. As you scan the titles listed here, you will notice that some works deal with other closely related aspects of the subject, such as energy, environmental studies, pollution, and even environmental engineering. In truth, many more resources are available, some of which are devoted to very specific topics such as solar energy or noise pollution. These tools may be found by looking under the authorized subject headings in your library's catalog. Also keep in mind that the whole broad field of ecology continues to expand and many new reference works are published each year.

S   Allaby, Michael. *A Dictionary of the Environment.* New York: Van Nostrand Reinhold, 1977. 532p. (QH540.4; 301.3103 / 1. Ecology – Dictionaries. 2. Natural history – Dictionaries.)

S   *Annual Review of Ecology and Systematics.* Palo Alto, Calif.: Annual Reviews, 1970- , v.1- . Annual. (QH540; ___ / 1. Ecology – Periodicals. 2. Biology – Classification – Periodicals.)

A   Burke, John Gordon, and Reddig, Jill Swanson. *Guide to Ecology Information and Organizations.* New York: H. W. Wilson, 1976. 292p. (Z5861; 016.30131 / 1. Human ecology – Bibliography. 2. Human ecology – Directories. 3. Ecology – Bibliography. 4.

Ecology – Directories. 5. Environmental protection – Bibliography.
6. Environmental protection – Directories.)

S   Durrenberger, Robert W., comp. *Dictionary of the Environmental
       Sciences.* Palo Alto, Calif.: National Press Books, 1973. 282p. (QE5;
       550.3 / 1. Earth sciences – Dictionaries. 2. Natural resources – Dic-
       tionaries. 3. Natural history – Dictionaries.)

SA   *Encyclopedia of Environmental Science and Engineering.*
       Eds., James R. Pfafflin and Edward N. Ziegler. New York: Gordon
       and Breach, 1976. 2v. bibl. (TD9; 628.5 / 1. Environmental
       engineering – Dictionaries.)

SA   *The Energy Source Book.* Alexander McRae and Janice L.
       Dudas, eds. Germantown, Md.: Aspen Systems, 1977. 724p. bibl.
       (TJ163.25.U6; 333.7 / 1. Power resources – United States. 2. Energy
       policy – United States.)

SA   *Energy Technology Handbook.* Douglas M. Considine, ed. in
       chief. New York: McGraw-Hill, 1977. 1884p. bibl. (TJ163.9; 621 /
       1. Power (Mechanics) – Handbooks, manuals, etc. 2. Power
       resources – Handbooks, manuals, etc.)

SA   *Environmental Engineers' Handbook.* Béla G. Lipták, ed.
       Radnor, Pa.: Chilton, 1973–1974. 3v. bibl. (TD145; 628 / 1. En-
       vironmental engineering – Handbooks, manuals, etc. 2. Pollu-
       tion – Handbooks, manuals, etc.)

SA   *Grzimek's Encyclopedia of Ecology.* Bernhard Grzimek,
       ed. in chief. New York: Van Nostrand Reinhold, c1976. 705p. bibl.
       (QH541; 574.503 / 1. Ecology.)

SA   Holum, John R. *Topics and Terms in Environmental Problems.*
       New York: Wiley, c1977. 729p. bibl. (TD173; 363.6 / 1. Pollu-
       tion – Dictionaries. 2. Man – Influence on nature – Dictionaries. 3.
       Environmental protection – Dictionaries.)

SA   Hunt, V. Daniel. *Energy Dictionary.* New York: Van
       Nostrand Reinhold, c1979. 518p. bibl. (TJ163.2; 621 / 1. Power
       resources – Dictionaries. 2. Power (Mechanics) – Dictionaries.)

SA   Lewis, Walter H. *Ecology Field Glossary: A Naturalist's
       Vocabulary.* Westport, Conn.: Greenwood Press, 1977. 152p. bibl.
       (QH540.4; 574.5014 / 1. Ecology – Dictionaries. 2. Natural
       history – Dictionaries.)

SA   Loftness, Robert L. *Energy Handbook.* New York: Van
       Nostrand Reinhold, c1978. 741p. bibl. (TJ163.2; 333.7 / 1. Power
       resources – Handbooks, manuals, etc. 2. Power (Mechanics) – Hand-
       books, manuals, etc. 3. Environmental protection – Handbooks,
       manuals, etc.)

SA   *McGraw-Hill Encyclopedia of Energy.* Sybil P. Parker,
       ed. in chief. 2d ed. New York: McGraw-Hill, 1980. 840p. bibl.
       (TJ163.2; 333.790321 / 1. Power resources – Dictionaries. 2. Power
       (Mechanics) – Dictionaries.)

SA   *McGraw-Hill Encyclopedia of Environmental Science.* Sybil

P. Parker, ed. in chief. 2d ed. New York: McGraw-Hill, c1980.
754p. bibl. (QH540.4; 304.203 / 1. Ecology–Dictionaries. 2.
Man–Influence on nature–Dictionaries. 3. Environmental protection–Dictionaries.)

SA Onyx Group, Inc. *Environment U.S.A.: A Guide to Agencies,*
People, and Resources. Comp. and ed. by the Onyx Group. Glenn L.
Paulson, advisory ed. New York: R. R. Bowker, 1974. 451p. bibl.
(TD171; 333.7202573 / 1. Environmental protection–United
States–Directories. 2. Conservation of natural resources–United
States–Directories.)

A *Sourcebook on the Environment: A Guide to the Literature.*
Ed. by Kenneth A. Hammond, George Macinko, and Wilma B.
Fairchild. Chicago: University of Chicago Press, 1978. 613p.
(Z5861; 016.30131 / 1. Human ecology–Bibliography. 2. En-
vironmental protection–Bibliography.)

SA United States. Library of Congress. Science Policy
Research Division. *Energy Facts.* Prepared for the Subcommittee on
Energy of the Committee on Science and Astronautics, U.S. House
of Representatives. Washington, D.C.: Government Printing Office,
1973. 539p. bibl. (HD9545; 333.70973 / 1. Power resources–United
States.)

S *The World Energy Book: An A-Z, Atlas, and Statistical*
Source Book. Consultant eds. and principal contributors, David
Crabbe and Richard McBride. Cambridge, Mass.: MIT Press, 1979,
c1978. 259p. (HD9502.A2; 333.7 / 1. Energy policy–Dictionaries.
2. Power resources–Dictionaries. 3. Power resources–Statistics.)

Mathematics

The mathematics student can turn to the library's reference collection and find a number of types of reference tools available. At the
community college level, the most useful resources are the handbooks, books of mathematical tables and formulas, and dictionaries of
specialized terms. The more advanced student will also want to take
advantage of the bibliographic guides cited in this section since they
will note what other, more specialized tools exist.

SA Assaf, Karen, and Assaf, Said A. *Handbook of Mathematical*
Calculations for Science Students and Researchers. Ames: Iowa State
University Press, 1974. 309p. bibl. (QA40; 510.202 / 1.
Mathematics–Handbooks, manuals, etc.)

S Burington, Richard Stevens. *Handbook of Mathematical*
Tables and Formulas. 5th ed. New York: McGraw-Hill, 1973. 500p.
(QA47; 510.83 / 1. Mathematics–Tables, etc.)

SA *CRC Handbook of Mathematical Sciences.* Ed. by William

H. Beyer. 5th ed. West Palm Beach, Fla.: CRC Press, c1978. 982p.
bibl. (QA47; 510.212 / 1. Mathematics–Tables.)

S   Grazda, Edward E., ed. *Handbook of Applied Mathematics.*
Morris Brenner and William R. Minrath, associate eds. 4th ed.
Princeton: Van Nostrand, 1966. 1119p. (TA330; 510.0202 / 1.
Engineering mathematics. 2. Shop mathematics. 3. Business
mathematics.)

SA   Karush, William. *The Crescent Dictionary of Mathematics.*
Oscar Tarov, general ed. New York: Macmillan, 1962. 313p. bibl.
(QA5; 510.3 / 1. Mathematics–Dictionaries.)

SA   Merritt, Frederick S. *Mathematics Manual: Methods and
Principles of the Various Branches of Mathematics for Reference, Prob-
lem Solving, and Review.* New York: McGraw-Hill, 1962. 378p. bibl.
(QA40; 510.2 / 1. Mathematics–Handbooks, manuals, etc.)

S   Millington, T. Alaric, and Millington, William. *Dictionary
of Mathematics.* New York: Barnes & Noble, 1971, c1966. 259p.
(QA5; 510.3 / 1. Mathematics–Dictionaries.)

SA   Nihon Sūgakkai. *Encyclopedic Dictionary of Mathematics.*
By the Mathematical Society of Japan. Cambridge, Mass.: MIT
Press, 1977. 2v. bibl. (QA5; 510.3 / 1. Mathematics–Dictionaries.)

A   Parke, Nathan Grier. *Guide to the Literature of
Mathematics and Physics Including Related Works on Engineering
Science.* 2d rev. ed. New York: Dover, 1958. 436p. (Z6651; 016.51 /
1. Mathematics–Bibliography. 2. Physics–Bibliography. 3.
Engineering–Bibliography.)

SA   Schaefer, Barbara Kirsch. *Using the Mathematical
Literature: A Practical Guide.* New York: Dekker, c1979. 141p. bibl.
(QA41.7; 510.72 / 1. Mathematical literature.)

SA   Tuma, Jan J. *Engineering Mathematics Handbook:
Definitions, Theorems, Formulas, Tables.* 2d enl. and rev. ed. New
York: McGraw-Hill, c1979. 394p. bibl. (TA332; 510.212 / 1.
Engineering mathematics–Handbooks, manuals, etc.)

S   *Universal Encyclopedia of Mathematics.* Foreword by James
R. Newman. New York: Simon & Schuster, 1964. 715p. (QA5;
510.3 / 1. Mathematics–Dictionaries. 2. Mathematics–Formulae.
3. Mathematics–Tables, etc.)

S   *The VNR Concise Encyclopedia of Mathematics.* W. Gellert
and others, eds. New York: Van Nostrand Reinhold, 1977. 760p.
(QA40; 510.202 / 1. Mathematics–Handbooks, manuals, etc.)

Oceanography

The oceanography student has a number of reference tools
available. The encyclopedic source tool predominates the list, but
there are also some atlases, two dictionaries, and a handbook. You
will notice that while no bibliographic guides are cited, there are some

source/access tools listed that include bibliographies with which you can expand your searching. Also note that the tools mentioned below deal not just with oceanography, but also with marine biology, marine resources, and even fisheries.

S   Barton, Robert. *Atlas of the Sea.* New York: John Day,
          1974. 128p. (GC21; 551.46 / 1. Oceanography. 2. Marine
          resources.)

SA   *CRC Handbook of Marine Science.* Cleveland: CRC Press,
          1976- . v. bibl. (GC24; 551.46008 / 1. Oceanography—Handbooks,
          manuals, etc. 2. Marine biology—Handbooks, manuals, etc. 3.
          Ocean engineering—Handbooks, manuals, etc.)

SA   Fairbridge, Rhodes Whitmore. *The Encyclopedia of
          Oceanography.* New York: Reinhold, 1966. 1021p. bibl. (GC9;
          551.46003 / 1. Oceanography—Dictionaries.)

SA   Firth, Frank E., ed. *The Encyclopedia of Marine Resources.*
          New York: Van Nostrand Reinhold, 1969. 740p. bibl. (SH201;
          551.46003 / 1. Fisheries—Dictionaries. 2. Marine resources—
          Dictionaries.)

S   Food and Agricultural Organization of the United Nations.
          Department of Fisheries. *Atlas of the Living Resources of the Sea.*
          Rome: FAO; New York: Unipub, 1972. 1v. in various pagings.
          (G2801.L1; 912.157492 / 1. Marine resources—Maps.)

S   Groves, Donald G., and Hunt, Lee M. *Ocean World Encyclopedia.*
          New York: McGraw-Hill, c1980. 443p. (GC9; 551.46003 / 1.
          Oceanography—Dictionaries.)

SA   Hunt, Lee M., and Groves, Donald G., eds. *A Glossary
          of Ocean Science and Undersea Technology Terms.* Arlington, Va.:
          Compass Publications, 1965. 173p. bibl. (GC9; 551.46 / 1.
          Oceanography—Dictionaries.)

SA   *McGraw-Hill Encyclopedia of Ocean and Atmospheric Sciences.*
          Ed. by Sybil P. Parker. New York: McGraw-Hill, 1980. 580p. bibl.
          (GC9; 551.46003 / 1. Oceanography—Dictionaries. 2. At-
          mosphere—Dictionaries.)

S   *The Rand McNally Atlas of the Oceans.* New York: Rand
          McNally, 1977. 208p. (G2800; 912.155146 / 1.
          Oceanography—Maps.)

S   Tver, David F. *Ocean and Marine Dictionary.* Centreville,
          Md.: Cornell Maritime Press, 1979. 358p. (GC9; 551.46003 / 1.
          Oceanography—Dictionaries. 2. Marine engineering—Dictionaries.
          3. Marine biology—Dictionaries.)

Physics

The dictionary of specialized terms predominates the list of tools for the physics student. But there is also an encyclopedic source, a handbook, a book of physics and mathematical formulas, and even a bibliographic guide that will give you access to many other tools not listed here. Because physics is closely related to mathematics, you should also consult that section in this chapter to find other tools – particularly books of tables and formulas – of interest to you.

SA   Besançon, Robert M., ed. *The Encyclopedia of Physics.*
      2d ed. New York: Van Nostrand Reinhold, 1974. 1067p. bibl.
      (QC5; 530.03 / 1. Physics – Dictionaries.)

SA   Condon, Edward Uhler, and Odishaw, Hugh. *Handbook of
      Physics.* 2d ed. New York: McGraw-Hill, 1967. 1v. in various pag-
      ings. bibl. (QC21; 530 / 1. Physics.)

SA   Gray, Harold James, and Isaacs, Alan, eds. *A New
      Dictionary of Physics.* 2d ed. New York: Longman, 1975. 619p. bibl.
      (QC5; 530.03 / 1. Physics – Dictionaries.)

S   *McGraw-Hill Dictionary of Physics and Mathematics.* Daniel
      N. Lapedes, ed. in chief. New York: McGraw-Hill, 1978. 1074p.
      (QC5; 530.03 / 1. Physics – Dictionaries. 2. Mathematics – Dic-
      tionaries. 3. Science – Dictionaries.)

SA   Menzel, Donald Howard, ed. *Fundamental Formulas of Physics.*
      New York: Dover, 1960. 2v. bibl. (QA401; 530.15 / 1.
      Mathematical physics. 2. Mathematics – Formulas.)

S   *The Penguin Dictionary of Physics.* Valerie H. Pitt, ed.
      New York: Penguin, 1977. 428p. (QC5; 530.03 / 1. Physics –
      Dictionaries.)

S   Thewlis, James. *Concise Dictionary of Physics and Related Subjects.*
      2d ed., rev. and enl. Oxford: Pergamon, 1979. 370p. (QC5; 530.03 /
      1. Physics – Dictionaries.)

A   Whitford, Robert Henry. *Physics Literature: A Reference
      Manual.* 2d ed. Metuchen, N.J.: Scarecrow, 1968. 272p. (Z7141;
      016.53 / 1. Physics – Bibliography. 2. Physics – Study and teaching.)

HEALTH SCIENCES AND OCCUPATIONS

Health care professionals have long recognized the critical need for up-to-date medical and technical information, so it is not surprising that most students majoring in one of the health-related fields are enthusiastic and intelligent library users. What many beginning students are surprised to learn is that so many reference works are available to them. Besides the large number cited below, there are tools listed under the specific subject areas such as dental assisting, respiratory therapy, or nursing.

Regardless of whether you're majoring in paramedical studies, radiologic technology, or even medical-record technology, you will find most of the tools cited in this section to be useful. Listed below is everything from handbooks on diagnosis and atlases of anatomy to works on pharmacology and dictionaries of abbreviations. There are also bibliographic guides, an important index to health literature, some guides to the fields in health science, and even works on microbiology and physiology.

While you will occasionally find some dated materials listed here and under the more specific subjects within the health sciences, most of the works listed are likely to have been recently published. As in the pure sciences, current information is all important, so you should always make a point of consulting your library's catalog – or a reference librarian – to learn what new publications are available.

A   *Allied Health Education Directory.* Ed.1- . Chicago: Council on Medical Education, American Medical Association, 1971- . Annual. (RC745; 613.071 / 1. Paramedical education – United States – Directories.)

SA   American Hospital Association. *American Hospital Association Guide to the Health Care Field.* Chicago: American Hospital Association, 1972- . Annual. (RA977.A1; 362.11025 / 1. American Hospital Association – Yearbooks. 2. Hospitals – Directories – Yearbooks. 3. Hospitals – United States – Directories – Yearbooks. 4. Medical societies, etc. – Yearbooks. 5. Medical supplies – Directories – Yearbooks.)

SA   Berger, Karen J., and Fields, Willa L. *Pocket Guide to Health Assessment.* Reston, Va.: Reston, c1980. 146p. bibl. (RC76; 616.075 / 1. Physical diagnosis – Outlines, syllabi, etc. 2. Medical history taking – Outlines, syllabi, etc.)

SA   Bernstein, Lewis; Bernstein, Rosalyn S.; and Dana, Richard H. *Interviewing: A Guide for Health Professionals.* 2d ed. New York: Appleton-Century-Crofts, 1974. 197p. bibl. (RC65; 610.19 / 1. Medical history taking. 2. Nurse-patient relations. 3. Physician-patient relations.)

A   Blake, John Ballard, and Roos, Charles. *Medical Reference Works, 1679-1966: A Selected Bibliography.* Chicago: Medical Library Association, 1967. 343p. And its *Supplement 1.* Compiled by Mary Virginia Clark. Chicago: Medical Library Association, 1970. 46p. And its *Supplement 2, 1969-1972.* Chicago: Medical Library Association, 1973. 174p. (Z6658; 016.61 / 1. Medicine – Bibliography.)

S   *Blakiston's Gould Medical Dictionary.* Chairman of the editorial board, Arthur Osol. 3d ed. New York: McGraw-Hill, 1972. 1828p. (R121; 610.3 / 1. Medicine – Dictionaries.)

A   *Bowker's Medical Books and Serials in Print: Subject*

     Index, Author Index, Title Index. New York: R. R. Bowker, 1972- .
     Annual. (Z6658; 016.61 / 1. Medicine – Indexes – Periodicals.)
S   Burton, Benjamin T. *Human Nutrition.* 3d ed. New York:
     McGraw-Hill, 1976. 530p. (QP141; 612.3 / 1. Nutrition. 2. Diet in
     disease.)
S   *Butterworth's Medical Dictionary.* Ed. by Arthur Salusbury
     MacNalty. 2d ed. Woburn, Mass.: Butterworth Publishers, 1978.
     1942p. (R121; 610.3 / 1. Medicine – Dictionaries.)
S   *Current Medical Diagnosis & Treatment.* Los Altos, Calif.:
     Lange Medical, 1974- . (RC71; 616.07505 / 1.
     Diagnosis – Periodicals. 2. Therapeutics – Periodicals.)
S   *Current Medical Information and Terminology.* 4th- ed.
     Chicago: American Medical Association, 1971- . Triennial. (____;
     ____ / 1. Medicine – Terminology. 2. Semiology. 3. Nosology.)
S   Davidson, Henry Alexander. *Guide to Medical Writing:*
     A Practical Manual for Physicians, Dentists, Nurses, Pharmacists.
     New York: Ronald, 1957. 338p. (R119; 808.06 / 1. Medical writing.)
A   *Directory of Medical Specialists.* 1st- ed. Chicago:
     Marquis Who's Who, 1940- . Biennial. (R712.A1; 610.922 / 1.
     Medicine – Specialities and specialists – Directories. 2. Physi-
     cians – United States – Directories.)
S   Dox, Ida; Melloni, Biagio; and Eisner, Gilbert M.
     Melloni's Illustrated Medical Dictionary. Baltimore: Williams &
     Wilkins, 1979. 530p. (R121; 610.3 / 1. Medicine – Dictionaries.)
SA   Dreisbach, Robert H. *Handbook of Poisoning: Diagnosis*
     and Treatment. 9th ed. Los Altos, Calif.: Lange Medical, 1977.
     559p. bibl. (RA1211; 615.900202 / 1. Toxicology – Handbooks,
     manuals, etc.)
SA   *Encyclopedia of Bioethics.* Warren T. Reich, ed. in chief.
     New York: Macmillan, Free Press, 1978. 4v. bibl. (QH332; 174.2 /
     1. Bioethics – Dictionaries. 2. Medical ethics – Dictionaries.)
S   Grant, John Charles Boileau. *Grant's Atlas of Anatomy.*
     7th ed. by James E. Anderson. Baltimore: Williams & Wilkins,
     1978. 1v. in various pagings. (QM25; 611.00222 / 1. Anatomy,
     Human – Atlases.)
SA   Gray, Henry. *Gray's Anatomy.* 35th ed. Philadelphia:
     W. B. Saunders, 1973. 1471p. bibl. (QM23.2; 611 / 1. Anatomy,
     Human.)
SA   *Handbook of Non-Prescription Drugs.* 6th ed. Washington,
     D.C.: American Pharmaceutical Association, 1979. 488p. bibl.
     (RM671.A1; 615.1 / 1. Drugs, Nonprescription – Handbooks,
     manuals, etc. 2. Therapeutics – Handbooks, manuals, etc.)
S   Hendin, David. *The World Almanac Whole Health Guide.*
     New York: New American Library, 1977. 266p. (RC81; 362.1 / 1.
     Medicine, Popular. 2. Medical personnel and patient. 3. Medical

care – United States. 4. Medicine – Information services – United
States – Directories.)

S   Hughes, Harold K. *Dictionary of Abbreviations in Medicine
and the Health Sciences.* Lexington, Mass.: Lexington Books, 1977.
313p. (R121; 610.148 / 1. Medicine – Abbreviations.)

A   *Index Medicus.* Washington, D.C.: National Library of
Medicine, 1960- , v.1- . Monthly with annual cumulations. Also
available from January 1970- , as *Abridged Index Medicus.* Annual
cumulation called *Cumulated Index Medicus.* Chicago: American
Medical Association, 1961- . Annual. (Z6660; 016.61 / 1.
Medicine – Periodicals – Indexes – Periodicals.)

S   *The Johns Hopkins Atlas of Human Functional Anatomy.* Text
ed. by George D. Zuidema. Baltimore: Johns Hopkins University
Press, 1977. 108p. (QM23.2; 611 / 1. Anatomy, Human. 2.
Anatomy, Human – Atlases.)

S   Langley, Leroy L. *Review of Physiology.* 3d ed. New
York: McGraw-Hill, 1971. 726p. (QP31.2; 612 / 1. Physiology.)

S   Langman, Jan, and Woerdeman, M. W. *Atlas of Medical
Anatomy.* Philadelphia: W. B. Saunders, 1978. 523p. (QM25;
611.00222 / 1. Anatomy, Human – Atlases.)

S   Lingeman, Richard R. *Drugs from A to Z: A Dictionary.*
New York: McGraw-Hill, 1969. 277p. (HV5804; 613.8303 / 1. Drug
abuse – Dictionaries. 2. Drugs – Dictionaries.)

A   Lunin, Lois F. *Health Sciences and Services: A Guide
to Information Sources.* Detroit: Gale, 1979. 614p. bibl. (Z6658;
016.610973 / 1. Medicine – Bibliography. 2. Medicine – Information
services – United States – Directories. 3. Health – Bibliography. 4.
Health – Information services – United States – Directories.)

S   *Medical Abbreviations: A Cross Reference Dictionary.* 2d
ed., comp. by the Special Studies Committee of the Michigan Occupational Therapy Association. Ann Arbor, Mich.: Michigan Occupational Therapy Association, 1967. 165p. (R121; 610.148 / 1.
Medicine – Abbreviations. 2. Medicine – Dictionaries.)

S   *Medical and Health Annual.* Chicago: Encyclopaedia
Britannica, 1977- . Annual. (R5; 362.105 / 1.
Medicine – Periodicals. 2. Health – Periodicals.)

S   *Medical Risks: Patterns of Mortality and Survival.*
Richard B. Singer and Louis Levinson, eds. Sponsored by the
Association of the Life Insurance Medical Directors of America and
the Society of Actuaries. Lexington, Mass.: Lexington Books, 1976.
662p. (RA407; 312.2 / 1. Mortality – Tables. 2.
Death – Causes – Tables. 3. Life expectancy – Tables. 4. Medical
statistics.)

S   *Merck Manual of Diagnosis and Therapy.* 1st- ed. Rahway,
N.J.: Merck, 1899- . Irregular. (RC55; 615.02 / 1. Diagnosis. 2.

Therapeutics. 3. Medicine–Handbooks, manuals, etc.)

SA   Mettler, Frederick Albert. *The Medical Sourcebook: A*
     Reference Handbook for Legal, Legislative, and Administrative Person-
     nel. Boston: Little, 1959. 1000p. bibl. (RC41; 616 / 1.
     Medicine–Practice.)

SA   Meyers, Frederick H.; Jawetz, Ernest; and Goldfien, Alan.
     Review of Medical Pharmacology. 6th ed. Los Altos, Calif.: Lange
     Medical, 1978. 762p. bibl. (RM300; 615.1 / 1. Pharmacology.)

A   *National Health Directory.* 1st– ed. Washington, D.C.:
     Science and Health Publications, 1977– . Annual. (RA7.5;
     353.0084102573 / 1. Public health administration–United
     States–Directories.)

SA   National Health Education Committee. *Facts on the Major*
     Killing and Crippling Diseases in the United States Today. New York:
     National Health Education Committee, 1959– . Annual (irregular).
     bibl. (RA407.3; 614.59 / 1. United States–Statistics, Medical.)

S   *Physicians' Desk Reference to Pharmaceutical Specialities*
     and Biologicals. 1947– . Rutherford, N.J.: Medical Economics,
     1946– . Annual. (RS75; _____ / 1. Materia medica. 2.
     Drugs–Catalogs. 3. Biological products.)

S   *Physician's Handbook.* 1st– ed. Los Altos, Calif.: Lange
     Medical, 1941– . Irregular. (RC55; 616.075 / 1. Medicine–Hand-
     books, manuals, etc.)

SA   Postell, William Dosite. *Applied Medical Bibliography for Students.*
     Springfield, Ill.: Charles C. Thomas, 1955. 142p. (Z6658; 016.61 / 1.
     Medicine–Bibliography–Methodology. 2. Medical writing.)

S   Roody, Peter; Forman, Robert E.; and Schweitzer, Howard B.
     Medical Abbreviations and Acronyms. New York: McGraw-Hill,
     1977. 255p. (R121; 610.148 / 1. Medicine–Abbreviations. 2.
     Medicine–Acronyms.)

S   Snell, Richard S. *Atlas of Clinical Anatomy.* 1st ed.
     Boston: Little, Brown, c1978. 530p. (QM25; 611 / 1. Anatomy,
     Human–Atlases.)

S   Stacy, Ralph W. *Biological and Medical Electronics.*
     New York: McGraw-Hill, 1960. (QH324; 574.078 / 1. Biological ap-
     paratus and supplies. 2. Medical electronics.)

S   *Standard Medical Almanac.* 1st– ed. Chicago: Marquis
     Academic Media/Marquis Who's Who, 1977– . Annual. (R101;
     362.05 / 1. Medical care–United States–Yearbooks. 2. Medical
     care–United States–Statistics.)

S   Stedman, Thomas Lathrop. *Stedman's Medical Dictionary:*
     A Vocabulary of Medicine and Its Allied Sciences, with Pronunciations
     and Derivatives. 23d ed. Baltimore: Williams & Wilkins, 1976.
     1678p. (R121; 610.3 / 1. Medicine–Dictionaries.)

S   Taber, Clarence Wilbur. *Taber's Cyclopedic Medical*

Dictionary. 13th ed. Ed. by Clayton L. Thomas, Philadelphia: F. A.
Davis, 1977. 1781p. (R121; 610.3 / 1. Medicine – Dictionaries.)

S   *The United States Dispensatory*. Ed. by Arthur Osol and
Robertson Pratt. 27th ed. Philadelphia: Lippincott, 1973. 1292p.
bibl. (RS151.2; 615.1273 / 1. Dispensatories. 2. Pharmacopoeias – United States.)

S   *USPDI United States Pharmacopoeia Dispensing Information*.
Rockville, Md.: United States Pharmacopoeial Convention, 1980- .
Annual. (RS141.2; ____ / 1. Pharmacopoeias – United
States – Periodicals. 2. Medicine – United States – Formulae,
receipts, prescriptions. 3. Drugs – Periodicals.)

S   Volk, Wesley A. *Essentials of Medical Microbiology*.
Philadelphia: Lippincott, 1978. 654p. bibl. (QR46; 616.01 / 1.
Medical microbiology.)

SA   *Who's Who in Health Care*. 1st- ed. New York: Hanover
Publications, 1977- . (RA424.4; 362.10922 / 1. Health services administrators – United States – Biography. 2. Health services administrators – Canada – Biography. 3. Health services administrators –
United States – Directories. 4. Health services administrators – Canada – Directories.)

S   Willeford, George, comp. *Medical Word Finder*. 2d ed. West
Nyack, N.Y.: Parker, 1976. 490p. (R123; 610.14 / 1. Medicine –
Terminology. 2. Spellers. 3. Medical libraries – Directories.)

SA   Wischnitzer, Saul. *Barron's Guide to Medical, Dental, and
Allied Health Science Careers*. Completely rev. and updated 3d ed.
Woodbury, N.Y.: Barron's, 1977. 269p. bibl. (R690; 610.69 / 1.
Medicine – Vocational guidance. 2. Dentistry – Vocational guidance.
2. Allied health personnel – Vocational guidance.)

Dental Assistant

If you have already scanned the many pages devoted to reference
sources in the "Health Sciences and Occupations" section, you will
have discovered many useful titles. There are only a handful of tools
listed here, but they are designed to aid the dental assistant in preparing patients for treatment, handling dental records, assisting the dentist with instruments, and performing other similar duties typically re-
quired of the assistant. Because dental assistants sometimes have
several different clerical and secretarial duties assigned to them, you
may also wish to use some of the reference works listed earlier in this
chapter under "Secretarial Science." You will also find the titles listed
under both "Dental Hygienist" and "Dental Lab Technician" to be
useful.

A   *American Dental Directory.* Chicago: American Dental
       Association, 1947- . Annual. (RK37; ____ / 1. Dentists – United
       States – Directories.)
SA   Boucher, Carl O., ed. *Current Clinical Dental*
       Terminology: A Glossary of Accepted Terms in All Disciplines of Den-
       tistry. St. Louis: Mosby, 1974. 442p. bibl. (RK28; 617.703 / 1. Den-
       tistry – Dictionaries.)
SA   Castano, Francis, and Alden, Betsey. *Handbook of Expanded*
       Dental Auxiliary Practice. Philadelphia: Lippincott, 1973. 225p. bibl.
       (RK60.5; 617.60233 / 1. Dental assistants.)
S   Gelbier, Stanley, and Copley, Margaret A. H. *Handbook*
       for Dental Surgery Assistants and Other Ancillary
       Workers. 2d ed. Bristol: J. Wright, 1977. 244p. (RK60.5; 617.6 / 1.
       Dental assistants. 2. Dentistry.)
S   Reap, Charles A., Jr. *Complete Dental Assistant's,*
       Secretary's, and Hygienist's Handbook. West Nyack,
       N.Y.: Parker, 1973. 240p. (RK60.5; 651.96176 / 1. Dental
       assistants – Handbooks, manuals, etc. 2. Dental hygienists – Hand-
       books, manuals, etc.)

Dental Hygienist

Besides the many general tools listed under "Health Sciences and
Occupations," the dental hygienist has several tools that will aid him
or her in performing the various preventive and therapeutic services
in the dentist's office. There are handbooks of therapeutics and of
diagnosis, an index to periodical literature, a history of dentistry, and
a yearbook. There is even an atlas of oral diseases that you may find
useful. You may also wish to consult the lists of tools under both "Dental Assistant" and "Dental Lab Technician."

S   *Accepted Dental Therapeutics.* Ed.33- , 1969/70- .
       Chicago: American Dental Association, 1968- . Biennial. (RK701;
       617.60605 / 1. Therapeutics, Dental – Periodicals.)
A   *Index to Dental Literature.* 1939- . Chicago: American
       Dental Association, 1943- . Quarterly, with annual cumulations.
       (Z6668; 016.6176 / 1. Dentistry – Periodicals – Indexes.)
S   McElroy, Donald L., and Malone, William F. *Handbook of*
       Oral Diagnosis and Treatment Planning. Baltimore: Williams &
       Wilkins, c1969. 220p. (RK308; 617.6075 / 1.
       Teeth – Diseases – Diagnosis.)
SA   Pindborg, Jens J. *Atlas of Diseases of the Oral Mucosa.*
       2d enl. ed. Philadelphia: Saunders, 1973. 285p. bibl. (RC815;
       616.31 / 1. Mouth – Diseases. 2. Oral manifestations of general
       diseases.)

SA   Weinberger, Bernhard Wolf. *An Introduction to the History
      of Dentistry, with Medical and Dental Chronology and Bibliographic
      Data.* St. Louis: Mosby, 1948. 2v. bibl. (RK29; 617.609 / 1. Den-
      tistry – History. 2. Dentistry – Bibliography.)
S   *Year Book of Dentistry.* Chicago: Year Book Medical
      Publishers, 1936- . Annual. (RK16; 617.6058 / 1. Dentistry –
      Yearbooks.)

Dental Lab Technician

The tools listed below for the dental lab technician will be useful
primarily in answering questions about dental materials and devices
such as crowns and bridges, although there is also an atlas on teeth
and dentures. Note that with the exception of the atlas, all the tools
listed are of the source/access type so that you can learn what other information resources are available to you. Some of the general tools
listed under "Health Sciences and Occupations," as well as those titles
cited in the sections on "Dental Assistant" and "Dental Hygienist" may
also prove useful.

SA   American Dental Association. *Guide to Dental Materials
      and Devices.* Ed.1- , 1962/63- . Chicago: American Dental Association,
      1962- . Irregular. bibl. (____; ____ / 1. Dental materials.)
SA   Craig, Robert G., and Peyton, Floyd A., eds. *Restorative
      Dental Materials.* 5th ed. St. Louis: Mosby, 1975. 495p. bibl.
      (RK652.5; 617.695 / 1. Dental materials.)
SA   Johnston, John F.; Phillips, Ralph W.; and Dykema, Roland
      W. *Modern Practice in Crown & Bridge Prosthodontics.* 3d ed.
      Philadelphia: Saunders, 1971. 692p. bibl. (RK666; 617.692 / 1.
      Crowns (Dentistry). 2. Bridges (Dentistry.)
SA   Skinner, Eugene William. *Skinner's Science of Dental
      Materials.* By Ralph W. Phillips. 7th ed. Philadelphia: Saunders,
      1973. 682p. bibl. (RK652.5; 617.695 / 1. Dental materials.)
S   Wheeler, Russell C. *Atlas of Tooth Form.* 4th ed.
      Philadelphia: Saunders, 1969. 163p. (RK656; 611.314022 / 1. Teeth.
      2. Dentures.)

Medical Assistant

The medical assistant performs a variety of tasks: everything from
assisting a physician in the examination and treatment of patients to
performing administrative functions in the medical office. The tools
listed below will assist you in developing and refining such skills and
others besides. There are handbooks; guides to writing, shorthand,

typing, and transcribing; and even works on law and on insurance. Because you may be called upon to assist in such areas as first aid and filing medical records, you may want to consult the appropriate sections in this chapter such as "Paramedical Studies" and "Medical Records Technician," to name just two. Also of interest will be many of the dictionaries and diagnostic handbooks listed under "Health Sciences and Occupations" as well as some general works cited under "Secretarial Science."

SA   Alcazar, Carol C. *Medical Typist's Guide for Histories
      and Physicals.* 2d ed. Flushing, N.Y.: Medical Examination
      Publishing Co., 1974. 249p. bibl. (R728.8; 651.3741 / 1. Medical
      secretaries. 2. Medicine–Terminology.)

S   Bradbury, Peggy F., ed. *Transcriber's Guide to Medical
      Terminology.* Flushing, N.Y.: Medical Examination Publishing Co.,
      1973. 106p. (R123; 610.14 / 1. Medicine–Terminology.)

SA   Bredow, Miriam. *Medical Office Procedures.* 6th ed. New
      York: McGraw-Hill, 1973. 283p. bibl. (R728.8; 651.961 / 1. Medical
      secretaries. 2. Medicine–Terminology. 3. Medicine–Practice.)

SA   Cooper, Marian G., and Bredow, Miriam. *The Medical
      Assistant.* 4th ed. New York: McGraw-Hill, 1978. 501p. bibl.
      (R728.8; 610 / 1. Medical assistants.)

S   Davis, Phyllis E. *Medical Shorthand.* New York: Wiley-
      Medical, 1967. 317p. (Z56.3.M4; 653.4 / 1. Medical shorthand)

SA   Doyle, Jean Monty, and Dennis, Robert Lee. *The Complete
      Handbook for Medical Secretaries and Assistants.* 2d ed. Boston: Lit-
      tle, Brown, 1978. 619p. bibl. (R728.8; 651.3741 / 1. Medical
      secretaries–Handbooks, manuals, etc. 2. Medical
      assistants–Handbooks, manuals, etc.)

SA   Fishbein, Morris. *Medical Writing: The Technic and the
      Art.* 4th ed. Springfield, Ill.: Charles C. Thomas, 1972. 203p. bibl.
      (R119; 808.06661021 / 1. Medical writing.)

S   Fordney, Marilyn T. *Insurance Handbook for the Medical
      Office.* Philadelphia: Saunders, 1977. 646p. (HG9396;
      369.38002461 / 1. Insurance, Health–United States–Handbooks,
      manuals, etc. 2. Medical offices–Management–Handbooks,
      manuals, etc.)

SA   Morris, R. Crawford, and Moritz, Alan R. *Doctor and Patient
      and the Law.* 5th ed. St. Louis: Mosby, 1971. 554p. bibl. (KF2905;
      344.73041 / 1. Malpractice–United States. 2. Medical
      jurisprudence–United States. 3. Medical laws and legisla-
      tion–United States.)

SA   *Webster's Medical Office Handbook.* Anne H. Soukhanov,
      general ed. Springfield, Mass.: Merriam, 1979. 596p. bibl. (R728.8;
      651.961 / 1. Medical secretaries–Handbooks, manuals, etc. 2.

Medical offices – Management – Handbooks, manuals, etc.)

Medical Laboratory Assistant

The tools listed in this section will support the medical laboratory assistant in learning his or her primary task: how to analyze blood, tissues, and fluids by using various biomedical equipment. There are handbooks of microbiology and hematology, clinical data, and laboratory testing and technique. You will also find cited some diagnostic lab manuals and even a dictionary of terms in biomedical engineering. As with the other medical specializations, you may find many of the tools listed under "Health Sciences and Occupations" to be valuable. Also, you may want to look in your library's catalog – and in other access tools – under such subjects as bacteriology, serology, parasitology, blood banking, urinalysis, and clinical chemistry, all subjects of interest to the laboratory assistant.

SA   *Clinical Hematology.* By Maxwell M. Wintrobe [and others].
      7th ed. Philadelphia: Lea & Febiger, 1974. 1896p. bibl. (RB145;
      616.15 / 1. Hematology.)

SA   French, Ruth M. *Guide to Diagnostic Procedures.* 4th ed.
      New York: McGraw-Hill, 1975. 369p. bibl. (RB37; 616.075 / 1.
      Diagnosis. 2. Medicine, Clinical – Laboratory manuals, etc.)

S   Graf, Rudolf F., and Whalen, George J. *The Encyclopedia
      of Biomedical Engineering Terms.* Reston, Va.: Reston, 1977. 415p.
      (R856; 610.28 / 1. Biomedical engineering – Dictionaries.)

SA   *Handbook of Clinical Laboratory Data.* 2d ed. Coeditors:
      Willard R. Faulkner, John W. King, Henry C. Damm. Cleveland:
      Chemical Rubber Co., 1968. 710p. bibl. (RB37; 616.0260202 / 1.
      Medicine, Clinical – Handbooks, manuals, etc.)

SA   *The Laboratory in Clinical Medicine: Interpretation and
      Application.* Ed. by James A. Halstead. Philadelphia: Saunders,
      1976. 866p. bibl. (RC71; 616.075 / 1. Diagnosis. 2. Medicine.)

S   Oppenheim, Irwin A. *Textbook for Laboratory Assistants.*
      2d ed. St. Louis: Mosby, 1976. 162p. (RB37; 616.075028 / 1.
      Medical laboratories – Technique.)

SA   Todd, James Campbell. *Clinical Diagnosis and Management
      by Laboratory Methods.* Edited by John Bernard Henry. 16th ed.
      Philadelphia: Saunders, 1979. 2v. bibl. (RB37; 616.0756 / 1.
      Diagnosis, Laboratory.)

SA   Widmann, Francis K. *Clinical Interpretation of Laboratory
      Tests.* 8th ed. Philadelphia: F. A. Davis Co., 1979. 656p. bibl.
      (RB37; 616.075 / 1. Diagnosis, Laboratory.)

SA   Witton, Catherine Jones. *Microbiology.* Rewritten and

rev. by Genevieve Gray Young. 3d. ed. New York: McGraw-Hill,
1961. 586p. bibl. (QR46; 616.01 / 1. Microbiology.)

Medical Records Technician

Whether working in a hospital or in the office of a private physician,
the medical records technician will find the tools listed here helpful in
developing or enhancing the basic skills of transcribing, analyzing,
coding, and filing medical records. There are handbooks and guides
that deal with everything from the retention and preservation of
records to the transcription of data and the organization and release of
medical information. There are also wordbooks of medical terminology from Greek and Latin, of hospital terms, and even of abbreviations and symbols frequently encountered. Other useful tools
may be found listed under "Health Sciences and Occupations,"
"Medical Assistant," and even "Secretarial Science."

S   American Hospital Association. *Hospital Medical Records:*
         Guidelines for Their Use and the Release of Medical Information.
         Chicago: American Hospital Association, 1972. 64p. (RA976;
         651.5 / 1. Medical records.)

SA   American Hospital Association. *Medical Record Departments*
         in Hospitals: Guide to Organization. Chicago: American Hospital
         Association, 1972. 88p. bibl. (RA976; 651.5 / 1. Medical records.)

SA   American Medical Record Association. *Glossary of Hospital*
         Terms. 2d ed. Chicago: American Medical Record Association,
         1974. 111p. bibl. (____; 362.11014 / 1. Medicine–Terminology.)

S   American Medical Record Association. *An Instruction Guide*
         for Organizing Health Records. Chicago: American Medical Record
         Association, 1971. 52p. (____; ____ / 1. Medical records. 2. Hospital
         records.)

S   Kerr, Avice H. *Medical Hieroglyphs: Abbreviations and*
         Symbols. Chicago: Clissold Books, 1970. 383p. (R123; 610.148 / 1.
         Medicine–Abbreviations.)

S   *Medical Record Forms for Hospitals: Guide to Preparation.*
         Chicago: American Hospital Association, 1963. Unpaged. (____;
         362.1 / 1. Medical records.)

S   Patterson, Sandra R., and Thompson, Lawrence S. *Medical*
         Terminology from Greek and Latin. Troy, N.Y.: Whitston Publishing,
         1978. 275p. (____; ____ / 1. Medicine–Terminology. 2. English
         language–Foreign elements–Greek. 3. English language–Foreign
         elements–Latin.)

SA   Record Controls, Inc., and Hospital Financial Management
         Association. *Guide to the Retention and Preservation of Records (with*
         Destruction Schedules.) 5th hospital ed. Chicago: Record Controls

and Hospital Financial Management Association, 1978. 80p. bibl.
(HF5736; 651.51 / 1. Business records. 2. Hospital records.)

S   Sloane, Sheila B. *The Medical Word Book: A Spelling and
       Vocabulary Guide to Medical Transcription.* Philadelphia: Saunders,
       1973. 923p. (R123; 610.14 / 1. Medicine–Terminology.)

S   Thompson, Edward T., and Hayden, Adaline C., eds. *Standard
       Nomenclature of Diseases and Operations.* For the American Medical
       Association. New York: McGraw-Hill, 1959. 71p. (RB115; 616.012 /
       1. Nosology.)

Nursing

A wide variety of reference sources are available to the nursing student and practicing nurse. There are a number of handbooks devoted to various topics such as drugs, diagnosis, and even specific types of nursing such as pediatrics; eye, ear, nose, and throat; and even surgical nursing and postsurgical care. There are also some miscellaneous source tools that contain information and statistics about the nursing profession generally. And an important periodical index is devoted to nursing. Because of the many and varied tasks assigned to the contemporary nurse, it should come as no surprise that he or she may need to consult not only the section on "Health Sciences and Occupations," but also all of the other sections devoted to medical sciences in this chapter.

S   American Nurses' Association. Nursing Information Bureau.
       Facts About Nursing. New York: American Nurses' Association,
       1935– . Annual. (RT1; 610.73069 / 1. Nurses and train-
       ing–Societies, etc.)

S   Broadwell, Lucile, and Milutinovic, Barbara. *Medical-
       Surgical Nursing Procedures.* New York: Van Nostrand Reinhold,
       1977. 457p. (RT41; 610.73 / 1. Nursing. 2. Surgical nursing.)

SA   Brunner, Lillian Sholtis, and Suddarth, Doris Smith.
       The Lippincott Manual of Nursing Practice. 2d ed. Philadelphia: Lip-
       pincott, 1978. 1868p. bibl. (RT52; 610.73 / 1. Nursing–Handbooks,
       manuals, etc.)

SA   *Comprehensive Pediatric Nursing.* By Gladys M. Scipien
       [and others]. New York: McGraw-Hill, 1975. 975p. bibl. (RJ245;
       610.7362 / 1. Pediatric nursing.)

A   *Cumulative Index to Nursing & Allied Health Literature.*
       Glendale, Calif.: Seventh Day Adventist Hospital Association,
       1961– , v.1/5– . Bimonthly, with annual cumulations. (Z6675.N7;
       016.61 / 1. Nursing–Periodicals–Indexes. 2.
       Health–Periodicals–Indexes.)

S   *Current Drug Handbook.* Philadelphia: Saunders, 1958– .

Annual. (RM101; 615.1 / 1. Pharmacology. 2. Drugs.)

S   Goldman, Myer. *A Nurse's Guide to the X-Ray Department.*
       2d ed. Edinburgh, Scotland: Churchill Livingstone, 1972. 87p.
       (RC78; 616.07572 / 1. Radiography.)

S   Hansen, Helen F. *Encyclopedic Guide to Nursing.* New
       York: McGraw-Hill, Blakiston Division, 1957. 406p. (RT21;
       610.7303 / 1. Nurses and nursing – Dictionaries.)

SA   Jackson, Jane. *The Whole Nurse Catalog.* New York:
       Churchill Livingstone, 1980. 1v. bibl. (RT51; 610.73020219 / 1.
       Nursing – Handbooks, manuals, etc. 2. Nursing – Information ser-
       vices – United States – Directories. 3. Nursing – Bibliography. 4.
       Nursing – Equipment and supplies – Catalogs.)

SA   King, Eunice M. *Illustrated Manual of Nursing Techniques.*
       Philadelphia: Lippincott, 1977. 432p. bibl. (RT52; 610.730202 / 1.
       Nursing – Handbooks, manuals, etc.)

SA   Major, Ralph Herman. *Major's Physical Diagnosis.* Edited
       by Mahlon H. Delp and Robert T. Manning. 8th ed. Philadelphia:
       Saunders, 1975. 790p. bibl. (RC76; 616.0754 / 1. Physical
       diagnosis.)

S   *McGraw-Hill Nursing Dictionary.* New York: McGraw-Hill,
       1979. 1211p. (RT21; 610.3 / 1. Nursing – Dictionaries.)

S   Miller, Benjamin Frank, and Keane, Claire B. *Encyclopedia
       and Dictionary of Medicine and Nursing and Allied Health.* 2d ed.
       Philadelphia: Saunders, 1978. 1148p. (R121; 610.3 / 1.
       Medicine – Dictionaries. 2. Nursing – Dictionaries.)

S   National League for Nursing. Division of Research.
       *NLN Nursing Data Book: Statistical Information on Education and
       Newly Licensed Nurses.* 1st ed. New York: National League for
       Nursing, c1978. 86p. (RT79; 610.73071173 / 1. Nursing – Study and
       teaching – United States – Statistics. 2. Nurses – United
       States – Statistics.)

SA   *The Nurse's Drug Handbook.* By Suzanne Loebl [and others].
       New York: Wiley, 1977. 803p. bibl. (RM125; 615.58 / 1.
       Therapeutics – Handbooks, manuals, etc. 2. Drugs – Handbooks,
       manuals, etc. 3. Nursing – Handbooks, manuals, etc.)

S   *Nurse's Guide to Drugs.* Horsham, Pa.: Intermed
       Communications, c1979. 1355p. (RM300; 615.1 / 1. Drugs. 2. Phar-
       macology. 3. Nursing.)

SA   *Nursing Care in Eye, Ear, Nose, and Throat Disorders.*
       William H. Havener [and others]. 3d ed. St. Louis: Mosby, 1974.
       459p. bibl. (RE88; 610.736 / 1. Ophthalmic nursing. 2.
       Otolaryngological nursing.)

SA   *Nursing Care of the Patient with Medical-Surgical Disorders.*
       Harriet Costen Moidel [and others], eds. 2d ed. New York:
       McGraw-Hill, 1976. 1193p. bibl. (RT65; 610.73677 / 1. Nurses and
       nursing. 2. Surgical nursing.)

S   Raus, Elmer E., and Raus, Madonna M. *Manual of History
      Taking, Physical Examinations and Record Keeping.* Philadelphia: Lip-
      pincott, 1974. 588p. (RC65; 616.075 / 1. Medical history tak-
      ing—Handbooks, manuals, etc. 2. Physical diagnosis—Handbooks,
      manuals, etc.)
S   Rowland, Howard S. *The Nurse's Almanac.* Germantown, Md.:
      Aspen Systems Corp., 1978. 844p. (RT41; 610.73 / 1. Nursing. 2.
      Nursing—United States.)

Paramedical Studies

Not surprisingly, the overwhelming majority of tools listed here
under paramedical studies relates to emergency care and transportation and to first aid. The paramedic—sometimes also called an
"emergency medical technician"—will also find two dictionaries and a
useful handbook on the use of drugs in medical emergencies. The
paramedic may also want to consult some of the reference works
listed in this chapter under "Health Sciences and Occupations," "Nursing," and "Respiratory Therapy."

SA   American Academy of Orthopaedic Surgeons. Committee on
      Injuries. *Emergency Care and Transportation of the Sick and Injured.*
      Chicago: American Academy of Orthopaedic Surgeons, 1971. 304p.
      bibl. (RC87; 616.025 / 1. Medical emergencies. 2. Transport of sick
      and wounded.)
SA   Barber, Janet Miller. *Handbook of Emergency Pharmacology.*
      St. Louis: Mosby, 1978. 139p. bibl. (RM300; 616.025 / 1.
      Drugs—Handbooks, manuals, etc. 2. Medical emergencies—Hand-
      books, manuals, etc.)
S   Cole, Warren Henry, and Puestow, Charles B. *First Aid
      Diagnosis and Management.* 6th ed. New York: Appleton, 1965.
      445p. (RD131; 614.88 / 1. Wounds—Treatment. 2. First aid in ill-
      ness and injury.)
SA   *Emergency Care.* Editor, Alan B. Gazzaniga. Reston, Va.:
      Reston, 1979. 704p. bibl. (RC86.7; 616.025 / 1. Medical emergen-
      cies. 2. Allied health personnel.)
SA   Henderson, John. *Emergency Medical Guide.* 3d ed. New
      York: McGraw-Hill, 1973. 651p. bibl. (RC87; 614.88 / 1. First aid
      in illness and injury.)
SA   London, Peter Stanford. *A Practical Guide to the Care of
      the Injured.* Edinburgh, Scotland: Churchill Livingstone, 1967.
      777p. bibl. (RC87; 617.1 / 1. Medical emergencies. 2. Wounds.)
SA   *MGH Textbook of Emergency Medicine: Emergency Care As
      Practiced at the Massachusetts General Hospital.*
      Ed., Earle W. Wilkins, Jr. Baltimore: Williams & Wilkins, 1978.

829p. bibl. (RC86.7; 616.025 / 1. Medical emergencies. 2.
Hospitals–Emergency service. 3. Emergency medicine.)

S   Red Cross. United States American National Red Cross.
Advanced First Aid and Emergency Care. Garden City, N.Y.: Doubleday, 1973. 318p. (RC87; 614.88 / 1. First aid in illness and injury.
2. Medical emergencies.)

S   Red Cross. United States American National Red Cross.
Standard First Aid and Personal Safety. Garden City, N.Y.: Doubleday, 1973. 268p. (RC87; 614.88 / 1. First aid in illness and injury.)

S   Schmidt, Jacob E. *Index of Paramedical Vocabulary: An
Index-Indicator Enabling the User Not Versed in Greek and Latin to
Locate the Terminology of Any Given Subject in a Paramedical,
Medical, or Biological Dictionary.* Springfield, Ill.: Charles C.
Thomas, 1974. 324p. (R123; 610.14 / 1. Medicine–Terminology.)

S   Schmidt, Jacob E. *Visual Aids for Paramedical Vocabulary.*
Springfield, Ill.: Charles C. Thomas, 1973. 182p. (R121; 612 / 1.
Medicine–Dictionaries. 2. Medicine–Terminology.)

SA   Snyder, Donald Rowe. *Handbook for Emergency Medical
Personnel.* New York: McGraw-Hill, 1978. 212p. bibl. (RC86.7;
616.025 / 1. Medical emergencies–Handbooks, manuals, etc. 2.
First aid in illness and injury–Handbooks, manuals, etc.)

SA   Wilson, David H., and Hall, Maurice H. *Casualty Officer's
Handbook.* 4th ed. Boston: Butterworth's, 1979. 294p. bibl. (RD93;
617.1 / 1. Wounds–Treatment. 2. Medical emergencies.)

S   Young, Carl B. *First Aid for Emergency Crews: A Manual
on Emergency First Aid Procedures. . . .* Springfield, Ill.: Charles C.
Thomas, 1965. 165p. (RC87; 614.88 / 1. First aid in illness and
injury.)

Physical Therapist Assistant

Without exception, the tools listed here for the physical therapist
assistant are of the source/access type, not only providing information
but also leading you to other sources of information. The topics range
from physical medicine and rehabilitation to neurology and the administration and management of physical therapy. You may also wish
to consult many of the tools–particularly those relating to human
anatomy and physiology–listed in this chapter under "Health
Sciences and Occupations" and "Nursing."

SA   American Physical Therapy Association. *Physical Therapy
Administration and Management.* Robert Hickok, ed. Baltimore:
Williams & Wilkins, 1974. 214p. bibl. (RM700; 658.916158 / 1.
Physical therapy.)

SA   Cash, Joan, ed. *Neurology for Physiotherapists.* 2d ed.
     Philadelphia: Lippincott, 1977. 495p. bibl. (RC346; 616.8046 / 1.
     Nervous system – Diseases. 2. Physical therapy.)

SA   Garrett, James F., and Levine, Edna S., eds. *Rehabilitative*
     Practices with the Physically Disabled. New York: Columbia Univer-
     sity Press, 1973. 569p. bibl. (HD7256.U5; 362.4 / 1. Physically
     handicapped – Rehabilitation – United States – Addresses, essays,
     lectures. 2. Physically handicapped – Rehabilitation – Addresses,
     essays, lectures.)

SA   Krusen, Frank Hammond. *Handbook of Physical Medicine*
     and Rehabilitation. 2d ed. Philadelphia: Saunders, 1971. 920p. bibl.
     (RM700; 615.8 / 1. Physical therapy. 2. Physically hand-
     icapped – Rehabilitation.)

SA   Nagler, Willibald W. *Manual for Physical Therapy*
     Technicians. Chicago: Year Book Medical Publications, 1974. 181p.
     bibl. (RM700; 615.82 / 1. Physical therapy.)

SA   Rush, Howard A. *Rehabilitation Medicine.* 4th ed. St.
     Louis: Mosby, 1977. 675p. bibl. (RM700; 615.8 / 1. Medicine,
     Physical. 2. Rehabilitation.)

SA   Shestack, Robert. *Handbook of Physical Therapy.* 3d ed.
     New York: Springer Publications, 1977. 216p. bibl. (RM700; 615.8 /
     1. Physical therapy.)

SA   Stryker, Ruth. *Rehabilitative Aspects of Acute and*
     Chronic Nursing Care. 2d ed. Philadelphia: Saunders, 1977. 272p.
     bibl. (RT120.R4; 610.73 / 1. Rehabilitation nursing.)

SA   Washburn, Kenneth B. *Physical Medicine and Rehabilitation.*
     Flushing, N.Y.: Medical Examination Publishing Co., 1976. 153p.
     bibl. (RM700; 615.82 / 1. Medicine, Physical – Handbooks,
     manuals, etc. 2. Rehabilitation – Handbooks, manuals, etc.)

Radiologic Technician

The tools listed here will assist the radiologic technician in operating
X-ray equipment. There are handbooks of radiographic processing
and radiation hygiene as well as works on radiological anatomy and a
radiographic atlas. You will even find a dictionary of specialized
terms used in radiology and nuclear medicine and a work on cardiac
catheterization. Because the radiologic technician is also sometimes
interested in other general works on anatomy, physiology, and nursing procedures, the tools listed under "Health Sciences and Occupations" and "Nursing" may prove useful.

SA   Eastman, Terry R. *Radiographic Fundamentals and Technique*
     Guide. St. Louis: Mosby, 1979. 175p. bibl. (RC78; 616.0757 / 1.

Radiography, Medical. 2. Radiography – Processing.)
S   Etter, Lewis E. *Glossary of Words and Phrases Used in Radiology, Nuclear Medicine, and Ultrasound.* 2d ed. Springfield, Ill.: Charles C. Thomas, 1970. 355p. (RM849; 616.075703 / 1. Radiology, Medical – Dictionaries.)

SA Fuchs, Arthur W. *Principles of Radiographic Exposure and Processing.* 2d ed. Springfield, Ill.: Charles C. Thomas, 1958. 284p. bibl. (RC78; 616.0757 / 1. Radiography.)

S   Goldman, Myer. *A Nurse's Guide to the X-Ray Department.* 2d ed. Edinburgh, Scotland: Churchill Livingstone, 1972. 87p. (RC78; 616.07572 / 1. Radiography.)

S   Hamilton, William James; Simon, George; and Hamilton, S. G. Ian. *Surface and Radiological Anatomy for Students and General Practitioners.* 5th ed. Baltimore: Williams & Wilkins, 1971. 397p. (QM23.2; 611 / 1. Anatomy, Surgical and topographical. 2. Radiography, Medical.)

SA Kory, Ross C.; Tsagaris, Theofilos J.; and Bustamante, Rodrigo A. *A Primer of Cardiac Catheterization.* Springfield, Ill.: Charles C. Thomas, 1965. 114p. bibl. (RC683.5.C25; 616.12075 / 1. Cardiac catheterization.)

SA Lusted, Lee B., and Keats, Theodore E. *Atlas of Roentgenographic Measurement.* 3d ed. Chicago: Year Book Medical Publications, 1972. 296p. bibl. (QM25; 616.07572 / 1. Radiography. 2. Anatomy, Human.)

SA Merrill, Vinita. *Atlas of Roentgenographic Positions and Standard Radiologic Procedures.* 4th ed. St. Louis: Mosby, 1975. 3v. bibl. (RC78.4; 616.07572 / 1. Radiography, Medical – Positioning – Atlases.)

SA Paul, Lester W., and Juhl, John H. *The Essentials of Roentgen Interpretation.* 3d ed. New York: Harper & Row, c1972. 1138p. bibl. (RC78; 616.07572 / 1. Diagnosis, Radioscopic.)

SA Powell, Nieta Whitman. *Handbook for Radiologic Technologists and Special Procedures Nurses in Radiology.* Springfield, Ill.: Charles C. Thomas, 1974. 105p. bibl. (RM849; 616.0757 / 1. Radiologic technologists.)

SA *Radiation Hygiene Handbook.* Hanson Blatz, ed. New York: McGraw-Hill, 1959. 1v. in various pagings. bibl. (RA1231.R2; 614.715 / 1. Radiation – Physiological effect.)

SA Selman, Joseph. *The Fundamentals of X-Ray and Radium Physics.* 6th ed. Springfield, Ill.: Charles C. Thomas, 1977. 586p. bibl. (QC481; 537.535 / 1. X-rays. 2. Radium. 3. Radiography.)

Respiratory Therapist

The respiratory therapist – sometimes also called an inhalation therapist–needs information to assist him or her in treating patients with cardiorespiratory problems. The tools listed here are designed to do just that. There are handbooks on lung diseases, electrocardiography, oxygen therapy, ventilators, and pulmonary-function testing. All of these are in addition to several general handbooks on respiratory therapy as well as a combination dictionary and reference guide to the field. The respiratory therapist will also find useful reference sources listed under "Health Sciences and Occupations," "Nursing," and even "Paramedical Studies."

SA   Bates, David V.; Macklem, Peter T.; and Christie, Ronald V.
      Respiratory Function in Disease. 2d ed. Philadelphia: Saunders, 1971.
      584p. bibl. (RC756; 616.24 / 1. Lungs–Diseases.)
SA   Comroe, Julius H. [and others]. *The Lung: Clinical*
      Physiology and Pulmonary Function Tests. 2d ed. Chicago: Year Book
      Medical Publishers, 1962. 390p. bibl. (RC733; 616.24075 / 1.
      Lungs. 2. Lungs–Diseases–Diagnosis.)
SA   Dobkin, Allen B., ed. *Ventilators and Inhalation Therapy.*
      2d ed. Boston: Little, Brown, 1972. 269p. bibl. (RM161; 615.836 /
      1. Inhalation therapy. 2. Respirators.)
SA   Egan, Donald F. *Fundamentals of Respiratory Therapy.*
      3d ed. St. Louis: Mosby, 1977. 551p. bibl. (RM161; 615.836 / 1. In-
      halation therapy.)
SA   Kacmaret, Robert M.; Dimas, Steven; and Mack, Craig W.
      The Essentials of Respiratory Therapy. Chicago: Year Book Medical
      Publishers, 1979. 359p. bibl. (RC735.I5; 615.836 / 1. Inhalation
      therapy. 2. Respiration.)
SA   Krasowski, J. Owen. *Dictionary/Reference Guide for*
      Respiratory Therapy. Chicago: Year Book Medical Publishers, 1977.
      114p. bibl. (RC732; 615.83063 / 1. Respiratory
      organs–Diseases–Terminology. 2. Inhalation therapy–
      Terminology.)
S   Lyon, Leonard J. *Basic Electrocardiography Handbook.*
      New York: Van Nostrand Reinhold, 1977. 175p. (RC683.5.E5;
      616.120754 / 1. Electrocardiography.)
SA   Nose, Yukihiko. *The Oxygenator.* Volume 2 of *Manual on*
      Artificial Organs. St. Louis: Mosby, 1973. 350p. bibl. (RM666.O8;
      616.836 / 1. Oxygen therapy–Apparatus and supplies.)
SA   *Principles and Practices of Respiratory Therapy.* Jimmy
      Albert Young and Dean Crocker, eds. 2d ed. Chicago: Year Book
      Medical Publishers, 1976. 777p. bibl. (RM161; 615.836 / 1. Inhala-
      tion therapy.)
SA   Ruppel, Gregg. *Manual of Pulmonary Function Testing.*
      2d ed. St. Louis: Mosby, 1979. 162p. bibl. (RC734.P84; 616.24075 /
      1. Pulmonary function tests.)

SA   Safar, Peter, ed. *Respiratory Therapy.* Philadelphia:
        F. A. Davis Co., 1965. 419p. bibl. (RD81.A1; 615.836 / 1. Inhala-
        tion therapy. 2. Resuscitation.)

SA   Shapiro, Barry A.; Harrison, Ronald; and Trout, Carole.
        Clinical Application of Respiratory Care. Chicago: Year Book Medical
        Publishers, c1975. 454p. bibl. (RM161; 616.2 / 1. Inhalation
        therapy.)

SA   Symposium on Oxygen Measurements in Blood and Tissues
        and Their Significance, London, 1964. *A Symposium on Oxygen
        Measurements in Blood and Tissues and Their Significance.* Edited by
        J. P. Payne and D. W. Hill. Boston: Little, Brown, 1966. 274p. bibl.
        (QP535.O1; 612.01524 / 1. Oxygen in the body—Congresses. 2.
        Blood—Analysis and chemistry—Congresses.)

Surgical Assistant

The surgical assistant can use the informational tools listed here to support him or her in learning how to assist both surgeons and anesthesiologists before, during, and after surgery. Of most value are the several handbooks that deal with both operating room and surgical nursing. There is also a tool that outlines basic surgical techniques and even an atlas of surgical operations. Students of surgical assisting may also want to consult the sections on "Health Sciences and Occupations" and "Nursing," where other related tools on such topics as anatomy, physiology, and microbiology are cited.

SA   Alexander, Edythe Louise. *Alexander's Care of the Patient
        in Surgery.* 6th ed. Ed. by Marie J. Rhodes and Barbara J.
        Gruendemann. St. Louis: Mosby, 1978. 886p. bibl. (RD32.3;
        610.73677 / 1. Operating room nursing.)

SA   Berry, Edna Cornelia, and Kohn, Mary Louise. *Introduction
        to Operating-Room Technique.* 4th ed. New York: McGraw-Hill,
        1972. 342p. bibl. (RD32; 617.91 / 1. Operating room nursing.)

SA   Ginsberg, Frances; Brunner, Lillian; and Cantlin, Vernita.
        Manual of Operating Room Technology. Philadelphia: Lippincott,
        1966. 276p. bibl. (RD32.3; 610.73677 / 1. Surgical nursing. 2.
        Surgery, Operative.)

SA   Hoeller, Mary Louise. *Surgical Technology: Basis for
        Clinical Practice.* 3d ed. St. Louis: Mosby, 1974. 386p. bibl. (RD99;
        617.9 / 1. Operating room technicians.)

S   Kirk, Raymond M. *Basic Surgical Techniques.* 2d ed.
        Edinburgh, Scotland; New York: Churchill Livingstone, 1978.
        168p. (RD32; 617.91 / 1. Surgery, Operative.)

SA   LeMaitre, George D., and Finnegan, Janet A. *The Patient
        in Surgery: A Guide for Nurses.* 3d ed. Philadelphia: Saunders, 1975.

506p. bibl. (RD99; 610.73677 / 1. Surgical nursing.)

S   Zollinger, Robert M., and Zollinger, Robert M., Jr. *Atlas of Surgical Operations.* 4th ed. New York: Macmillan, 1975. 392p. (RD41; 617.91 / 1. Surgery, Operative – Atlases.)

AGRICULTURAL TECHNOLOGY

The student of agricultural technology has a wide variety of tools available, regardless of whether his or her major is agribusiness, forestry, horticulture, or any other of the specific subjects found in this section. There are two important periodical indexes, handbooks of agricultural engineering, encyclopedic source tools on agricultural history and production, and miscellaneous almanac-type tools containing important statistics. Besides these, you will also find an atlas of resources, an important agricultural yearbook (each issue of which is devoted to a specific subject), and even a directory of information resources. These tools, used in conjunction with the more specific titles listed under your major, should satisfy most of your information needs. Your librarian can point you toward other sources not listed here.

A   Agricultural Sciences Information Network. *Directory of Information Resources in Agriculture and Biology.* Beltsville, Md.: National Agricultural Library, 1971. 523p. (QH321; 630.72073 / 1. Biological laboratories – United States – Directories. 2. Agricultural research – United States – Directories.)

A   *Biological and Agricultural Index: A Cumulative Subject Index to Periodicals in the Fields of Biology, Agriculture, and Related Sciences.* v.50- . New York: H. W. Wilson, 1964- . Continues *Agricultural Index,* 1916-1964. Monthly, with quarterly and annual cumulations. (Z5073; 016.57405 / 1. Agriculture – Periodicals – Indexes. 2. Agriculture – Bibliography – Periodicals. 3. Biology – Periodicals – Indexes. 4. Biology – Bibliography – Periodicals.)

A   Brown, Mary Ruth; Moss, Eugenie Lair; and Bright, Karin Drudge. *Agriculture Education in a Technical Society: An Annotated Bibliography of Resources.* Chicago: American Library Association, 1973. 228p. (Z5071; 016.63 / 1. Agriculture – Bibliography.)

S   *Dictionary of Agricultural and Food Engineering.* Editor in chief, Arthur W. Farrall. 2d ed. Danville, Ill.: Interstate Printers & Publishers, c1979. 437p. (S674; 631.03 / 1. Agricultural engineering – Dictionaries. 2. Food industry and trade – Dictionaries.)

A   Farm and Garden Index. Jan./Mar. 1978- , v.1- .
       Mankato, Minn.: Minnesota Scholarly Press, 1978- . Quarterly.
       (Z5071; ____ / ____.)
SA   Farrall, Arthur W., and Albrecht, Carl F. Agricultural
       Engineering: A Dictionary and Handbook. Danville, Ill.: Interstate
       Printers & Publishers, 1965. 434p. bibl. (S674; 631.03 / 1.
       Agricultural engineering – Dictionaries. 2. Agricultural engineer-
       ing – Tables, etc.)
S   McGraw-Hill Encyclopedia of Food, Agriculture & Nutrition.
       Daniel N. Lapedes, ed. in chief. New York: McGraw-Hill, 1977.
       732p. (TX349; 641.03 / 1. Food – Dictionaries. 2. Agriculture – Dic-
       tionaries. 3. Nutrition – Dictionaries.)
S   Rasmussen, Wayne David, ed. Agriculture in the United
       States: A Documentary History. Westport, Conn.: Greenwood Press,
       1975. 4v. (S441; 630.073 / 1. Agriculture – United
       States – History – Sources.)
SA   Richey, C. B. [and others]. Agricultural Engineers'
       Handbook. New York: McGraw-Hill, 1961. 880p. bibl. (S675; 631 /
       1. Agricultural engineering.)
SA   Schapsmeier, Edward L., and Schapsmeier, Frederick H.
       Encyclopedia of American Agricultural History. Westport, Conn.:
       Greenwood Press, 1975. 467p. bibl. (S441; 630.973 / 1.
       Agriculture – United States – History – Dictionaries. 2.
       Agriculture – Dictionaries.)
S   United States. Department of Agriculture. Agricultural
       Statistics. Washington, D.C.: Government Printing Office, 1936- ,
       v.1- . Annual. (HD1751; 338.10973 / 1. Agriculture – United
       States – Statistics.)
SA   United States. Department of Agriculture. Office of
       Governmental and Public Affairs. Fact Book of U.S. Agriculture.
       Rev. Nov. 1978. Washington, D.C.: Government Printing Office,
       1978. 119p. bibl. (S21; 630.8 / 1. Agriculture – United States. 2.
       Agriculture – Economic aspects – United States.)
SA   Van Royen, William. Atlas of the World's Resources. New
       York: Prentice-Hall for the University of Maryland, Department of
       Geography, 1952-1954. 2v. bibl. (G1046.G3; 338 / 1. Natural
       resources. 2. Geography, Economic – Maps.)
S   Yearbook of Agriculture. Washington, D.C.: U.S. Department
       of Agriculture, 1926- . Annual. (S21; 630.58 / 1. Agriculture –
       Yearbooks.)

Agribusiness

The student of agribusiness is, of course, concerned with the financial and managerial side of contemporary agriculture. Besides the

more general tools listed under "Agricultural Technology," there are some very specific sources to be consulted: guides to farm management, to marketing of products, to commodity markets, and to consumer demand; handbooks of financial calculations, economic analysis, and law; and even a handbook for farm builders. These reference works may also be supplemented by some of the general works cited earlier in this chapter under "Business and Office Occupations," "Business and Management," and "Economics."

SA   Beuscher, Jacob Henry. *Beuscher's Law and the Farmer.*
4th ed. rev., updated, and expanded by Harold W. Hannah. New York: Springer, 1975. 452p. bibl. (KF390.F3; 343.73076 / 1. Farm law – United States.)

S   Bishop, Charles E., and Toussaint, William D. *Introduction to Agricultural Economic Analysis.* New York: Wiley, 1958. 258p. (HF1411; 338.1 / 1. Agriculture – Economic aspects.)

S   Botts, Ralph Rudolph. *Farmers' Handbook of Financial Calculations and Physical Measurements.* Rev. Nov. 1966. Washington, D.C.: U.S. Farm Production Economics Division, Economic Research Service, 1966. 54p. (S413; ____ / 1. Agriculture – Tables and ready-reckoners. 2. Physical measurements.)

SA   Dahl, Dale C., and Hammond, Jerome W. *Market and Price Analysis: The Agricultural Industries.* New York: McGraw-Hill, 1977. 323p. bibl. (HD9005; 380.1410973 / 1. Agricultural industries – United States. 2. Agricultural prices – United States.)

S   Doane Agricultural Service, St. Louis. *Doane's Facts & Figures for Farmers.* 3d ed. St. Louis: Doane Agricultural Service, c1977. 345p. (S501.2; 630.20112 / 1. Agriculture – Handbooks, manuals, etc. 2. Agriculture – United States – Handbooks, manuals, etc.)

S   Doane Agricultural Service, St. Louis. *Doane's Farm Management Guide.* 11th ed. St. Louis: Doane Agricultural Service, c1976. 336p. (S561; 658.930973 / 1. Farm management. 2. Farm management – United States.)

SA   George, P. S., and King, G. A. *Consumer Demand for Food Commodities in the United States with Projections for 1980.* Berkeley: California Agricultural Experiment Station, 1971. 161p. bibl. (HD1407.C27; 338.108 / 1. Food supply – United States – Statistics. 2. Food consumption – United States – Statistics.)

S   *Guide to World Commodity Markets.* Consultants, John Edwards and Brian Reidy; editor, Ethel de Keyser. 2d ed. New York: Nichols Publishing Co., 1979. 383p. (HG6046; 332.644 / 1. Commodity exchanges.)

SA   Kohls, Richard Louis, and Uhl, Joseph N. *Marketing of*

Agricultural Products. 5th ed. New York: Macmillan, c1980. 612p.
bibl. (HD9000.5; 381.41 / 1. Produce trade. 2. Produce
trade – United States. 3. Farm produce – Marketing.)

S   Luening, R. A., and Mortenson, William P. *The Farm
Management Handbook.* 6th ed. Danville, Ill.: Interstate Printers &
Publishers, c1979. 513p. (S561; 630.68 / 1. Farm management. 2.
Farm management – United States.)

S   Lytle, R. J. *Farm Builder's Handbook.* 3d ed. Farmington,
Mich.: Structures Publishing Co., c1978. 288p. (TH4916; 690.89 /
1. Farm buildings – Handbooks, manuals, etc.)

SA   Marion, Bruce W., and Handy, Charles R. *Market Performance:
Concepts and Measures.* Washington, D.C.: Economic Research Service, U.S. Department of Agriculture, 1973. 130p. bibl. (HD1751;
338.108 / 1. Production (Economic theory). 2. Competition. 3.
Markets.)

SA   McCoy, John Henry. *Livestock and Meat Marketing.* 2d ed.
Westport, Conn.: Avi Publishing Co., c1979. 479p. bibl. (HD9415;
381.41600973 / 1. Meat industry and trade – United States.)

SA   Roy, Ewell Paul; Corty, Floyd L.; and Sullivan, Gene D.
Economics: Applications to Agriculture and Agribusiness. 2d ed. Dan-
ville, Ill.: Interstate Printers & Publishers, c1975. 569p. bibl.
(HD1411; 338.10973 / 1. Agriculture – Economic aspects. 2.
Agriculture – Economic aspects – United States.)

SA   Shepherd, Geoffrey Seddon; Futrell, Gene A.; and Strain,
J. Robert. *Marketing Farm Products: Economic Analysis.* 6th ed.
Ames: Iowa State University Press, 1976. 485p. bibl. (HD9006;
338.13 / 1. Produce trade – United States. 2. Farm produce – Marketing.)

SA   Tomek, William G., and Robinson, Kenneth L. *Agricultural
Product Prices.* Ithaca, N.Y.: Cornell University Press, 1972. 376p.
bibl. (HD9000.5; 338.13 / 1. Agricultural prices.)

Animal Science

The animal scientist is concerned with breeding, raising, and
marketing various farm animals, particularly livestock. Listed below
are some general works on animal science, but also reference sources
for specific animals: swine, dairy and beef cattle, horses, sheep, and
chickens. Also cited are works on livestock health and even on
livestock equipment. Other useful works may be found under
"Veterinary Science," "Conservation and Wildlife Management," and
"Agricultural Technology."

S   Baker, James K., and Juergenson, Elwood M. *Approved*

      Practices in Swine Production. 6th ed. Danville, Ill.: Interstate
      Printers & Publishers, c1979. 432p. (SF395; 636.4 / 1. Swine.)

SA   *Dairy Cattle: Principles, Practices, Problems, Profits.*
      Donald L. Bath [and others]. 2d ed. Philadelphia: Lea & Febiger,
      1978. 574p. bibl. (SF208; 636.214 / 1. Dairy cattle. 2. Dairy
      farming.)

SA   Ensminger, M. Eugene. *Animal Science.* 7th ed. Danville,
      Ill.: Interstate Printers & Publishers, 1977. 1047p. bibl. (SF61;
      636.08 / 1. Livestock. 2. Livestock – United States.)

SA   Ensminger, M. Eugene. *Beef Cattle Science.* 5th ed.
      Danville, Ill.: Interstate Printers & Publishers, 1976. 1556p. bibl.
      (SF207; 636.213 / 1. Beef cattle.)

SA   Ensminger, M. Eugene. *Breeding and Raising Horses.*
      Washington, D.C.: Agricultural Research Service, U.S. Department
      of Agriculture, 1972. 81p. bibl. (S21.A37; 338.108 / 1. Horses.)

SA   Ensminger, M. Eugene. *Horses and Horsemanship.* 5th ed.
      Danville, Ill.: Interstate Printers & Publishers, 1977. 546p. bibl.
      (SF285; 636.1 / 1. Horses.)

S   Ensminger, M. Eugene. *The Stockman's Handbook.* 5th ed.
      Danville, Ill.: Interstate Printers & Publishers, 1978. 1192p. (SF61;
      636.08 / 1. Livestock.)

SA   Ensminger, M. Eugene. *Swine Science.* 4th ed. Danville,
      Ill.: Interstate Printers & Publishers, 1970. 881p. (SF395; 636.4 / 1.
      Swine. 2. Swine – United States.)

S   Juergenson, Elwood M. *Approved Practices in Sheep
      Production.* 3d ed. Danville, Ill.: Interstate Printers & Publishers,
      1973. 406p. (SF375; 636.3 / 1. Sheep.)

S   Juergenson, Elwood M. *Handbook of Livestock Equipment.*
      2d ed. Danville, Ill.: Interstate Printers & Publishers, c1979. 371p.
      (SF92; 636.08028 / 1. Livestock – Equipment and supplies.)

SA   Levie, Albert. *Meat Handbook.* 4th ed. Westport, Conn.:
      Avi Publishing Co., c1979. 338p. bibl. (TS1955; 664.92 / 1. Meat. 2.
      Meat industry and trade.)

SA   Melby, Edward C., and Altman, Norman H., eds. *CRC
      Handbook of Laboratory Animal Science.* Cleveland: CRC Press,
      1974–1976. 3v. bibl. (QL55; 636.0885 / 1. Laboratory animals. 2.
      Zoology, Experimental – Technique. 3. Medicine, Experimen-
      tal – Technique.)

S   North, Mack O. *Commercial Chicken Production Manual.*
      2d ed. Westport, Conn.: Avi Publishing Co., c1978. 692p. (SF487;
      636.5 / 1. Chickens.)

S   Schwartz, L. Dwight. *Pennsylvania Poultry Health
      Handbook.* University Park: Pennsylvania State University, College
      of Agriculture, c1972. 148p. (____; 636.50896 / 1.
      Poultry – Diseases.)

SA   Scott, George E. *The Sheepman's Production Handbook.*
     Prepared and edited by Dr. Hudson A. Glimp. 2d ed. Denver:
     Sheep Industry Development, c1970. 246p. bibl. (____; ____ / 1.
     Sheep.)
SA   Seiden, Rudolph. *Livestock Health Encyclopedia.* Ed. by
     W. James Gough. 3d ed. New York: Springer, 1968. 628p. bibl.
     (SF609; 636.08903 / 1. Veterinary medicine – Dictionaries.)

Conservation and Wildlife Management

The conservation and wildlife management student has a number of
reference works available to assist him or her in studying animal
resources to determine the best methods of conservation and propaga-
tion. There are several handbooks and histories on wildlife management and on conservation, as well as guides and atlases to wildlife.
You will also find directories to conservation and environmental
organizations, a work on land use and wildlife resources, and even a
biographical dictionary on prominent conservationists. Besides the
general works cited under "Agricultural Technology," the student of
wildlife management may find useful tools listed elsewhere in this
chapter under "Biology" and "Ecology."

SA   Borland, Hal Glen. *The History of Wildlife in America.*
     Washington, D.C.: National Wildlife Federation, c1975. 197p. bibl.
     (QH104; 591.973 / 1. Natural history – United States. 2. Wildlife
     conservation – United States – History. 3. Man – Influence on
     nature – United States – History. 4. United States – History.)
SA   Burger, George Vanderkarr. *Practical Wildlife Management.*
     New York: Winchester Press, 1973. 218p. bibl. (SK353; 639.9 / 1.
     Wildlife management.)
SA   Clepper, Henry Edward. *Leaders of American Conservation.*
     New York: Ronald Press, 1971. 353p. bibl. (S926.A2; 333.720922 /
     1. Conservationists – United States.)
SA   *Conservation and Agriculture.* Ed. by J. G. Hawkes.
     Montclair, N.J.: Allenheld, 1978. 284p. bibl. (S912; 333.76 / 1. Con-
     servation of natural resources – Congresses. 2. Agriculture
     ecology – Congresses. 3. Agricultural conservation – Congresses. 4.
     Forests and forestry – Environmental aspects – Congresses. 5. Forest
     conservation – Congresses. 6. Land use, Rural – Environmental
     aspects – Congresses.)
S   *Conservation Directory.* Washington, D.C.: National Wildlife
     Federation, 1956– . Annual. (S920; 333.95025733337 / 1. Conserva-
     tion of natural resources – Directories.)
SA   Dasmann, Raymond Frederick. *Environmental Conservation.*

4th ed. New York: Wiley, c1976. 427p. bibl. (S938; 333.72 / 1.
Conservation of natural resources. 2. Ecology. 3. Human ecology.)

S   Gabrielson, Ira N. *Wildlife Conservation.* 2d ed. New
York: Macmillan, 1959. 244p. (SK353; 799.0973 / 1. Wildlife
conservation.)

SA   Giles, Robert H. *Wildlife Management.* San Francisco:
W. H. Freeman, c1978. 416p. bibl. (SK353; 639.9 / 1. Wildlife
management.)

SA   Hanenkrat, Frank T. *Wildlife Watcher's Handbook.* New
York: Winchester Press, c1977. 241p. bibl. (QL60; 591 / 1. Wildlife
watching.)

S   Jordan, Emil Leopold. *Animal Atlas of the World.* Maplewood,
N.J.: Hammond, 1969. 224p. (QL50; 599 / 1. Animals. 2.
Zoogeography.)

S   McHenry, Robert, comp. *A Documentary History of Conservation
in America.* With Charles Van Doren. New York: Praeger, 1972.
422p. (S930; 333.720973 / 1. Conservation of natural
resources – United States – History – Sources. 2. Ecology – United
States – History – Sources.)

SA   National Research Council. Committee on Agricultural Land
Use and Wildlife Resources. *Land Use and Wildlife Resources.*
Washington, D.C.: National Academy of Sciences, 1970. 262p. bibl.
(SK353; 333.70973 / 1. Wildlife management. 2. Land use.)

S   Ovington, Ray. *Wildlife Illustrated.* Northfield, Ill.:
Digest Books, 1974. 256p. (QL151; 596.097 / 1. Game and game-
birds – North America. 2. Fishes – North America.)

SA   *The Rand McNally Atlas of World Wildlife.* New York:
Rand McNally, c1973. 208p. bibl. (____; 591.9 / 1. Zoogeography.)

SA   Schoenfeld, Clarence Albert, and Hendee, John C. *Wildlife
Management in Wilderness.* Pacific Grove, Calif.: Boxwood Press,
1978. 172p. bibl. (____; 639.9 / 1. Wilderness areas – Management.
2. Wildlife management – United States.)

S   Street, Philip. *Wildlife Preservation.* Chicago: H.
Regnery Co., c1970. 141p. (S962; 639.9 / 1. Wildlife conservation.)

SA   Trippensee, Reuben Edwin. *Wildlife Management.* 1st ed.
New York: McGraw-Hill, 1948-1953. 2v. bibl. (SK353; 333.78 / 1.
Wildlife conservation – North America. 2. Game – North America.)

S   *World Directory of Environmental Organizations.* Ed. by
Thaddeus C. Trzyna and Eugene V. Coan. Claremont, Calif.: Se-
quoia Institute, 1973- , v.1- . (S920; 333.72025 / 1. Conservation of
natural resources – Directories – Periodicals. 2. Environmental protection – Directories – Periodicals.)

S   *The World Wildlife Guide.* Edited by Malcolm Ross-Macdonald.
New York: Viking Press, c1971. 416p. (SB481; 910.202 / 1. National parks and reserves. 2. Wildlife refuges. 3. Parks.)

Culinary Arts

The student in culinary arts is interested in tools that will deal not only with large quantity cooking, but also with beverage preparation, nutritional quality, and even kitchen supervision. The tools listed here meet those needs exactly: there are guides to alcoholic and nonalcoholic beverages, handbooks on nutritional contents in foods, guides to preparation of fast foods and even desserts, and, of course, some standard cookbooks. There is even a work on kitchen operations and staff management. It probably goes without saying that some of the tools cited under "Agricultural Technology" may prove useful occasionally. You may also find some useful works listed in the following section, "Food Technology."

S   Adams, Catherine F. *Encyclopedia of Food & Nutrition.*
       New York: Drake Publishers, 1977. 175p. (TX551; 641.103 / 1.
       Food – Composition – Tables.)

SA   American Home Economics Association. Food and Nutrition
       Section. Terminology Committee. *Handbook of Food Preparation.*
       6th ed. Washington, D.C.: American Home Economics Association,
       1971. 116p. bibl. (TX535; 330.973 / 1. Food. 2. Cookery.)

SA   Grossman, Harold J. *Grossman's Guide to Wines, Beers,*
       and Spirits. 6th rev. ed., rev. by Harriet Lembeck. New York:
       Scribner, c1977. 634p. bibl. (TP505; 641.2 / 1. Alcoholic beverages.)

SA   Hardwick, Geraline B., and Kennedy, Robert L. *Fundamentals*
       of Quantity Food Preparation: Desserts and Beverages. Jule Wilkin-
       son, ed. Boston: Cahners Books, 1975. 338p. bibl. (TX820; 641.86 /
       1. Quantity cookery. 2. Desserts. 3. Beverages.)

SA   Lichine, Alexis. *Lichine's Encyclopedia of Wines &*
       Spirits. In collaboration with William Fifield. Enlarged and com-
       pletely rev. ed. London: Cassell, 1979. 716p. bibl. (TP546;
       641.2220321 / 1. Wine and wine-making – Dictionaries.)

S   Montagné, Prosper. *The New Larousse Gastronomique: The*
       Encyclopedia of Food, Wine & Cookery. American editor, Charlotte
       Turgeon. New York: Crown, c1977. 1064p. (TX349; 641.03 / 1.
       Cookery – Dictionaries – French. 2. Food – Dictionaries – French. 3.
       Cookery, French.)

SA   Pennington, Jean A. Thompson. *Dietary Nutrient Guide.*
       Westport, Conn.: Avi Publishing Co., 1976. 276p. bibl. (QP141;
       641.1 / 1. Nutrition – Tables. 2. Dietary supplements – Tables. 3.
       Nutrition – Bibliography.)

S   Rietz, Carl A. *Rietz Master Food Guide.* Ed. by Norman
       W. Desrosier. Westport, Conn.: Avi Publishing Co., c1978. 445p.
       (TX651; 641.5 / 1. Food. 2. Cookery. 3. Gastronomy.)

S   Rombauer, Irma von Starkloff, and Becker, Marion Rombauer.
     Joy of Cooking. Indianapolis, Ind.: Bobbs-Merrill, 1975. 915p.
     (TX715; 641.5 / 1. Cookery, American.)

SA   Simon, André Louis, and Howe, Robine. *Dictionary of
     Gastronomy.* New York: Overlook Press, c1970. ca. 400p. bibl.
     (TX349; 641.03 / 1. Food–Dictionaries. 2. Cookery–Dictionaries.)

SA   Thorner, Marvin Edward. *Convenience and Fast Food
     Handbook.* Westport, Conn.: Avi Publishing Co., 1973. 358p. bibl.
     (TX820; 641.57 / 1. Quantity cookery. 2. Convenience foods.)

SA   Thorner, Marvin Edward, and Herzberg, Ronald J. *Non-Alcoholic
     Food Service Beverage Handbook.* 2d ed. Westport, Conn.: Avi
     Publishing Co., c1978. 343p. bibl. (TX815; 642.5 / 1. Beverages. 2.
     Food service.)

SA   Van Duyn, J. A. *Successful Kitchen Operations and Staff
     Management Handbook.* Englewood Cliffs, N.J.: Prentice-Hall, 1979.
     234p. bibl. (TX911.3.M27; 658.9164795 / 1. Restaurant manage-
     ment. 2. Food service management.)

SA   Watt, Bernice Kunerth, and Merrill, Annabel L. *Handbook
     of the Nutritional Contents of Foods.* Prepared for the United States
     Department of Agriculture. New York: Dover, 1975. 190p. bibl.
     (TX551; 641.1 / 1. Food–Composition–Tables.)

Food Technology

The student of food technology–or food science–is interested in learning how to buy, process, preserve, package, grade, and market food products. The tools listed here, while few in number, will assist the food technician in accomplishing those tasks. There are general encyclopedic sources on food science; dictionaries of food and food engineering; handbooks on food additives, flavor ingredients, and food products; and a nutritional quality index. Some of the tools cited under both "Agricultural Technology" and "Culinary Arts" may also prove helpful to the prospective food technician.

SA   *CRC Handbook of Food Additives.* Editor, Thomas E. Furia.
     2d ed. Cleveland: CRC Press, c1972. 998p. bibl. (TX553.A3;
     664.06 / 1. Food additives–Handbooks, manuals, etc.)

S   *Encyclopedia of Food Science.* Ed. by Martin S. Peterson,
     Arnold H. Johnson. Westport, Conn.: Avi Publishing Co., c1978.
     1005p. (TP368.2; 664.003 / 1. Food industry and trade–
     Dictionaries.)

SA   Fenaroli, Giovanni. *Fenaroli's Handbook of Flavor Ingredients.*
     Edited, translated, and rev. by Thomas E. Furia and Nicolo Bellan-
     ca. 2d ed. Cleveland: CRC Press, 1975. 2v. bibl. (TP418; 664.5 / 1.

         Flavoring essences – Handbooks, manuals, etc.)
S   *Food Products Formulary.* Westport, Conn.: Avi Publishing Co.,
         1974–1976. 3v. (TP370.4; 664.028 / 1. Food industry and
         trade – Handbooks, manuals, etc.)
SA   Hall, Carl W.; Farrall, A. W.; and Rippen, A. L.
         Encyclopedia of Food Engineering. Westport, Conn.: Avi Publishing
         Co., 1971. 755p. bibl. (TP369; 664.003 / 1. Food industry and
         trade – Dictionaries.)
SA   Hansen, Roger Gaurth; Wyse, Bonita W.; and Sorenson, Ann W.
         Nutritional Quality Index of Foods. Westport, Conn.: Avi Publishing
         Co., c1979. 636p. bibl. (TX353; 641.1 / 1. Food. 2. Nutrition. 3.
         Food – Composition – Tables.)
SA   Johnson, Arnold Harvey, and Peterson, Martin S. *Encyclopedia
         of Food Technology.* Westport, Conn.: Avi Publishing Co., 1974.
         993p. bibl. (TP368.2; 664.003 / 1. Food industry and trade –
         Dictionaries.)
SA   Ockerman, Herbert W. *Source Book for Food Scientists.*
         Westport, Conn.: Avi Publishing Co., c1978. 926p. bibl. (TX349;
         664.003 / 1. Food – Dictionaries. 2. Food – Composition – Tables.)

Forestry

   Regardless of whether you plan to work in the care, management,
harvesting, or replanting of forests or in the production of wood-
derived products, you will find tools of use to you listed below. There
are several guides to trees, a statistical yearbook on forest products, an
atlas of trees, and an organizational directory of the U.S. Forest Service. You will also find dictionaries of terms used not just in forestry
but also in logging, and even a bibliography for access to works on the
identification of trees and shrubs. Keep in mind that your library may
well have specific guides to trees in your region as well as the more
general ones listed here. Also remember that the titles cited under
"Agricultural Technology" may prove useful to you.

SA   Forbes, Reginald Dunderdale. *Forestry Handbook.* Ed. for
         the Society of American Foresters. New York: Ronald Press, 1955.
         1v. in various pagings. bibl. (SD371; 634.9 / 1. Forests and
         forestry.)
S   Leathart, Scott. *Trees of the World.* New York: A. &
         W. Publishers, c1977. 224p. (QK475.6; _____ / 1. Trees – Pictorial
         works.)
SA   Little, Elbert Luther. *Check List of Native and Naturalized
         Trees of the United States (Including Alaska).* Prepared under the
         direction of the Forest Service Tree and Range Plant Name Com-
         mittee. Washington, D.C.: U.S. Department of Agriculture, Forest

    Service, 1953. 472p. bibl. (QK481; 582.16581973 / 1. Trees – United
States. 2. Trees – Nomenclature (Popular). 3.
Botany – Nomenclature.)

A   Little, Elbert Luther, and Honkala, Barbara H. *Trees
and Shrubs of the United States: A Bibliography for Identification.*
Washington, D.C.: U.S. Department of Agriculture, Forest Service,
1976. 56p. (S21.A46; 630.8 / 1. Trees – United States – Identification – Bibliography. 2. Shrubs – United States – Identification – Bibliography.)

S   McCulloch, Walter Fraser. *Woods Words: A Comprehensive
Dictionary of Loggers Terms.* Portland, Oreg.: Oregon Historical
Society, 1958. 219p. (PE3727.L8; 427.9 / 1. English
language – Slang – Dictionaries. 2. Lumbermen – Language (New
words, slang, etc.). 3. Lumbering – Terminology.)

SA   Nicholson, Barbara Evelyn. *The Oxford Book of Trees.*
Text by A. R. Clapham. London: Oxford University Press, 1975.
216p. bibl. (QK488; 582.160941 / 1. Trees – Great Britain – Identification. 2. Trees – Great Britain – Pictorial works.)

SA   Rendle, B. J. *World Timbers.* London: E. Benn, 1969–1970.
3v. bibl. (SD536; 674 / 1. Wood.)

SA   Society of American Foresters. Committee on Forestry
Terminology. *Forestry Terminology: A Glossary of Technical Terms
Used in Forestry.* 3d ed. Washington, D.C.: Society of American
Foresters, 1958. 97p. bibl. (SD126; 634.903 / 1. Forests and
forestry – Dictionaries.)

SA   United States. Division of Timber Management Research.
Silvics of Forest Trees of the United States. Compiled and revised by
H. A. Fowells. Washington, D.C.: U.S. Department of Agriculture,
Forest Service, 1965. 762p. bibl. (SD395; 582.160973 / 1. Forest
ecology. 2. Trees – United States.)

SA   United States. Forest Service. *Atlas of United States Trees.* Washington,
D.C.: U.S. Department of Agriculture, Forest Service, 1971– ,
v.1– . bibl. (S21.A46; 630.8 / 1. Trees – United States –
Maps.)

A   United States. Forest Service. *Forest Service
Organizational Directory.* Washington, D.C.: U.S. Department of
Agriculture, Forest Service. (___; ___ / ___.)

S   *Yearbook of Forest Products: Annuaire statistique des
produits forestiers.* Washington, D.C.: Food and Agriculture
Organization of the United Nations, 1947– . Annual. (HD9750.4;
___ / 1. Forest products – Yearbooks. 2. Forest
products – Statistics.)

Horticulture/Floriculture

There are a variety of specializations for the horticulture/

floriculture major: everything from nursery management to landscaping. And in this section you will find listed many tools that will
support your studies, regardless of your particular specialization. There
are numerous works identifying plants and flowers of all types,
specialized works in botany, popular works on gardening, and guides
to plant diseases and pests. You will also find a directory of horticulture, a guide to botanical gardens, and even a handbook for
grounds maintenance. Keep in mind that there exist many regional
guides to wildflowers, types of plants, and so on, and your library is
likely to have some on its shelves. Also remember that some of the
tools listed under "Agricultural Technology" may prove useful.

SA   American Joint Committee on Horticultural Nomenclature.
      *Standardized Plant Names: A Revised and Enlarged Listing of Ap-
      proved Scientific and Common Names of Plants and Plant Products in
      American Commerce or Use.* 2d ed. Harrisburg, Pa.: J. Horace
      McFarland Company for American Joint Committee on Hor-
      ticultural Nomenclature, 1942. 675p. bibl. (QK11; 580.14 / 1.
      Botany–Nomenclature. 2. Plant names, Popular.)

S   Bailey, Liberty Hyde. *Manual of Cultivated Plants Most
      Commonly Grown in the Continental United States and Canada.* Rev.
      ed., completedly restudied. New York: Macmillan, 1949. 1116p.
      (QK110; 581.97 / 1. Botany–United States. 2. Botany–Canada. 3.
      Plants, Cultivated.)

SA   Bailey, Liberty Hyde. *The Standard Cyclopedia of Horticulture.*
      New ed. New York: Macmillan, 1928. 3v. bibl. (SB45; 716.03 / 1.
      Gardening–Dictionaries.)

S   Bailey, Liberty Hyde, and Bailey, Ethel Zoe. *Hortus
      Third: A Concise Dictionary of Plants Cultivated in the United States
      and Canada.* Rev. and expanded by the staff of the Liberty Hyde
      Bailey Hortorium. New York: Macmillan, 1976. 1290p. (SB45;
      582.061 / 1. Plants, Cultivated–North America–Dictionaries. 2.
      Gardening–North American–Dictionaries.)

S   Conover, Herbert S. *Grounds Maintenance Handbook.* 3d ed.
      New York: McGraw-Hill, 1977. 631p. (SB476; 635.9 / 1. Grounds
      maintenance.)

SA   Cunningham, John J., and Côté, Rosalie J. *Common Plants:
      Botanical and Colloquial Nomenclature.* New York: Garland, 1977.
      120p. bibl. (QK13; 581.014 / 1. Plant names, Popular. 2.
      Botany–Nomenclature. 3. Plant lore.)

A   *Directory of American Horticulture.* Mt. Vernon, Va.:
      American Horticultural Society, 1954– . Annual. (SB1; 635.02572 /
      1. Horticulture–United States–Directories. 2. Hor-
      ticulture–Canada–Directories. 3. Horticulture societies.)

S   *The Encyclopedia of Organic Gardening.* By the staff of

Organic Gardening magazine. New rev. ed. Emmaus, Pa.: Rodale Press, 1978. 1236p. (SB453.5; 631.58 / 1. Organic gardening – Dictionaries.)

S   Everett, Thomas H. *The New York Botanical Garden Illustrated Encyclopedia of Horticulture.* New York: Garland, 1980- , v.1- . (SB317.58; 635.90321 / 1. Horticulture – Dictionaries. 2. Gardening – Dictionaries. 3. Plants, Ornamental – Dictionaries. 4. Plants, Cultivated – Dictionaries.)

SA Featherly, Henry Ira. *Taxonomic Terminology of the Higher Plants.* Ames: Iowa State College Press, 1954. 166p. bibl. (QK9; 580.3 / 1. Botany – Dictionaries. 2. Botany – Dictionaries – Latin. 3. Latin language – Dictionaries – English.)

SA Graf, Alfred Byrd. *Tropica: Color Cyclopedia of Exotic Plants and Trees from the Tropics and Subtropics.* 1st ed. East Rutherford, N.J.: Roehrs Company, 1978. 1120p. bibl. (SB407; 635.9520222 / 1. Plants, Ornamental – Pictorial works. 2. Tropical plants – Pictorial works. 3. House plants – Pictorial works.)

S   Gray, Asa. *Manual of Botany: A Handbook of the Flowering Plants and Ferns of the Central and Northeastern United States and Adjacent Canada.* 8th centennial ed. Largely rewritten and expanded by Merritt Lyndon Fernald with assistance of specialists in some groups. New York: American Book Co., 1950. 1632p. (QK117; 581.973 / 1. Botany – United States.)

S   Hay, Roy, and Synge, Patrick M. *The Color Dictionary of Flowers and Plants for Home and Garden.* U.S. consultant: George Kalmbacher. New York: Crown, c1969. 373p. (SB407; 635.903 / 1. Plants, Ornamental – Pictorial works. 2. Plants, Ornamental – Dictionaries.)

SA Howes, Frank N. *A Dictionary of Useful and Everyday Plants and Their Common Names.* Based on material contained in J. C. Willis, *A Dictionary of the Flowering Plants and Ferns* (6th ed., 1931). New York: Cambridge University Press, 1974. 290p. bibl. (QK13; 581.03 / 1. Plant names, Popular – Dictionaries. 2. Botany, Economic – Dictionaries. 3. Plants, Ornamental – Dictionaries.)

S   Hutchinson, John. *The Families of Flowering Plants Arranged According to a New System Based on Their Probable Phylogeny.* 3d ed. Oxford: Clarendon Press, 1973. 968p. (QK97; 582.13012 / 1. Botany – Classification. 2. Angiosperms.)

S   Hyams, Edward S. *Great Botanical Gardens of the World.* 1st U.S. ed. New York: Macmillan, 1969. 288p. (QK71; 580.744 / 1. Botanical gardens.)

SA Kingsbury, John Merriam. *Poisonous Plants of the United States and Canada.* Englewood Cliffs, N.J.: Prentice-Hall, 1964. 626p. bibl. (SB617; 581.69 / 1. Poisonous plants. 2. Botany – North America.)

SA Moerman, Daniel E. *American Medical Ethnobotany: A*

      Reference Dictionary. New York: Garland, 1977. 527p. bibl.
      (E98.M4; 615.321 / 1. Indians of North America – Medicine – Dic-
      tionaries. 2. Ethnobotany – North America – Dictionaries. 3. Indians
      of North America – Medicine – Bibliography. 4.
      Ethnobotany – North America – Bibliography.)

SA   Pirone, Pascal P. *Diseases and Pests of Ornamental Plants.*
      5th ed. New York: Wiley, 1978. 566p. bibl. (SB603.5; 635.92 / 1.
      Plants, Ornamental – Diseases and pests.)

SA   Powell, Thomas, and Powell, Betty. *The Avant Gardener:*
      A Handbook and Sourcebook of All That's New and Useful in Garden-
      ing. Boston: Houghton Mifflin, 1975. 263p. bibl. (SB453; 635 / 1.
      Gardening.)

S   Rickett, Harold William. *Wild Flowers of the United States.*
      General ed., William C. Steere. 1st ed. New York: McGraw-Hill,
      1966-1973. 6v. in 14 pts. (QK115; 582.130973 / 1. Wild
      flowers – United States – Pictorial works.)

SA   Splittstoesser, Walter E. *Vegetable Growing Handbook.*
      Westport, Conn.: Avi Publishing Co., 1979. 298p. bibl. (SB321;
      635 / 1. Vegetable gardening.)

S   Usher, George. *A Dictionary of Botany: Including Terms*
      Used in Biochemistry, Soil Science and Statistics. London: Constable;
      New York: Van Nostrand, 1970. 408p. (QK9; 581.03 / 1.
      Botany – Dictionaries.)

SA   Westcott, Cynthia. *Westcott's Plant Disease Handbook.*
      4th ed., rev. by R. Kenneth Horst. New York: Van Nostrand
      Reinhold, c1979. 803p. bibl. (SB731; 632 / 1. Plant diseases. 2.
      Plant diseases – United States.)

S   Wyman, Donald. *Wyman's Gardening Encyclopedia.* Rev.
      and expanded ed. New York: Macmillan, 1977. 1221p. (SB45;
      635.03 / 1. Gardening – Dictionaries. 2. Plants, Cultivated –
      Dictionaries.)

Veterinary Science

    The tools listed here will be useful to the community college student
who is enrolled in a preveterinary science program. Some of these
resources may also be of interest to animal scientists and farmers.
There are handbooks of infectious diseases, drugs, and diagnosis, as
well as a yearbook on animal health and an encyclopedic source tool
on animal care. There is even a handbook of surgical instruments and
a bibliographic guide for access to other informational resources in
veterinary medicine. The interested student may find other useful
sources listed under "Animal Science" and "Agricultural Technology."

S   *Animal Health Yearbook: Annuaire de la santé animale:*
     Anuario de sanidad animal. [New York?] Food and Agriculture
     Organization of the United Nations, 1975- . Annual. (SF600;
     636.08944 / 1. Veterinary medicine – Yearbooks. 2. Communicable
     diseases in animals – Statistics – Yearbooks.)

S   *Encyclopedia of Animal Care.* 12th ed., edited by Geoffrey
     P. West. Baltimore: Williams & Wilkins, 1977. 867p. (SF609;
     636.08903 / 1. Veterinary medicine – Dictionaries.)

SA   Hagan, William Arthur. *Hagan's Infectious Diseases of*
     Domestic Animals. With special reference to etiology, diagnosis, and
     biologic therapy by Dorsey William Bruner and James Howard
     Gillespie. 6th ed. Ithaca, N.Y.: Comstock Publishing Associates,
     1973. 1385p. bibl. (SF781; 636.08969 / 1. Communicable diseases
     in animals. 2. Veterinary microbiology.)

S   Hurov, L. *Handbook of Veterinary Surgical Instruments and*
     Glossary of Surgical Terms. With the assistance of K. Knauer, R.
     Playter, R. Sexton. Philadelphia: Saunders, 1978. 214p. (SF913;
     636.08979178 / 1. Veterinary surgery – Instruments. 2. Veterinary
     surgery – Terminology.)

A   Kerker, Ann E., and Murphy, Henry T. *Comparative &*
     Veterinary Medicine: A Guide to the Resource Literature. Madison:
     University of Wisconsin Press, 1973. 308p. (Z7991; 016.61 / 1.
     Zoology – Bibliography. 2. Veterinary medicine – Bibliography. 3.
     Medicine – Bibliography.)

S   *The Merck Veterinary Manual: A Handbook of Diagnosis*
     and Therapy for the Veterinarian. O. H. Siegmund, ed. 4th ed.
     Rahway, N.J.: Merck, 1973. 1618p. (SF745; 636.0896 / 1.
     Veterinary medicine – Handbooks, manuals, etc.)

S   Rossoffl, Irving S. *Handbook of Veterinary Drugs: A*
     Compendium for Research and Clinical Use. New York: Springer,
     c1974. 730p. (SF917; 636.08951 / 1. Veterinary drugs.)

S   Spaulding, C. E. *A Veterinary Guide for Animal Owners:*
     Cattle, Goats, Sheep, Horses, Pigs, Poultry, Rabbits, Dogs, Cats. Em-
     maus, Pa.: Rodale Press, c1976. 420p. (SF745; 636.089 / 1.
     Veterinary medicine.)

TRADE, TECHNICAL, AND INDUSTRIAL OCCUPATIONS

If you scanned the Table of Contents, you will have noticed that the
broad area of "Trade, Technical, and Industrial Occupations" contains
a wide variety of subjects, everything from automotive maintenance
and repair and cosmetology to law enforcement and printing. Because
these subjects are almost totally unrelated, you will probably not be
surprised to see that there are no reference tools listed for this broad

area. Thus, you may turn directly to your specific subject, and, of course, to the general reference tools listed in Chapter 2.

Air-conditioning, Heating, and Refrigeration

While there are relatively few titles listed here for the student of air-conditioning, heating, and refrigeration, those listed are extremely useful. There is a manual for testing and balancing in air-conditioning, handbooks on air-conditioning, heating, and ventilating and on fuels and combustion, as well as a dictionary of specialized terms. One of the handbooks is authored by ASHRAE – the American Society of Heating, Refrigerating and Air-Conditioning Engineers. This particular organization issues other reputable publications you should look for in your library's catalog.

S   American Society of Heating, Refrigerating and Air-Conditioning
       Engineers. *ASHRAE Handbook & Product Directory.* New York:
       Society, 1973– . (TH7011; 697 / 1. Heat engineering – Handbooks,
       manuals, etc. 2. Ventilation – Handbooks, manuals, etc. 3. Air
       conditioning – Handbooks, manuals, etc. 4. Refrigeration
       and refrigerating machinery – Handbooks, manuals,
       etc.)

A   *Applied Science and Technology Index.* New York: H. W.
       Wilson, 1913– . Monthly, except July. Quarterly and annual
       cumulations. (Z7913; 016.6 / 1. Engineering – Periodicals – Indexes.
       2. Technology – Periodicals – Indexes. 3. Industrial
       arts – Periodicals – Indexes.)

SA   Gladstone, John. *Air Conditioning Testing and Balancing:
       A Field Practice Manual.* New York: Van Nostrand Reinhold, 1974.
       110p. bibl. (TH7687.7; 697.93 / 1. Air conditioning – Equipment
       and supplies – Testing – Handbooks, manuals, etc.)

SA   *Handbook of Air Conditioning, Heating, and Ventilating.*
       Eugene Stamper, ed. 3d ed. New York: Industrial Press, c1979.
       1366p. bibl. (TH7687; 697 / 1. Air conditioning – Handbooks,
       manuals, etc. 2. Heating – Handbooks, manuals, etc. 3. Ventila-
       tion – Handbooks, manuals, etc.)

SA   Johnson, Allen J., and Auth, George H. *Fuels and
       Combustion Handbook.* New York: McGraw-Hill, 1951. 915p. bibl.
       (TP318; 662.6 / 1. Fuel. 2. Combustion.)

S   Zurick, Timothy. *Air Conditioning, Heating & Refrigeration
       Dictionary.* Birmingham, Mich.: Business News Publishing Co.,
       1977. (TH7007; 697 / 1. Air conditioning – Dictionaries. 2.
       Heating – Dictionaries. 3. Refrigeration and refrigerating
       machinery – Dictionaries.)

Automotive Maintenance and Repair

The tools listed below will be of interest not just to the student of automotive maintenance and repair, but also to car buffs. There are handbooks on such topics as cooling systems, transistorized ignitions, emission controls, and automotive electronics as well as dictionaries of specialized terms, encyclopedias of automobiles, a bibliographic guide for access to further information, and even a work that lists serial numbers for U.S.-built cars from 1900 to 1975. You will notice that one work is authored and another published by the Society of Automotive Engineers (SAE). This professional association is an important source of information, and you should look for other publications by it in the catalog. Also, not listed but of equally vital interest are the many publications issued by Mitchell Manuals, Inc. This publisher issues a large number of works in service and repair, estimating, and speciality work for both domestic and foreign automobiles and trucks. These guides and handbooks may be accessed in the catalog either by subject or, frequently, under "Mitchell Manuals."

A   *Applied Science and Technology Index.* New York: H. W.
         Wilson, 1913- . Monthly, except July. Quarterly and annual
         cumulations. (Z7913; 016.6 / 1. Engineering – Periodicals – Indexes.
         2. Technology – Periodicals – Indexes. 3. Industrial
         arts – Periodicals – Indexes.)
S   Armento, Richard F. *Automotive Cooling System Training
         and Reference Manual.* Reston, Va.: Reston, c1979. 150p.
         (TL214.R3; 629.256028 / 1. Automobiles – Motors – Cooling
         systems – Maintenance and repair.)
S   Brant, Carroll A. *Transistor Ignition Systems.* 1st ed.
         Blue Ridge Summit, Pa.: G/L Tab Books, 1976. 250p. (TL213;
         629.254 / 1. Automobiles – Ignition – Maintenance and repair.)
S   Brigham, Grace. *The Serial Number Book for U.S. Cars,
         1900-1975.* Osceola, Wis.: Motorbooks International, c1979. 275p.
         (TL154; 388.3422 / 1. Automobiles – United States – Serial
         numbers.)
S   Chilton Book Company. Automotive Book Dept. *Chilton's
         Guide to Emission Controls and How They Work.* Ed. in Chief, John
         D. Kelly. 1st ed. Radnor, Pa.: Chilton, 1974. 160p. (TL214.P6;
         629.252 / 1. Automobiles – Pollution control devices.)
S   Chilton Book Company. Automotive Editorial Dept. *Chilton's
         Basic Auto Maintenance.* Radnor, Pa.: Chilton, 1976. 708p. (TL152;
         629.28722 / 1. Automobiles – Maintenance and repair.)

S   *Chilton's Motor/Age Professional Auto Heating and Air
     Conditioning Manual.* Radnor, Pa.: Chilton, c1979. 1184p. (TL271.5;
     ____ / 1. Automobiles – Air conditioning – Maintenance and repair.
     2. Automobiles – Heating and ventilation – Maintenance and repair.)

S   Crouse, William Harry, and Anglin, Donald L. *Automotive
     Technician's Handbook.* New York: McGraw-Hill, 1979. 664p.
     (TL152; 629.287 / 1. Motor vehicles – Maintenance and repair. 2.
     Automobiles – Maintenance and repair.)

S   Dinkel, John. *The Road & Track Illustrated Auto Dictionary.*
     1st ed. New York: Norton, c1977. 92p. (TL9; 629.203 / 1.
     Automobiles – Dictionaries.)

S   Evenson, A. E. *The Complete Handbook of Automotive Engines
     & Systems.* 1st ed. Blue Ridge Summit, Pa.: Tab Books, 1974. 252p.
     (TL210; 629.2504 / 1. Automobiles – Motors.)

S   Georgano, G. N. *The Complete Encyclopedia of Motorcars,
     1885 to the Present.* 2d ed. New York: Dutton, 1973. 751p. (TL15;
     629.222209 / 1. Automobiles – History.)

S   *Goodheart-Willcox Automotive Encyclopedia: Fundamental
     Principles, Operation, Construction, Service, Repair.* Ed. by William
     King Toboldt, Larry Johnson. South Holland, Ill.:
     Goodheart-Willcox Co., 1975. 768p. (TL205; 629.2222 / 1.
     Automobiles. 2. Automobiles – Maintenance and repair.)

S   Hallmark, Clayton. *Auto Electronics Simplified: A Complete
     Guide to Service/Repair of Automotive Electronic Systems.* 1st ed. Blue
     Ridge Summit, Pa.: Tab Books, 1975. 266p. (TL272.5; 629.254 / 1.
     Automobiles – Electronic equipment – Maintenance and repair.)

S   Heasley, Jerry. *The Production Figure Book for U.S. Cars.*
     Osceola, Wis.: Motorbooks International, c1977. 180p.
     (HD9710.U52; 338.476292220973 / 1. Automobile industry and
     trade – United States – Statistics.)

S   Jennings, Ralph E. *The Automotive Dictionary.* New York:
     William Dogan Annual Publications Associates, 1969. 277p.
     (TL9; 629.203 / 1. Automobiles – Dictionaries.)

S   *Motor's Emission Control Manual.* Editors, Joe Oldham and
     Lou Forier. New York: Motor, 1973- , v.1- . (TL214.P6; 629.252 /
     1. Motor vehicles – Pollution control devices – Handbooks,
     manuals, etc.)

S   *SAE Handbook.* New York: Society of Automotive Engineers,
     1926- . Annual. (TL151; ____ / 1. Automobile engineering – Hand-
     books, manuals, etc.)

A   Schipf, Robert G. *Automotive Repair and Maintenance.*
     Littleton, Colo.: Libraries Unlimited, 1973. 119p. (Z5173.M3;
     016.62928722 / 1. Automobiles – Maintenance and
     repair – Bibliography.)

S   Society of Automotive Engineers. Nomenclature Advisory
     Committee. *SAE Motor Vehicle, Safety, and Environmental Ter-*

minology. Warrendale, Pa.: Society of Automotive Engineers, c1977. 179p. (TL9; 629.231028 / 1. Automobiles – Dictionaries. 2. Automobiles – Safety measures – Dictionaries.)

S   *Whole Car Catalog.* By the editors of *Consumer Guide.* New York: Simon & Schuster, c1977. 320p. (TL152; 629.28822 / 1. Automobiles – Maintenance and repair.)

S   *The World of Automobiles: An Illustrated Encyclopedia of the Motor Car.* Executive ed., Ian Ward. Reference ed. Milwaukee: Purnell Reference Books, c1977. 22v. (TL9; 629.203 / 1. Automobiles – Dictionaries.)

Aviation Occupations

The majority of the titles listed here will be of interest primarily to the aviation student learning to fly, although some of the historical and aircraft identification guides will be of interest to the aviation maintenance technician. Among the tools cited below, you will find the following: dictionaries of specialized terms, encyclopedic sources, handbooks on private piloting, instrument flying, and even Federal Aviation Administration (FAA) regulations, and a who's-who type of biographical source. There is even a bibliographic guide that will lead you to many other sources of information.

S   Aero Publishers, Inc. *Federal Aviation Regulations for Pilots.* Fallbrook, Calif.: Aero Publishers, c1979. 112p. (KF2400; 343.73097 / 1. Aeronautics – Law and legislation – United States. 2. Air pilots – Legal status, laws, etc. – United States. 3. Airplanes – Piloting.)

S   *Airman's Information Manual.* Fallbrook, Calif.: Aero Publishers. Annual. (TL710; 629.132520973 / 1. Airplanes – Piloting. 2. Aids to air navigation – United States. 3. Airports – United States – Directories.)

A   *Applied Science and Technology Index.* New York: H. W. Wilson, 1913- . Monthly, except July. Quarterly and annual cumulations. (Z7913; 016.6 / 1. Engineering – Periodicals – Indexes. 2. Technology – Periodicals – Indexes. 3. Industrial arts – Periodicals – Indexes.)

S   *Aviation & Space Dictionary.* 1st- , 1940- . Los Angeles: Aero Publishers, 1940- . Irregular. (TL509; 629.1303 / 1. Aeronautics – Dictionaries. 2. Astronautics – Dictionaries.)

S   Briddon, Arnold E.; Champie, Ellmore A.; and Marraine, Peter A. *FAA Historical Fact Book: A Chronology, 1926-1971.* 2d ed. Washington, D.C.: Federal Aviation Administration, Office of Information Services, 1974. 315p. (TL521; 353.00877709 / 1. United

States. Federal Aviation Administration – History.)

S   *Encyclopedia of Aviation.* New York: Scribner's, 1977.
218p. (TL509; 387.703 / 1. Aeronautics – Dictionaries.)

S   Flatau, Courtney L., and Mitchell, Jerome. *Instrument Flying Handbook.* New York: Van Nostrand, 1979. (TL711.B6; 629.13252 / 1. Instrument flying.)

S   Foye, James, and Crane, Dale. *Aircraft Technical Dictionary.* 1st ed. Basin, Wyo.: Aviation Maintenance Publishers, c1978. 193p. (TL509; 629.13303 / 1. Airplanes – Dictionaries.)

S   Green, William, and Swanborough, Gordon. *The Observer's World Airlines and Airlines Directory.* London; New York: F. Warne, 1975. 384p. (TL512; 387.7025 / 1. Air lines – Directories. 2. Transport planes.)

S   *The International Encyclopedia of Aviation.* General ed., David Mondey. New York: Crown, 1977. 480p. (TL509; 629.1 / 1. Aeronautics – Dictionaries.)

S   *Jane's All the World's Aircraft.* New York: Franklin Watts, 1909- . Annual. (TL501; 629.105 / 1. Aeronautics – Yearbooks. 2. Airplanes – Yearbooks. 3. Rockets (Aeronautics) – Yearbooks. 4. Space vehicles – Yearbooks.)

S   Jeppesen Sanderson, Inc. *Jeppesen Sanderson Aviation Yearbook.* Denver: Jeppesen Sanderson. Annual. (TL501; 629.13005 / 1. Aeronautics – Yearbooks.)

S   *The Observer's Book of Aircraft.* New York: Warne, 1952- . Annual. (TL670; 629.133 / 1. Airplanes – Recognition.)

S   Polking, Kirk. *The Private Pilot's Dictionary and Handbook.* New York: Arco, 1974. 190p. (TL509; 629.132503 / 1. Aeronautics – Dictionaries. 2. Private flying – Dictionaries.)

A   Reister, Floyd Nester. *Private Aviation: A Guide to Information Sources.* Detroit: Gale, c1979. 140p. (Z5065.U5; 016.62913 / 1. Private flying – United States – Bibliography.)

S   Rolfe, Douglas. *Airplanes of the World, 1490 to 1976.* Historical introductions by Alexis Dawydoff; rev. by William Winter, William Byshyn, Hank Clark. Rev. and enl. ed. New York: Simon & Schuster, c1978. 482p. (TL670.3; 629.1333409 / 1. Airplanes – History.)

S   Taylor, John William Ransom, and Swanborough, Gordon. *Civil Aircraft of the World.* New York: Scribner's, c1974. 168p. (TL685; 387.733404230904 / 1. Transport planes. 2. Airplanes, Private.)

SA Taylor, John William Ransom; Taylor, Michael J. H.; and Mondey, David. *Air Facts & Feats.* Rev. ed. New York: Sterling Publishing Co., c1978. 240p. bibl. (TL515; 387.709 / 1. Aeronautics – History.)

S   United States. Federal Aviation Agency. *FAA Statistical Handbook of Aviation.* Washington, D.C.: Federal Aviation Agency,

1944- , v.1- . (TL521; ____ / 1. Aeronautics – United
States – Statistics.)

S   *Who's Who in Aviation.* New York: Harwood & Charles
Publishing Co., 1973- . (TL539; 629.1200922 / 1.
Aeronautics – Biography.)

S   *World Aviation Directory.* Washington, D.C.: American
Aviation Publications, 1940- , v.1- . Biennial. (TL512; ____ / 1.
Aeronautics – Directories.)

S   Wragg, David W. *A Dictionary of Aviation.* New York:
F. Fell Publishers, c1973. 286p. (TL509; 629.13003 / 1.
Aeronautics – Dictionaries.)

Construction Technology

The tools listed here are of value not only to students in construction technology, but also to those interested in the general building industry, civil engineering, and even cabinetry and carpentry. The list is predominated by handbooks devoted to various topics: everything from structural engineering and construction equipment maintenance to metric construction and foundation engineering. Besides these, there are also guides to estimating, works on different building materials – particularly wood – a directory of safety and construction codes, some encyclopedic source tools, and a dictionary. There are even two bibliographic guides that will lead you to many other sources of information. Depending on your specific interests within the field, you may also wish to consult the section on "Architecture" earlier in this chapter for other related tools.

S   Beckmann, John. *Handbook of Forms, Charts, and Tables
for the Construction Industry.* Englewood Cliffs, N.J.: Prentice-Hall,
c1979. 216p. (TH151; 690.0202 / 1. Building – Handbooks, manuals,
etc.)

S   Brooks, Hugh. *Illustrated Encyclopedic Dictionary of
Building and Construction Terms.* Englewood Cliffs, N.J.: Prentice-
Hall, c1976. 366p. (TH9; 690.03 / 1. Building – Dictionaries.)

S   De Chiara, Joseph, and Callender, John Hancock. *Time-Saver
Standards for Building Types.* 2d ed. New York: McGraw-Hill, 1980.
1277p. (NA2760; 729.2 / 1. Modular coordination (Architecture). 2.
Building materials – Standards.)

SA   Gaylord, Edwin Henry, and Gaylord, Charles N. *Structural
Engineering Handbook.* 2d ed. New York: McGraw-Hill, c1979. ca.
600p. in various pagings. bibl. (TA635; 624.1 / 1. Structural
engineering – Handbooks, manuals, etc.)

A   Godel, Jules B. *Sources of Construction Information: An*

*Annotated Guide to Reports, Books, Periodicals, Standards, and
Codes.* Metuchen, N.J.: Scarecrow, 1977- , v.1- . (Z5851; 016.624 /
1. Engineering – Bibliography. 2. Architecture – Bibliography. 3.
Construction industry – Bibliography.)

SA   *Handbook of Construction Equipment Maintenance.* Lindley
      R. Higgins, consulting engineer. New York: McGraw-Hill, c1979.
      ca. 650p. in various pagings. bibl. (TH900; 621.8 / 1. Construction
      equipment – Maintenance and repair.)

S   *Handbook of Heavy Construction.* Ed. by John A. Havers
      and Frank W. Stubbs, Jr. 2d ed. New York: McGraw-Hill, 1971.
      1v. in various pagings. (TA151; 624.0202 / 1. Engineering – Hand-
      books, manuals, etc.)

S   Hopf, Peter S. *Designer's Guide to OSHA: A Design Manual
      for Architects, Engineers, and Builders to the Occupational Safety and
      Health Act.* New York: McGraw-Hill, 1974. 289p. (KF5701;
      344.730465 / 1. Building laws – United States. 2. Industrial
      safety – Law and legislation – United States.)

SA   Levin, Ezra. *The International Guide to Wood Selection.*
      New York: Drake Publishers, 1972. 153p. bibl. (TA419; 691.1 / 1.
      Wood.)

S   Love, T. W. *Construction Manual: Finish Carpentry.*
      Solana Beach, Calif.: Craftsman Book Co. of America, 1974. 188p.
      (TH5604; 694.6 / 1. Carpentry – Handbooks, manuals, etc. 2. Wood-
      work – Handbooks, manuals, etc.)

SA   Lytle, R. J. *American Metric Construction Handbook.* 1st
      ed. Farmington, Mich.: Structures Pub. Co., 1976. 304p. bibl.
      (TH151; 690 / 1. Building – Handbooks, manuals, etc. 2. Metric
      system – Handbooks, manuals, etc.)

S   *McGraw-Hill's Dodge Manual for Building Construction
      Pricing and Scheduling.* New York: McGraw-Hill, 1980- . v.1- .
      (TH435; 692.50973 / 1. Building – Estimates – United
      States – Periodicals.)

SA   Merritt, Frederick S. *Building Construction Handbook.*
      3d ed. New York: McGraw-Hill, 1975. 1116p. in various pagings.
      bibl. (TH151; 690.0202 / 1. Building – Handbooks, manuals, etc.)

S   Mueller, Jerome F. *Standard Mechanical and Electrical
      Details.* New York: McGraw-Hill, 1980. 352p. (TH6010; 696 / 1.
      Buildings – Mechanical equipment – Handbooks, manuals, etc. 2.
      Buildings – Electric equipment – Handbooks, manuals, etc.)

S   *National Construction Estimator.* Solana Beach, Calif.:
      Craftsman Book Co. Appears irregularly. (____; 692.505 / 1.
      Building – Estimates – United States.)

SA   National Forest Products Association. *Wood Structural
      Design Data: A Manual for Architects, Builders, Engineers, and Others
      Concerned with Wood Construction.* Washington, D.C.: National
      Forest Products Association, 1970. 236p. bibl. (TA666; 691.1 / 1.
      Building, Wooden – Tables. 2. Wood.)

SA   O'Brien, James Jerome. *Construction Inspection Handbook.*
Fred C. Kreitzberg, technical editor. New York: Van Nostrand
Reinhold, 1974. 494p. bibl. (TH439; 690.2 / 1. Building inspec-
tion – Handbooks, manuals, etc.)

S   Paxton, Albert S. *National Repair and Remodeling Estimator,*
1979. Solana Beach, Calif.: Craftsman Book Co., c1978. 158p.
(TH4816; 690.8028 / 1. Dwellings – Remodeling – Costs.)

S   Scott, John S. *A Dictionary of Building.* 2d ed.
Harmondsworth, Eng.: Penguin Books, 1974. 392p. (TH9; 690.03 /
1. Building – Dictionaries.)

S   Siemon, Karl O. *Directory of Safety and Construction*
Codes, U.S.A. States and Cities. Westfield, N.J.: Code Publishing
Co., 1965. 264p. (_____; 340 / 1. Industrial safety – Law and legisla-
tion – United States – States. 2. Industrial hygiene – Law and legisla-
tion – United States – States. 3. Public health laws – United
States – States.)

S   Stein, J. Stewart. *Construction Glossary: An Encyclopedic*
Reference and Manual. New York: Wiley, 1980. 1013p. (TH9;
690.0319 / 1. Building – Dictionaries.)

S   Timber Engineering Company. *Timber Design and Construction*
Handbook. New York: F. W. Dodge Corp., 1956. 622p. (TA666;
624 / 1. Building, Wooden.)

SA   United States. Forest Products Laboratory, Madison, Wis.
The Encyclopedia of Wood: Wood as an Engineering Material. New
York: Drake Publishers, 1977. 376p. bibl. (TA419; 630.8 / 1.
Wood.)

SA   Waddell, Joseph J. *Concrete Construction Handbook.* 2d
ed. New York: McGraw-Hill, 1974. 1v. in various pagings. bibl.
(TA681; 624.1834 / 1. Concrete construction.)

A   Ward, Jack W. *Construction Information Source and Reference*
Guide: Listings of Texts, Manuals, Handbooks, Associations, Societies,
Institutes, Periodicals, Publishers & Book Sources. 3d ed. Phoenix:
Construction Publications, 1973. 190p. (Z7914.B9; 016.624 / 1.
Building – Bibliography.)

S   Winslow, Taylor F. *Construction Industry Production Manual.*
Los Angeles: Craftsman Book Co., 1972. 165p. (TH435; 692.5 / 1.
Building – Estimates.)

SA   Winterkorn, Hans Friedrich, and Fang, Hsai-Yang. *Foundation*
Engineering Handbook. New York: Van Nostrand Reinhold, 1975.
751p. bibl. (TA775; 624.15 / 1. Foundations – Handbooks, manuals,
etc. 2. Soil mechanics – Handbooks, manuals, etc.)

Cosmetology

Almost all of the tools listed here for the cosmetology student are
handbooks that cover skin care, hairstyling and hair care, and skin

diseases. There is also a directory of equipment and supplies for beauty parlors and barbershops that you should find useful. Since three of the handbooks include bibliographies, they may also be used to locate other sources of information.

S   *The AMA Book of Skin and Hair Care.* Ed. by Linda Allen
        Schoen. Prepared in consultation with members of the AMA Com-
        mittee on Cutaneous Health and Cosmetics. Philadelphia: Lippin-
        cott, c1976. 352p. (RL87; 646.72 / 1. Skin – Care and hygiene. 2.
        Hair – Care and hygiene. 3. Toilet preparations.)
SA   Dalton, John W. *The Professional Cosmetologist.* 2d ed.
        St. Paul, Minn.: West Publishing, 1979. 463p. bibl. (TT957;
        646.72 / 1. Beauty culture.)
SA   *Modern's Market Guide.* Chicago: Vance Publishing,
        1967- . (HD9999.B253; 688.50257 / 1. Beauty shops – Equipment
        and supplies – Directories. 2. Barbers' supplies – Directories.)
SA   Sauer, Gordon C. *Manual of Skin Diseases.* 4th ed.
        Philadelphia: Lippincott, c1980. bibl. (RL71; 616.5 / 1.
        Skin – Diseases.)
SA   Tremblay, Suzanne. *The Professional Skin Care Manual.*
        New York: Prentice-Hall, 1978. 231p. bibl. (TT958; 642.726 / 1.
        Beauty culture. 2. Skin – Care and hygiene.)

Electronics

The tools listed in this section will be of value not just to the electronics student, but also to those interested in electrical engineering and in electrician work. There are several general handbooks as well as more specialized works on circuits and circuit design, components, formulas and symbols, and even oscilloscopes and operational amplifiers. Besides these, there are also several works on the National Electrical Code – including the code itself – an encyclopedic source on scientific and engineering instruments, several dictionaries, and even a phone directory for the electronics industry. Because of rapid advancements in the industry, there is an ever-increasing need for new technical material and for newer editions of standard works. Checking frequently in your library's catalog will help keep you aware of new technical literature as it appears.

S   *American Electricians' Handbook: A Reference Book for the*
        Practical Electrical Man. John H. Watt, ed. 9th ed. New York:
        McGraw-Hill, 1970. 1v. in various pagings. (TK151; 621.3 / 1. Elec-
        tric engineering – Handbooks, manuals, etc.)
A   *Applied Science and Technology Index.* New York: H. W.

Wilson, 1913- . Monthly, except July. Quarterly with annual
cumulations. (Z7913; 016.6 / 1. Engineering – Periodicals – Indexes.
2. Technology – Periodicals – Indexes. 3. Industrial
arts – Periodicals – Indexes.)

S   Brand, John R. *Handbook of Electronics Formulas, Symbols,*
and Definitions. New York: Van Nostrand Reinhold, c1979. 359p.
(TK7825; 621.3810202 / 1. Electronics – Handbooks, manuals, etc.)

SA   Buchsbaum, Walter H. *Buchsbaum's Complete Handbook of*
Practical Electronic Reference Data. Englewood Cliffs, N.J.: Prentice-
Hall, 1973. 529p. bibl. (TK7825; 621.381 / 1. Electronics – Hand-
books, manuals, etc.)

SA   Coombs, Clyde F., ed. *Printed Circuits Handbook.* 2d ed.
New York: McGraw-Hill, c1979. 629p. in various pagings. bibl.
(TK7868.P7; 621.38174 / 1. Printed circuits.)

A   *EITD: Electronic Industry Telephone Directory.* Cleveland:
Harris Publishing Co., [1974?]- . Annual. (HD9696.A3; 384.6 / 1.
Electronic industries – United States – Directories.)

SA   *Encyclopedia of Instrumentation and Control.* Ed. in chief,
Douglas M. Considine. New York: McGraw-Hill, 1971. 788p. bibl.
(Q185; 502.8 / 1. Scientific apparatus and instruments – Dictionaries. 2. Engineering instruments – Dictionaries. 3. Automatic
control – Dictionaries.)

SA   Fink, Donald G. *Electronics Engineers' Handbook.* 1st
ed. New York: McGraw-Hill, 1975. 2144p. in various pagings. bibl.
(TK7825; 621.3810202 / 1. Electronics – Handbooks, manuals, etc.)

S   Furlow, Bill. *Circuit Design Idea Handbook.* Boston:
Cahners Books, 1974. 209p. (TK7867; 621.38153 / 1. Electronic
circuits.)

S   Garland, J. D. *National Electrical Code Reference Book.*
Englewood Cliffs, N.J.: Prentice-Hall, 1977. 561p. (TK260;
621.31924021 / 1. Electric engineering – Insurance requirements.)

S   Goodman, Robert L. *Indexed Guide to Modern Electronic*
Circuits. 1st ed. Blue Ridge Summit, Pa.: G/L Tab Books, 1974.
216p. (TK7867; 621.38153 / 1. Electronic circuits.)

S   Graf, Rudolf F. *Electronic Databook: A Guide for*
Designers. New York: Van Nostrand Reinhold, 1974. 312p.
(TK7825; 621.3810212 / 1. Electronics – Tables. 2. Elec-
tronics – Graphic methods.)

S   Grolle, Carl G. *Electronic Technician's Handbook of Time-*
Savers and Shortcuts. West Nyack, N.Y.: Parker Publishing Co.,
1974. 238p. (TK7870; 621.381 / 1. Electronic apparatus and appliances – Maintenance and repair. 2. Electronic apparatus and appliances – Testing.)

S   *Handbook for Electronics Engineering Technicians.* Editors,
Milton Kaufman, Arthur H. Seidman. New York: McGraw-Hill,
c1976. 515p. in various pagings. (TK7825; 621.38 / 1. Elec-

tronics – Handbooks, manuals, etc.)

SA   *Handbook of Components for Electronics.* Charles A. Harper,
ed. in chief. New York: McGraw-Hill, c1977. 1097p. in various
pagings. bibl. (TK7870; 621.381028 / 1. Electronic apparatus and
appliances – Handbooks, manuals, etc.)

SA   *Handbook of Electronics Calculations for Engineers and
Technicians.* Editors, Milton Kaufman, Arthur H. Seidman. New
York: McGraw-Hill, c1979. ca. 550p. in various pagings. bibl.
(TK7825; 621.3810202 / 1. Electronics – Handbooks, manuals, etc.)

S   Hansteen, Henry B. *Electrician's Vest Pocket Reference
Book.* Rev. ed. Englewood Cliffs, N.J.: Prentice-Hall, 1973. 189p.
(TK3205; 621.31924 / 1. Electric wiring – Tables.)

SA   Harman, Thomas L., and Allen, Charles E. *Guide to the
National Electrical Code.* Englewood Cliffs, N.J.: Prentice-Hall,
c1979. 388p. bibl. (KF5704; 343.73078 / 1. Electric engineering – Law and legislation – United States.)

S   Herrick, Clyde N. *Oscilloscope Handbook.* Reston, Va.:
Reston, 1974. 214p. (TK7878.7; 621.381548 / 1. Cathode ray
oscilloscopes – Handbooks, manuals, etc. 2. Electronic
measurements – Handbooks, manuals, etc.)

S   Institute of Electrical and Electronics Engineers.
IEEE Standard Dictionary of Electrical and Electronics Terms. Frank
Jay, ed. in chief. 2d ed. New York: Institute of Electrical and Electronics Engineers, 1977. 882p. (TK9; 621.303 / 1. Electric engineering – Dictionaries. 2. Electronics – Dictionaries.)

SA   Jones, Thomas H. *Electronic Components Handbook.* Reston,
Va.: Reston, c1978. 391p. bibl. (TK7870; 621.3815 / 1. Electronic
apparatus and appliances – Handbooks, manuals, etc.)

S   Lenk, John D. *Handbook of Electronic Circuit Designs.*
Englewood Cliffs, N.J.: Prentice-Hall, c1976. 307p. (TK7871.9;
621.381530422 / 1. Transistor circuits. 2. Electronic circuit design.)

S   Ludwig, Raymond H. *Illustrated Handbook of Electronic
Tables, Symbols, Measurements, and Values.* West Nyack, N.Y.:
Parker Publishing, c1977. 352p. (TK7825; 621.381 / 1. Elec-
tronics – Handbooks, manuals, etc.)

S   Mandl, Matthew. *Directory of Electronic Circuits, with a
Glossary of Terms.* Rev. and enl. Englewood Cliffs, N.J.: Prentice-
Hall, c1978. 321p. (TK7867; 621.38153 / 1. Electronic circuits.)

S   Markus, John. *Electronics Dictionary: Accurate, Easy-
to-Understand, and Up-to-Date Definitions for 17,090 Terms Used in
Solid-State Electronics, Computers, Television, Radio, Medical Electronics, Industrial Electronics, Satellite Communication, and Military
Electronics.* 4th ed. New York: McGraw-Hill, c1978. 745p. (TK7804;
621.38103 / 1. Electronics – Dictionaries. 2. Nuclear engineering – Dictionaries.)

SA   Markus, John. *Modern Electronic Circuits Reference*

      Manual. New York: McGraw-Hill, 1980. 1238p. bibl. (TK7867;
      621.38153 / 1. Electronic circuits – Handbooks, manuals, etc. 2. In-
      tegrated circuits – Handbooks, manuals, etc.)

S   Markus, John. *Sourcebook of Electronic Circuits.*
      New York: McGraw-Hill, c1968. 888p. (TK7867; 621.381530202 /
      1. Electronic circuits – Handbooks, manuals, etc. 2. Transistor cir-
      cuits – Handbooks, manuals, etc.)

S   *McGraw-Hill's Leaders in Electronics.* By *Electronics* magazine.
      New York: McGraw-Hill, c1979. 651p. (TK7806; 621.3810922 / 1.
      Electronics – Biography. 2. Electronic industries –
      Biography.)

S   *Modern Dictionary of Electronics.* Compiled by Rudolf
      F. Graf. 5th ed. Indianapolis, Ind.: H. W. Sams, c1977. 832p.
      (TK7804; 621.38103 / 1. Electronics – Dictionaries.)

S   Moon, Hugh. *Simplified Guide to Electronic Circuits,*
      Test Procedures and Troubleshooting. West Nyack, N.Y.: Parker
      Publishing, 1975. 250p. (TK6550; 621.38412 / 1. Radio. 2. Televi-
      sion. 3. Electronic circuits.)

S   National Fire Protection Association. *The National*
      Electrical Code Handbook. Boston: National Fire Protection Associa-
      tion, 1978- . v.1- . (TK260; 621.30202 / 1. Electric engineering – In-
      surance requirements. 2. Electric engineering – Handbooks,
      manuals, etc.)

SA   Robinson, Vester. *Handbook of Electronic Instrumentation,*
      Testing, and Troubleshooting. Reston, Va.: Reston, 1974. 358p. bibl.
      (TK7878.4; 621.381028 / 1. Electronic instruments. 2. Electronic
      measurements. 3. Electronic apparatus and appliances –
      Maintenance and repair.)

S   *Standard Handbook for Electrical Engineers.* 1st- ed.
      New York: McGraw-Hill, 1908- . (TK151; 621.3 / 1. Electric
      engineering – Handbooks, manuals, etc.)

S   Stout, David F. *Handbook of Operational Amplifier Circuit*
      Design. Ed. by Milton Kaufman. New York: McGraw-Hill, c1976.
      448p. in various pagings. (TK7871.58.O6; 621.381535 / 1. Opera-
      tional amplifiers. 2. Electronic circuit design.)

S   Thomas, Harry Elliot. *Handbook for Electronic Engineers*
      and Technicians. New York: Gernsback Library, c1965. 427p. (____;
      621.381 / 1. Electronics – Handbooks, manuals, etc.)

S   Thomas, Harry Elliot. *Handbook of Electronic Circuit*
      Design Analysis. Reston, Va.: Reston, 1972. 502p. (TK7867;
      621.38153 / 1. Electronic circuit design. 2. Electronic apparatus and
      appliances.)

S   Thomas, Harry Elliot, and Clarke, Carole A. *Handbook of*
      Electronic Instruments and Measurement Techniques. Englewood
      Cliffs, N.J.: Prentice-Hall, 1967. (TK7878.4; 621.38154 / 1. Elec-
      tronic instruments. 2. Electronic measurements.)

Fire Science

The majority of tools available to the fire science student – or, for that matter, to the practicing fire officer – fall into the handbook category. There are manuals on everything from fire-resistant fabrics to the flammability of plastics. Also listed is a dictionary of specialized terms, a guide to safety, and the National Fire Code. You will notice that some of the works listed have the National Fire Protection Association as either author or publisher, or both. This important professional association issues a number of different publications that may be accessed through the catalog directly under the association's name.

S   *Fire Protection Guide on Hazardous Materials.* 1st- ed.
           Boston: National Fire Protection Association, 1966- . (TH9115;
           614.8310212 / 1. Hazardous substances – Fires and fire preven-
           tion – Collected works.)

SA   *Fire Protection Handbook.* 1st- ed. Boston: National
           Fire Protection Association, 1896- . bibl. (TH9150; 614.84 / 1. Fire
           prevention.)

SA   Hilado, Carlos J. *Flammability Handbook for Plastics.*
           2d ed. Westport, Conn.: Technomic Publishing Co.,
           1974. 201p. bibl. (TH9446.P55; 628.922 / 1. Plastics. 2.
           Oxygen index of materials. 3. Flame spread. 4.
           Fire-testing.)

S   Kuvshinoff, B. W. *Fire Sciences Dictionary.* New York:
           Wiley, 1977. 439p. (TH9116; 628.9203 / 1. Fire prevention – Dic-
           tionaries. 2. Fire extinction – Dictionaries.)

S   National Fire Protection Association. *National Fire*
           Code. Boston: National Fire Protection Association, 1938- . Annual.
           (TH9111; 614.8410973 / 1. Fire prevention – United
           States – Periodicals. 2. Fire extinction – Periodicals.)

SA   Reeves, Wilson A.; Drake, G. L.; and Perkins, R. M.
           Fire Resistant Textiles Handbook. Westport, Conn.: Technomic
           Publishing Co., 1974. 241p. bibl. (TP267; 677.689 / 1. Fireproofing
           of fabrics.)

SA   Sax, Newton Irving. *Dangerous Properties of Industrial*
           Materials. Assisted by Robert D. Bruce [and others]. 4th ed. New
           York: Van Nostrand Reinhold, 1975. 1258p. bibl. (T55.3.H3;
           604.7 / 1. Hazardous substances.)

SA   Soros, Charles C. *Fire Officer's Guide to Safety in the*
           Fire Service. Boston: National Fire Protection Association, 1979.
           334p. bibl. (TH9182; 363.37028 / 1. Fire-departments – Safety
           measures – Handbooks, manuals, etc.)

Law Enforcement

The student of law enforcement has a number of different tools he or she may consult, some of which deal with the related fields of criminology and penology. The tools listed below are dominated by the handbook, with topics ranging from narcotics control and fingerprints to forensic science and search and evidence. There are also dictionaries of specialized terms, several bibliographies, a bibliographic guide, and statistical sources on crime and criminals in the United States. Those law enforcement students interested in the law itself will find some of the tools listed earlier in this chapter under "Legal Assistant" to be valuable.

S   Beckman, Erik. *The Criminal Justice Dictionary*. Ann
        Arbor, Mich.: Pierian Press, 1979. 215p. (HV6017; 364.03 / 1.
        Criminal justice, Administration of – Dictionaries. 2. Correc-
        tions – Dictionaries. 3. Crime and criminals – Dictionaries. 4. Police
        administration – Dictionaries. 5. Law enforcement – Dictionaries.)

S   Brodie, Thomas G. *Bombs and Bombings: A Handbook to*
        Detection, Disposal, and Investigation for Police and Fire Departments.
        Springfield, Ill.: Charles C. Thomas, 1972. 183p. (TP270; 628.9 / 1.
        Bombs. 2. Explosives. 3. Bomb reconnaissance.)

A   Felkenes, George T., and Becker, Harold K. *Law Enforcement:*
        A Selected Bibliography. 2d ed. Metuchen, N.J.: Scarecrow, 1977.
        329p. (KF9201; 016.364973 / 1. Criminal procedure – United
        States – Bibliography. 2. Criminal law – United
        States – Bibliography. 3. Law enforcement – Bibliography. 4.
        Police – Bibliography.)

SA   Fox, Richard H., and Cunningham, Carl L. *Crime Scene*
        Search and Physical Evidence Handbook. Washington, D.C.: U.S.
        Department of Justice, Law Enforcement Assistance Administra-
        tion, National Institute of Law Enforcement and Criminal Justice,
        1974. 189p. bibl. (HV8073; 364.12 / 1. Criminal investigation. 2.
        Crime laboratories.)

SA   Gunn, Rodger S. *Glossary Handbook for Law Enforcement*
        Education: 333 Selected Terms for the Law Enforcement Officer and
        Student. 1st ed. Provo, Utah: Printed for the Political Science Dept.
        by the Brigham Young University Printing Service, 1973. 80p. bibl.
        (KF9217; 345.73003 / 1. Criminal law – United States – Dictionaries.
        2. Law enforcement – United States – Dictionaries.)

A   *Index to Legal Periodicals*. 1908- . Published for
        the American Association of Law Libraries. New York:
        H. W. Wilson, 1909- . Monthly, except September, with annual
        and triennial cumulations. (K9; 016.34705 / 1.

Law – Periodicals – United States – Indexes. 2.
Law – Periodicals – Indexes.)

A   Johnson, Emily. *Basic Sources in Criminal Justice: A
     Selected Bibliography.* Marjorie Kravitz, supervising editor.
     Washington, D.C.: National Institute of Law Enforcement and
     Criminal Justice, Law Enforcement Assistance Administration, U.S.
     Department of Justice, 1978. 182p. (Z5703.5.U5; 016.364973 / 1.
     Criminal justice, Administration of – United States – Bibliography.)

SA   Pace, Denny F., and Styles, Jimmie C. *Handbook of Narcotics
     Control.* Englewood Cliffs, N.J.: Prentice-Hall, 1972. 95p. bibl.
     (HV5825; 363.45 / 1. Drug abuse – United States. 2. Narcotics,
     Control of – United States. 3. Drug abuse and crime – United
     States.)

A   Parisi, Nicolette. *Sources of National Criminal Justice
     Statistics: An Annotated Bibliography.* Washington, D.C.: U.S.
     Department of Justice, Law Enforcement Assistance Administra-
     tion, National Criminal Justice Information and Statistics Service,
     c1977. 65p. (Z5703.5.U5; 364.973 / 1. Criminal justice, Administra-
     tion of – United States – Statistics – Bibliography. 2. Criminal
     statistics – United States – Bibliography.)

A   Prostano, Emanuel T., and Piccirillo, Martin L. *Law
     Enforcement: A Selective Bibliography.* Littleton, Colo.: Libraries
     Unlimited, 1974. 203p. (Z7164.P76; 016.3632 / 1. Law en-
     forcement – Bibliography. 2. Criminal justice, Administration
     of – Bibliography. 3. Police – Bibliography. 4. Crime and
     criminals – Bibliography.)

S   Rush, George Eugene. *Dictionary of Criminal Justice.*
     Boston: Holbrook Press, c1977. 374p. (HV6017; 364.03 / 1.
     Criminal justice, Administration of – Dictionaries.)

S   *Sourcebook of Criminal Justice Statistics.* Washington, D.C.:
     National Criminal Justice Information and Statistics Service,
     1973– . Annual. (HV7245; 364.973 / 1. Criminal justice, Ad-
     ministration of – United States – Statistics – Periodicals. 2. Criminal
     statistics – United States – Periodicals. 3. Corrections – United
     States – Statistics – Periodicals.)

S   United States. Federal Bureau of Investigation. *The
     Science of Fingerprints: Classification and Uses.* Washington, D.C.:
     U.S. Department of Justice, Federal Bureau of Investigation, 1977.
     209p. (HV6074; 364.125 / 1. Fingerprints.)

S   United States. Federal Bureau of Investigation. Laboratory.
     Handbook of Forensic Science. Washington, D.C.: Federal Bureau of
     Investigation, 1978. 133p. (HV8073; 364.12 / 1. Chemistry, Foren-
     sic. 2. Criminal investigation.)

SA   Williams, Vergil L. *Dictionary of American Penology:
     An Introductory Guide.* Westport, Conn.: Greenwood Press, 1979.
     530p. bibl. (HV9304; 365.973 / 1. Corrections – United States – Dic-

tionaries. 2. Prisons – United States – Dictionaries. 3. Criminal
justice, Administration of – United States – Dictionaries. 4. Corrections – United States – Statistics.)

A   Wolfgang, Marvin E.; Figlio, Robert M.; and Thornberry,
Terence P. *Criminology Index: Research and Theory in Criminology in
the United States, 1945-1972.* New York: Elsevier Scientific
Publishing Co., 1975. 2v. (Z5118.C9; 016.364973 / 1. Crime and
criminals – United States – Bibliography. 2. Crime and
criminals – Research – United States – Bibliography.)

SA   Wright, Martin. *Use of Criminology Literature.* Hamden,
Conn.: Archon Books, 1974. 242p. (Z5118.C9; 016.364 / 1. Crime
and criminals – Bibliography – Addresses, essays, lectures. 2.
Police – Bibliography – Addresses, essays, lectures. 3. Corrections – Bibliography – Addresses, essays, lectures.)

Library Technician

The literature of librarianship is well developed, so the prospective
library technician will have little difficulty in finding information on
almost any aspect of the profession. Listed here are source and
source/access tools on almost all aspects of library work such as acquisitions, reference, serials, cataloging, and interlibrary loan. Also
listed are two encyclopedic sources, two annuals, two specialized dictionaries, and an important index to periodical literature.

S   *ALA World Encyclopedia of Library and Information Services.*
Chicago: American Library Association, 1980. 601p. (Z1006; 020.3 /
1. Library science – Dictionaries. 2. Information science –
Dictionaries.)

S   American Library Association. *The ALA Yearbook.* Chicago:
American Library Association, 1976- . Annual. (Z673.A5;
020.62273 / 1. American Library Association.)

S   American Library Association. Editorial Committee.
Subcommittee on Library Terminology. *A.L.A. Glossary of Library
Terms.* . . . By Elizabeth H. Thompson. Chicago: American Library
Association, 1943. 159p. (Z1006; 020.3 / 1. Library science –
Dictionaries.)

SA   American Library Association. Subcommittee on the ALA Rules for
Filing Catalog Cards. *ALA Rules for Filing Catalog Cards.* Pauline A.
Seely, chairman and editor. 2d ed. Chicago: American Library
Association, 1968. 260p. bibl. (Z695.95; 025.37 / 1. Alphabeting.)

A   *American Library Directory: A Classified List of Libraries
in the United States and Canada with Personnel and Statistical Data.*
Ed.1- . New York: R. R. Bowker, 1923- . Biennial. (Z731;
021.002573 / 1. Libraries – Directories. 2. Libraries – United

States – Directories. 3. Libraries – Canada – Directories.)

S   *Anglo-American Cataloguing Rules.* 2d ed. Prepared by
    the American Library Association, the British Library, the
    Canadian Committee on Cataloguing, the Library Association, the
    Library of Congress. Edited by Michael Gorman and Paul W.
    Winkler. Chicago: American Library Association, 1978. 620p.
    (Z694; 025.32 / 1. Descriptive cataloging – Rules.)

S   *A Biographical Directory of Librarians in the United
    States and Canada.* Lee Ash, ed. 5th ed. Chicago: American Library
    Association, 1970. 1250p. (Z720.A4; 020.922 / 1. Librarians – United
    States – Directories. 2. Librarians – Canada – Directories.)

SA Bloomberg, Marty. *Introduction to Public Services for
    Library Technicians.* 2d ed. Littleton, Colo.: Libraries Unlimited,
    1977. 278p. bibl. (Z711; 025.5 / 1. Libraries and readers. 2. Library
    technicians.)

SA Bloomberg, Marty, and Evans, G. Edward. *Introduction to
    Technical Services for Library Technicians.* 2d ed. Littleton, Colo.:
    Libraries Unlimited, 1974. 253p. bibl. (Z688.5; 025.02 / 1. Process-
    ing (Libraries).)

S   *The Bowker Annual of Library and Book Trade Information.*
    New York: R. R. Bowker, 1955/56- . Annual. (Z731; 020.58 / 1.
    Book industries and trade – United States – Yearbooks. 2.
    Libraries – United States – Yearbooks.)

SA *Dictionary of American Library Biography.* Ed. by Bohdan
    S. Wynar. Littleton, Colo.: Libraries Unlimited, 1978. 596p. bibl.
    (Z720.A4; 020.922 / 1. Librarians – United States – Biography.)

SA *Encyclopedia of Library and Information Science.* Eds.,
    Allen Kent and Harold Lancour. New York: Dekker, 1968- , v.1- .
    bibl. (Z1006; 020.3 / 1. Library science – Dictionaries. 2. Informa-
    tion science – Dictionaries.)

SA Evans, G. Edward. *Developing Library Collections.*
    Littleton, Colo.: Libraries Unlimited, 1979. 340p. bibl. (Z687;
    025.2 / 1. Collection development (Libraries).)

SA Gates, Jean Key. *Introduction to Librarianship.* 2d ed.
    New York: McGraw-Hill, c1976. 288p. bibl. (Z721; 021 / 1.
    Libraries. 2. Library science – Vocational guidance.)

S   Harrod, Leonard Montague. *The Librarians' Glossary of
    Terms Used in Librarianship, Documentation, and the Book Crafts,
    and the Reference Book.* 4th rev. ed. Boulder, Colo.: Westview
    Press, 1977. 903p. (Z1006; 020.3 / 1. Library science – Dictionaries.
    2. Bibliography – Dictionaries. 3. Book industries and trade –
    Dictionaries.)

SA Katz, William A. *Introduction to Reference Work.* 3d ed.
    New York: McGraw-Hill, 1978. 2v. bibl. (Z711; 011.02 / 1.
    Reference services (Libraries). 2. Reference books.)

A   *Library Literature.* 1933/35- . New York: H. W.

Wilson, 1934- . Bimonthly, with annual cumulations. (Z666;
016.02 / 1. Library science – Indexes – Periodicals. 2. Information
science – Indexes – Periodicals. 3.
Bibliography – Bibliography – Periodicals.)

SA Miller, Shirley. *The Vertical File and Its Satellites:*
A Handbook of Acquisition, Processing, and Organization.
2d ed. Littleton, Colo.: Libraries Unlimited, 1979. 251p. bibl.
(Z691; 025.172 / 1. Vertical files (Libraries).)

SA Osborn, Andrew Delbridge. *Serial Publications: Their*
Place and Treatment in Libraries. 3d ed. Chicago: American Library
Association, 1980. bibl. (Z692.S5; 025.173 / 1. Periodicals. 2. Serials
control systems.)

SA Shera, Jesse Hauk. *Introduction to Library Science:*
Basic Elements of Library Service. Littleton, Colo.: Libraries
Unlimited, 1976. 208p. bibl. (Z665; 020 / 1. Library science. 2.
Libraries. 3. Information services.)

SA Thomson, Sarah Katharine. *Interlibrary Loan Procedure*
Manual. Chicago: Interlibrary Loan Committee, American Library
Association, 1970. 116p. bibl. (Z713; 024.60973 / 1. Inter-library
loans – Handbooks, manuals, etc.)

Mechanical Engineering

The tools listed here will be of interest not just to the student of
mechanical engineering, but also to the aspiring machinist. There are
handbooks – both source and source/access – on such topics as
metallic properties, machinery design, machine-shop practice, valves,
and pumps. Also cited are an encyclopedic source on engineering
materials and a dictionary of specialized mechanical terms. You will
notice that the first handbook listed is authored by ASME – the
American Society of Mechanical Engineers. This professional association authors other important publications that you should look for
under its name in the catalog.

SA American Society of Mechanical Engineers. *ASME Handbook.*
1st ed. New York: McGraw-Hill, 1953-1958. 4v. bibl. (TJ233;
620.18 / 1. Metals. 2. Machinery – Design. 3. Mechanical engineering – Handbooks, manuals, etc.)

A *Applied Science and Technology Index.* New York: H. W.
Wilson, 1913- . Monthly, except July. Quarterly with annual
cumulations. (Z7913; 016.6 / 1. Engineering – Periodicals – Indexes.
2. Technology – Periodicals – Indexes. 3. Industrial
arts – Periodicals – Indexes.)

S *Audels New Mechanical Dictionary for Technical Trades:*

  Containing 11,000 Definitions of Commonly Used Terms in
  Mechanical Trades, Physics, Chemistry, Electricity, etc. New York:
  T. Audel, 1960. 736p. (T9; 620.3 / 1. Technology – Dictionaries.)

S   *Encyclopedia of Engineering Materials and Processes.* Ed.
  in chief, H. R. Clauser. New York: Reinhold, 1963. 787p. (TA403;
  620.11 / 1. Materials – Dictionaries. 2. Production engineering –
  Dictionaries.)

SA Flügge, Wilhelm. *Handbook of Engineering Mechanics.* 1st
  ed. New York: McGraw-Hill, 1962. 1v. in various pagings. bibl.
  (TA350; 620.1002 / 1. Mechanics, Applied.)

SA *ISA Handbook of Control Valves: A Comprehensive Reference*
  Book Containing Application and Design Information. Ed. in chief, J.
  W. Hutchison. 2d ed. Pittsburgh: Instrument Society of America,
  c1976. 533p. bibl. (TJ223.V3; 629.8315 / 1. Valves – Handbooks,
  manuals, etc.)

SA Kent, William. *Mechanical Engineers' Handbook.* 12th ed.
  New York: Wiley, 1950. 2v. bibl. (TJ151; 621.02 / 1. Mechanical
  engineering – Handbooks, manuals, etc.)

S   Le Grand, Rupert. *The New American Machinist's Handbook.*
  New York: McGraw-Hill, 1955. 1v. (TJ1165; 621.75 / 1. Machine-
  shop practice.)

S   *Machinery's Handbook: A Reference Book for the Mechanical*
  Engineer, Draftsman, Toolmaker and Machinist. By Erik Oberg,
  Franklin D. Jones, and Holbrook L. Horton. 20th ed. New York:
  Industrial Press, 1973. 2482p. (TJ151; 621.802 / 1. Mechanical
  engineering – Handbooks, manuals, etc.)

S   *Marks' Standard Handbook for Mechanical Engineers.* 8th-
  ed. New York: McGraw-Hill, 1978- . Continues *Mechanical*
  Engineers' Handbook and *Standard Handbook for Mechanical*
  Engineers. (TJ151; 621.8 / 1. Mechanical engineering – Handbooks,
  manuals, etc.)

S   Perry, Robert H. *Engineering Manual: A Practical Reference*
  of Design Methods and Data in Building Systems, Chemical, Civil,
  Electrical, Mechanical, and Environmental Engineering and Energy
  Conversion. 3d ed. New York: McGraw-Hill, c1976. 971p. in
  various pagings. (TA151; 620.00202 / 1. Engineering – Handbooks,
  manuals, etc.)

SA *Pump Handbook.* Ed. by Igor J. Karassik. New York: McGraw-
  Hill, c1976. 1102p. in various pagings. bibl. (TJ900; 621.6 / 1.
  Pumping machinery – Handbooks, manuals, etc.)

S   Weingartner, C. *Machinists' Ready Reference.* New rev.
  and enl. ed. Ann Arbor, Mich.: Prakken Publications, c1977. 219p.
  (TJ1165; 621.80212 / 1. Shop mathematics – Tables.)

Mortuary Science

There are all too few works of reference value for the mortuary science student, although that situation is slowly beginning to change. Bibliographic guides are available on death, dying, and separation and loss, as well as on the funeral service itself. You will also find listed a source/access work on mortuary services in the United States, a work on the legal aspects of burial, and an encyclopedic source on funeral services. While the bibliographic guides give you access to many other sources of information, you should also check in your library's catalog under similar, related terms such as cremation, mourning customs, and embalming.

SA   Bernard, Hugh Yancey. *The Law of Death and Disposal of the Dead.* Dobbs Ferry, N.Y.: Oceana Publications, 1966. 113p. bibl. (_____; 344.73045 / 1. Undertakers and undertaking – Laws and legislation – United States. 2. Burial laws – United States.)

A   Bernstein, Joanne E. *Books to Help Children Cope with Separation and Loss.* New York: R. R. Bowker, 1977. 255p. (Z7204.S45; 155.937 / 1. Separation (Psychology) – Juvenile literature – Bibliography. 2. Bereavement – Psychological aspects – Juvenile literature – Bibliography. 3. Bibliotherapy.)

A   Fulton, Robert Lester. *Death, Grief, and Bereavement: A Bibliography, 1845-1975.* New York: Arno Press, 1977. 253p. (Z5725; 016.1285 / 1. Death – Bibliography. 2. Grief – Bibliography. 3. Bereavement – Bibliography.)

A   Harrah, Barbara K., and Harrah, David F. *Funeral Service: A Bibliography of Literature on Its Past, Present, and Future, the Various Means of Disposition, and Memorialization.* Metuchen, N.J.: Scarecrow, 1976. 383p. (Z5994; 016.61460973 / 1. Undertakers and undertaking – Bibliography. 2. Undertakers and undertaking – United States – Bibliography. 3. Funeral rites and ceremonies – Bibliography. 4. Funeral rites and ceremonies – United States – Bibliography. 5. Dead – Bibliography.)

SA   Mitford, Jessica. *The American Way of Death.* New York: Simon & Schuster, 1978. 324p. bibl. (HD9999.U53; 338.4761460973 / 1. Undertakers and undertaking – United States. 2. Funeral rites and ceremonies – United States.)

S   Wallis, Charles L., ed. *The Funeral Encyclopedia: A Source Book.* New York: Harper, 1953; reprinted, Grand Rapids, Mich.: Baker Book House, 1973. 327p. (BV4275; 252.1 / 1. Funeral sermons. 2. Funeral service.)

Printing

For the student of printing, a variety of reference works are available. Predictably, most of the tools deal with type and typefaces and styles; other works concentrate on paper, graphic arts, and proofreading. There are also several works that deal with the history of the book and contemporary bookmaking, as well as a bibliography of works on printing so that you have access to other sources beyond those listed here.

S   Allen, Edward Monington. *Harper's Dictionary of the*
       Graphic Arts. New York: Harper, 1963. 295p. (Z118; 655.303 / 1.
       Printing – Dictionaries. 2. Graphic arts – Dictionaries.)
SA   American Paper and Pulp Association. *The Dictionary of*
       Paper: Including Pulp, Paperboard, Paper Properties, and Related
       Papermaking Terms. 3d ed. New York: Association, 1965. 500p.
       bibl. (TS1085; 676.03 / 1. Paper – Dictionaries. 2. Paper making and
       trade – Dictionaries.)
S   Biegeleisen, Jacob Israel. *Art Directors' Workbook of*
       Type Faces: For Artists, Typographers, Letterers, Teachers & Students.
       3d ed. New York: Arco, 1976. 247p. (Z250; 686.224 / 1. Print-
       ing – Specimens. 2. Type and type-founding.)
SA   *The Bookman's Glossary.* 5th ed. Ed. by Jean Peters.
       New York: R. R. Bowker, 1975. 169p. bibl. (Z118; 010.3 / 1. Book
       industries and trade – Dictionaries. 2. Printing – Dictionaries. 3.
       Bibliography – Dictionaries.)
S   Collins, Frederick Howard. *Authors and Printers Dictionary.*
       11th ed., rev. by Stanley Beale. New York: Oxford University
       Press, 1973. 474p. (PE1628; 423 / 1. English language – Usage –
       Dictionaries.)
SA   Glaister, Geoffrey Ashall. *Glaister's Glossary of the*
       Book: Terms Used in Papermaking, Printing, Bookbinding and
       Publishing. . . . 2d ed., completely rev. Berkeley: University of
       California Press, 1979. 551p. bibl. (Z118; 686.20319 / 1.
       Books – Dictionaries. 2. Printing – Dictionaries. 3. Publishers and
       publishing – Dictionaries.)
SA   Lasky, Joseph. *Proofreading and Copy-Preparation: A*
       Textbook for the Graphic Arts. New York: Agathon Press, 1971,
       c1941. 656p. bibl. (Z254; 686.2255 / 1. Proof-reading. 2. Printing,
       Practical – Style manuals.)
A   Lehmann-Haupt, Hellmut. *One Hundred Books About Bookmaking:*
       A Guide to the Study and Appreciation of Printing. Westport, Conn.:
       Greenwood Press, 1975, c1949. 83p. (Z117; 016.6862 / 1. Print-
       ing – Bibliography. 2. Books – Bibliography. 3. Book industries and
       trade – Bibliography.)
S   Mackay (W. and J.) and Company, Ltd. *Type for Books:*
       A Designer's Manual. New ed. London: Bodley Head for Mackays,
       1976. 280p. (Z250; 686.224 / 1. Printing – Specimens.)
SA   McMurtrie, Douglas Crawford. *The Book: The Story of*
       Printing and Bookmaking. New York: Oxford University Press,

1943. 676p. bibl. (Z4; 002 / 1. Books. 2. Printing – History.)

SA   Ryder, John. *Flowers & Flourishes: Including a Newly Annotated Edition of "A Suite of Fleurons."* London: Bodley Head for Mackays, 1976. 168p. bibl. (Z250.3; 686.224 / 1. Type ornaments.)

SA   Skillin, Marjorie E., and Gay, Robert M. *Words into Type.* 3d ed., completely rev. Englewood Cliffs, N.J.: Prentice-Hall, 1974. 585p. bibl. (PN160; 808.02 / 1. Authorship – Handbooks, manuals, etc. 2. Printing, Practical – Style manuals.)

SA   Stevenson, George A. *Graphic Arts Encyclopedia.* 2d ed. New York: McGraw-Hill, c1979. 483p. bibl. (Z118; 686.203 / 1. Printing – Dictionaries. 2. Graphic arts – Dictionaries.)

SA   Updike, Daniel Berkeley. *Printing Types: Their History, Forms, and Use: A Study in Survivals.* 3d ed. Cambridge, Mass.: Belknap Press, 1962. 2v. bibl. (Z250.A2; 655.24 / 1. Type and typefounding. 2. Printing – History. 3. Printing – Specimens.)

S   V & M Typographical, Inc. *The Type Specimen Book: 544 Different Typefaces with over 3,000 Sizes Shown in Complete Alphabets.* New York: Van Nostrand Reinhold, 1974. 622p. (Z250; 686.224 / 1. Printing – Specimens.)

Transportation

The student of transportation and transportation engineering is likely to be interested in a variety of reference works, as indicated in this section. There are, of course, handbooks devoted to different topics: everything from highway engineering to traffic engineering. There are also works devoted to several other modes of transportation, such as rail, ship, and truck, as well as a bibliography on transportation and the distribution of goods. Also included are two statistical sources on roads in the United States.

SA   Baker, Robert Fulton. *Handbook of Highway Engineering.* New York: Van Nostrand Reinhold, 1975. 894p. bibl. (TE151; 625.7 / 1. Highway engineering – Handbooks, manuals, etc.)

A   Davis, Bob J. *Information Sources in Transportation, Material Management, and Physical Distribution: An Annotated Bibliography and Guide.* Westport, Conn.: Greenwood Press, 1976. 715p. (Z7164.T8; 016.658781 / 1. Transportation – Bibliography. 2. Materials management – Bibliography. 3. Physical distribution of goods – Bibliography.)

S   *Jane's World Railways.* 1st– ed. London: Jane's Yearbooks, 1950/1951– . Annual. (TF1; ____ / 1. Railroads – Yearbooks.)

S   *The Observer's Book of Commercial Vehicles.* New ed., compiled by Nick Baldwin. London: F. Warne, 1978. 192p. (TL230;

> 629.224 / 1. Motor-trucks.)

S *The Oxford Companion to Ships & the Sea.* Ed. by Peter
Kemp. London: Oxford University Press, 1976. 972p. (V23;
387.03 / 1. Naval art and science – Dictionaries. 2. Navigation – Dictionaries. 3. Naval history – Dictionaries.)

S Rand McNally & Company. *The Rand McNally Encyclopedia
of Transportation.* Chicago: Rand McNally, 1976. 256p. (TA1009;
380.503 / 1. Transportation – Dictionaries.)

SA *Transportation and Traffic Engineering Handbook.* By the
Institute of Traffic Engineers, John E. Baerwald, ed. Englewood
Cliffs, N.J.: Prentice-Hall, c1976. 1080p. bibl. (HE333; 387.31 / 1.
Traffic engineering. 2. Transportation.)

S United States. Federal Highway Administration. *Highway
Statistics.* Washington, D.C.: Government Printing Office. v.
(HE355.A3; 388.10973 / 1. Roads – United
States – Statistics – Periodicals. 2. Motor fuels – Taxation – United
States – Periodicals. 3. Transportation, Automotive – United
States – Statistics – Periodicals.)

S United States. Federal Highway Administration. *Highway
Statistics: Summary to 1975.* Washington, D.C.: Government Printing Office, 1977. 286p. (HE355.A3; 388.10973 / 1. Roads – United
States – Statistics.)

SA Woods, Kenneth Brady [and others]. *Highway Engineering
Handbook.* 1st ed. New York: McGraw-Hill, 1960. 1v. in various
pagings. bibl. (TE145; 625.7 / 1. Roads.)

Welding

The most important citation in this section is the first listing, the
Welding Handbook, a multivolume source/access tool of standard
reference value. Also listed are works on welding symbols and a
welding code for steel. The welding student cannot fail to notice that
all those publications have the same author, the American Welding
Society. This professional association publishes over 100 works on
specifications, codes, and recommended practices; so you should
check under the society's name in the catalog for other works.

SA American Welding Society. *Welding Handbook.* Charlotte
Weisman, editor. 7th ed. Miami, Fla.: American Welding Society,
c1976- , v.1- . bibl. (TS227; 671.52 / 1. Welding.)

S American Welding Society. Committee on Definitions, Symbols,
and Metric Practice. *Symbols for Welding and Nondestructive Testing.*
Miami, Fla.: American Welding Society, c1976. 70p. (TS227.2;
671.520148 / 1. Welding – Notation. 2. Non-destructive
testing – Notation.)

S   American Welding Society. Structural Welding Committee.
     Structural Welding Code—Steel. 3d ed. Miami, Fla.: American
     Welding Society, c1978. 223p. (TS227; 672.52 / 1. Welding. 2.
     Welded steel structures.)

PHYSICAL EDUCATION AND RECREATION

The tools listed below will be of interest not just to the physical
education and recreation major, but also to the sports buff. There are
general handbooks, encyclopedic sources, and dictionaries as well as
works on sports rules and on sports scoring and record keeping. Also
listed are sports and recreation directories for the United States, a
biographical source tool, and even a bibliography and an index for access to other works. Keep in mind that there exist many more tools
than listed here, most of which are devoted to individual sports. You
may access those works in your library's catalog by looking directly
under the name of the sport.

S   *The Big Book of Halls of Fame in the United States and
     Canada.* Compiled and edited by Paul Soderberg, Helen
     Washington, Jaques Cattell Press. New York: R. R. Bowker,
     1977- , v.1- . (CT215; 973 / 1. Biography. 2. Halls of fame—United
     States. 3. Halls of fame—Canada. 4. United States—Biography. 5.
     Canada—Biography.)

S   Diagram Group. *The Official World Encyclopedia of Sports
     and Games: The Rules, Techniques of Play and Equipment for over 400
     Sports and 1,000 Games.* New York: Paddington Press, 1979. 543p.
     (GV1201; 790 / 1. Games—Rules. 2. Sports—Rules.)

S   Frommer, Harvey. *Sports Lingo: A Dictionary of the Language
     of Sports.* 1st ed. New York: Atheneum, 1979. 302p. (GV567;
     796.03 / 1. Sports—Dictionaries.)

SA   Hickok, Ralph. *New Encyclopedia of Sports.* New York:
     McGraw-Hill, 1977. 543p. bibl. (GV567; 796.097 / 1. Sports—North
     America—Dictionaries.)

S   McWhirter, Norris Dewar. *Guinness Sports Record Book,
     1979-1980.* Rev. ed. New York: Sterling Publishing Co., c1979.
     192p. (GV741; 796.0212 / 1. Sports—Records.)

S   Menke, Frank Grant. *The Encyclopedia of Sports.* 6th rev.
     ed., revisions by Pete Palmer. South Brunswick, N.J.: A. S. Barnes,
     1978. 1132p. (GV567; 796.03 / 1. Sports—Dictionaries.)

A   Norback, Craig T., and Norback, Peter. *The New American
     Guide to Athletics, Sports & Recreation.* New York: New American
     Library, c1979. 659p. (GV583; 796.02573 / 1. Sports—United
     States—Directories. 2. Recreation—United States—Directories.)

A   Nunn, Marshall E. *Sports.* Littleton, Colo.: Libraries
        Unlimited, 1976. 217p. (Z7511; 016.796 / 1. Sports – Bibliography.)
S   *Official Rules of Sports and Games.* London: N. Kaye,
        1949- , v.1- . (GV731; 796 / 1. Sports.)
S   *The Oxford Companion to World Sports & Games.* Ed. by
        John Arlott. New York: Oxford University Press, 1975. 1143p.
        (GV207; 796.03 / 1. Physical education and training – Dictionaries.
        2. Sports – Dictionaries. 3. Games – Dictionaries. 4.
        Athletes – Biography.)
A   *Recreation and Outdoor Life Directory: A Guide to National,*
        International, State, and Regional Organizations, Federal Grant
        Sources, Foundations, Consultants, Special Libraries, and Information
        Centers, Research Centers, Educational Programs, Journals, and
        Periodicals, and State and Federal Leisure Activity Facilities. Paul
        Wasserman, managing ed. 1st ed. Detroit: Gale, 1979. 469p.
        (GV191.35; 333.7802573 / 1. Outdoor recreation – United
        States – Directories. 2. Recreation – United States – Directories. 3.
        Federal aid to outdoor recreation – United States – Directories.)
S   Richards, Jack W., and Hill, Danny. *Complete Handbook*
        of Sports Scoring and Record Keeping. West Nyack, N.Y.: Parker
        Publishing Co., 1974. 266p. (GV741; 796.0212 / 1.
        Sports – Statistics. 2. Sports – Records. 3. Sports officiating.)
SA   *Thrill Sports Catalog.* By the editors of *Consumer Guide.*
        New York: Dutton, c1977. 192p. bibl. (GV191.6; 016.796 / 1. Out-
        door recreation – Handbooks, manuals, etc. 2. Sports – Handbooks,
        manuals, etc. 3. Outdoor recreation – Equipment and sup-
        plies – Handbooks, manuals, etc. 4. Sports – Equipment and sup-
        plies – Handbooks, manuals, etc. 5. Outdoor recrea-
        tion – Bibliography. 6. Sports – Bibliography.)
A   Turner, Pearl. *Index to Outdoor Sports, Games, and*
        Activities. Westwood, Mass.: F. W. Faxon, c1978. 409p. (GV191.6;
        796 / 1. Outdoor recreation – Indexes. 2. Sports – Indexes.)
SA   United States. Children's Bureau. *Handbook for Recreation.*
        Detroit: Gale, 1976. 148p. bibl. (GV1201; 790 / 1. Recreation. 2.
        Games.)
S   *Webster's Sports Dictionary.* Springfield, Mass.: Merriam, c1976. 503p.
        (GV567; 796.03 / 1. Sports – Dictionaries.)

Appendix: Common Bibliographical Abbreviations

arr.	Arranged or arranger
augm.	Augmented
bibl.	Bibliography
bull.	Bulletin
cm.	Centimeter(s)
comp.	Compiler or compiled
c	Copyright
ca.	Circa (i.e., approximately)
corr.	Corrected
dist.	Distributor or distributed
ed.	Edition or editor
enl.	Enlarged
front., fronts.	Frontispiece(s)
ill. or illus.	Illustration(s) or illustrator(s)
ISBN	International standard book number
l. or *l.*	Leaf or leaves

n.d.	No date (of publication)
n.p.	No place (of publication)
no.	Number
p.	Page(s)
port., ports.	Portrait(s)
pt., pts.	Part(s)
pref.	Preface
prep.	Prepared
pub. or publ.	Publisher, published, publishing
rev.	Revised
s.l.	*Sine loco* (i.e., no place of publication)
s.n.	*Sine nomine* (i.e., no name of publisher)
suppl.	Supplement(s)
t.p.	Title page
tr. or trans.	Translator or translation
v., vol., vols.	Volume(s)

Index

This index is arranged alphabetically in the letter-by-letter mode of filing, which is discussed on page 31. The index includes author entries (in regular type), title entries (in italics), and subject entries (in boldface).

Abbreviations: bibliographical, 239–240; **in filing,** 32; **dictionaries of.** *See* **Dictionaries and books on language**

Abercrombie, Michael, 170

Abrams, Alan E., 115

Abridged dictionaries. *See* **Dictionaries and books on language**

Abridged Index Medicus. See Index Medicus

Abstracting services. *See* **Indexing and abstracting services**

Academic American Encyclopedia, 53, 55–56

Accent marks, in filing, 32

Accepted Dental Therapeutics, 186

Access, Film and Video Equipment: A Directory, 117

Access: The Supplementary Index to Periodicals, 70, 72–74

Access type reference tools, 43–45

Accountants' Handbook, 150

Accounting, 150–151

Accounting Desk Book: The Accountant's Everyday Instant Answer Book, 150

Accounting: Information Sources, 150

Acronyms, in filing, 32

Acronyms, Initialisms, and Abbreviations Dictionary, 47, 52

Adams, Catherine F., 206

Adams, Charles J., 111

Added entries, 9, 17–19

Advanced First Aid and Emergency Care, 194

Advertising, 151–152

Aero Publishers, Inc., 217

Aesthetics and Clothing: An Annotated Bibliography, 124

Aesthetics for Dancers: A Selected Annotated Bibliography, 97

Afro-American Literature and Culture since World War II: A Guide to Information Sources, 130

Afro-American studies, 129–130

Agribusiness, 200–202

Agricultural Engineering: A Dictionary and Handbook, 200

Agricultural Engineers' Handbook, 200

Agricultural Index. See Biological and Agricultural Index

Agricultural Product Prices, 202

Agricultural Sciences Information Network, 199

Agricultural Statistics, 200

Agricultural technology, 199–213

Agriculture Education in a Technical Society, 199

Agriculture in the United States: A Documentary History, 200

AICPA Professional Standards, 150

Air-conditioning, heating, and

241

refrigeration, 214-215
Air Conditioning, Heating & Refrigeration Dictionary, 214
Air Conditioning Testing and Balancing, 214
Aircraft maintenance. *See* **Aviation occupations**
Aircraft Technical Dictionary, 218
Air Facts & Feats, 218
Airman's Information Manual, 217
Airplanes of the World, 1490 to 1976, 218
A.L.A Glossary of Library Terms, 229
ALA Rules for Filing Catalog Cards, 30, 229
ALA World Encyclopedia of Library and Information Services, 229
ALA Yearbook, The, 229
Albrecht, Carl F., 200
Alcazar, Carol C., 188
Alden, Betsey, 186
Alexander, Edythe Louise, 198
Alexander, Franz Gabriel, 142
Alexander's Care of the Patient in Surgery, 198
Allaby, Michael, 175
Allen, Charles E., 224
Allen, David, 169
Allen, Edward Monington, 234
Allen, Robert D., 143
Allied Health Education Directory, 181
Allied health occupations. *See* **Health sciences and occupations**
Almanac of American Politics, The, 139
Almanac of British and American Literature, 106
Almanacs, 63-66
Alphanumeric Filing Rules for Business Documents, 165
Alred, Gerald J., 149
Altick, Richard Daniel, 102
Altman, Norman H., 203
Altman, Philip L., 170
AMA Book of Skin and Hair Care, The, 222
AMA Committee on Cutaneous Health and Cosmetics, 222
Amateur Astronomer's Glossary, The, 168
Americana Annual, An Encyclopedia of Current Events, 64-65

American Academy of Orthopaedic Surgeons, Committee on Injuries, 193
American Art Directory, 119
American Authors 1600-1900: A Biographical Dictionary of American Literature, 104
American Counties, The, 135
American Dental Association, 187
American Dental Directory, 186
American Drama Criticism: Interpretations, 1890-1977, 98
American Electricians' Handbook, 222
American Fabric Magazine, 124
American Geological Institute, 174
American Handbook of Psychiatry, 142
American Heritage, 136
American Heritage Dictionary of the English Language, 46, 49-51
American Heritage Pictorial Atlas of United States History, The, 136
American Historical Association, 136
American Home Economics Association: Food and Nutrition Section, Terminology Committee, 206; Textiles and Clothing Section, 124
American Hospital Association, 181, 190
American Hospital Association Guide to the Health Care Field, 181
American Institute of Architects, 120
American Institute of Certified Public Accountants, 150
American Institute of Real Estate Appraisers, 163
American Joint Committee on Horticultural Nomenclature, 210
American Junior Colleges, 132
American Library Association, 229, 230: Editorial Committee, Subcommittee on Library Terminology, 229; Subcommittee on the ALA Rules for Filing Catalog Cards, 229
American Library Directory, 229-230
American Medical Ethnobotany: A Reference Dictionary, 211-212
American Medical Record Association, 190
American Men and Women of Science, 166: Social and Behavioral Sciences, 128

American Metric Construction Handbook, 220

American Musical Theatre: A Chronicle, 108

American Nurses' Association, Nursing Information Bureau, 191

American Paper and Pulp Association, 234

American Physical Therapy Association, 194

American Place Names: A Concise and Selective Dictionary for the Continental United States of America, 135

American Political Dictionary, The, 140

American Political Terms: An Historical Dictionary, 141

American Reference Books Annual (ARBA), 89, 91

American Society of Heating, Refrigeration and Air-Conditioning Engineers, 214

American Society of Mechanical Engineers, 231

American Society of Picture Professionals, 123

American Theatre Association, 99

American Universities and Colleges, 132

American Usage and Style: The Consensus, 48, 53

American Votes: A Handbook of Contemporary American Election Statistics, 138

American Way of Death, The, 233

American Welding Society, 236: Committee on Definitions, Symbols, and Metric Practice, 236; Structural Welding Committee, 236

Amerongen, C. Van. *See* Van Amerongen, C.

Ammer, Christine, 155

Ammer, Dean S., 155

Anderson, James E., 182

Anderson, Michael, 98

Anderson, Peter Joseph, 115, 140

Anderson, William S., 161

Andriot, John L., 145

Anglin, Donald L., 216

Anglo-American Cataloging Rules, 41 n.1, 230

Animal Atlas of the World, 205

Animal Health Yearbook, 213

Animal science, 202–204

Annotated Journalism Bibliography, 1958–1968, An, 116

Annual Bibliography of English Language and Literature, 105

Annual Review of Anthropology, 130

Annual Review of Earth and Planetary Sciences, 174

Annual Review of Ecology and Systematics, 175

Annual Review of Psychology, 142

Annual Review of Sociology, 144

Annuals. *See* **Yearbooks**

Anthropology, 130–131

Antony, Arthur, 171

Apel, Willi, 107

Applied Medical Bibliography for Students, 184

Applied Science and Technology Index, 166, 214, 215, 217, 222–223, 231

Approved Practices in Sheep Production, 203

Approved Practices in Swine Production, 202–203

ARBA. *See American Reference Books Annual*

Architectural and Building Trades Dictionary, 121

Architectural Graphic Standards, 121

Architecture, 120–122

Architecture Through the Ages, 121

Argumentation and Debate: A Classified Bibliography, 118

Arieti, Silvano, 142

Arkin, Herbert, 150

Arlott, John, 238

Armento, Richard F., 215

Arnold, Alvin L., 163

Arnold, W., 142

Arnold Encyclopedia of Real Estate, The, 163

Aronson, Joseph, 125

Art, 122–123

Art Books, 1950–1979, 119

Art Directors' Workbook of Type Faces, 234

Articles, in filing, 32

Art Index, 119

Artists' and Illustrators' Encyclopedia, 120

Artist's Handbook of Materials and Techniques, The, 122–123
Artist's Market, 122
Art Reproductions, 122, 126–127
Ash, Lee, 230
ASHRAE Handbook & Product Directory, 214
ASME Handbook, 231
Assaf, Karen, 177
Assaf, Said A., 177
Association for Educational Communications and Technology, Task Force on Definition and Terminology, 132
Astronomy, 168–169
Astronomy: A Handbook, 169
Astronomy Data Book, 169
Athletics. *See* **Physical education and recreation**
Atlases, 60–63
Atlas for Anthropology, 131
Atlas of Clinical Anatomy, 184
Atlas of Diseases of the Oral Mucosa, 186
Atlas of Landforms, 175
Atlas of Medical Anatomy, 183
Atlas of Roentgenographic Measurement, 196
Atlas of Roentgenographic Positions and Standard Radiologic Procedures, 196
Atlas of Surgical Operations, 199
Atlas of the Early Christian World, 113
Atlas of the Historical Geography of the United States, 138
Atlas of the Living Resources of the Sea, 179
Atlas of the Planets, 168
Atlas of the Sea, 179
Atlas of the World's Resources, 200
Atlas of Tooth Form, 187
Atlas of United States Trees, 209
Atlas of World History, 138
Atlas of World Population History, 146
Attwater, Donald, 111
Audels New Mechanical Dictionary for Technical Trades, 231–232
Audio-visual materials. *See* **Media**
Auer, John Jeffery, 118
Auth, George H., 214
Author numbers, 35
Authors and Printers Dictionary, 234

Auto Electronics Simplified, 216
Automotive Cooling System Training and Reference Manual, 215
Automotive Dictionary, The, 216
Automotive maintenance and repair, 215–217
Automotive Repair and Maintenance, 216
Automotive Technician's Handbook, 216
Avant Gardener, The, 212
Aviation & Space Dictionary, 217
Aviation occupations, 217–219
Ayer Glossary of Advertising and Related Terms, 151
A-Z of Astronomy, The, 168

Babb, Janice B., 163
Backhouse, Duncan, 127
Badger, Ralph E., 159
Baerwald, John E., 236
Bailey, Ethel Zoe, 210
Bailey, F. Lee, 161
Bailey, Liberty Hyde, 210
Baker, James K., 202
Baker, Robert Fulton, 235
Baker, Theodore, 108
Baker's Biographical Dictionary of Musicians, 108
Balachandran, M., 159
Baldwin, James Mark, 110
Baldwin, Nick, 235
Ball, Robert Hamilton, 97
Ballentine, James Arthur, 161
Ballentine's Law Dictionary with Pronunciations, 161
Bannock, G., 155
Barber, Janet Miller, 193
Barker, William Pierson, 112
Barnes, John A., 146
Barnes, Leo, 160
Barnet, Sylvan, 102
Barnhart, Clarence L., 47
Barnhart, Robert K., 47
Barnouw, Erik, 116
Barone, Michael, 139
Barraclough, Geoffrey, 136
Barron's Guide to Medical, Dental, and Allied Health Science Careers, 185
Bartholomew (John) and Son, Ltd., 60
Bartlett, John, 102
Barton, Robert, 179

Barton, Roger, 151
Barzun, Jacques, 48, 136
Basic Books in the Mass Media, 114
Basic Electrocardiography Handbook, 197
Basic Handbook on Mental Illness, 143
Basic Music Library: Essential Scores and Books, A, 109
Basic Sources in Criminal Justice, 228
Basic Surgical Techniques, 198
Basic Tables in Business and Economics, 149
Basic Tools of Research: An Annotated Guide for Students of English, 107
Baskin, Wade, 129
Bates, David V., 197
Bath, Donald L., 203
Batz, Laila, 160
Bauman, Lawrence, 172
Baxter, R. E., 155
Bayne, Pauline Shaw, 109
Bazin, Germain, 122
Beale, Stanley, 234
Beau, Dennis La. *See* La Beau, Dennis
Beauty culture. *See* **Cosmetology**
Beck, Emily Morison, 102
Becker, Harold K., 227
Becker, Marion Rombauer, 207
Becker, Samuel L., 97
Beckman, Erik, 227
Beckmann, John, 219
Bedford, Norton M., 150
Beef Cattle Science, 203
Beer, Arthur, 169
Bell, James Edward, 142
Bellanca, Nicolo, 207
Benet, William Rose, 95
Berger, Karen J., 181
Berke, Beverly, 124
Berman, Morton, 102
Bernard, Hugh Yancey, 233
Bernero, Jacqueline, 146
Bernstein, Joanne E., 233
Bernstein, Lewis, 181
Bernstein, Rosalyn S., 181
Berry, Edna Cornelia, 198
Besançon, Robert M., 180
Best Plays [of 1894/99-   ] and Year Book of the Drama in America, The, 97
Best's Insurance Reports: Life-Health Edition, 158; *Property-Casualty Edition,* 158
Betteridge, Harold T., 100
Beuscher, Jacob Henry, 201
Beuscher's Law and the Farmer, 201
Beyer, William H., 145, 177–178
Bible, the, 111
Bibliographical abbreviations, 239–240
Bibliographical Guide to Research in Speech and Dramatic Art, A, 98
Bibliographic guides, 89–91
Bibliographic Index, 68
Bibliographic sources, 67–69
Bibliographies, trade, 67–69
Bibliography of Geography: Part I, Introduction to General Aids, 134–135
Bibliography of Place-name Literature: United States and Canada, 135
Bickerman, Elias Joseph, 136
Biegeleisen, Jacob Israel, 234
Big Book of Halls of Fame in the United States and Canada, The, 237
Biographical Dictionaries and Related Works (and its *Supplement*), 58
Biographical Dictionaries Master Index, 71, 78–79
Biographical Dictionary of American Science: The Seventeenth Through the Nineteenth Centuries, 167
Biographical Directory of Librarians in the United States and Canada, A, 230
Biographical Directory of the American Psychological Association. See Directory of the American Psychological Association
Biographical sources of information, 57–60, 71, 78–79
Biography Index, 71, 78–79
Biological and Agricultural Index, 170, 199
Biological and Medical Electronics, 184
Biology, 169–171
Biology Data Book, 170
BIP. See Books in Print
Bishop, Charles E., 201
Bittmer, Dorothy S., 170
Black, Henry Campbell, 161
Black American Reference Book, The, 130
Black Americans: A Study Guide and

Sourcebook, 130
Black American studies. *See*
  Afro-American studies
Black's Law Dictionary, 161
Blake, John Ballard, 181
Blakiston's Gould Medical Dictionary, 181
Blatz, Hanson, 196
Blom, Eric, 108
Bloomberg, Marty, 230
Blum, Eleanor, 114
Blumenthal, Lassor A., 165
Boatner, Mark Mayo, 136
Boaz, Joseph N., 121
Boger, Louise Ade, 128
Boggs, Ralph Steele, 101
Bollier, John A., 112
Bombs and Bombings, 227
Bond, Otto F., 101
Book collection, 5
Book: The Story of Printing and
  Bookmaking, The, 234-235
Bookman's Glossary, The, 234
Book of American Rankings, The, 145
Book of Costume, The, 124
Book of the Dance, 97
Book of the States, 139
Book of World Rankings, The, 145
Book Review Digest, 70, 76, 78
Book Review Index, 70, 78
Book review indexes, 70, 76, 78
Books, parts of, 38-39
Books in Print (BIP), 67-69
Books to Help Children Cope with
  Separation and Loss, 233
Borchardt, Dietrich Hans, 110
Bordman, Gerald, 108
Borgatta, Edgar F., 142
Borland, Hal Glen, 204
Botany. *See* **Horticulture/floriculture**
Botts, Ralph Rudolph, 201
Boucher, Carl O., 186
Boulding, Elise, 147
Boundaries of the United States and the
  Several States, 135
Bowker Annual of Library and Book Trade
  Information, The, 230
Bowker (R. R.) Company, New York,
  119
Bowker's Medical Books and Serials in
  Print, 181-182

Bowman, Walter Parker, 97
Boyce, Byrl N., 163
Bradbury, Malcolm, 105
Bradbury, Peggy F., 188
Brand, John R., 223
Brant, Carroll A., 215
Bredow, Miriam, 188
Breed, Paul Francis, 97
Breeding and Raising Horses, 203
Bréhier, Émile, 111
Brenner, Morris, 178
Breslau, Michael, 173
Brewer, J. Gordon, 134
Briddon, Arnold E., 217
Briggs, Martin Shaw, 120
Brigham, Grace, 215
Bright, Karin Drudge, 199
Britannica Book of the Year, 64-65
Britannica Encyclopedia of American Art,
  The, 119
Britannica Yearbook of Science and the
  Future, 166
British Authors Before 1800: A
  Biographical Dictionary, 104
British Authors of the 19th Century, 104
British Library, 230
Broadcast Communications Dictionary,
  The, 114
Broadwell, Lucile, 191
Brock, Clifton, 139
Brockett, Oscar Gross, 97
Brodie, Thomas G., 227
Brooks, Hugh, 219
Brooks, Tim, 116
Brown, J. Buchanan-. *See*
  Buchanan-Brown, J.
Brown, Les, 116
Brown, Mary Ruth, 199
Brown, Stanley M., 152
Browsing, 35, 38
Bruce, Robert D., 226
Bruner, Dorsey William, 213
Brunner, Lillian Sholtis, 191, 198
Brussel, James Arnold, 142
Bryant, Donald C., 97-98
Buchanan-Brown, J., 103
Buchsbaum, Walter, 223
Buchsbaum's Complete Handbook of
  Practical Electronic Reference Data,
  223

Building Construction Handbook, 220
Building trades. *See* **Construction technology**
Bull, Storm, 108
Bulletin of the Public Affairs Information Service, 129
Burchfield, R. W., 47
Burger, George Vanderkarr, 204
Burington, Richard Stevens, 145, 177
Burke, John Gordon, 175
Bursaw, Charles T., 149
Burton, Benjamin T., 182
Burton, William, 102
Bury, J. B., 136
Business and Financial Planning Tables Desk Book, 149
Business and management, 153–155
Business and office occupations, 148–165
Business Books and Serials in Print, 149
Business Communication for Better Human Relations, 165
Business Executive's Handbook, 152
Business Management Handbook, 149
Business Periodicals Index, 149
Business Writer's Handbook, The, 149
Bustamente, Rodrigo, A., 196
Butler, Audrey, 137
Butterick Fabric Handbook, The, 124
Butterworth's Medical Dictionary, 182
Byshyn, William, 218

Cabinetry. *See* **Construction technology**
Callatäy, Vincent de, 168
Callender, John Hancock, 121, 129
Call numbers, 34
Cambridge Ancient History, 136
Cambridge Encyclopedia of Astronomy, The, 168
Cambridge History of American Literature, 102
Cambridge History of English Literature, 102
Cambridge Mediaeval History, 136
Camera Work, 127
Campbell, Don G., 163
Canadian Committee on Cataloguing, 230
Cantlin, Vernita, 198

Cantor, M. Catherine, 164
Cantzlaar, George La Fond, 142
Card catalogs. *See* **Catalogs**
Carlson, G. E., 121
Carpentry. *See* **Construction technology**
Carruth, Gorton, and associates, 136
Casey, William J., 150, 158, 161, 163
Cash, Joan, 195
Cashin, James A., 150
Cassell's Encyclopaedia of World Literature, 97, 102
Cassell's German-English, English-German Dictionary, 100
Cassell's Italian-English, English-Italian Dictionary, 101
Castano, Francis, 186
Castillo, Carlos, 101
Casualty Officer's Handbook, 194
Catalog of the Universe, 169
Catalogs, 5, 7–32: **dictionary,** 8; **divided,** 8; **physical formats of,** 8
CBI. See Cumulative Book Index
Cestre, Charles, 100
Challinor, John, 174
Chamberlin, Mary Walls, 119
Chamber's Biographical Dictionary, 57, 59
Champie, Ellmore A., 217
Chandor, Anthony, 173
Check List of Native and Naturalized Trees of the United States (Including Alaska), 208–209
Chemical Technician's Ready Reference Handbook, 172
Chemistry, 171–172
Chen, Philip, S., 171
Chiara, Joseph De. *See* De Chiara, Joseph
Chicago, University of, Press, 48
Chilton Book Company: Automotive Book Dept., 215; Automotive Editorial Dept., 215
Chilton's Basic Auto Maintenance, 215
Chilton's Guide to Emission Controls and How They Work, 215
Chilton's Motor/Age Professional Auto Heating and Air Conditioning Manual, 216
Christie, Ronald V., 197
Chronology of the Ancient World, 136

Chronology of the United States, 136
Chujoy, Anatole, 96
Circuit Design Idea Handbook, 223
Circulation desk, 4–5
City directories, 66
Civil Aircraft of the World, 218
Civil War Dictionary, The, 136
Clapham, A. R., 209
Clapp, Jane, 122, 126
Clark, Donald Thomas, 152
Clark, Hank, 218
Clark, Mary Virginia, 181
Clarke, Mary, 96
Classical Music Recordings for Home and
    Library, 108
Classification of library materials,
    32–38
Clauser, H. R., 232
Clements, John, 136
Clepper, Henry Edward, 204
Clinical Application of Respiratory Care,
    198
Clinical Diagnosis and Management by
    Laboratory Methods, 189
Clinical Hematology, 189
Clinical Interpretation of Laboratory Tests,
    189
Clothing. See Fashion design
Coan, Eugene V., 205
Cohen, Morris L., 161
Cohen, Ronald, 131
Colby, Vineta, 104, 105
Cole, Warren Henry, 193
Collation, of a book, 16–17
Collegiate Dictionary of Zoology, 171
Collins, Frederick Howard, 234
Collins, George William, 160
Collocott, T. C., 167
Color Dictionary of Flowers and Plants for
    Home and Garden, The, 211
Columbia Dictionary of Modern European
    Literature, 103
Columbia Encyclopedia. See New Columbia
    Encyclopedia, The
Columbia Lippincott Gazetteer of the
    World, 61, 63
Coman, Edwin Truman, 149
Commager, Henry Steele, 137, 139
Commercial Artist's Handbook, 123

Commercial Chicken Production Manual,
    203
Common Plants: Botanical and Colloquial
    Nomenclature, 210
Common Sense Guide to Professional
    Advertising, A, 152
Communications, 114–118
Communications/Research/Machines,
    Inc., 142
Comparative & Veterinary Medicine, 213
Comparative International Almanac, The,
    145
Complete Book of Personal Letter-Writing
    and Modern Correspondence, The, 165
Complete Dental Assistant's, Secretary's,
    and Hygienist's Handbook, 186
Complete Directory of Prime Time
    Network TV Shows, 1946–Present,
    The, 116
Complete Encyclopedia of Motorcars, 1885
    to the Present, The, 216
Complete Encyclopedia of Popular Music
    and Jazz, 1900–1950, The, 108–109
Complete Guide to Furniture Styles, The,
    125
Complete Guide to Investment Analysis,
    The, 159
Complete Guide to Modern Dance, The, 97
Complete Handbook for Medical
    Secretaries and Assistants, The, 188
Complete Handbook of Automotive Engines
    & Systems, The, 216
Complete Handbook of Sports Scoring and
    Record Keeping, 238
Complete Manual of Criminal Forms:
    Federal and State, 161
Complete Secretary's Handbook, 165
Composite Index for CRC Handbooks, 166
Comprehensive Dictionary of Psychological
    and Psychoanalytical Terms: A Guide
    to Usage, 143
Comprehensive Pediatric Nursing, 191
Computer-assisted searching, 75
Computer Dictionary and Handbook, 173
Computer Glossary for Students and
    Teachers, 173
Computer science, 172–174
Computer Yearbook, 173
Comroe, Julius H., 197

Concise Atlas of the Universe, The, 169
Concise Cambridge Bibliography of English Literature, 600-1950, The, 107
Concise Cambridge Italian Dictionary, The, 101
Concise Desk Book of Business Finance, 153
Concise Desk Guide to Real Estate Practice and Procedure, 163
Concise Dictionary of Interior Decorating, The, 126
Concise Dictionary of Physics and Related Subjects, 180
Concise Encyclopedia of Astronomy, 169
Concise Oxford Dictionary of Ballet, The, 96
Concise Oxford Dictionary of Opera, The, 109
Concrete Construction Handbook, 221
Condensed Chemical Dictionary, The, 171
Condensed Computer Encyclopedia, 173
Condon, Edward Uhler, 180
Congress and the Nation, 139
Congressional District Data Book, 141
Congressional Quarterly Almanac, 139
Congressional Quarterly, Inc., 139
Congressional Quarterly's Guide to Congress, 139
Congressional Staff Directory, 139
Connor, Billie M., 99
Connor, John M., 99
Conover, Herbert S., 210
Conservation and Agriculture, 204
Conservation and wildlife management, 204-205
Conservation Directory, 204
Considine, Douglas M., 167-168, 176, 223
Construction Glossary, 221
Construction Industry Production Manual, 221
Construction Information Source and Reference Guide, 221
Construction Inspection Handbook, 221
Construction Manual: Finish Carpentry, 220
Construction technology, 219-221
Consumer Demand for Food Commodities in the United States with Projections for 1980, 201
Consumer Guide, 217, 238
Contemporary Architects, 120-121
Contemporary Authors: A Bio-Bibliographical Guide to Current Authors and Their Works, 103
Contemporary Dramatists, 99
Contemporary Literary Criticism, 97, 103
Contemporary Novelists, 107
Contemporary Poets, 103
Contento, William, 103
Convenience and Fast Food Handbook, 207
Cook, Dorothy Elizabeth, 103
Cooking. *See* **Culinary arts**
Cooley, C. Earl, 156
Coombs, Clyde F., 223
Coon, Carleton Stevens, 131
Cooper, Marian G., 188
Copley, Margaret A. H., 186
Copperud, Roy H., 48
Corporate authors, 10, 12, 13
Corpus Juris Secundum, 161
Corty, Floyd L., 202
Cosmetology, 221-222
Côté, Rosalie J., 210
Council of Chief State School Officers, 132
Council of State Governments, 139
Countries of the World and Their Leaders, 139
County and City Data Book, 146
Cowan, Henry J., 121
Cox, Edwin Burk, 149
CQ Weekly Report, 139-140
Crabbe, David, 177
Craig, Robert G., 187
Craigie, Sir William Alexander, 46
Crane, Dale, 218
CRC Handbook of Food Additives, 207
CRC Handbook of Laboratory Animal Science, 203
CRC Handbook of Marine Science, 179
CRC Handbook of Mathematical Sciences, 177-178
CRC Handbook of Tables for Probability and Statistics, 145
Crescent Dictionary of Mathematics, The, 178

*Crime Scene Search and Physical Evidence
    Handbook,* 227
Criminal Justice. *See* **Law
    enforcement**
Criminal Justice Dictionary, The, 227
Criminology Index, 229
Crippen, Cynthia, 148
Crispin, Frederic Swing, 166
Crobaugh, Clyde J., 158
Crocker, Dean, 197
Croix, Horst de la. *See* De la Croix,
    Horst
Cross, F. L., 113
Crouse, William Harry, 216
*Crowell's Handbook of Contemporary
    Drama,* 98
Crowley, Ellen T., 47, 153
Cuddon, John A., 103
Culinary arts, 206–207
*Cumulated Index Medicus. See Index
    Medicus*
Cumulative Book Index (CBI), 67, 69
*Cumulative Index to Nursing & Allied
    Health Literature,* 191
Cunningham, Carl L., 227
Cunningham, John J., 210
Cunningham, William E., 161
Curran, H. Allen, 175
Current biographical tools, 58
Current Biography Yearbook, 57, 59
Current Book Review Citations, 70, 78
Current Clinical Dental Terminology, 186
Current Drug Handbook, 191–192
Current events indexes, 70, 76
Current Medical Diagnosis & Treatment,
    182
*Current Medical Information and
    Terminology,* 182

Dahl, Dale C., 201
Daiches, David, 106
*Dairy Cattle: Principles, Practices,
    Problems, Profits,* 203
Dalton, John W., 222
Damm, Henry C., 189
Dana, Richard H., 181
Dance, 96–97
Dance Catalog, The, 96
Dance Encyclopedia, The, 96

Dance Magazine, 96
Dance World, 96
*Dangerous Properties of Industrial
    Materials,* 226
Daniel, Howard, 122
*Dartnell Advertising Manager's Handbook,
    The,* 152
Dartnell Corporation, 153
Dartnell International Trade Handbook,
    153
*Dartnell Office Administration Handbook,
    The,* 165
*Dartnell Personnel Administration
    Handbook, The,* 153
Dasmann, Raymond Frederick, 204
Data processing. *See* **Computer
    science**
*Data Processing Secretary's Complete
    Handbook,* 173
Davenport, Millia, 124
Davids, Lewis E., 158
Davidson, Henry Alexander, 182
Davidson, Sidney, 151
Davis, Bob J., 235
Davis, Phyllis E., 188
Dawydoff, Alexis, 218
Dean, John A., 172
*Death, Grief, and Bereavement: A
    Bibliography, 1845–1975,* 233
De Callatäy, Vincent. *See* Callatäy,
    Vincent de
De Chiara, Joseph, 219
Decker, O'Neill, Lois. *See* O'Neill, Lois
    Decker
Decoration. *See* **Interior decoration
    and design**
Deighton, Lee C., 133
De Keyser, Ethel. *See* Keyser, Ethel de
De la Croix, Horst, 119
Delp, Mahlon H., 192
Demarest, Rosemary R., 150
*Demographic Yearbook/Annuaire
    démographique,* 145
Dennis, Robert Lee, 188
Dental assistant, 185–186
Dental hygienist, 186–187
Dental lab technician, 187
**Depositories, for U.S. government
    publications,** 80
Der Meer, Frederic van. *See* Meer,

Frederic van der
Designer's Guide to OSHA, 220
Desrosier, Norman W., 206
Developing Library Collections, 230
De Vries, Mary A., 165
Dewey decimal classification, 5,
   33–38
Diacritical marks, in filing, 32
Diagram Group, 108, 237
DIALOG, 75
Diamant, Lincoln, 114
Dictionaries and books on language,
   46–53. *See also* **Languages**
Dictionary for Accountants, A, 151
*Dictionary of Abbreviations in Medicine
   and the Health Sciences*, 183
Dictionary of Advertising Terms, 152
*Dictionary of Agricultural and Food
   Engineering*, 199
*Dictionary of Altitudes in the United
   States*, 134
Dictionary of American Biography, 58, 60
*Dictionary of American English on
   Historical Principles*, 46, 51–52
Dictionary of American History, 137
*Dictionary of Americanisms on Historical
   Principles, A*, 46, 51–52
Dictionary of American Library Biography,
   230
Dictionary of American Penology, 228–229
Dictionary of American Slang, 47, 52
Dictionary of Anthropology, 131
Dictionary of Applied Geology, 175
Dictionary of Architectural Science, 121
Dictionary of Architecture, A, 121
*Dictionary of Architecture and
   Construction*, 121
*Dictionary of Art Terms and Techniques,
   A*, 119
Dictionary of Astronomical Terms, 169
Dictionary of Aviation, A, 219
Dictionary of Basic Geography, A, 134
Dictionary of Behavioral Science, 143
Dictionary of Biology, A, 170
Dictionary of Black Culture, 129
Dictionary of Botany, A, 212
Dictionary of Building, A, 221
Dictionary of Business and Economics, 155
Dictionary of Business and Finance, 152–
   153

Dictionary of Business and Industry, The,
   154
Dictionary of Business and Management,
   149
*Dictionary of Business Finance and
   Investment*, 160
Dictionary of Computers, 173
Dictionary of Contemporary Music, 110
Dictionary of Contemporary Photography,
   127–128
Dictionary of Costume, The, 125
Dictionary of Criminal Justice, 228
Dictionary of Data Processing, 173
*Dictionary of Economic and Statistical
   Terms*, 146–147
Dictionary of Economics, 150
Dictionary of Education, 133
Dictionary of Gastronomy, 207
Dictionary of Genetics, A, 170
Dictionary of Geological Terms, 174
Dictionary of Geology, A, 174
*Dictionary of Hymnology Setting Forth the
   Origin and History of Christian Hymns
   of All Ages and Nations, A*, 112
Dictionary of Insurance, 158
Dictionary of Interior Design, The, 126
Dictionary of Life Sciences, A, 170
*Dictionary of Literary, Dramatic, and
   Cinematic Terms, A*, 97, 102
Dictionary of Literary Terms, A, 103
Dictionary of Logical Terms and Symbols,
   173
Dictionary of Management, 153
Dictionary of Management Terms, 153
Dictionary of Mathematics, 178
Dictionary of Modern English Usage, 48,
   53
Dictionary of Modern Painting, 122
Dictionary of Modern Sculpture, 122
Dictionary of Paper, The, 234
Dictionary of Philosophy, A, 111
Dictionary of Philosophy and Psychology,
   110
Dictionary of Politics, 140–141
Dictionary of Psychology, A, 142
Dictionary of Religion and Ethics, 113
Dictionary of Science and Technology, 167
Dictionary of Scientific Biography, 167
*Dictionary of Slang and Unconventional
   English, A*, 47, 52

Dictionary of Social Science, 129
Dictionary of Technical Terms, 166–167
Dictionary of the Biological Sciences, The,
    170
Dictionary of the Dance, 97
Dictionary of the Decorative Arts, 126
Dictionary of the Environment, A, 175
Dictionary of the Environmental Sciences,
    176
Dictionary of the Flowering Plants and
    Ferns, A, 211
Dictionary of the History of Ideas: Studies
    of Selected Ideas, 111
Dictionary of the Natural Environment, A,
    135
Dictionary of the Social Sciences, A, 129
Dictionary of Useful and Everyday Plants
    and Their Common Names, 211
Dictionary/Outline of Basic Statistics, 145
Dictionary/Reference Guide for Respiratory
    Therapy, 197
Dietary Nutrient Guide, 206
Digest of Educational Statistics, 132
Digests of Great American Plays, 99
Dimas, Steven, 197
Dinkel, John, 216
Direct Mail List Rates and Data, 151
Directories, 64, 66–67
Directory of Afro-American Resources, 130
Directory of American Horticulture, 210
Directory of American Scholars: A
    Biographical Directory, 132
Directory of Electronic Circuits, with a
    Glossary of Terms, 224
Directory of Information Resources in
    Agriculture and Biology, 199
Directory of Medical Specialists, 182
Directory of Safety and Construction
    Codes, U.S.A. States and Cities, 221
Directory of the American Psychological
    Association, 142
Diseases and Pests of Ornamental Plants,
    212
Dixson, Joseph I., 101
Doane Agricultural Service, St. Louis,
    201
Doane's Facts & Figures for Farmers, 201
Doane's Farm Management Guide, 201
Dobkin, Allen B., 197
Doctor and Patient and the Law, 188

Documentary History of Conservation in
    America, A, 205
Documents of American History, 137, 139
Dollfus, Audouin, 168
Dordick, Beverly F., 163
Doren, Charles Van. *See* Van Doren,
    Charles
Doris, Lillian, 152, 165
Doubleday, Nelson, 156
Douglas, James Dixon, 112
Dow Jones Investor's Handbook, The, 160
Dow Jones-Irwin, 149
Dow Jones-Irwin Business Almanac, 149
Dox, Ida, 182
Doyle, Jean Monty, 188
Drake, G. L., 226
Drama, 97–100
Drama A to Z: A Handbook, 99
Dramatic Criticism Index, 97
Dreisbach, Robert H., 182
Drever, James, 142
Dreyfuss, Henry, 122
Drugs from A to Z: A Dictionary, 183
Drury, Francis Keese Wynkoop, 98
Drury's Guide to Best Plays, 98
Dubois, Marguerite-Marie, 100
Duckles, Vincent Harris, 108
Dudas, Janice L., 176
Dudley, D. R., 105
Dun & Bradstreet's Guide to Your
    Investments, 160
Dunn, Lynn P., 130
Durrenberger, Robert W., 134, 176
Duyn, J. A. Van. *See* Van Duyn, J. A.
Dykema, Roland W., 187

Eagle, Dorothy, 104
Earl of Harewood, 109
Earth sciences, 174–175
Eastern Definitions: A Short Encyclopedia
    of Religions of the Orient, 113
Eastman, Terry R., 195
Ebony Handbook, The, 130
Eckersley-Johnson, Anna L., 165
Ecology, 175–177
Ecology Field Glossary, 176
Economic Indicators, 156
Economic Report of the President
    Transmitted to the Congress, 156

Economics, 155-156
Economics: Applications to Agriculture and Agribusiness, 202
Economics: Encyclopedia, 155
Eddleman, Floyd Eugene, 98
Edgerton, Harold A., 145
Editing by Design, 116
Edition statements for books, 14-16
Education, 131-134
Educational Research Information Center (ERIC), 132, 133
Educational Technology: Definitions and Glossary of Terms, 132
Education Directory, 134
Education Index, 132
Education in the States, 132
Education Yearbook, 133
Educators Guide to Free Films, 82, 89
Educators Guide to Free Filmstrips, 83, 89
Edwards, John, 201
Edwards, Paul, 111
Egan, Donald F., 197
Ehresmann, Donald L., 119
Eisner, Gilbert M., 182
EITD: Electronic Industry Telephone Directory, 223
Electrical engineering. *See* **Electronics**
Electrician. *See* **Electronics**
Electrician's Vest Pocket Reference Book, 224
Electronic Components Handbook, 224
Electronic Databook, 223
Electronics, 222-225
Electronics Dictionary, 224
Electronics Engineers' Handbook, 223
Electronics magazine, 225
Electronic Technician's Handbook of Time-Savers and Shortcuts, 223
Elements of Style, The, 48, 53
Elliott, Clark A., 167
Ellwood, L. W., 163
Ellwood, R. Terry, 116
Ellwood Tables for Real Estate Appraising and Financing, 163
Elrick, George, 103
Elving, Bruce F., 116
Emanuel, Muriel, 120
Emergency Care, 193
Emergency Care and Transportation of the Sick and Injured, 193

Emergency Medical Guide, 193
Emergency medical technician. *See* **Paramedical studies**
Encyclopaedia Britannica. See New Encyclopaedia Britannica
Encyclopaedia Judaica, 112
Encyclopaedia of Educational Media Communications and Technology, The, 133
Encyclopaedia of Religion and Ethics, 112
Encyclopaedia of the Social Sciences, 128
Encyclopedia Americana, 53, 55-56
Encyclopedia and Dictionary of Medicine and Nursing and Allied Health, 192
Encyclopedia International, 54-56
Encyclopedia of Accounting Systems, 150
Encyclopedia of Advertising, 151-152
Encyclopedia of American Agricultural History, 200
Encyclopedia of American Architecture, 121
Encyclopedia of American Facts and Dates, The, 136
Encyclopedia of American History, 137
Encyclopedia of American Religions, The, 113
Encyclopedia of Animal Care, 213
Encyclopedia of Anthropology, 131
Encyclopedia of Architectural Technology, 121
Encyclopedia of Associations, 64, 67
Encyclopedia of Auditing Techniques, 151
Encyclopedia of Aviation, 218
Encyclopedia of Banking and Finance, 160
Encyclopedia of Biochemistry, The, 171
Encyclopedia of Bioethics, 182
Encyclopedia of Biomedical Engineering Terms, The, 189
Encyclopedia of Business Information Sources, 153
Encyclopedia of Business Letters in Four Languages, 165
Encyclopedia of Chemistry, The, 171
Encyclopedia of Computer Science, 173
Encyclopedia of Computer Science and Technology, 173
Encyclopedia of Dance & Ballet, The, 96
Encyclopedia of Decorative Arts, 1890-1940, The, 125-126
Encyclopedia of Education, The, 133

Encyclopedia of Engineering Materials and Processes, 232

Encyclopedia of Environmental Science and Engineering, 176

Encyclopedia of Folk, Country and Western Music, 110

Encyclopedia of Food & Nutrition, 206

Encyclopedia of Food Engineering, 208

Encyclopedia of Food Science, 207

Encyclopedia of Food Technology, 208

Encyclopedia of Furniture, The, 125

Encyclopedia of Human Behavior, The, 143

Encyclopedia of Instrumentation and Control, 223

Encyclopedia of Jazz, The, 108

Encyclopedia of Library and Information Science, 230

Encyclopedia of Management, The, 153

Encyclopedia of Marine Resources, The, 179

Encyclopedia of Microscopy and Microtechnique, The, 170

Encyclopedia of Oceanography, The, 179

Encyclopedia of Organic Gardening, The, 210-211

Encyclopedia of Painting, 122

Encyclopedia of Philosophy, 111

Encyclopedia of Physics, The, 180

Encyclopedia of Pop, Rock and Soul, 109-110

Encyclopedia of Practical Photography, 128

Encyclopedia of Prehistoric Life, The, 131

Encyclopedia of Psychology, 142

Encyclopedia of Real Estate Forms, 163

Encyclopedia of Science Fiction and Fantasy Through 1968, The, 106

Encyclopedia of Sociology, 144

Encyclopedia of Sports, The, 237

Encyclopedia of Textiles, 124

Encyclopedia of the American Revolution, 136

Encyclopedia of the Biological Sciences, The, 170

Encyclopedia of Themes and Subjects in Painting, 122

Encyclopedia of the Third World, 140

Encyclopedia of Wood, The, 221

Encyclopedia of World Art, 119

Encyclopedia of World Costume, The, 125

Encyclopedia of World History, 137

Encyclopedia of World Theater, The, 98

Encyclopedia of World Travel, 156

Encyclopedias, general, 53-57

Encyclopedic Dictionary of Business Finance, 154

Encyclopedic Dictionary of Business Law, 154

Encyclopedic Dictionary of Mathematics, 178

Encyclopedic Dictionary of Real Estate Practice, 164

Encyclopedic Dictionary of Systems and Procedures, 149

Encyclopedic Guide to Nursing, 192

Energy. *See* **Ecology**

Energy Dictionary, 176

Energy Facts, 177

Energy Handbook, 176

Energy Source Book, The, 176

Energy Technology Handbook, 176

Engelbrektson, Sune, 169

Engineering Manual, 232

Engineering Mathematics Handbook, 178

English, Ava C., 143

English, Horace Bidwell, 143

English Association, 103

English literature. *See* **Literature**

Ensminger, M. Eugene, 203

Environmental Conservation, 204-205

Environmental Engineers' Handbook, 176

Environmental studies. *See* **Ecology**

Environment U.S.A., 177

ERIC. *See* Educational Research Information Center

Ernst, Morris Leopold, 145

Ervin H. Pollack's Fundamentals of Legal Research, 162

Esquire's Encyclopedia of 20th Century Men's Fashions, 125

Essay and General Literature Index, 102, 103

Essentials of Medical Microbiology, 185

Essentials of Respiratory Therapy, The, 197

Essentials of Roentgen Interpretation, The, 196

Esslin, Martin, 98

Ethnographic Atlas, 131

Etter, Lewis E., 196

Etymological dictionaries. *See*
Dictionaries and books on
language
Europa Year Book, The, 140
European Authors: 1000-1900, 104
Evaluating books, 38-39
Evans, G. Edward, 230
Evenson, A. E., 216
Everett, Thomas H., 211
Everyday Spanish Idioms, 101
Everyman's Concise Encyclopaedia of
Architecture, 120
Everyman's Dictionary of Dates, 137
Everyman's Dictionary of Music, 108
Everyman's Dictionary of Pictorial Art, 122
Ewbank, Henry Lee, 118
Ewen, David, 108
Exhaustive Concordance of the Bible,
113-114
Eysenck, Hans Jürgen, 142, 143

FAA Historical Fact Book, 217-218
FAA Statistical Handbook of Aviation,
218-219
Fabric Almanac, 124
Fabric Catalog, The, 124
Fact Book of U.S. Agriculture, 200
Facts About Nursing, 191
Facts About the Presidents, 140
Facts on File Dictionary of Astronomy,
The, 168
Facts on File: Weekly World News Digest
with Cumulative Index, 70, 76
Facts on File Yearbook, 64-66
Facts on the Major Killing and Crippling
Diseases in the United States Today,
184
Fairbridge, Rhodes Whitmore, 179
Fairchild, Wilma B., 177
Fairchild's Dictionary of Textiles, 124
Familiar Quotations, 102
Families of Flowering Plants Arranged
According to a New System Based on
Their Probable Phylogeny, The, 211
Famous First Facts, 64, 66
Fang, Hsai-Yang, 221
Farber, Eduard, 171
Farm and Garden Index, 200
Farm Builder's Handbook, 202
Farmers' Handbook of Financial

Calculations and Physical
Measurements, 201
Farm management. *See* **Agribusiness**
Farm Management Handbook, The, 202
Farrall, Arthur W., 199, 200, 208
Farrell, Maurice L., 160
Fashion design, 123-125
Fashion Dictionary, The, 125
Fashion Production Terms, 124
Faulkner, Willard R., 189
Featherly, Henry Ira, 211
Federal Aviation Regulations for Pilots,
217
Feldman, Stephen, 160
Felkenes, George T., 227
Feminist Quotations, 147
Fenaroli, Giovanni, 207
Fenaroli's Handbook of Flavor Ingredients,
207-208
Ferguson, Elizabeth, 158
Fernald, Merritt Lyndon, 211
Fiction Catalog, 107
Fidell, Estelle A., 98, 107
Field, Stanley, 117
Fieldbook of Natural History, 171
Fields, Willa L., 181
Fifield, William, 206
Figlio, Robert M., 229
Figure Types & Size Ranges, 124
Filing, in a catalog, 30-32
Films, guides to, 82, 84-89
Filmstrips, guides to, 83
Finding and evaluating books, 32-39
Fine Art Reproductions of Old & Modern
Masters, 123
Fine arts, 118-128
Fine Arts: A Bibliographic Guide to Basic
Reference Works, Histories, and
Handbooks, 119
Fink, Donald G., 223
Finnegan, Janet A., 198
Fire Officer's Guide to Safety in the Fire
Service, 226
Fire Protection Guide on Hazardous
Materials, 226
Fire Protection Handbook, 226
Fire Resistant Textiles Handbook, 226
Fire science, 226
Fire Sciences Dictionary, 226
First Aid Diagnosis and Management, 193

First Aid for Emergency Crews, 194
Firth, Frank E., 179
Fishbein, Morris, 188
FitzGerald, Ann, 147
Flammability Handbook for Plastics, 226
Flammarion, Camille, 168
Flammarion Book of Astronomy, 168
Flatau, Courtney L., 218
Fleming, John, 121, 126
Fletcher, John, 150
Flexner, Stuart Berg, 47
Floriculture. *See* **Horticulture/
   floriculture**
Flowers & Flourishes, 235
Flügge, Wilhelm, 232
Flying. *See* **Aviation occupations**
FM Atlas and Station Directory, 116–117
*Focal Dictionary of Photographic
   Technologies, The,* 127
*Focal Encyclopedia of Film and Television
   Techniques,* 117
Focal Encyclopedia of Photography, 127
Fodor's Modern Guides, 156
Follett, Wilson, 48
Food Products Formulary, 208
Food Technology, 207–208
Forbes, Reginald Dunderdale, 208
Ford, Richard A., 172
Fordney, Marilyn T., 188
Foreign languages. *See* **Languages**
Forestry, 208–209
Forestry Handbook, 208
Forestry Terminology, 209
Forest Service Organizational Directory,
   209
Forier, Lou, 216
Forman, Robert E., 184
*Forms and Functions of Twentieth-Century
   Architecture,* 121
Foskett, D. J., 133
Foundation Engineering Handbook, 221
1400 Ideas for Speakers and Toastmasters,
   118
Fowells, H. A., 209
Fowler, Henry Watson, 48
Fowler, H. Seymour, 171
Fox, Richard H., 227
Foye, James, 218
Franco, Jean, 105
Frantz, Charles, 131

Freidel, Frank, 137
French, 100
French, Derek, 153
French, Ruth M., 189
Freund, John E., 145
Frommer, Harvey, 237
Fuchs, Arthur W., 196
Fuels and Combustion Handbook, 214
Fuller, Edgar, 132
Fulton, Robert Lester, 233
Fundamental Formulas of Physics, 180
*Fundamentals of Legal Research. See Ervin
   H. Pollack's Fundamentals of Legal
   Research*
*Fundamentals of Quantity Food
   Preparation: Desserts and Beverages,*
   206
Fundamentals of Respiratory Therapy, 197
*Fundamentals of X-Ray and Radium
   Physics,* 196
Funeral Encyclopedia, The, 233
Funeral service. *See* **Mortuary science**
*Funeral Service: A Bibliography of
   Literature on Its Past, Present, and
   Future, the Various Means of
   Disposition, and Memorialization,* 233
*Funk & Wagnalls Guide to Modern World
   Literature,* 106
Furia, Thomas E., 207
Furlow, Bill, 223
Furniture. *See* **Interior decoration
   and design**
Futrell, Gene A., 202

Gabrielson, Ira N., 205
Gale, William, 125
Gale Research Company, 47
Gannett, Henry, 134
Garcia, F. L., 160
Garcia-Pelayo y Gross, Ramon, 101
Gardner, Helen, 119
Gardner's Art Through the Ages, 119
Garland, J. D., 223
Garner, Philippe, 126
Garrett, James F., 195
Gary, Margaret, 174
Gassan, Arnold, 127
Gassner, John, 98
Gaster, Adrian, 104
Gaunt, William, 122

Gaustad, Edwin Scott, 112
Gay, Robert M., 235
Gaylord, Charles N., 219
Gaylord, Edwin Henry, 219
Gazetteers, 61, 63
Gazzaniga, Alan B., 193
Gelbier, Stanley, 186
Gellert, W., 178
General Science Index, 167
Geographical Research and Writing, 134
Geographical sources: general, for nongeography students, 60–63; **specialized, for geography students,** 134–135
Geology. *See* **Earth sciences**
Georgano, G. N., 216
George, P. S., 201
German, 100–101
Gibb, H.A.R., 113
Gifis, Steven H., 162
Giles, Robert H., 205
Gillespie, James Howard, 213
Gillispie, Charles Coulston, 167
Ginsberg, Frances, 198
Gioello, Debbie Ann, 124
Girard, Denis, 100
Gladstone, John, 214
Glaister, Geoffrey Ashall, 234
Glaister's Glossary of the Book, 234
Glimp, Hudson A., 204
Gloag, John, 126
Glossary Handbook for Law Enforcement Education, 227
Glossary of Art, Architecture and Design Since 1945, 120
Glossary of Astronomy and Astrophysics, 168
Glossary of Chemical Terms, 172
Glossary of Geology, 174
Glossary of Hospital Terms, 190
Glossary of Mapping, Charting, and Geodetic Terms, 135
Glossary of Ocean Science and Undersea Technology Terms, 179
Glossary of Words and Phrases Used in Radiology, Nuclear Medicine, and Ultrasound, 196
Godel, Jules B., 219
Goldenson, Robert M., 143
Goldfien, Alan, 184

Goldman, Myer, 192, 196
Good, Carter Victor, 133
Goodheart-Willcox Automotive Encyclopedia, 216
Goodman, Robert L., 223
Goodman, Steven E., 133
Gordon, Arnold J., 172
Gordon, Frank S., 162
Gordon, Thomas Frank, 114
Gorman, Michael, 230
Gottfried, Bert A., 152
Gough, W. James, 204
Gove, Philip Babcock, 46
Government. *See* **Political science**
Government publications, 79–82
Gowers, Sir Ernest, 48
GPO. *See* U.S. Government Printing Office
Graf, Alfred Byrd, 211
Graf, Rudolf F., 189, 223, 225
Graff, Henry F., 136
Graham, Irvin, 151
Graham, John, 173
Granger, Edith, 104
Granger's Index to Poetry, 104
Granger's Index to Poetry, 1970–1977, 106
Grant, Gail, 96
Grant, John Charles Boileau, 182
Grant's Atlas of Anatomy, 182
Graphic arts. *See* **Art; Printing**
Graphic Arts Encyclopedia, 235
Gray, Asa, 211
Gray, Dorothy A., 167
Gray, Harold James, 180
Gray, Henry, 182
Gray, Peter, 170
Gray, Richard A., 167
Gray's Anatomy, 182
Grazda, Edward E., 178
Great Botanical Gardens of the World, 211
Great Chemists, 171–172
Great Psychologists, from Aristotle to Freud, The, 143
Green, William, 218
Greenberg, Milton, 140
Greenfield, Stanley R., 64
Greenstein, Carol Horn, 173
Greenwald, Douglas, 155
Gregg, Davis W., 158
Gregg Reference Manual, The, 149–150

Greisman, Bernard, 149
Gresswell, R. Kay, 174
Grogan, Denis Joseph, 167
Grolle, Carl G., 223
Gross, Jerome S., 163
Gross, Ramon Garcia-Pelayo y. *See*
    Garcia-Pelayo y Gross, Ramon
Grossman, Harold J., 206
Grossman's Guide to Wines, Beers, and
    Spirits, 206
Grounds Maintenance Handbook, 210
Grout, Donald Jay, 108
Groves, Donald G., 179
Gruendemann, Barbara J., 198
Grzimek, Bernhard, 170, 176
Grzimek's Animal Life Encyclopedia, 170
Grzimek's Encyclopedia of Ecology, 176
Guedes, Pedro, 121
Guercio, Francis M., 101
Guide to Architectural Information, 121
Guide to Art Reference Books, 119
Guide to Basic Information Sources in
    Chemistry, 171
Guide to Basic Information Sources in the
    Visual Arts, 120
Guide to Dental Materials and Devices,
    187
Guide to Diagnostic Procedures, 189
Guide to Ecology Information and
    Organizations, 175
Guide to Fashion Merchandise Knowledge,
    125
Guide to Great Plays, 99
Guide to Historical Literature, 136
Guide to Historical Method, A, 138
Guide to Historical Reading: Non-Fiction,
    A, 137
Guide to Library Research in Psychology,
    A, 142
Guide to Medical Writing, 182
Guide to Microforms in Print, 82, 85
Guide to Play Selection, 99
Guide to Reference Books (and its
    Supplement), 89–91
Guide to Reference Materials, 90–91:
    Volume 1: Science and Technology,
    168
Guide to Sources of Educational
    Information, A, 134

Guide to the Literature of Astronomy, A,
    169
Guide to the Literature of Mathematics
    and Physics Including Related Works
    on Engineering Science, 178
Guide to the Literature of the Life
    Sciences, 171
Guide to the National Electrical Code, 224
Guide to the Retention and Preservation of
    Records (with Destruction Schedules),
    190–191
Guide to Trade and Securities Statistics, A,
    159
Guide to U.S. Government Statistics, 145
Guide to World Commodity Markets, 201
Guinness Book of World Records, 64, 66
Guinness Sports Record Book, 1979–1980,
    237
Gunn, Rodger S., 227
Guralnik, David B., 46

Hagan, William Arthur, 213
Hagan's Infectious Diseases of Domestic
    Animals, 213
Haight, Timothy R., 115
Hairstyling. *See* **Cosmetology**
Hall, Carl W., 208
Hall, Maurice H., 194
Hallmark, Clayton, 216
Halsey, Richard Sweeney, 108
Halstead, James A., 189
Hamilton, S. G. Ian, 196
Hamilton, William James, 196
Hamlin, Talbot Faulkner, 121
Hammond, Jerome W., 201
Hammond, Kenneth A., 177
Hammond, N.G.L., 137
Hampel, Clifford A., 171, 172
Handbook for Auditors, 150
Handbook for Chemical Technicians, 172
Handbook for Dental Surgery Assistants
    and Other Ancillary Workers, 186
Handbook for Discussion Leaders, 118
Handbook for Electronic Engineers and
    Technicians, 225
Handbook for Electronics Engineering
    Technicians, 223–224
Handbook for Emergency Medical

Personnel, 194
Handbook for Radiologic Technologists and Special Procedures Nurses in Radiology, 196
Handbook for Recreation, 238
Handbook of Abnormal Psychology, 143
Handbook of Advertising Management, 151
Handbook of Air Conditioning, Heating, and Ventilating, 214
Handbook of Applied Mathematics, 178
Handbook of Architectural Practice, 120
Handbook of Business Administration, 153
Handbook of Chemistry and Physics, 172
Handbook of Clinical Laboratory Data, 189
Handbook of Clinical Psychology, 143
Handbook of Components for Electronics, 224
Handbook of Construction Equipment Maintenance, 220
Handbook of Contemporary Photography, A, 127
Handbook of Educational Administration, 134
Handbook of Educational Research: A Guide to Methods and Materials, 133
Handbook of Electronic Circuit Design Analysis, 225
Handbook of Electronic Circuit Designs, 224
Handbook of Electronic Instrumentation, Testing, and Troubleshooting, 225
Handbook of Electronic Instruments and Measurement Techniques, 225
Handbook of Electronics Calculations for Engineers and Technicians, 224
Handbook of Electronics Formulas, Symbols, and Definitions, 223
Handbook of Emergency Pharmacology, 193
Handbook of Engineering Mechanics, 232
Handbook of Expanded Dental Auxiliary Practice, 186
Handbook of Food Preparation, 206
Handbook of Forensic Science, 228
Handbook of Forms, Charts, and Tables for the Construction Industry, 219
Handbook of General Psychology, 143–144

Handbook of Heavy Construction, 220
Handbook of Highway Engineering, 235
Handbook of Insurance, 158
Handbook of International Data on Women, 147
Handbook of Labor Statistics, 155
Handbook of Livestock Equipment, 203
Handbook of Mathematical Calculations for Science Students and Researchers, 177
Handbook of Mathematical Tables and Formulas, 177
Handbook of Method in Cultural Anthropology, A, 131
Handbook of Modern Accounting, 151
Handbook of Modern Rhetorical Terms, A, 118
Handbook of Narcotics Control, 228
Handbook of Non-Prescription Drugs, 182
Handbook of Operational Amplifier Circuit Design, 225
Handbook of Oral Diagnosis and Treatment Planning, 186
Handbook of Personal Insurance Terminology, A, 158–159
Handbook of Personality Theory and Research, 142
Handbook of Physical Medicine and Rehabilitation, 195
Handbook of Physical Therapy, 195
Handbook of Physics, 180
Handbook of Pictorial Symbols, 123
Handbook of Poisoning: Diagnosis and Treatment, 182
Handbook of Probability and Statistics, 145
Handbook of Psychological Terms, 143
Handbook of Real Estate Investment, The, 163
Handbook of Sampling for Auditing and Accounting, 150
Handbook of Social and Cultural Anthropology, 131
Handbook of Statistical Tables, 146
Handbook of the Nutritional Contents of Foods, 207
Handbook of Theological Terms, A, 112
Handbook of Veterinary Drugs, 213
Handbook of Veterinary Surgical

Instruments and Glossary of Surgical Terms, 213

Handbook of Wealth Management, 160

Handbook on Contemporary Education, 133

Handbooks, 64–66

Handbook to Literature, A, 104

Handy, Charles R., 202

Hanenkrat, Frank T., 205

Hannah, Harold W., 201

Hansen, Helen F., 192

Hansen, Roger Gaurth, 208

Hansteen, Henry B., 224

Hardingham, Martin, 124

Hardwick, Geraline B., 206

Harewood, Earl of. *See* Earl of Harewood

Harling, Robert, 126

Harman, Thomas L., 224

Harper, Charles A., 224

Harper Dictionary of Contemporary Usage, 48, 53

Harper Encyclopedia of the Modern World, 137

Harper's Bible Dictionary, 113

Harper's Dictionary of Hinduism, 114

Harper's Dictionary of the Graphic Arts, 234

Harrah, Barbara K., 233

Harrah, David F., 233

Harriman, Philip Lawrence, 143

Harris, Chauncy D., 134

Harris, Cyril M., 121

Harrison, Henry S., 164

Harrison, Ronald, 198

Harrod, Leonard Montague, 230

Hart, James David, 104

Hartnoll, Phyllis, 98

Harvard Books on Astronomy, 168

Harvard Concise Music Dictionary, 109

Harvard Dictionary of Music, 107

Harvard Guide to American History, 137

Harvey, Anthony P., 131

Harvey, Sir Paul, 104

Harvey, Van Austin, 112

Harwood, Mary, 127

Hastings, James, 112

Haupt, Hellmut Lehmann-. *See* Lehmann-Haupt, Hellmut

Havener, William H., 192

Havers, John A., 220

Havlice, Patricia P., 108

Hawkes, J. G., 204

Hawley, Gessner G., 171, 172

Hay, Roy, 211

Haycraft, Howard, 104

Hayden, Adaline C., 191

Hayward, Arthur L., 101

Headings, on catalog cards, 14

Health Insurance Institute, 159

Health sciences and occupations, 180–199

Health Sciences and Services: A Guide to Information Sources, 183

Heasley, Jerry, 216

Heath, Gerald R., 158

Heating. *See* **Air-conditioning, heating, and refrigeration**

Hedgecoe, John, 127

Hedlund, Mary F., 113

Heffner, Hubert C., 98

Heise, Jon O., 157

Hemnes, Thomas M. S., 162

Hendee, John C., 205

Henderson, John, 193

Hendin, David, 182

Henry, John Bernard, 189

Herrick, Clyde N., 224

Herzberg, Ronald J., 207

Heyel, Carl, 153

Hickman, C. J., 170

Hickok, Ralph, 237

Hickok, Robert, 194

Higgins, Lindley R., 220

Highway engineering. *See* **Transportation**

Highway Engineering Handbook, 236

Highway Statistics, 236

Highway Statistics: Summary to 1975, 236

Hilado, Carlos J., 226

Hill, Ann, 123

Hill, Danny, 238

Hill, D. W., 198

Hillway, Tyrus, 133

Historian's Handbook: A Descriptive Guide to Reference Works, The, 138

Historical Atlas, 60, 63

Historical Atlas of Religion in America, 112

Historical dictionaries. *See*
Dictionaries and books on
language
Historical Statistics of the United States:
Colonial Times to 1970, 146
Historic Architecture Sourcebook, 121
History, 135–138
History and Criticism of American Public
Address, A, 118
History of Art, 119
History of Broadcasting in the United
States, A, 116
History of Philosophy, The, 111
History of Psychiatry, The, 142
History of Western Music, A, 108
History of Wildlife in America, The, 204
History of World Sculpture, The, 122
Hochman, Stanley, 137
Hoeller, Mary Louise, 198
Hoffman, Herbert H., 165
Holler, Frederick L., 140
Holman, Clarence Hugh, 104
Holum, John R., 176
Home Book of Bible Quotations, The, 113
Home Book of Proverbs, Maxims, and
Familiar Phrases, The, 106
Home Book of Quotations, Classical and
Modern, The, 106
Honigmann, John Joseph, 131
Honkala, Barbara H., 209
Honour, Hugh, 121, 126
Hopf, Peter S., 220
Hopkins, Jeanne, 168
Horses and Horsemanship, 203
Horst, R. Kenneth, 212
Horticulture/floriculture, 209–212
Horton, Holbrook L., 232
Hortus Third, 210
Hospital Financial Management
Association, 190
Hospital Medical Records, 190
Hotel and Motel Red Book, 156
Hotel & Travel Index, 156
Hotel/motel and travel/tourism,
156–157
Houses: The Illustrated Guide to
Construction, Design, and Systems,
164
Housing Construction Statistics, 1889–
1964, 164

Howard, Neale E., 168
Howe, George Frederick, 136
Howe, Robine, 207
Howes, Frank N., 211
How to Find Chemical Information, 172
How to Find Information About
Companies, 154
How to Find Out: Educational Research,
133
How to Find Out in Philosophy and
Psychology, 110–111
How to Write Scientific and Technical
Papers, 167
Hudson, Michael C., 141
Hughes, Harold K., 183
Hughes, Marija Matich, 147
Hulbert, James R., 46
Humanities, 95–114
Humanities: A Selective Guide to
Information Sources, The, 96
Humanities Index, 95
Human Nutrition, 182
Humphreys, Christmas, 112
Hunt, Lee M., 179
Hunt, V. Daniel, 176
Hunt, William Dudley, 121
Hunter, David E., 131
Hurlbut, Cornelius S., Jr., 175
Hurov, L., 213
Hurrel, Ron, 117
Hutchison, J. W., 232
Hutchinson, John, 211
Huxley, Anthony Julian, 174
Hyams, Edward S., 211

IEEE Standard Dictionary of Electrical and
Electronics Terms, 224
Illingworth, Valerie, 168
Illustrated Dictionary of Broadcast-CATV-
Telecommunications, The, 116
Illustrated Dictionary of Ornament, An,
120
Illustrated Dictionary of Photography, 127
Illustrated Encyclopedia of Mankind, The,
131
Illustrated Encyclopedic Dictionary of
Building and Construction Terms, 219
Illustrated Encyclopedic Dictionary of Real
Estate Terms, 163–164
Illustrated Handbook of Electronic Tables,

Symbols, Measurements, and Values, 224

Illustrated Manual of Nursing Techniques, 192

Imprint, of a book, 16

Index, defined, 7–8

Indexed Guide to Modern Electronic Circuits, 223

Indexes to government publications, 79–82

Indexing and abstracting services, 70–79

Index Medicus, 183

Index of Paramedical Vocabulary, 194

Index to Biographies of Contemporary Composers, Volume II, 108

Index to Book Reviews in the Humanities, 78–95

Index to Dental Literature, 186

Index to Educational Audio Tapes, 83

Index to Educational Overhead Transparencies, 83

Index to Educational Records, 84

Index to Educational Slides, 83

Index to Educational Video Tapes, 83

Index to 8mm Motion Cartridges, 82

Index to Legal Periodicals, 162, 227

Index to Outdoor Sports, Games, and Activities, 238

Index to Plays in Periodicals, 98

Index to Science Fiction Anthologies and Collections, 103

Index to 16mm Educational Films, 82–89

Index to 35mm Educational Filmstrips, 83

Industrial occupations. *See* **Trade, technical, and industrial occupations**

Information Please Almanac, 63, 65

Information science. *See* **Computer science**

Information Sources in Advertising History, 152

Information Sources in Transportation, Material Management, and Physical Distribution, 235

Information Sources of Political Science, The, 140

Inglis, J. Gall, 169

Inglis, R.M.G., 169

Inhalation therapist. *See* **Respiratory therapist**

Initials, in filing, 32

Inkeles, Alex, 144

Institute for Business Planning, Inc., 149

Institute of Electrical and Electronics Engineers, 224

Institute of Life Insurance, 159

Instruction Guide for Organizing Health Records, An, 190

Instrument Flying Handbook, 218

Insurance, 158–159

Insurance Almanac, 158

Insurance Handbook for the Medical Office, 188

Insurance Inspection and Underwriting: A Non-Technical Encyclopedic Handbook, 159

Insurance Words and Their Meanings, 158

Interior decoration and design, 125–126

Interior Design and Decoration: A Bibliography, 126

Interior Painting, Wallpapering, and Paneling: A Beginner's Approach, 126

Interlibrary loan, 40

Interlibrary Loan Procedure Manual, 231

International Authors and Writers Who's Who, The, 104

International Dictionary of Education, 133

International Encyclopedia of Aviation, The, 218

International Encyclopedia of Chemical Science, 172

International Encyclopedia of Higher Education, 133

International Encyclopedia of Psychiatry, Psychology, Psychoanalysis & Neurology, 143

International Encyclopedia of Statistics, 145

International Encyclopedia of the Social Sciences, 128

International Geographic Encyclopedia and Atlas, The, 135

International Guide to Wood Selection, The, 220

International standard book number (ISBN), 17

International Television Almanac, 117

International Who's Who, 57, 59

International Yearbook and Statesmen's Who's Who, 140

Interpreter's Bible, 112
Interpreter's Dictionary of the Bible, The, 112
Interviewing: A Guide for Health Professionals, 181
Introduction to Agricultural Economic Analysis, 201
Introduction to Librarianship, 230
Introduction to Library Science, 231
Introduction to Operating-Room Technique, 198
Introduction to Public Services for Library Technicians, 230
Introduction to Reference Work, 230
Introduction to Technical Services for Library Technicians, 230
Introduction to the History of Dentistry, An, 187
Introduction to United States Public Documents, 79, 82
Investment Companies: Mutual Funds and Other Types, 160
Investments, 159–161
Irwin, Graham W., 137
Irwin, Leonard Bertram, 137
Isaacs, Alan, 180
ISA Handbook of Control Valves, 232
ISBN. *See* **International standard book number**
Italian, 101

Jablonski, Donna M., 154
Jackson, Jane, 192
Jackson, Joseph Hollister, 168
Jacobstein, J. Myson, 162
Jane's All the World's Aircraft, 218
Jane's World Railways, 235
Janson, Dora Jane, 119
Janson, Horst Woldemar, 119
Jaques Cattell Press, 237
Jawetz, Ernest, 184
Jay, Frank, 224
Jazz. *See* **Music**
Jennings, Ralph E., 216
Jeppesen Sanderson Aviation Yearbook, 218
Jeppesen Sanderson, Inc., 218
J. K. Lasser's Standard Handbook for Accountants, 151
Johns Hopkins Atlas of Human Functional Anatomy, The, 183

Johnsich, John Robert, 164
Johnson, Allen J., 214
Johnson, Anna L. Eckersley-. *See* Eckersley-Johnson, Anna L.
Johnson, Arnold H., 207, 208
Johnson, Elden, 131
Johnson, Emily, 228
Johnson, Larry, 216
Johnson, M. L., 170
Johnson, Russell E., 134
Johnson, Thomas Herbert, 137
Johnston, John F., 187
Jones, Franklin D., 232
Jones, Kenneth K., 98
Jones, Richard, 146
Jones, Thomas H., 224
Jordain, Philip B., 173
Jordan, Emil Leopold, 205
Journalism, 115–116
Journalist Biographies Master Index, 115
Joy of Cooking, 207
Judge, Clark S., 145
Juergenson, Elwood M., 202, 203
Juhl, John H., 196
Julian, John, 112
Juvenile encyclopedias. *See* **Encyclopedias, general**

Kacmaret, Robert M., 197
Kalmbacher, George, 211
Kalvelage, Carl, 140
Kane, Joseph Nathan, 64, 135, 140
Kaprelian, Mary H., 97
Karassik, Igor J., 232
Karpinski, Leszek M., 113
Karush, William, 178
Katz, William A., 68, 230
Kaufman, Milton, 223, 225
Keane, Claire B., 192
Keats, Theodore E., 196
Kell, Walter G., 150
Keller, Dean H., 98
Keller, Helen Rex, 104
Kelly, John D., 215
Kemp, Peter, 236
Kennedy, James R., 113
Kennedy, Robert L., 206
Kent, Allen, 230
Kent, Ruth K., 115
Kent, William, 232
Kerekes, Gabriel T., 160

Kerker, Ann E., 213
Kerr, Avice H., 190
Keyser, Ethel de, 210
King, Eunice M., 192
King, G. A., 201
King, John W., 189
King, Robert C., 170
Kingsbury, John Merriam, 211
Kinkle, Roger D., 108
Kirk, Raymond M., 198
Kirk, Thomas G., Jr., 170
Kiser, Donald J., 161
Klapper, Marvin, 124
Kleeberg, Irene Cumming, 124
Klein, Barry T., 143
Knauer, K., 213
Knowles, Asa S., 133
Kobbé, Gustave, 109
Koegler, Horst, 96
Kohler, Eric Louis, 151
Kohls, Richard Louis, 201
Kohn, Mary Louise, 198
Kory, Ross C., 196
Kraeling, Emil Gottlieb Heinrich, 113
Kramers, J. H., 113
Krasowski, J. Owen, 197
Kravitz, Marjorie, 228
Kreitzberg, Fred C., 221
Krichmar, Albert, 147
Krikler, Bernard, 137
Kruger, Arthur N., 118
Krusen, Frank Hammond, 195
Kruskal, William H., 145
Kuhn, Ryan A., 148
Kunitz, Stanley J., 104
Kurian, George Thomas, 140, 145
Kurtz, Albert K., 145
Kusnet, Jack, 163
Kuvshinoff, B. W., 226

La Beau, Dennis, 114
Laboratory in Clinical Medicine, The, 189
Lacey, Alan Robert, 111
Lackschewitz, Gertrud, 126
La Croix, Horst de. *See* De la Croix,
    Horst
Laird, Eleanor S., 173
Lake, Carlton, 122
Lambert, Eleanor, 124
Lambert, William W., 142

Lancour, Harold, 230
Landon, Grelun, 110
Landscaping. *See* **Horticulture/**
    floriculture
Land Use and Wildlife Resources, 205
Lang, D. M., 105
Lange, Norbert Adolph, 172
*Langenscheidt's Concise German
    Dictionary*, 101
Langer, William Leonard, 137
Lange's Handbook of Chemistry, 172
Langley, Leroy L., 183
Langman, Jan, 183
*Language of Journalism: A Glossary of
    Print Communication Terms, The*, 115
Language of Wall Street, The, 160–161
Languages, 100–101
Lansford, Edwin M., 171
Lapedes, Daniel N., 167, 171, 175, 180,
    200
Laqueur, Walter, 137
Larousse, Pierre, 101
Larousse Encyclopedia of Animal Life, 171
Larrick, Nancy, 152
Lasky, Joseph, 234
Lasser, Jacob Kay, 149
Lasser (J.K.) Institute, New York, 151
Lavidge, Arthur W., 152
Law. *See* **Law enforcement; Legal**
    assistant
Law Dictionary, 162
Law enforcement, 227–229
Law Enforcement: A Selected Bibliography,
    227
*Law Enforcement: A Selective
    Bibliography*, 228
*Law of Death and Disposal of the Dead,
    The*, 233
Lawyer's Desk Book, 161
Layman's Dictionary of Psychiatry, The,
    142
LC classification. *See* **Library of**
    Congress classification
*LCSH. See Library of Congress Subject
    Headings*
Leaders of American Conservation, 204
Leathart, Scott, 208
Lee, Jo Ann, 165
Legal assistant, 161–162
Legal Research in a Nutshell, 161

Legal Secretary's Encyclopedic Dictionary, 162
Legal Secretary's Word Finder and Desk Book, 162
Legal Word Book, The, 162
Legge, Nancy, 117
Le Grand, Rupert, 232
Lehmann-Haupt, Hellmut, 234
LeMaitre, George D., 198
Lembeck, Harriet, 206
Lenk, John D., 224
Letter-by-letter filing, 31
Levie, Albert, 203
Levin, Ezra, 220
Levine, Edna S., 195
Levinson, Louis, 183
Levy, Michael H., 158
Lewis, H.A.G., 169
Lewis, Leslie L., 153
Lewis, Walter H., 176
Liberty Hyde Bailey Hortorium, 210
Librarians, 40–41
Librarians' Glossary of Terms Used in Librarianship, 230
Libraries, defined, 3
Library Association, 230
Library Literature, 230–231
Library of Congress, 230
Library of Congress classification, 5, 33–34
Library of Congress Subject Headings (LCSH), 27–30
Library Research Guide to Biology, 170
Library Research Guide to Religion and Theology, 113
Library technician, 229–231
Lichine, Alexis, 206
Lichine's Encyclopedia of Wines & Spirits, 206
Life and Health Insurance Handbook, 158
Life Insurance Desk Book, 158
Life Insurance Fact Book, 159
Life sciences. *See* **Biology**
Lincoln, Walter Osborn, 159
Lindemann, A. J., 153
Lingeman, Richard R., 183
Linton, George E., 124
Lippincott Manual of Nursing Practice, The, 191
Lipták, Béla G., 176

List of Worthwhile Life and Health Insurance Books, A, 159
Literary History of the United States, 106
Literature, 101–107
Literature of Geography: A Guide to Its Organization and Use, The, 134
Literature of Journalism: An Annotated Bibliography, The, 115
Literature of Political Science, The, 139
Literature of Theology: A Guide for Students and Pastors, The, 112
Little, Elbert Luther, 208, 209
Livestock and Meat Marketing, 202
Livestock breeding. *See* **Animal science**
Livestock Health Encyclopedia, 204
Livingstone, E. A., 113
Loebl, Suzanne, 192
Loftness, Robert L., 176
London, Peter Stanford, 193
Long Term Economic Growth, 1860–1965: A Statistical Compendium, 156
Loose-leaf services, defined, 76
Love, T. W., 220
Lovell, John, 99
Lucas, Vane B., 158
Ludwig, Raymond H., 224
Luening, R. A., 202
Lundberg, Donald E., 156
Lundgren, Earl F., 153
Lung: Clinical Physiology and Pulmonary Function Tests, The, 197
Lunin, Lois F., 183
Lusted, Lee B., 196
Lyon, Leonard J., 197
Lytle, R. J., 202, 220

Macdonald, Malcolm Ross-. *See* Ross-Macdonald, Malcolm
Machinery's Handbook, 232
Machine shop practice. *See* **Mechanical engineering**
Machinists' Ready Reference, 232
Macinko, George, 177
Mack, Craig W., 197
Mack, William, 161
Mackay (W. and J.) and Company, Ltd., 234
Macklem, Peter T., 197
MacNalty, Arthur Salusbury, 182

Magazine Index, The, 70, 74–75
Magazines. See Periodicals
Magazines for Libraries, 68–69
Magill, Frank Northen, 105
Magill's Bibliography of Literary Criticism, 105
Mai, Ludwig H., 155
Maillard, Robert, 122
Main entry, 8–27: for books, 9–18; for media, 22, 23–25; for microforms, 18, 22; for periodicals, 18; for sound recordings, 22, 26–27
Maizell, Robert E., 172
Major, Ralph Herman, 192
Major's Physical Diagnosis, 192
Making the Media Revolution: A Handbook for Video-Tape Production, 117
Malinowsky, Harold Robert, 167
Management. See Business and management
Manchester, P. W., 96
Mandl, Matthew, 224
Manning, Robert T., 192
Manual for Lawyers and Legal Assistants: Real Estate, 164
Manual for Physical Therapy Technicians, 195
Manual for Writers of Term Papers, Theses, and Dissertations, A, 48, 53
Manual of Botany, 211
Manual of Cultivated Plants Most Commonly Grown in the Continental United States and Canada, 210
Manual of Documents and Forms for the Legal Secretary. See Sletwold's Manual of Documents and Forms for the Legal Secretary
Manual of History Taking, Physical Examinations and Record Keeping, 193
Manual of Operating Room Technology, 198
Manual of Pulmonary Function Testing, 197
Manual of Skin Diseases, 222
Manual of Style, A, 48, 53
Manual on Artificial Organs, 197
Manuals. See Handbooks
Maps, in libraries, 61–62. See also Atlases

Maps for America: Cartographic Products of the U.S. Geological Survey and Others, 135
March, Robert T., 151
Marcuse, Sibyl, 109
Marine science. See Oceanography
Marion, Bruce W., 202
Mark, Charles, 144
Market and Price Analysis: The Agricultural Industries, 201
Marketing Farm Products: Economic Analysis, 202
Marketing of Agricultural Products, 201
Market Performance: Concepts and Measures, 202
Marks' Standard Handbook for Mechanical Engineers, 232
Markus, John, 224, 225
Marr, Warren, 130
Marraine, Peter A., 217
Marsh, Earle, 116
Martin, E. A., 170
Martin, John Joseph, 97
Martindale-Hubbell Law Directory, 162
Mass Communication Effects and Processes: A Comprehensive Bibliography, 1950–1975, 114
Mass communications. See Communications
Mass Media: Aspen Institute Guide to Communication Industry Trends, The, 115
Masterpieces of World Literature in Digest Form, 105
Materials and Techniques of Painting, The, 123
Mathematics, 177–178
Mathematics Manual, 178
Mathews, Mitford M., 46
Mathews, Shailer, 113
Matlaw, Myron, 99
Matthews, Douglas, 139
May, Donald Curtis, 145
Mayer, Ralph, 119, 122
Maynard, Harold Bright, 153
Maynard, Jeff, 173
McAfee, Robert, 174
McAleese, Ray, 133
McBride, Richard, 177
McCavitt, William E., 117
McCoy, John Henry, 202

McCulloch, Walter Fraser, 209
McDonagh, Don, 97
McElroy, Donald L., 186
McEvedy, Colin, 146
McGraw-Hill Dictionary of Art, 119–120
McGraw-Hill Dictionary of Modern Economics, 155
McGraw-Hill Dictionary of Physics and Mathematics, 180
McGraw-Hill Dictionary of Scientific and Technical Terms, 167
McGraw-Hill Dictionary of the Life Sciences, 171
McGraw-Hill Encyclopedia of Energy, 176
McGraw-Hill Encyclopedia of Environmental Science, 176–177
McGraw-Hill Encyclopedia of Food, Agriculture & Nutrition, 200
McGraw-Hill Encyclopedia of Ocean and Atmospheric Sciences, 179
McGraw-Hill Encyclopedia of Science and Technology, 167
McGraw-Hill Encyclopedia of the Geological Sciences, 174–175
McGraw-Hill Encyclopedia of World Biography, The, 58, 60
McGraw-Hill Encyclopedia of World Drama, 99
McGraw-Hill Nursing Dictionary, 192
McGraw-Hill Real Estate Pocket Guide, The, 164
McGraw-Hill's Dodge Manual for Building Construction Pricing and Scheduling, 220
McGraw-Hill's Leaders in Electronics, 225
McGraw-Hill Yearbook of Science and Technology, 167
McHenry, Robert, 205
McInnis, Raymond G., 128
McKee, Kathleen Burke, 147
McMahan, John, 164
McMurtrie, Douglas Crawford, 234
McPhee, Carol, 147
McRae, Alexander, 176
McWhirter, Norris Dewar, 237
Meat Handbook, 203
Mechanical engineering, 231–232
Mechanical Engineers' Handbook, 232
Media: cataloging of, 22–25; **in libraries**, 6–7; **reference works for**, 82–89

Media Review Digest, 84, 89
Medical Abbreviations: A Cross Reference Dictionary, 183
Medical Abbreviations and Acronyms, 184
Medical and Health Annual, 183
Medical assistant, 187–189
Medical Assistant, The, 188
Medical careers. *See* **Health sciences and occupations**
Medical Hieroglyphs, 190
Medical laboratory assistant, 189–190
Medical Office Procedures, 188
Medical Record Departments in Hospitals, 190
Medical Record Forms for Hospitals, 190
Medical records technician, 190–191
Medical Reference Works, 1679–1966, 181
Medical Risks: Patterns of Mortality and Survival, 183
Medical Shorthand, 188
Medical Sourcebook, The, 184
Medical-Surgical Nursing Procedures, 191
Medical Terminology from Greek and Latin, 190
Medical Typist's Guide for Histories and Physicals, 188
Medical Word Book, The, 191
Medical Word Finder, 185
Medical Writing: The Technic and the Art, 188
Meer, Frederic van der, 113
Meili, R., 142
Melby, Edward C., 203
Melcher, Daniel, 152
Melloni, Biagio, 182
Melloni's Illustrated Medical Dictionary, 182
Melton, J. Gordon, 113
Melzi, Gian Battista, 101
Men and Ideas in Economics: A Dictionary of World Economists Past and Present, 155
Menke, Frank Grant, 237
Mental health. *See* **Psychology**
Mental Health Almanac, The, 143
Mental Health Yearbook/Directory, The, 143
Menzel, Donald Howard, 180
Merck Index: An Encyclopedia of Chemicals and Drugs, 172

Merck Manual of Diagnosis and Therapy, 183–184

Merck Veterinary Manual, The, 213

Merrill, Annabel L., 207

Merrill, Vinita, 196

Merritt, Frederick S., 178, 220

Mersand, Joseph, 99

Mersky, Roy M., 162

Messinger, Heinz, 101

Mettler, Frederick Albert, 184

Meyers, Frederick H., 184

MGH Textbook of Emergency Medicine, 193–194

Miall, Laurence Mackenzie, 172

Michigan Occupational Therapy Association, 183

Microbiology, 189–190

Microforms: cataloging of, 18, 21–22; **defined (fiche and film),** 6; **in libraries,** 6; **reference works for,** 82, 85

Miller, Benjamin Frank, 192

Miller, Besse May, 165

Miller, John Lane, 113

Miller, Madeleine Sweeny, 113

Miller, Shirley, 231

Millington, T. Alaric, 178

Millington, William, 178

Milt, Harry, 143

Milutinovic, Barbara, 191

Minrath, William R., 178

Mitchell, Geoffrey Duncan, 128

Mitchell, Jerome, 218

Mitford, Jessica, 233

Mitton, Simon, 168

MLA Handbook for Writers of Research Papers, Theses, and Dissertations, 48, 53

MLA International Bibliography of Books and Articles on the Modern Languages and Literatures, 97, 105

MoCat. See Monthly Catalog of United States Government Publications

Modern American Usage: A Guide, 48, 53

Modern Dictionary of Electronics, 225

Modern Dictionary of Sociology, A, 144

Modern Electronic Circuits Reference Manual, 224–225

Modern French-English Dictionary, 100

Modern Humanities Research Association, 105

Modern Language Association of America, 48, 105

Modern Practice in Crown & Bridge Prosthodontics, 187

Modern Real Estate Dictionary, 164

Modern Researcher, The, 136

Modern's Market Guide, 222

Modern Textile and Apparel Dictionary, The, 124–125

Modern Theatre Practice, 97, 98

Modern World Drama: An Encyclopedia, 99

Modley, Rudolf, 123

Moerman, Daniel E., 211

Moffat, Donald W., 153

Mohrmann, Christine, 113

Moidel, Harriet Costen, 192

Mondey, David, 218

Monkhouse, Francis John, 135

Monro, Isabel Stevenson, 103

Monro, Kate M., 165

Montagné, Prosper, 206

Monthly Catalog of United States Government Publications (MoCat), 79–82

Monthly Periodical Index (MPI), 70, 72, 74

Moody's Handbook of Widely Held Common Stocks, 160

Moon, Hugh, 225

Moore, Norman D., 160

Moore, Patrick, 168, 169

Morehead, Joe, 79, 82

Morison, Samuel Eliot, 137

Moritz, Alan R., 188

Morris, Dan, 140

Morris, Inez, 140

Morris, R. Crawford, 188

Morris, Richard Brandon, 137

Morris, William, 46, 48

Mortenson, William P., 202

Mortuary science, 232–233

Moss, Eugenie Lair, 199

Moss, Martha, 127

Motion pictures. *See* **Films, guides to**

Motor's Emission Control Manual, 216

Mottram, Eric, 105

MPI. See Monthly Periodical Index

Muehsam, Gerd, 120
Mueller, Jerome F., 220
Muirden, James, 169
Multi-Media Reviews Index. See Media Review Digest
Municipal Year Book, 140
Munn, Glenn Gaywaine, 160
Murdin, Paul, 169
Murdoch, John, 146
Murdock, George Peter, 131
Murphy, Henry T., 213
Murray, Sir James Augustus Henry, 47
Music, 107–110
Musical Instruments of the World: An Illustrated Encyclopedia, 108
Musicians Since 1900: Performers in Concert and Opera, 108
Music Index: The Key to Current Music Periodical Literature, 109
Music Library Association, Subcommittee on Basic Music Collection, 109
Music Reference and Research Materials: An Annotated Bibliography, 108
Myers, Bernard S., 119, 122

Nagler, Willibald W., 195
Names and Numbers: A Journalist's Guide to the Most Needed Information Sources, 115
Nanassy, Louis C., 165
Naroll, Raoul, 131
National Atlas of the United States, The, 60, 62
National Basic Intelligence Factbook, 141
National Construction Estimator, 220
National Directory of Addresses and Telephone Numbers, 64, 67
National Electrical Code, 222
National Electrical Code Handbook, The, 225
National Electrical Code Reference Book, 223
National Fire Code, 226
National Fire Protection Association, 225, 226
National Forest Products Association, 220
National Health Directory, 184

National Health Education Committee, 184
National Information Center for Educational Media (NICEM), 82–89
National League for Nursing, Division of Research, 192
National Repair and Remodeling Estimator, 1979, 221
National Research Council, Committee on Agricultural Land Use and Wildlife Resources, 205
National Trade and Professional Associations of the United States, and Labor Unions, 153
National Union Catalog, 68
NCTE Liaison Committee, 99
Neblette, Carroll Bernard, 127
Neblette's Handbook of Photography and Reprography, 127
Negro Almanac: A Reference Work on the Afro American, The, 130
Negro in American History, The, 130
Neilson, William Allan, 46
Nelson, Archibald, 175
Nelson, Kenneth Davies, 175
Network Rates and Data, 151
Neurology for Physiotherapists, 195
New Acronyms, Initialisms, and Abbreviations, 47, 52
New American Guide to Athletics, Sports & Recreation, The, 237
New American Machinist's Handbook, The, 232
New Cambridge Bibliography of English Literature, The, 105
New Cambridge Modern History, The, 137
New Cassell's French Dictionary: French-English, English-French, 100
New Catholic Encyclopedia, 113
New Columbia Encyclopedia, The, 54, 56
New Complete Book of the American Musical Theater, 108
New Dictionary of Chemistry, A, 172
New Dictionary of Physics, A, 180
New Dictionary of the Social Sciences, A, 128–129
New Encyclopaedia Britannica, 54–57
New Encyclopedia of Sports, 237
New Encyclopedia of the Opera, The, 108
New Encyclopedic Dictionary of Business

Law—With Forms, 154
New English Dictionary on Historical
   Principles (and its *Supplement*), 47, 51
New Grove Dictionary of Music and
   Musicians, The, 109
New Handbook of Chemistry, A, 171
New International Dictionary of the
   Christian Church, The, 112
New Kobbé's Complete Opera Book, The,
   109
New Larousse Gastronomique, The, 206
Newman, James R., 178
New Oxford History of Music, 109
New Schöffler-Weis German and English
   Dictionary, The, 101
New Serial Titles, 68
Newspaper indexes, 70, 76–77
New words, books on. *See*
   Dictionaries and books on
   language
New York Botanical Garden Illustrated
   Encyclopedia of Horticulture, The, 211
New York Graphic Society, 123
New York Times Encyclopedia of
   Television, The, 116
New York Times Index, The, 70, 76–77
NICEM. *See* National Information
   Center for Educational Media
Nicholls, Peter, 106
Nicholson, Barbara Evelyn, 209
Nihon Sūgakkai, 178
1970 Census of Housing, 164
NLN Nursing Data Book, 192
Non-Alcoholic Food Service Beverage
   Handbook, 207
Norback, Craig T., 237
Norback, Peter, 237
Nordland, Rod, 115
North, Mack O., 203
Norton, Arthur Philip, 169
Nose, Yukihiko, 197
Notable Names in the American Theatre,
   99
Notes area of a catalog card, 17
Novak, Stephen R., 150
Novissimo Melzi: Dizionario Enciclopedico
   Italiano, Il, 101
Novotny, Ann, 123
Numbers, in filing, 32
Nunn, Marshall E., 238
Nurse's Almanac, The, 193

Nurse's Drug Handbook, The, 192
Nurse's Guide to Drugs, 192
Nurse's Guide to the X-Ray Department,
   A, 192, 196
Nursing, 191–193
Nursing Care in Eye, Ear, Nose, and
   Throat Disorders, 192
Nursing Care of the Patient with Medical-
   Surgical Disorders, 192
Nutritional Quality Index of Foods, 208

Oberg, Erik, 232
O'Brien, James Jerome, 221
Observer's Book of Aircraft, The, 218
Observer's Book of Commercial Vehicles,
   The, 235–236
Observer's World Airlines and Airlines
   Directory, The, 218
Ocean and Marine Dictionary, 179
Oceanography, 178–179
Ocean World Encyclopedia, 179
Ockerman, Herbert W., 208
Odeh, Robert E., 146
Odishaw, Hugh, 180
Office Management Handbook, 165
Office occupations. *See* **Business and**
   office occupations
Official Airline Guide, Worldwide Edition,
   157
Official Congressional Directory, 141
Official Guide of the Railways and Steam
   Navigation Lines of the United States,
   Puerto Rico, Canada, Mexico and
   Cuba, The, 157
Official Hotel & Resort Guide, The, 157
Official Meeting Facilities Guide, 157
Official Rules of Sports and Games, 238
Official Steamship Guide, 157
Official World Encyclopedia of Sports and
   Games, The, 237
Oldham, Joe, 216
Oliu, Walter E., 149
One Hundred Books about Bookmaking,
   234
O'Neill, Lois Decker, 148
One-volume encyclopedias. *See*
   Encyclopedias, general
Onions, Charles Talbut, 47
On-line computer searches, 75
Onyx Group, Inc., 177
Opera. *See* **Music**

Operating room assistant. *See*
    Surgical assistant
Oppenheim, Irwin A., 189
Organic Gardening, 211
Origin of Races, The, 131
Orton, Charles William Previté-. *See*
    Previté-Orton, Charles William
Osborn, Andrew Delbridge, 231
Osborne, Harold, 120
Oscilloscope Handbook, 224
Osol, Arthur, 181, 185
Ottemiller, John Henry, 99
Ottemiller's Index to Plays in Collections,
    99
Our Magnificent Earth, 175
Oversize books, 7
Ovington, Ray, 205
Owen, Donald Bruce, 146
Oxford Book of Trees, The, 209
Oxford Classical Dictionary, The, 137
Oxford Companion to American History,
    The, 137
Oxford Companion to American Literature,
    The, 104
Oxford Companion to Art, The, 120
Oxford Companion to English Literature,
    The, 104
Oxford Companion to Ships & Sea, The,
    236
Oxford Companion to the Theatre, The, 98
Oxford Companion to World Sports &
    Games, The, 238
Oxford Dictionary of English Etymology,
    47, 51
Oxford Dictionary of English Proverbs, 105
Oxford Dictionary of Quotations, The, 105
Oxford Dictionary of the Christian Church,
    The, 113
Oxford Economic Atlas of the World, 155
Oxford History of the American People,
    The, 137
Oxford Regional Economic Atlas: The
    United States and Canada, 155
Oxford University Press, 155
Oxygenator, The, 197

Pace, Denny F., 228
Page, G. Terry, 133
Painter's Dictionary of Materials and
    Methods, The, 123
Painting. *See* **Art**

Painting in America: The Story of 450
    Years, 123
Palen, Jennie M., 151
Paleontology. *See* **Anthropology**
Palmer, E. Laurence, 171
Palmer, Pete, 237
Palmer, R. R., 138
Pan Am's World Guide, 157
Para-Legal and the Lawyer's Library, The,
    161–162
Paramedical studies, 193–194
Parisi, Nicolette, 228
Parke, Nathan Grier, 178
Parker, Sybil P., 176–177, 179
Parkhurst, Charles Chandler, 165
Partnow, Elaine, 147
Partridge, Eric, 47
Patient in Surgery: A Guide for Nurses,
    The, 198–199
Patterson, Sandra R., 190
Paul, Lester W., 196
Paullin, Charles Oscar, 138
Paulsen, Kathryn, 148
Paulson, Glenn L., 177
Paxton, Albert S., 221
Payne, J. P., 198
Peake, Dorothy Margaret, 98, 100
Pearson, Jim B., 132
Peavy, Charles D., 130
Pegler, Martin, 126
Pelayo y Gross, Ramon Garcia-. *See*
    Garcia-Pelayo y Gross, Ramon
Penguin Companion to American
    Literature, The, 105
Penguin Companion to Classical, Oriental
    & African Literature, The, 105
Penguin Companion to English Literature,
    The, 106
Penguin Companion to European
    Literature, The, 106
Penguin Dictionary of Economics, The, 155
Penguin Dictionary of Physics, The, 180
Penguin Dictionary of Saints, The, 111–
    112
Pennak, Robert William, 171
Pennington, Jean A. Thompson, 206
Pennsylvania Poultry Health Handbook,
    203
Pequeño Larousse Ilustrado, 101
Periodicals: cataloging of, 18, 20;
    indexes to, 70–75; **in libraries,** 5

Perkins, R. M., 226
Perry, Robert H., 232
Pescow, Jerome K., 150
Peters, Jean, 234
Peterson, Martin S., 207, 208
*Petit Larousse Illustré: Dictionnaire
    Encyclopédique Pour Tous*, 100
Pevsner, Nikolaus, 121
Peyton, Floyd A., 187
Pfafflin, James R., 176
*Phaidon Dictionary of Twentieth-Century
    Art*, 123
Phillips, Margaret, 121
Phillips, Ralph W., 187
Philosophy, 110–111
Photographer's Handbook, 127
Photographer's Market, 126, 127
Photography, 126–128
Photography Books Index, 127
Photography Year, 127
Photo-Lab-Index, 127
Physical education and recreation,
    237–238
Physical Medicine and Rehabilitation, 195
Physical therapist assistant, 194–195
*Physical Therapy Administration and
    Management*, 194
*Physician's Desk Reference to
    Pharmaceutical Specialities and
    Biologicals*, 184
Physician's Handbook, 184
Physics, 179–180
Physics Literature: A Reference Manual,
    180
Piccirillo, Martin L., 228
Picken, Mary (Brooks), 125
Pickett, Calder M., 116
Pictorial Guide to the Planets, 168
*Picture Sources: Collections of Prints and
    Photographs in the U.S. and Canada*,
    123, 127
Pindborg, Jens J., 186
Pirone, Pascal P., 212
Pitt, Valerie H., 180
*Place-name Changes Since 1900: A World
    Gazetteer*, 135
Place-name dictionaries. *See*
    Gazetteers
Planet We Live On, The, 175
Plano, Jack C., 140

Play Index 1949–1952, 100
Play Index 1953–1960, 98
Play Index 1961–1967, 98
Play Index 1968–1972, 98
Play Index 1973–1977, 98
Plays. *See* **Drama**
Playter, R., 213
Ploski, Harry A., 130
Pocket Book of Statistical Tables, 146
Pocket Guide to Health Assessment, 181
*Poisonous Plants of the United States
    and Canada*, 211
Police science. *See* **Law enforcement**
*Political Handbook and Atlas of the
    World*, 140
Political science, 138–141
Political Science Dictionary, 140
Politics in America, 139
Polk, R. L., & Company, Kansas City, 66
Polking, Kirk, 218
Pollack, Ervin Harold, 162
Pollard, Arthur, 107
Pollay, Richard W., 152
*Poor's Register of Corporations, Directors
    and Executives, United States and
    Canada*, 153–154
Popular Dictionary of Buddhism, A, 112
Popular Periodical Index, 70, 73–74
Popular Song Index (and its *First
    Supplement*), 108
Posner, Judith A., 145
Postell, William Dosite, 184
Poulton, Helen J., 138
Powell, Betty, 212
Powell, Nieta Whitman, 196
Powell, Thomas, 212
*Practical Guide to the Care of the
    Injured, A*, 193
Practical Wildlife Management, 204
Pratt, Robertson, 185
Preminger, Alex, 106
Prenis, John, 173
Prentice-Hall, Inc., 149, 151, 154, 162,
    164
Previté-Orton, Charles William, 138
Price, Warren C., 115, 116
Primer of Cardiac Catheterization, A,
    196
*Princeton Encyclopedia of Poetry and
    Poetics*, 106

Principles and Practices of Respiratory Therapy, 197
Principles of Radiographic Exposure and Processing, 196
Printed Circuits Handbook, 223
Printing, 233–235
Printing and Promotion Handbook, 152
Printing of a book, compared with edition, 16
Printing Types: Their History, Forms, and Use, 235
Private Aviation: A Guide to Information Sources, 218
Private Pilot's Dictionary and Handbook, The, 218
Prochnow, Herbert Victor, 118
Production Figure Book for U.S. Cars, The, 216
Professional Broadcast Writer's Handbook, 117
Professional Cosmetologist, The, 222
Professional Skin Care Manual, The, 222
Proofreading and Copy-Preparation, 234
Prostano, Emanuel T., 228
Psychological Abstracts, 73
Psychology, 141–144
Psychosources: A Psychology Resource Catalog, 142
Public Affairs Information Service, 128, 129
Publishers, addresses of, 68–69
Puestow, Charles B., 193
Pump Handbook, 232
Pure sciences, 166–180
Putnam, R. E., 121

Quick, John, 120
Quinn, Edward, 98
Quotable Woman, 1800–1975, The, 147

Race Relations Information Center, Nashville, 130
Radiation Hygiene Handbook, 196
Radio Amateur's Handbook, The, 117
Radio and television, 116–117
Radio and Television: A Selected, Annotated Bibliography, 117
Radiographic Fundamentals and Technique Guide, 195–196
Radiologic technician, 195–196

Raffé, Walter George, 97
Rafferty, Max, 134
Ralston, Anthony, 173
Ramsey, Charles George, 121
Randel, Don Michael, 109
Rand McNally & Co., 60, 138, 154, 236
Rand McNally Atlas of the Oceans, 179
Rand McNally Atlas of World Wildlife, The, 205
Rand McNally Bible Atlas, 113
Rand McNally Commercial Atlas and Marketing Guide, 60, 62–63, 154
Rand McNally Cosmopolitan World Atlas, 60, 62
Rand McNally Encyclopedia of Transportation, The, 236
Random House Dictionary of the English Language, 46, 49, 51
Random House Encyclopedia, The, 54, 56–57
Rasmussen, Wayne David, 200
Raus, Elmer E., 193
Raus, Madonna M., 193
Raymond, Walter J., 140
Reader's Adviser, The, 97, 106
Reader's Digest of Books, 104
Reader's Encyclopedia, The, 95
Reader's Encyclopedia of World Drama, The, 98
Reader's Guide to Contemporary History, A, 137
Reader's Guide to Periodical Literature, The, 70–75
Reader's Guide to the Great Religions, A, 111
Reading, Hugo F., 129
Ready-reference: questions, defined, 54; sources of information, 63–67
Real estate, 162–164
Real Estate Appraisal Bibliography, 163
Real Estate Appraisal Terminology, 163
Real Estate Handbook, The, 164
Real Estate Information Sources, 163
Real Estate Investment Tables, 163
Real Estate Sales Handbook, 164
Realtors National Marketing Institute, 164
Reap, Charles A., Jr., 186
Rebora, Piero, 101
Record Controls, Inc., 190

Records, guides to. *See* **Sound
recordings, guides to**
Recreation. *See* **Physical education
and recreation**
Recreation and Outdoor Life Directory,
238
Red Cross, United States American
National, 194
Reddig, Jill Swanson, 175
Rees, R., 155
Reeves, Wilson A., 226
Reference Development Corporation,
133
*Reference Encyclopedia of American
Psychology and Psychiatry*, 143
Reference Manual for Office Workers, 165
**Reference tools: defined and
described, 43–46; in libraries, 5**
Refrigeration. *See* **Air-conditioning,
heating, and refrigeration**
Rehabilitation Medicine, 195
*Rehabilitative Aspects of Acute and
Chronic Nursing Care*, 195
*Rehabilitative Practices with the Physically
Disabled*, 195
Reich, Warren T., 182
Reid, W. Malcolm, 171
Reidy, Brian, 201
Reilly, Theresa M., 162
Reister, Floyd Nester, 218
Religion, 111–114
*Religious Life of Man: Guide to Basic
Literature, The*, 113
Rendle, B. J., 209
Research, defined, 1–2
*Research Guide for Undergraduates in
Political Science*, 140
Research Guide in Journalism, 115
Research Guide in Speech, 118
Research in Education. *See Resources in
Education*
Reserve collection, 7
Resources in Education, 132, 133
Respiratory Function in Disease, 197
Respiratory therapist, 196–198
Respiratory Therapy, 198
Restorative Dental Materials, 187
Retrospective biographical tools, 58
Review of Medical Pharmacology, 184
Review of Physiology, 183

Reynolds, Barbara, 101
Reynolds, Nancy, 96
Rezzuto, Tom, 98
Rhetoric. *See* **Speech**
Rhodes, Marie J., 198
Rice, Edward, 113
Rich, Maria F., 110
Richards, Berry G., 68
Richards, Jack W., 238
Richards, J. M., 121
Richardson, Edgar Preston, 123
Richey, C. B., 200
Richter, G. R., 153
Rickett, Harold William, 212
Rietz, Carl A., 206
Rietz Master Food Guide, 206
Rippen, A. L., 208
*Road & Track Illustrated Auto Dictionary,
The*, 216
Robinson, J. Hedley, 169
Robinson, Kenneth L., 202
Robinson, Vester, 225
Rock Encyclopedia, 109
Rock music. *See* **Music**
Rogers, A. Robert, 96
Roget's International Thesaurus, 48, 52
Rolfe, Douglas, 218
Rombauer, Irma von Starkloff, 207
Roody, Peter, 184
Room, Adrian, 135
Roos, Charles, 181
Rosenberg, Jerry Martin, 149
Rosenthal, Harold, 109
Ross, Martin J., 154
Ross-Macdonald, Malcolm, 205
Rossoffl, Irving S., 213
Roth, Günter Dietmar, 169
Rothblatt, Henry B., 161
Rowland, Howard S., 193
Rowley, H. H., 113
Roxon, Lillian, 109
Roy, Ewell Paul, 202
Royen, William Van. *See* Van Royen,
William
Runes, Richard N., 129
*Running Press Glossary of Accounting
Language*, 151
*Running Press Glossary of Banking
Language*, 160
Running Press Glossary of Computer

Terms, 173
Running Press Glossary of Photography Language, 127
Ruppel, Gregg, 197
Rush, George Eugene, 228
Rush, Howard A., 195
Russell's Official National Motor Coach Guide, 157
Ryder, John, 235

Sabin, William A., 149
Sadie, Stanley, 109
SAE Handbook, 216
SAE Motor Vehicle, Safety, and Environmental Terminology, 216-217
Safar, Peter, 198
Safire, William L., 141
Safire's Political Dictionary, 141
Salem, James M., 98
Sanderlin, David, 138
Sanders, William B., 144
Sauer, Gordon C., 222
Saward, Heather, 153
Sax, Newton Irving, 226
Schaefer, Barbara Kirsch, 178
Schapsmeier, Edward L., 200
Schapsmeier, Frederick H., 200
Schatz, Walter, 130
Scheer, Wilbert E., 153
Schipf, Robert G., 216
Schmalz, Larry C., 173
Schmidt, Jacob E., 194
Schmieder, Allen A., 134
Schoeffler, O. E., 125
Schoen, Linda Allen, 222
Schoenfeld, Clarence Albert, 205
Schöffler, Herbert, 101
Schwann Record & Tape Guide, 84, 89
Schwartz, L. Dwight, 203
Schwartz, Robert J., 154
Schweitzer, Howard B., 184
Science and Engineering Literature: A Guide to Reference Sources, 167
Science and Technology: An Introduction to the Literature, 167
Science Fiction Encyclopedia, The, 106
Science Fiction Handbook for Readers and Writers, 103
Science of Fingerprints, The, 228
Sciences. *See* **Pure sciences**

Science Year: The World Book Science Annual, 167
Scientific and Technical Books and Serials in Print, 167
Scipien, Gladys M., 191
Scott, George E., 204
Scott, James W., 128
Scott, John S., 221
Scullard, H. H., 137
Sculpture. *See* **Art**
Sculpture Index, 122
Seal, Robert A., 169
Sealock, Richard Burl, 135
Sears, Minnie Earl, 109
Second Barnhard Dictionary of New English, The, 47, 52
Secretarial science, 164-165
Secretary's Handbook: A Manual of Correct Usage, The, 165
Security Dealers of North America, 160
Seely, Pauline Augusta, 135, 229
Segal, Morley, 140
Seiden, Rudolph, 204
Seidman, Arthur H., 223
Selbie, John A., 112
Selden, William, 165
Seldin, Maury, 164
Selective Bibliography for the Study of English and American Literature, 102
Selesnick, Sheldon T., 142
Seligman, Edwin R. A., 128
Selman, Joseph, 196
Serial. *See* **Periodicals**
Serial Number Book for U.S. Cars, 1900-1975, The, 215
Serial Publications, 231
Series statement, for a book, 17
Seward, Peter G., 164
Sexton, R., 213
Sexual Barrier: Legal, Medical, and Social Aspects of Sex Discrimination, The, 147
Seymour-Smith, Martin, 106
Shafer, Robert Jones, 138
Shapiro, Barry A., 198
Sharp, D.W.A., 172
Sheehy, Eugene Paul, 89
Sheepman's Production Handbook, The, 204
Shepherd, Geoffrey Seddon, 202

Shepherd, William Robert, 60
Shera, Jesse Hauk, 231
Shertzer, Margaret D., 165
Shestack, Robert, 195
Shipley, Joseph Twadell, 99
Short Dictionary of Furniture, A, 126
Shorter Encyclopedia of Islam, 113
Short Story Index (including Supplements
    and Annuals), 103
Showers, Victor, 146
Showman, Richard K., 137
Shugar, Gershon J., 172
Shugar, Ronald A., 172
Siegmund, O. H., 213
Siemon, Karl O., 221
Sills, David L., 128
Silvics of Forest Trees of the United
    States, 209
Simon, André Louis, 207
Simon, George, 196
Simplified Guide to Electronic Circuits,
    Test Procedures and Troubleshooting,
    225
Simpson, Marian G., 165
Singer, Richard B., 183
Sippl, Charles J., 173
Sippl, Charles P., 173
6,000 Words: A Supplement to Webster's
    Third New International Dictionary,
    47, 52
Skillin, Marjorie E., 235
Skinner, Eugene William, 187
Skinner's Science of Dental Materials, 187
Slang, dictionaries of. See
    Dictionaries and books on
    language
Sleeper, Harold R., 121
Sletwold, Evangeline, 162
Sletwold's Manual of Documents and
    Forms for the Legal Secretary, 162
Slides, guides to, 83
Sloan, Harold Stephenson, 150
Sloane, Sheila B., 191
Slocum, Robert, 58
Slonimsky, Nicolas, 108
Small, John, 135
Smith, Gerald Birney, 113
Smith, Horatio, 103
Smith, Martin Seymour-. See Seymour-
    Smith, Martin

Smith, Roger Cletus, 171
Smith, William James, 104, 106
Smythe, Mabel M., 130
Snell, Richard S., 184
Sniderman, Florence M., 97
Snyder, Donald Rowe, 194
Snyder, John, 123
Social Science Research Handbook, 128
Social sciences, 128–148
Social Sciences and Humanities Index.
    See Humanities Index; Social Sciences
    Index
Social Sciences Index, 129
Society of American Foresters,
    Committee on Forestry Terminology,
    209
Society of Automotive Engineers, 215:
    Nomenclature Advisory Committee,
    216
Sociologist as Detective: An Introduction
    to Research Methods, The, 144
Sociology, 144
Sociology of America: A Guide to
    Information Sources, 144
Soderberg, Paul, 237
Song Index, 109
Sorenson, Ann W., 208
Soros, Charles C., 226
Soukhanov, Anne H., 188
Sound recordings: cataloging of, 22,
    26–27; guides to, 83–84, 89;
    in libraries, 7
Source-access type reference tools,
    43–45
Source Book for Food Scientists, 208
Sourcebook of Criminal Justice Statistics,
    228
Sourcebook of Electronic Circuits, 225
Sourcebook of Equal Educational
    Opportunity, 133
Sourcebook on the Environment, 177
Sources of Business Information, 149
Sources of Construction Information,
    219–220
Sources of Information in the Social
    Sciences: A Guide to the Literature,
    129
Sources of Insurance Statistics, 158
Sources of National Criminal Justice
    Statistics, 228

Source type reference tools, 43–45
Spanish, 101
Spaulding, C. E., 213
Special Libraries Association, Picture
    Division, 123, 127
Speech, 117–118
Speech Association of America, 118
Speech Communication Association, 99
Speech Index (and its *Supplements*), 118
Spencer, Douglas Arthur, 122
Spencer, Robert F., 131
Sperber, Hans, 141
Spiller, Robert E., 106
Splittstoesser, Walter E., 212
Sports. *See* **Physical education and
    recreation**
Sports, 238
Sports Lingo, 237
Spottiswoode, Raymond, 117
Sprinchorn, Evert, 99
*SPSE Handbook of Photographic Science
    and Engineering,* 128
Stacks, defined, 38
Stacy, Ralph W., 184
Stafford, Maureen, 120
Stambler, Irwin, 109, 110
Stamper, Eugene, 214
Standard & Poor's Corporation, 160
Standard Cyclopedia of Horticulture, The,
    210
*Standard Dictionary of Computers and
    Information Processing,* 174
Standard Directory of Advertisers, 52
*Standard Directory of Advertising
    Agencies,* 152
Standard Education Almanac, 134
*Standard Encyclopedia of the World's
    Mountains,* 174
*Standard Encyclopedia of the World's
    Oceans and Islands,* 174
*Standard Encyclopedia of the World's
    Rivers and Lakes,* 174
Standard First Aid and Personal Safety,
    194
*Standard Handbook for Electrical
    Engineers,* 225
*Standard Handbook for Mechanical
    Engineers. See Marks' Standard
    Handbook for Mechanical Engineers*
Standardized Plant Names, 210

*Standard Mechanical and Electrical
    Details,* 220
Standard Medical Almanac, 184
*Standard Nomenclature of Diseases and
    Operations,* 191
Standard Rate and Data Service, 151
Stansfield, Richard H., 152
*Star Atlas and Reference Handbook (Epoch
    1950) for Students and Astronomers,*
    169
Stark, John O., 106
*State Bluebooks and Reference Publications
    (A Selected Bibliography),* 139
Statesman's Year-Book, 146
Statistical Abstract of the United States,
    146
*Statistical Dictionary of Terms and
    Symbols,* 145–146
*Statistical Tables for Science, Engineering,
    Management and Business Studies,* 146
Statistical Yearbook/Annuaire statistique,
    146
Statistics, 144–147
Statistics Sources, 146
Stedman, Thomas Lathrop, 184
Stedman's Medical Dictionary, 184
Steel, Rodney, 131
Steere, William C., 212
Stein, Jess, 46
Stein, J. Stewart, 221
Steinberg, Cobett, 117
Steinmetz, Sol, 47
Sterling, Christopher H., 115
Stevenson, Burton, 106, 113
Stevenson, George A., 235
Stewart, George Rippey, 135
Stieglitz, Alfred, 127
Stock Exchange: International Directory,
    160
Stockman's Handbook, The, 203
Stock Market Encyclopedia, 160
Stock Market Handbook, The, 160
Stoops, Emery, 134
Stout, David F., 225
Strain, J. Robert, 202
Strauss, Howard J., 172
Street, Philip, 205
Stroebel, Leslie, 127
Strong, James, 113
Structural Engineering Handbook, 219

Structural Welding Code—Steel, 236
Strunk, William, 48
Stryker, Ruth, 195
Stubbs, Frank W., 220
Student Anthropologist's Handbook, The,
    131
Student Dictionary of Biology, 170
Studio Dictionary of Design and
    Decoration, 126
Stutley, James, 114
Stutley, Margaret, 114
Style, books of. *See* **Dictionaries and**
    books on language
Styles, Jimmie C., 228
Subject entries, 9, 17–19
Subject Guide to Books in Print, 67, 69
Subject Guide to Microforms in Print,
    82, 85
Subject searching, 27–30
Successful Kitchen Operations and Staff
    Management Handbook, 207
Suddarth, Doris Smith, 191
SUDOCS. *See* U.S. Superintendent of
    Documents
Sullivan, Gene D., 202
Surface and Radiological Anatomy for
    Students and General Practitioners,
    196
Surgical assistant, 198–199
Surgical Technology, 198
Survey of Contemporary Literature, 105
Survey of Current Business, 154
Survey of Musical Instruments, A, 109
Sutton, Roberta Briggs, 118
Swanborough, Gordon, 218
Swine Science, 203
Symbols for Welding and Nondestructive
    Testing, 236
Symbol Sourcebook, 122
Symposium on Oxygen Measurements in
    Blood and Tissues and Their
    Significance, A, 198
Syndicated Columnists, 116
Synge, Patrick M., 211
Synonyms and antonyms,
    dictionaries of. *See* **Dictionaries**
    and books on language

Taber, Clarence Wilbur, 184
Taber's Cyclopedic Medical Dictionary,
    184–185

Taintor, Sarah Augusta, 165
Tandberg, Gerilyn, 118
Tansey, Richard G., 119
Tanur, Judith M., 145
Tatham-Laird and Kudner, 152
Taubes, Frederic, 123
Taxonomic Terminology of the Higher
    Plants, 211
Taylor, Charles Lewis, 141
Taylor, Herb, 128
Taylor, John William Ransom, 218
Technical Book Review Index, 78
Technical Manual and Dictionary of
    Classical Ballet, 96
Technical occupations. *See* **Trade,**
    technical, and industrial
    occupations
Technical reading, 38–39
Telephone directory, as a reference
    tool, 43–44
Telescope Handbook and Star Atlas, The,
    168
Television. *See* **Radio and television**
Television Factbook, 117
Tested Secretarial Techniques for Getting
    Things Done, 165
Textbook for Laboratory Assistants, 189
Textile Fabrics and Their Selection, 125
Textile Handbook, 124
Textiles. *See* **Fashion design**
Theater. *See* **Drama**
Theatre, Film and Television Biographies
    Master Index, 114–115
Theatre Language: A Dictionary of Terms
    in English of the Drama and Stage
    from Medieval to Modern Times, 97
Theodorson, Achilles G., 144
Theodorson, George A., 144
Thewlis, James, 180
Thomae, Betty Kennedy, 162
Thomas, Clayton L., 185
Thomas, Harry Elliot, 225
Thomas, J. B., 133
Thomas, Joseph, 111
Thomas, Robert C., 47
Thomas, Woodlief, 128
Thomas Register of American
    Manufacturers and Thomas Catalog
    File, 154
Thompson, Edward T., 191
Thompson, Elizabeth H., 229

Thompson, Lawrence S., 190
Thompson, Morris Mordecai, 135
Thomson, Sarah Katherine, 231
Thorlby, Anthony, 106
Thornberry, Terence P., 229
Thorne, J. O., 57
Thorner, Marvin Edward, 207
Thrill Sports Catalog, 238
Timber Design and Construction Handbook, 221
Timber Engineering Company, 221
Times Atlas of the Moon, The, 169
Times Atlas of the World, The, 60, 62-63
Times Atlas of World History, The, 136
Time-Saver Standards for Architectural Design Data, 121
Time-Saver Standards for Building Types, 219
Tisdale, George W., 159
Toboldt, William King, 216
Todd, Hollis N., 127
Todd, James Campbell, 189
Tolman, Ruth, 125
Tomek, William G., 202
Tooley, Ronald Vere, 135
Tooley's Dictionary of Mapmakers, 135
Topics and Terms in Environmental Problems, 176
Tourist Business, The, 156
Tourist industry. *See* **Hotel/motel and travel/tourism**
Toussaint, William D., 201
Tracings, on a catalog card, 17-18
Trade bibliographies, 67-69
Trade Names Dictionary, 153
Trade, technical, and industrial occupations, 213-237
Traffic engineering. *See* **Transportation**
Transcriber's Guide to Medical Terminology, 188
Transistor Ignition Systems, 215
Transparencies, guides to, 83
Transportation, 235-236
Transportation and Traffic Engineering Handbook, 236
Traveler's Almanac, 156, 157
Travel Guidebooks in Review, 157
Travel Marketing, 157
Travel Market Yearbook. See Travel Marketing
Travel/tourism. *See* **Hotel/motel and travel/tourism**
Travel Weekly's World Travel Directory, 157
Trees and Shrubs of the United States: A Bibliography for Identification, 209
Trees of the World, 208
Trelease, Sam Farlow, 167
Tremblay, Suzanne, 222
Trent, William Peterfield, 102
Trippensee, Reuben Edwin, 205
Trittschuh, Travis, 141
Tropica, 211
Trout, Carole, 198
Trzyna, Thaddeus C., 205
Tsagaris, Theofilos J., 196
Tuck, Donald H., 106
Tuma, Jan J., 178
Turabian, Kate L., 48
Turgeon, Charlotte, 206
Turner, Pearl, 238
TV. *See* **Radio and television**
Tver, David F., 179
TV Facts, 117
Twentieth Century Authors: A Biographical Dictionary of Modern Literature (and its *First Supplement*), 104-105
Twentieth-Century Literary Criticism, 97, 107
20th-Century Plays in Synopsis, 99
Type for Books: A Designer's Manual, 234
Type Specimen Book, The, 235

Uhl, Joseph N., 201
Ujifusa, Grant, 139
Ulrich's International Periodical Directory, 68-69
Unabridged dictionaries. *See* **Dictionaries and books on language**
Undertakers and undertaking. *See* **Mortuary science**
Union List of Serials, 68
United Nations, Food and Agricultural Organization, Department of Fisheries, 179
United Nations, Statistical Office, 146, 154
United States Code Annotated, 162
United States Dispensatory, The, 185

United States Government Manual, 141
Universal Encyclopedia of Mathematics,
    178
University of Chicago Press. See
    Chicago, University of, Press
University of Chicago Spanish Dictionary,
    The, 101
Unwin, Derick, 133
Updike, Daniel Berkeley, 235
Urdang, Laurence, 152
U.S. Aeronautical Chart and Information
    Center, St. Louis, 169
Usage, books on. See Dictionaries
    and books on language
U.S. Army Topographic Command, 135
U.S. Bureau of Economic Analysis, 154
U.S. Bureau of Labor Statistics, 155
U.S. Bureau of the Census, 141, 146,
    156, 164
U.S. Central Intelligence Agency, 141
U.S. Children's Bureau, 238
U.S. Congress, 141
U.S. Council of Economic Advisors, 156
U.S. Department of Agriculture, 200:
    Office of Governmental and Public
    Affairs, 200
U.S. Department of Commerce, Office of
    the Assistant Secretary for Economic
    Affairs, 146
U.S. Division of Timber Management
    Research, 209
Use of Criminology Literature, 229
Use of Economics Literature, The, 150
U.S. Federal Aviation Agency, 218
U.S. Federal Bureau of Investigation,
    228: Laboratory, 228
U.S. Federal Highway Administration,
    236
U.S. Forest Products Laboratory,
    Madison, Wis., 221
U.S. Forest Service, 209
U.S. Geological Survey, 60
U.S. Government Printing Office (GPO),
    79
Usher, George, 212
U.S. history. See History
Using the Mathematical Literature, 178
U.S. laws, statutes, etc., 162
U.S. Library of Congress, Science Policy
    Research Division, 177

U.S. Military Academy, West Point,
    Department of Earth, Space, and
    Graphic Sciences, 175
U.S. Office of Education, 134
USPDI United States Pharmacopoeia
    Dispensing Information, 185
U.S. president, 156
U.S. Superintendent of Documents
    (SUDOCS), 79

Van Amerongen, C., 173
Van der Meer, Frederic. See Meer,
    Frederic van der
V & M Typographical, Inc., 235
Van Doren, Charles, 205
Van Duyn, J. A., 207
Van Nostrand Reinhold Manual of
    Television Graphics, 117
Van Nostrand's Scientific Encyclopedia,
    167–168
Van Royen, William, 200
Van Zandt, Franklin K., 135
Vaughan, David, 96
Vaughn, Jack A., 99
Vegetable Growing Handbook, 212
Ventilators and Inhalation Therapy, 197
Verna, Mary Ellen, 114
Vertical File and Its Satellites, The, 231
Vertical files, 5
Veterinary Guide for Animal Owners, A,
    213
Veterinary science, 212–213
Videotapes, guides to, 83
Vinson, James, 99, 103, 107
Vinton, John, 110
Visual Aids for Paramedical Vocabulary,
    194
Visual Dictionary of Art, A, 123
Vitale, Philip H., 107
Vital Speeches of the Day (and its 25
    Year Index), 118
VNR Concise Encyclopedia of
    Mathematics, The, 178
Volk, Wesley A., 185
Von Kaas, H. K., 153
Vries, Mary A. De. See De Vries,
    Mary A.

Waddell, Joseph J., 221
Wakeman, John, 107

Walford, Albert John, 90, 168
Walker, John A., 120
Wallenquist, Åke, 169
Waller, A. R., 102
Wallerstein, Harvey, 142
Wallis, Charles L., 233
Ward, A. W., 102
Ward, Diana Powell, 156
Ward, Ian, 217
Ward, Jack W., 221
Ware, Dora, 120
Warrack, John, 109
Washburn, Kenneth B., 195
Washington, Helen, 237
Washington Information Directory, 141
Washington Researchers, 154
Wasserman, Paul, 146, 153, 238
Watson, George, 107
Watson, Robert Irving, 143
Watt, Bernice Kunerth, 207
Watt, John H., 222
Way Things Work Book of the Computer,
The, 173–174
Webster's Biographical Dictionary, 57, 59
Webster's Collegiate Thesaurus, 48, 52
Webster's Guide to American History, 138
Webster's Medical Office Handbook,
188–189
Webster's New Collegiate Dictionary, 46,
50
Webster's New Dictionary of Synonyms,
48, 52
Webster's New Geographical Dictionary,
61, 63
Webster's New International Dictionary of
the English Language, 46, 49–50
Webster's New World Companion to
English and American Literature, 107
Webster's New World Dictionary of the
American Language, 46, 50–51
Webster's Secretarial Handbook, 165
Webster's Sports Dictionary, 238
Webster's Third New International
Dictionary of the English Language,
46, 50
Weekly Newspaper Rates and Data, 151
Wehlte, Kurt, 123
Weigert, A., 169
Weik, Martin H., 174
Weinberger, Bernhard Wolf, 187

Weiner, Peter Mark, 117
Weiner, Richard, 116
Weingartner, C., 232
Weis, Erich, 101
Weis, Erwin, 101
Weisman, Charlotte, 236
Weiss, Lillian, 126
Welding, 236–237
Welding Handbook, 236
Wentworth, Harold, 47
West, Dorothy Herbert, 100
West, Geoffrey P., 213
Westcott, Cynthia, 212
Westcott's Plant Disease Handbook, 212
Westrup, Sir Jack, 108
Whalen, George J., 189
Wheeler, Gershon J., 126
Wheeler, Russell C., 187
White, Carl Milton, 129
White, E. B., 48
White, Jan V., 116
Whitford, Robert Henry, 180
Whitten, Phillip, 131
Whole Car Catalog, 217
Whole Nurse Catalog, The, 192
Who's Who, 59
Who's Who Among Innkeepers, 157
Who's Who in America, 57, 59–60
Who's Who in American Art, 120
Who's Who in American Politics, 141
Who's Who in Architecture from 1400 to
the Present Day, 121–122
Who's Who in Aviation, 219
Who's Who in Church History, 112
Who's Who in Finance and Industry,
154–155
Who's Who in Health Care, 185
Who's Who in Insurance, 159
Who's Who in Opera, 110
Who's Who in Religion, 114
Who's Who in Rock Music, 110
Who's Who in the West, 59
Who's Who of American Women, 147–148
Who Was Who in American Politics, 140
Who Was Who in the Theatre, 1912–1976,
100
Widmann, Frances K., 189
Wiener, Philip P., 111
Wilcox, Ruth Turner, 125
Wild Flowers of the United States, 212

Wildlife Conservation, 205
Wildlife Illustrated, 205
Wildlife management. *See*
    Conservation and wildlife
    management
Wildlife Management (Giles), 205
Wildlife Management (Trippensee), 205
Wildlife Management in Wilderness, 205
Wildlife Preservation, 205
Wildlife Watcher's Handbook, 205
Wilkins, Earle W., Jr., 193
Wilkinson, Jule, 156, 206
Willeford, George, 185
Williams, Frank J., 145
Williams, Roger John, 171
Williams, Vergil L., 228
Williamson, Robin, 173
Willis, J. C., 211
Wilson, David H., 194
Wilson, H. W., Firm, Publishers, 107
Windholz, Martha, 172
Wingate, Isabel B., 124, 125
Winick, Charles, 131
Winkler, Paul W., 230
Winslow, Taylor F., 221
Winter, William, 218
Winterkorn, Hans Friedrich, 221
Wintrobe, Maxwell M., 189
Wischnitzer, Saul, 185
Witton, Catherine Jones, 189
Wixon, Rufus, 150
Woerdeman, M. W., 183
Wolf, Carol L., 174
Wolfgang, Marvin E., 229
Wolman, Benjamin B., 143
Woman's Almanac: 12 How-To Handbooks
    in One, 148
Women, 1965-1975, 148
Women's Book of World Records and
    Achievements, The, 148
Women's Organizations & Leaders
    Directory, 148
Women's Rights Almanac, 148
Women's Rights Movement in the United
    States, 1848-1970: A Bibliography and
    Sourcebook, The, 147
Women's studies, 147-148
Women Studies Abstracts, 148
Women's Studies: A Guide to Reference
    Sources, 147

Woodbury, Marda, 134
Woods, Kenneth Brady, 236
Woodson, Linda, 118
Wood Structural Design Data, 220
Woods Words: A Comprehensive
    Dictionary of Loggers Terms, 209
Word-by-word filing, 30-31
Words into Type, 235
Working Press of the Nation, The, 116
World Almanac and Book of Facts, The,
    63, 65
World Almanac Whole Health Guide, The,
    182-183
World Authors, 1970-1975, 107
World Aviation Directory, 219
World Book Encyclopedia, 54-56
World Communications: A 200-Country
    Survey of Press, Radio, Television
    and Film, 115
World Directory of Environmental
    Organizations, 205
World Energy Book, The, 177
World Facts and Figures, 146
World Handbook of Political and Social
    Indicators, 141
World history. *See* **History**
World literature. *See* **Literature**
Worldmark Encyclopedia of the Nations,
    141
World of Automobiles, The, 217
World of Fashion: People, Places,
    Resources, 124
World Timbers, 209
World Trade Annual, 154
World Travel Directory. See Travel
    Weekly's World Travel Directory
World Who's Who in Finance and
    Industry. See Who's Who in Finance
    and Industry
World Wildlife Guide, The, 205
Wragg, David W., 219
Wright, Andrew, 102
Wright, John K., 138
Wright, Martin, 229
Writer's Market, 115
Writing the History Paper, 138
Wyckoff, Peter, 160
Wylie, Harry L., 165
Wyman, Donald, 212
Wyman's Gardening Encyclopedia, 212

Wynar, Bohdan S., 230
Wyse, Bonita W., 208

Yarwood, Doreen, 125
Yearbook of Agriculture, 200
*Yearbook of American and Canadian
    Churches*, 114
Yearbook of Astronomy, 169
Year Book of Dentistry, 187
*Yearbook of Equal Educational
    Opportunity. See Sourcebook of Equal
    Educational Opportunity*
Yearbook of Forest Products, 209
Yearbook of Higher Education, 134
*Yearbook of International Trade
    Statistics*, 154
Yearbooks, 64–66
Year in Music, The, 110
Year's Work in English Studies, The, 103
*Yesterday and Today: A Dictionary of
    Recent American History*, 137
York, William, 110

Young, Carl B., 194
Young, Genevieve Gray, 190
Young, Jimmy Albert, 197
*Your Investments. See Dun & Bradstreet's
    Guide to Your Investments*

Zadrozny, John Thomas, 129
Zandt, Franklin K. Van. *See* Van Zandt,
    Franklin K.
Zarb, Frank G., 160
Zelko, Marjorie, 156
Ziegler, Edward N., 176
Ziff-Davis Publishing Company, Public
    Transportation and Travel Division,
    157
Zimmerman, H., 169
Zollinger, Robert M., 199
Zollinger, Robert M., Jr., 199
Zuidema, George D., 183
Zurcher, Arnold J., 150
Zurick, Timothy, 214